PRAISE FOR ANXIETY RX

"Full of truth and humor, *Anxiety Rx* takes the reader on a healing journey, with a deep dive into Dr Kennedy's own personal recovery from decades of chronic anxiety. This deeply insightful and ultimately practical book gives the reader a new and natural prescription to healing, using an approach Dr Kennedy has used in himself and countless patients. Russ specifically addresses what many therapies miss: the fundamental role of old unresolved trauma stored in the body as the cause of the anxieties of the mind. Creating that awareness, using strategies effective for both allows the mind and body to reconnect and resolve the mind-body disconnect that fuels and sustains anxiety. The insights and simple practices in this book will put you on the path to self-healing and keep you there. *Anxiety Rx* is unlike any book on anxiety and a must-read for anyone who suffers from chronic worry."

Nicole LePera, MD

The Holistic Psychologist

"The vulnerability matched with the depth in which Russell opens up about his life experiences, and battles with anxiety, leads the reader to feel safe to explore their own struggles while gaining invaluable knowledge. The personal approach Russ takes allowed me to feel I was getting to know him as a doctor and as a very real person, with a history that is like so many others. Trauma and anxiety can hit anyone at anytime of their life, they do not discriminate. This book and the knowledge and understanding gained is for everyone."

Ginger Henderson, RTC/MTC

Master Therapeutic Counsellor

Clinical Counselling Supervisor

"Advocating for a more integrated mind-body approach to mental health, Dr. Kennedy offers a framework for understanding anxiety in a revolutionary way. *Anxiety Rx* combines developmental science, attachment research and somatic principles, to create a masterpiece that is trauma-informed, infused with personal story, and accented with comedic overtones. A must-read for clinicians and everyday overthinkers alike!"

Kim Fraser-Harrison, MA Couns. Psych, RCC

Registered Clinical Counsellor, Psychotherapist

Individual and Family Therapist

"One of the most integrated and holistic formulations of anxiety available, *Anxiety Rx* allows the reader to peer into the complex interplay of mind and body, and learn effective techniques to become consciously aware, connected and free. Dr. Kennedy's personal journey of trauma, emotional pain, self-discovery and triumph is a beacon of hope for anyone entrapped by anxiety. By the way, this doctor and neuroscientist is also a comedian, so get ready to burst out laughing while mastering your worries."

Michael Mulvey, BSc, MD, FRCPC

Fellow of the Royal College of Physicians & Surgeons of Canada

Staff Psychiatrist in the Department of Psychiatry at St. Paul's Hospital, Vancouver, BC

Specialist in mood disorders and anxiety disorders

"It's rare I come across a non-fiction book that makes me laugh and cry, and the crying feels good! Thank you for having the tenacity to complete your life's work & the courage to bare your soul in print. You have translated your life experience into learnings that will benefit all of us, and for that, I am eternally grateful. Not only have your words and insight benefitted me as your friend & colleague, but now anyone who reads this can really take the messages easily as practical steps, and your generous nature means it will only cost them under 30 dollars, a box of tissues & a few afternoons glued to an armchair."

Dr Jenny Draper, MB BS DCH FRACGP ACAAM

Anxiety R_x

Anxiety R_x

A New Prescription for Anxiety Relief

From the Doctor Who Created It

Russell Kennedy, MD

AWAKEN
VILLAGE
PRESS

This is a work of nonfiction. All of Dr. Kennedy's stories as told are true. Any resemblance to persons living or dead is intended, as what would be the point of just making stuff up? That said, when other people are referenced, names and distinguishing characteristics are changed to protect confidentiality, and some "patients" may be an amalgamation of persons with similar clinical presentations.

The content of this book is for general instruction only. Each person's physical, emotional, and spiritual condition is unique. The instruction in this book is not intended to replace, supersede, or interrupt the reader's relationship with a physician or other mental health professional, especially where medications are concerned.

The information in this book is for humans only, not dogs, cats, sheep, honey badgers, or any other mammal, reptile, or fish, regardless of whether they seem angry or upset.

Printed in the United States of America.

Editing by Awaken Village Press
Design by Tim Murray and Daniel Holloway
Author photo by Michelle Koebke
Illustrations by Andrea Vásquez Aguilarte

ISBN 978-1-7344265-4-0 (paperback)

Library of Congress Cataloging-in-Publication Data

Published by Awaken Village Press, Sioux Falls, SD
www.awakenvillagepress.com

ATTENTION: Quantity discounts are available to health organizations, hospitals, clinics, rehab facilities, conferences, or for educational purposes, reselling, gifts, or fundraiser campaigns. Please contact www.dr-russ.com for more information or you can email Dr. Kennedy directly at theanxietymd@gmail.com.

For my Dad,
It wasn't your fault; it's no one's fault.
Your life had meaning; it's here in these pages.
You can rest now.

For my Mum,
You always did what you had to do.
The cost was immeasurable.
Thank you.

For Rusty, my younger self,
I have you now.
I love you now.
You can rest.

TABLE OF CONTENTS

Preface

On a muggy, late summer day in 1973, twelve-year-old me didn't know very much about what anxiety was, but I did know for certain I did not feel safe. My father had attempted suicide, and I was watching the ambulance drive off to take him away to the hospital. Even with the drama and trauma of my father's schizophrenia and bipolar illness, I knew my parents loved my younger brother and me, but the pressures were just too great to provide a stable home life. Looking back, I have often jokingly said my father was psychotic and my mother was neurotic, so my own psyche didn't stand much of a chance.

If you are looking at this book because you have anxiety, chances are you have some old wounding stored in you from your past and you haven't found a way to heal it yet. Anxiety can be the biggest challenge in a person's life. If you had managed to heal from chronic worry and anxiety, you would likely be looking at books on overcoming much easier challenges like becoming a blindfolded bomb diffuser or an amateur astronaut.

If you suffered in your past and you are still suffering now, I *feel* you. I really, really do. For decades I suffered from crippling anxiety and looked to every type of therapy—and was disappointed at every turn. I know the deep frustration of being promised relief and walking away empty-handed.

I wrote this book as a way to turn my dad's pain and suffering (and the suffering of my mother, brother, and me) into something for good, to create a healing message for others arising out of our pain. When I was a boy, my dad told me of his plans for the future. Mental illness stole those plans and burned them right in front of him. He could only stomp out the flames so many times until he went up in them. Watching the ambulance take my dad away that late summer day in 1973, I swore to myself that his pain, and the chaos, confusion, and heartbreak we suffered as his family, was going to stand for something. Although his potential was taken from him, I have taken that vow of my twelve-year-old self and rode the energy of his spirit and what he taught me to become a doctor. I told myself that if I was a physician, I could help others in a way I was never able to help my father.

My qualifications for guiding you on this healing journey:

University degrees in medicine and neuroscience.

Master's level training in developmental psychology at the Neufeld Institute in Vancouver.

Over a hundred thousand patient encounters.

Personal insights into anxiety from ayahuasca, LSD, psilocybin, and MDMA.

Hundreds of books on anxiety from highly spiritual to hard-core neuroscience.

Lived at a temple in India studying the science of spirit.

Certified yoga and meditation teacher.

Countless conferences on anxiety and mental health.

Many academic and spiritual retreats to explore mind-body mental and physical health.

Lived with anxiety every day for many years.

Overcame my own anxiety to become a professional stand-up comedian.

By the way, do you know what they call the person who graduates dead last in their medical class?

"Doctor."

Despite my extensive academic experience above, probably my biggest credential in helping others with anxiety is that I personally suffered from the dreaded condition for decades. The unusual position of being both anxiety doctor *and* anxiety patient has given me a unique ability to see what works and what doesn't from multiple perspectives. I don't have to go back to the doctor to report my progress; I *am* the doctor!

What we are currently doing in psychology and psychiatry is taking two very separate things, the anxious thoughts of the mind and the alarmed feeling in the body, and reducing them to one diagnosis: Anxiety. Most anxiety treatments have limited success because most treat the anxiety of the mind but neglect the bigger issue—the alarm signals of old trauma stored in the body.

There is a story about the organic chemist Friedrich Kekulé. He was struggling with finding a chemical formula for benzene, now known to be a six-carbon ring. Try as he might, he couldn't figure out how the six carbons would fit together. Chemical structures were thought to be linear, with the atoms fitting together like the boxcars on a train. Benzene was known to have six of these boxcars, but it was also known that the structure could not be linear. One night while dreaming, Kekulé had a vision of a snake biting its own tail, leading him to the idea that benzene's structure was not a linear but circular one.

In a similar manner, I had a vision while on LSD that went against conventional theory: much of my anxiety was not in my mind but rather in my body. Traditional therapies were looking in the wrong place! That psychedelic-induced vision has allowed me to develop the theory upon which this book is based.

While this book can't change the pain from your past, it can help you perceive it differently, both in your mind and in your body. When you change your perception of your past and especially of your "self," you change your future. This book is as unique as it is practical and not just a rehash of conventional therapies that do not work.

In my own healing from chronic worry, I have had to become my own doctor, therapist, and shaman. This book is exceptional in its amalgamation of the neuroscientific principles of the mind and the spirit of the body. I've used thousands of hours in scientific training to explain what I found unexplainable in my "out of mind" experiences in India and on psychedelics. What most approaches to treat anxiety miss, and this book addresses specifically, is the critical role of accessing the healing power and wisdom stored in the body. While more "medical" mind-based approaches are important and helpful (and I'll address those as well), you will only fully heal when you commit to a pointed focus on connecting to your body. Finding and soothing the alarm stored in your body is critical to you healing from chronic worry.

We need to know what we are treating to have the best treatments. Anxiety is an endless feedback loop of painful feeling in the body and anxious thinking in the mind. Each energizes the other. I'll show you how to break that destructive cycle so you can get back to living your life.

Leaving your anxiety behind requires a simple shift in your perception from mind to body, so you get out of the frightening predictions of your mind and into the grounded security of your body. Once you become practiced in this renewal of *perception*, you may well be able to talk to your doctor about the renewal of your *prescription*.

My father never got off medication, and in fact, it was medication that ultimately killed him, thirteen years after that summer day I watched the ambulance take him in 1973. It was me that found him, the first of many dead bodies I would see in my medical career. He left a note behind, beside his lifeless body that I found on January 12, 1987.

The note said "It's not your fault, it's no one's fault."

But I do feel at fault in a way. I could never help him; no one could. He was just too sick. I wasn't even a doctor while he was alive. He died five months before I could tell him that I gained admission to medical school.

I couldn't help my dad with his emotional pain, but I am fully committed to helping you with yours.

*"It's not your fault; it's no one's fault,
Love Dad."*

- Beverly Lorne Germa, January 12, 1987

Introduction

Many years ago, I had a patient send me an email that said: "Dear Dr. Kennedy, I am almost out of my anxiety medication, and I need you to renew my perception." She had meant to say "renew my *prescription*"! When I read that, I thought: if she could truly renew her perception, she probably wouldn't need the prescription.

That story is the reason "Renew Your Perception, Not Your Prescription" is written on the back cover. I loved this story so much and it captures the heart of what I would love to see for you, to be empowered to change your perception of yourself and your anxiety so much that you no longer need medication. Now, let me say clearly that I am not against medication; I am a medical doctor after all. I used to prescribe it every single day as a practicing physician. In many cases medication is an invaluable part of treatment, and I am not recommending in any way that you stop taking any medications without consulting your doctor. Further, this book is not intended to be medical advice because very little of what I am going to share with you has anything to do with what I learned in medical school. Being a trained and licensed physician certainly helped me in understanding the physiology of anxiety, but It was my training in neuroscience and developmental psychology along with my own diverse life experience learning to treat my own anxiety in very non-traditional ways that formed this book.

It is also important to note I am not a psychiatrist. Psychiatrists do at least five years of additional training in psychiatry after graduating from medical school, and, in my opinion, they are guided down a specific pharmacological path and usually stay within it for their entire careers. As a generalist, I had the freedom to pursue many different ideas that were well outside of conventional medicine, and as you'll soon see, I do not think like a medical doctor when it comes to anxiety. I think like a medical doctor when it comes to physical ailments, but when it comes to emotional ones, the medical model has significant limitations. I respect the work of psychiatrists because I know they often get the patients with the most severe illness, and that is a very tough burden to bear. Psychiatry is changing with the increasing use of psychedelics, and some psychiatrists are starting to accept the role of somatic therapies, but it is the rare psychiatrist that embraces the mind-body connection as I do.

Five years ago, I myself came completely off SSRI/SSNI type medications using the methods I will show you in this book, and I had taken those medications for over twenty-five years. My hope is that when you embrace the hard-won concepts I'll show you, you may well be able to reduce or come off your prescriptions as well. But again, and I cannot state this clearly enough, only reduce or come off your prescription medications under the guidance of your own doctor.

In this book, I want to help you renew your perception and look at yourself and your anxiety in a completely new way. It is what saved my life and just might save yours.

One of the biggest problems I've had as a doctor helping people heal from anxiety is the term *anxiety* has no consistent definition. Google "What is anxiety?" and you'll see a mishmash of physical and emotional symptoms in a very long list. How are you supposed to treat something when you don't know what that something is? When most people, including doctors and therapists, use the term "anxiety," they refer to a list of worrisome thoughts and painful feelings that you can pick and choose from like some kind of neurotic smorgasbord.

That is not a definition; that's a Costco list—and one that results in a bag of chips, some golf balls, a couple of frozen dinners, and maybe a backpack and a microwave oven. How do you effectively treat a list of disparate symptoms that you may or may not have? In my medical opinion, you can't. As a doctor, I know the more precisely I define and describe an illness or condition, the better I can treat it. The opposite is even more true: the less defined something is, the harder it is to treat. And anxiety has been notoriously hard to treat because we have no consistent and predictable way of pinning it down.

So here it goes. Are you ready for a consistent and predictable definition?

Please stay with me, as your quality of life depends on it.

Anxiety is a thinking process of the mind.

That's it.

Ready for another revelation?

Anxiety is not painful.

This may surprise you and may even cause you to doubt my credibility. If you feel resistance to this concept of anxiety being a painless thought process, let me assure you making this distinction has allowed me (and many others) to heal from chronic, relentless, persistent worrisome—or fear-inducing—thoughts.

Quite simply, anxiety itself doesn't hurt. The painful part comes from anxiety's evil twin: alarm. And I would tell you that you are confusing anxiety (the process that produces potentially fearful *thoughts* in your mind) with a painful *feeling* in your body. The thoughts themselves are not painful. Just as the brain itself has no pain sensation (I've been in the operating room during neurosurgery where I saw you can operate directly on the brain with only the anesthesia of the overlying skull and scalp), anxious thoughts are equally painless.

Why, then, does anxiety *feel* so uncomfortable?

You'll see, as this book unfolds, the pain you feel is not coming from the anxious thoughts of your mind but from a sense of alarm stored in your body. Alarm is a combination of misaligned energy of your fight-or-flight sympathetic nervous system, with an activating energy originating from unresolved emotional pain that has been repressed within your body. If you struggle with anxiety, your worry aggravates the alarm in your body, and it is the sense of alarm that is the source of your discomfort. Just because worries *activate* the alarm does not mean the worries are the cause.

For one more clarifying example, imagine your toaster short-circuits and starts a fire in your house, and then you throw lit matches on the flames. The matches make the fire worse, but they did not cause the fire in the first place. If you stop throwing matches on the fire, the problem is still there in the form of a fire in progress—started by the toaster, not the matches.

The alarm stored in our bodies is the toaster with the exposed wire. The matches are our worries. To heal, we must address the root problem (the toaster) and stop blaming the matches for a fire they surely aggravated but did not start. Even once we extinguish the fire, the problem may reoccur if we don't replace the toaster. But with the illusion that the matches (the anxious thoughts) are the problem, we may direct our efforts at removing all the matches from the house while leaving the broken toaster in place.

In 2015, I was at an anxiety conference in Vancouver, British Columbia. I know that sounds like a bunch of nervous people in the same room, but it was a group of doctors, social workers, teachers, and psychologists listening to various presentations on how to heal anxiety. Much of it was predictable and not new to me, but when developmental psychologist Dr. Gordon Neufeld spoke, what he said rocked my world.

"All anxiety is separation anxiety."

That, along with many other things Dr. Neufeld said, has stuck with me to this day. Anxiety and alarm almost always result from a break in attachment during childhood—in other words, an experience of separation.

When we are separated from our attachment figures, either physically or emotionally, our bodies go into a state of alarm. This is an activated state, a fight-or-flight type reaction the body mounts automatically when we sense real or perceived separation. However, instead of fighting or fleeing, that activated response is initially not about fighting or fleeing at all. It is an activated reaction to mobilize us to pursue a lost connection. That's right, the reason for our fight-or-flight reactions is usually not about a threat to our *physical* safety. In our modern world, it is much more often about a threat to our *emotional* safety. According to Dr. Neufeld—and I agree completely—this state of alarm is not about flight (moving away) but about pursuit (moving toward). In reaction to real or perceived separation, we engage in this alarm-based pursuit as a reflexive attempt to reconnect to our attachment figures. If the pursuit fails and, despite our best efforts, we still feel separate from our attachment figures, the alarm intensifies and the body stays in a state of alarm for an extended period.

This state of alarm, which started as a reaction to a real or perceived separation, becomes intensified and prolonged by the anxious thoughts of the mind. Over time, if we are subject to an alarming state of affairs (e.g., abuse, loss, abandonment, or rejection) we are unable to resolve, or if we don't have access to a caregiver that can love and calm us, that alarm state becomes stored in our bodies.

If you struggle with chronic anxious thoughts, it is highly probable you have a version of this state of alarm in your system, likely from a time in your life where you felt separated from your attachment figures and you were unable to close the gap. For me, my emotional separation from my schizophrenic father caused my body to go into an alarmed, activated state of pursuit to reconnect with him. As I was unable to decrease the separation because his mind was too fractured for him to connect with me, my alarm level increased.

This alarm energy became a chronic state in my body, where it would energize more false, worrisome thoughts in my mind. At the same time, the alarm energy would create a sense of my survival being threatened, which would impair my brain's ability to recognize those thoughts as false. As a result, I would believe, or give power to, the false worries I had created, thus increasing the sense of alarm, which then created more worrisome thoughts. I was trapped in a feedback loop I call the **alarm-anxiety cycle**, where the alarm in my body generated anxious thoughts in my mind and those thoughts generated more alarm.

Does this cycle sound familiar?

What we call *anxiety* is a combination of an alarm state in the body and anxious thoughts in the mind. I have found immeasurable relief in addressing the alarm of the body separately from the anxious thoughts of the mind. A considerable part of my healing was due to using the term *anxiety* simply to refer to the anxious thoughts of the mind. In this way, I divorced anxiety of the mind from the alarm state in the body. In distilling alarm and anxiety down to their essence, I was able to break the cycle by showing the component parts were separate and therefore separable.

I will continue to use the term *anxiety* in this book only to refer to the machinations and worrisome thoughts of the mind. The reason why most of the treatments for our generalized understanding of anxiety have failed or been of limited benefit is they have focused on treating the anxious thoughts of the mind (which is the *effect* of the alarm in the system) and virtually ignored the true underlying *cause*—the alarm in the body. In other words, we have been trying to get rid of all the matches in the house while ignoring the short-circuiting toaster!

When I was living at a temple in rural India and later teaching yoga classes in downtown Vancouver, I saw a lot of people with a string of prayer beads around their necks. These strings of beads, called *japa malas*, are often used by Hindus and Buddhists to help maintain focus during meditation and prayer. (They are also used by hipsters to appear spiritual.) The traditional *japa mala* has 108 beads. The number 108 is held as a sacred number said to be found in the ratios of our solar system, with the diameter of the sun being 108 times the diameter of the earth and the distance from the earth to the moon being equivalent to 108 diameters of the moon. (I did the math, and it's very close but by no means exact.)

What I can say for sure is 108 is a three-digit multiple of three (three times thirty-six) and its components add up to nine (three times three). Three is also purported to be the number of balance, as you can see with the tripod base on any drum stool. The drummer may be all over the place, but he sits in a place of balance to do that.

This book is about me going all over the world in search of emotional balance as a salve to my unending anxiety. The farther I travelled out into the world, the further it took me inside to myself. To quote Elizabeth Gilbert in her book *Eat, Pray, Love*: "I also like the idea of stringing these stories along the structure of a *japa mala* because it is so … structured. Sincere spiritual investigation is, and always has been, an endeavor of methodical discipline. Looking for Truth is not some kind of spazzy free-for-all, not even during this, the great age of the spazzy free-for-all." Although it may not be popular for a guy to say this, I really loved that book. I thought if I ever wrote a book, I was going to use that structure as well, and here we are.

In the first thirty-six chapters, we travel to the land of **Awareness of Mind**. I'll show you that you must be able to see your anxiety with a new outlook because you can't change what you can't see. Through awareness, I show you the fundamental cycle that anxiety runs on and how you can break it. I'll also show you how to use awareness to examine your anxious thoughts or, perhaps more importantly, to just let … them … go. I'll show you how anxious thoughts cannot survive in the light of awareness, which disarms the anxiety half of the anxiety/alarm cycle.

In the middle thirty-six chapters, we visit the faraway land of **Awareness of Body**, which is devoted to recognizing and relieving the alarm part of the cycle. I will show you how to use breath and other body-based methods to ground you in the moment, calming your nervous system and keeping you out of your (always future-based) worrisome thoughts. This helps disarm the alarm half of the anxiety/alarm cycle.

On the last leg of the journey, **Awareness of Self**, we return to the place our connection to ourselves was interrupted. We will focus on re-connecting and cultivating a compassionate connection with ourselves. I believe we all have compassion for ourselves, but our life experiences and underlying temperament cause us to lose touch with what truly heals anxiety—namely, a sense of connection and care for ourselves. The reason you became anxious is that once upon a time you left yourself, often to look after a parent or it was just too unbearable to be in your body. As a result, you learned to **judge**, **abandon, blame**, and **shame** yourself (in short, take JABS at yourself). Those JABS insidiously set traps or blocks to self-compassion and self-care—blocks that prevent you from having a mind and body that are in sync. As a result, you are blocked from becoming securely attached to yourself, and this separation energy creates what you have called "anxiety." To heal, you need to reestablish this secure attachment to yourself so your mind and body get back in sync.

The last thirty-six chapters are devoted to strategies to resolve the split that created the alarm in the first place. Once you heal the split, you can then connect the mind and body in a constructive, adaptive, and fulfilling way. In states of anxiety or alarm, the mind and body are not operating in harmony. There *is* a connection between them, but the connection is destructive rather than constructive. The mind and body learned to connect with excessive worry and alarm, giving rise to the alarm-anxiety cycle as a coping strategy of a child that needed to survive. We need to reconnect with ourselves, and in that new mind-body connection, we move from a focus on survival (and thus fear of growth) to moving toward true progress.

In short, we go from surviving to thriving.

As we take this journey together, you'll learn how to remove those blocks your mind creates. We will isolate and expose those JABS you take at yourself and, perhaps for the first time, you'll learn how to be truly connected to yourself. As your relationship with others can be no better than the relationship you have with yourself, your own mind-body connection allows you to become connected to others, which in turn provides you with the attachment you need to soothe the alarm. Since anxiety depends on the alarm created by the mind-body separation and cannot survive without that separation, once you are truly connected, what you call your "anxiety" has no choice but to retreat.

Healing in the mind leads to healing in the body and vice versa—and each opens a new door for the healing of the other. If you try to heal just one (as in doing yoga ten hours a day for the body or psychotherapy ten hours a day for the mind), you won't heal nearly as effectively or efficiently as when you do an hour a day of each.

Seeing the difference between anxiety and alarm will help you immeasurably in understanding how they form a reciprocating loop, each one feeding off the other like two siblings fighting in the backseat of a car. And once the anxiety of the mind is separated from the alarm in the body, each loses its respective energy source. At that point, the anxiety of the mind and the alarm in the body can be treated separately and the fight stops, just like the two siblings who are now separated by a caring parent. As you'll learn, that parent is you.

It is imperative for you to know there is nothing wrong with you. In fact, your mind and body are working as they should, which might sound weird to you, especially if you have been suffering for a long time. You have simply learned to automatically believe your thoughts because a part of you thinks that indiscriminate belief in your worries is keeping you safe. You are being tricked by your own perception—a perception that tells you you must be hypervigilant and keep on worrying to keep yourself safe. That may have had an element of truth in your childhood, but you are not a child anymore, and that vigilance that once helped you survive is now incredibly harmful.

You do not have a disease. You have simply learned a pattern of perception that is creating what you call anxiety. This is simply a coping strategy; it is not who you are. Anxiety is an adaptation to a stress (usually chronic) that was too much for your mind and body to bear.

It is inevitable that we all carry some form of emotional trauma from childhood. Here's an example I often use. Let's say, for the sake of argument and a slightly awkward metaphor, the child's mind can hold "one cupful" of emotional trauma. Death of the family pet, a grandparent who lives in another city passes away, or starting at a new school. Now, let's pour "two cupfuls" of trauma into that child's life. A parent is very sick or addicted, their parents divorce, or they are chronically bullied at school. The trauma not contained by the first cup runs over, and the excess trauma runs into the body and is stored there, where it must eventually be addressed and metabolized in order for us to truly heal.

This book is about showing you ways your body and mind can unlearn that trauma pattern and renew that faulty perception with a healthier one, based in greater truth and awareness. In doing so, you can learn to accept you do not have to believe everything you think and come to see and know a peaceful place where you need not think at all.

Returning to *Eat, Pray, Love* for a moment: "Every *japa mala* has a special, extra bead—the 109th bead—which dangles outside that balanced circle of 108 like a pendant. When your fingers reach this marker during prayer, you are meant to pause from your absorption in meditation and thank your teachers."

As I reach the 109th bead and publish this book, I acknowledge Elizabeth Gilbert for inspiring me to create the framework for this book and all of my teachers who have gone before me on the path. Looking for truth in my search to heal from chronic anxiety *has* been a bit of a "spazzy free-for-all," for I, too, realize I am a seeker and a writer. Perhaps most importantly, as I reach the 109th bead, I must acknowledge anxiety as my greatest teacher. I am grateful for the trust the universe has placed in me to experience it in the presence of so many other teachers. I am grateful for the learnings, both scientifically and spiritually based, in the hope I may be the teacher for others.

PART 1
AWARENESS OF MIND

1
My Trauma

In the summer of 1973, I was a skinny, distraught twelve-year-old with yellow blond hair, buck teeth, and bell-bottoms, watching through my bedroom window as an ambulance was preparing to take my father to the hospital, feeling helpless and hopelessly confused. By that time, I had had a vague suspicion something was not right about my dad for a few years, but like most children, I took what I was given and accepted it, as I didn't know anything different. Many have said I made the best of it. I would say I, like many of my fellow worriers, made the worst of it.

My father was loving and caring, with a great sense of playfulness and humour. He was a relatively small man, about five foot seven, but he had a big voice. He had his own radio show around the time I was born in 1960—no mean feat for a man of twenty-seven years old. The newscaster Peter Jennings, I'm told by my mother, said my father had the smoothest voice he had ever heard.

Now, it is 1973 and he is on his way to yet another admission to the hospital because, along with his own smooth-as-silk radio voice, he heard other voices too.

My dad was never abusive or violent, but he would lose touch with reality and believe things like he was the smartest person in the world or that he was able to talk directly to world leaders or that he was a cat. Okay, I made up the part about the cat, but he *was* certifiable. In fact, he was "certified" (the term we doctors use to commit someone to a mental health facility against their wishes) on more than one occasion.

I had always been a sensitive child, but I believe seeing my father descend into psychotic depression as a pre-adolescent is when my anxiety really began to take root. In some ways, one might say, because of my father, I developed an anxiety disorder.

It wasn't his fault. I loved him, and I knew he loved me, but over time his behaviour became too erratic for me to develop any sense of security. Often he was quite lucid and nurturing for months at a time, showing me how to hit a ball, ride a bike, and play chess. However, it's like accidentally being bitten by the family dog; it takes a hundred positive encounters with the dog to counteract that one negative one, and if the pooch bites you one more time, you'll likely never trust that dog again—especially if that dog thinks he is a chess-playing cat.

I was "bitten" many times by my father. He would regain my trust only to lose it again. If you had a parent or caregiver who was sick, addicted, alcoholic, or just plain not there—or worse, mentally, physically, or sexually abusive—you know what I mean by being "bitten." The more bites you sustain, the more you are at risk of developing anxiety. This anxiety develops because we lose our boundaries—the lines become blurry and we lose sight of where our parent ends and we begin. We divert energy from learning who we are and, instead, devote our attention to reading and assessing our parent (or caregiver) so we can look after their needs first—because if our parent isn't safe, neither are we.

Many of us have anxiety because we gave to others before ourselves. We are called things like highly sensitive people, empaths, and people-pleasers. We lost touch with what we needed because we perceived our survival was predicated on someone else being okay. Many of us are good at giving other people care and attention, but the sense of what we ourselves need has atrophied from disuse. We adopted those caregiving roles and honed them because it gave us a sense of power in situations where we otherwise felt powerless or immobilized. Over time, we lost touch with what we truly need, and we slowly but surely lost touch with ourselves. When you lose touch with yourself, you are like a cork bobbing in the waves of the ocean, at the whim of external forces, unable to find your own port.

When you are attached to a parent in a healthy way, you develop a sense of knowing yourself because your parent expresses an interest in knowing you. In secure attachment, parts of your brain develop so you can self-soothe and see the big picture. When conditions get stormy, you can go into the deep, still part of yourself that is unaffected by the rough waves on the surface of your life.

Without that care as a child, the best you learn is how to surf the waves, and you get tossed around. A lot.

As I watched the ambulance take my father away to the hospital, I felt completely frozen and immobilized, both physically and emotionally. I later came to understand this moment sowed the seeds for my desire to become a doctor so I would never have to feel that powerless again.

2
Challenges

1987 was the toughest year of my life. In the span of nine months, I lost my father, had to finish the final term of my neuroscience degree (and get exceptional grades in order to make the cut to enter medical school), got married, moved four thousand kilometres away, found a new home with a new wife and an eighteen-month-old daughter, and began medical school. And I was a nervous wreck throughout.

I still look back on this time of my life with a combination of pride and incredulity that I actually made it.

My father's bipolar disorder and schizophrenia had devastated his mind and body to the point that he took his own life by intentional prescription drug overdose on January 12, 1987. I had a deep sense that morning something was wrong and called my brother, Scott. We went over to his place, and it was no surprise to either of us to find his body. I was not yet a doctor or even a medical student at the time, and my father's was the first dead body I had ever encountered. I remember saying to my brother, "Well, that's it for dad."

When a boy loses his father, there is a sense of losing a protector, even though it was probably more accurate that I had been my dad's protector for many years prior to his death. Even though I was a twenty-six-year-old man at the time of his passing, the little boy in me never stopped hoping my dad would come back and be the man who had taken me fishing and taught me to ride a bike and hit a baseball. His death sparked a deep conflict in me. I remember simultaneously feeling incredible pain and tremendous relief that he was gone.

Pain that I'd lost my father, and relief his suffering had come to an end.

About a week later, my daughter, Leandra, had her first birthday. I was not married to her mother, and there was some question as to whether they would follow me to medical school if I was admitted to a university far away. Leandra and I have always been very close, and the thought of her and her mother not being with me was excruciating.

By May of that year, my anxiety was escalating. I did finish my degree, and despite the tragedy of losing my dad, I was able to get excellent grades. I applied to a number of medical schools, some close and some farther away.

The first round of acceptances had gone out, and a few of my friends had been granted early admission to various medical schools. I had not. As I write this, I can still feel the painful self-doubt. I had done my best and had done very well with good scores on the Medical College Admission Test (MCAT) and finished in the top one percent of my graduating class. But even with that, there was no guarantee. I felt vulnerable and weak and inferior. I was barely eating or sleeping, and with the stress of exams over, I had started having flashbacks about seeing my father's lifeless body. In my anxious and fractured state, I wondered if I was showing early signs of a serious mental illness. I wondered if the same fate of psychosis and suicide awaited me.

I was a mess.

Words cannot express how disappointed and disillusioned I was by June. Things were happening to me that made me question my sanity. I would have periods of what is called depersonalization, which is essentially the feeling you aren't inside of yourself. It is like you are hearing your own voice as someone else would or watching yourself drink a glass of water—as if you are outside of yourself, watching yourself do things. This sent me into a complete panic because my biggest fear was winding up schizophrenic or bipolar.

On more than one occasion, I used becoming a doctor as a type of lifeline. I remember thinking many times if I could get into medical school and become a doctor, that would prove once and for all I wasn't mentally ill. Becoming a doctor would be my "get out of jail free" card. (Little did I know then that being a doctor would become a jail of its own.)

The days dragged on, and as each day passed, I became more and more despondent. Part of me seriously considered quitting the whole idea of being a doctor. Then I got a break. On the morning of June 5, 1987, I got a phone call from the admissions office at the University of Western Ontario asking me if I was still interested in a position in their incoming class. They said I was on the waitlist and they were checking to see if everyone on the list still wanted to be considered.

One of the hallmarks of anxiety is being caught between two opposing paths of action. If I got in, there was a good chance I would be doing it alone, as my partner (and daughter's mother) didn't like the idea of moving so far away, and in my current state, I did not see that as a possibility. If I didn't get a spot, I would be in limbo, left in doubt of whether I would ever get into med school. To say I was pulled in different directions would be an understatement.

To make a long story short, I got accepted, and my partner and I decided to marry and form an official family unit that would uproot and make the journey from warm Victoria, British Columbia, to freezing cold London, Ontario.

Getting into med school was a battle, but getting through the first two years was a war. For the first year and a half of med school, I was a nervous wreck. I would sit in class and feel the drip, drip, drip of sweat run down my arms from the chronic state of fight-or-flight alarm in my body. Every day I felt crippling self-doubt. During orientation week, my anxious thoughts relentlessly told me I didn't deserve to be there and I had somehow gotten accepted by accident.

In your life, I'm sure you've faced huge obstacles—times when you felt completely overwhelmed. Hell, having a seemingly insurmountable challenge that completely overwhelmed you is probably why you developed an issue with anxiety in the first place, especially if that challenge occurred while you were a child or young teen.

If you were to ask me ten years ago what had been the biggest challenge in my life, I would have pointed to my childhood wounding, or medical school, or my two divorces. But I know now none of those are it. The biggest challenge I have faced in my life is dealing with uncertainty. Those of us with excruciating uncertainty in our childhoods will do just about anything to maximize our sense of certainty in adulthood. Unfortunately, as you'll soon see, worrying is a habit that gives the illusion of certainty but comes at a tremendous cost.

Many people who experience anxiety had a lot of uncertainty in their lives in childhood or at a time they were least able to handle it. Uncertainty is a huge unconscious trigger and is unbearable for many of us worriers because it reminds us of a time when we experienced tremendous, excruciating, desta-bilizing confusion and pain. When uncertainty revs up my worry, I know now this is the reactivation of the uncertainty of a thirteen-year-old who did not know what was coming next or what his father was doing and feeling. Because we will do anything to avoid it, uncertainty is often the birthplace of anxiety and worry.

Uncertainty was uncomfortable for us as children and still is for us as adults—and that discomfort in the body makes us feel we must *do* something about it. We feel we need to minimize uncertainty at all costs. The other name for minimizing uncertainty is control. The need to control shows up in many different ways and doesn't always show up as the busybody trying to do one hundred things at once or the person with an impeccably clean house. I am a self-proclaimed control freak, and if you ask my wife, my condo was often a complete mess. So perhaps a better name for it would be a "certainty freak."

In our attempt to control and limit uncertainty, we don't go out. We avoid places, people, and things that may create an undesirable reaction in us. Consciously, we are aware that control and certainty are an illusion, but unconsciously, where much of our motivation originates, we revert back to a time when we struggled to achieve control and certainty in any way, shape, or form.

3
Becoming a Doctor

Becoming a doctor was massively important to me. Overtly, the reason for this was I wanted the power to help people so they did not have to suffer as I had. I felt powerless to help my father, and I know how helpless and powerless it feels to be in chronic anxiety and alarm. Covertly, however, I would tell you now that being a doctor gave me a sense of power and control I never had growing up.

As a child, I never felt like I mattered. My father's tentative wellness and obvious sickness usurped most of the family's energy and attention. I adopted the role of caregiver for my parents and got some positive affirmation and identity that way. I have seen that many of my patients with anxiety carried responsibilities as children that were too much for them and made them grow up too fast. On one hand, you are inflated by the feeling of having a sense of purpose and importance. But on the other hand, when you carry too much responsibility too soon and part of you knows you're in way over your head, your nervous system goes into a state of chronic alarm.

By becoming a doctor, I was looking to recapture the inflated sense of importance I received from the responsibility I had taken on prematurely as an adolescent. I was going back to a well that had initially given me relief from my thirst for control, but I couldn't see the well was not full of pure water—but rather a mixture of water and toxins. All that responsibility I thought was feeding me as a teenager was in reality slowly poisoning me. As I continued to place caring for others above caring for myself, bit by bit, the mix became more poison and less water, but it was such an ingrained habit that I couldn't stop.

As I'll say many times, you can't change what you can't see, and I just couldn't see that my need to care for others before myself played a huge role in my increasing emotional and physical distress.

Helping my mother and father with their emotional needs was a coping strategy, and for a time, it helped me feel empowered amidst the chaos when my father got sick. But one of the definitions of neurosis is taking something that worked once and sticking with it forever. Part of me believed (and this is not unusual among doctors and worriers in general) that serving others would feed my own needs. But all coping strategies are only a temporary fix. Being a caregiver to my dad gave me a sense of power, and that made me feel I mattered. As I was young and impressionable, that caregiving behaviour created a program in me so that I could feel important when I looked after others. But in true neurotic fashion, I rode it until the wheels fell off and created the sense that I only felt good when I looked after others and therefore my own needs didn't matter. This mindset drove me right into medical school where looking after others before looking after yourself is par for the course (a little doctor golfing joke for you there).

When I qualified and began practicing as a doctor, I felt tricked. Instead of my elevated status and recognition as a physician decreasing my anxiety, the difficult memories associated with the caregiving role actually increased the feeling of instability and alarm, especially when there were patients that were not getting better despite my best efforts. When a patient failed to improve or got worse, there was an echo of my impotence at not being able to help my father. I had come all this way to be a doctor and I was *still* powerless? WTF?

I had viewed becoming a doctor as killing two birds with one stone. I could be important *and* help others with their suffering. But it soon became apparent the only thing being killed was me.

I probably went into medicine for the wrong reasons because I started to burn out early. It's a badge of honour worn by many doctors to work for thirty-six hours in one stretch, deliver babies at all hours, be on call for Christmas and holidays, and generally sacrifice for our patients. Part of me loved being a doctor and helping people, and part of me resented myself (although I wasn't consciously aware of it) for maintaining that debilitating childhood pattern of putting the needs of others before my own. It didn't help that my people-pleasing, rescuer personality was beginning to see the limitations of what I could actually do to help others. I felt impotent and frustrated with myself after working so hard and still being unable to help some of my patients.

Yet I didn't want to walk away. Being a doctor was part of my identity and, no matter how much it was hurting me, I couldn't willingly let it go. I'd have to be forced to let go—and as you'll see, I was.

4
Let Go of the Banana

Have you heard the story about how to catch a monkey? There is a see-through wire fence with a series of holes in it. The holes are just big enough to fit a monkey's hand and forearm. On the other side of the fence is a banana. The monkey can reach in and grab the banana, but the hole isn't big enough for the monkey to pull his hand out while still holding on.

The monkey sees the banana and grabs it—and then the person walks up and grabs *him*. The monkey could easily escape if he would let go of the banana, free his hand, and run. But because he can't bring himself to release the banana, he is trapped by his own hand and unable to see the simple solution to his predicament.

Do you chronically sacrifice for others? Are you holding on to worry under the illusion that it is keeping you safe and minimizing uncertainty because you are always prepared for the worst? Are you holding on to your identity of being anxious, as I clung to the identity of a doctor? Most likely you are fighting your thoughts on their own turf and aren't willing to let them go, as you falsely believe those worries are protecting you—just as I thought that being a doctor was killing two birds with one stone. Sure, in your adult mind, you know the worries make no sense, but in your child mind, where your deepest beliefs are, you unconsciously believe the worries are keeping you safe, and you are afraid to let them go.

Worrying gives us a sense of control and, in a way, it does actually make us feel better. We receive a small reward "hit" when something we've worried about does not come to pass. I will address this more later, but, essentially, worry does give us something and does serve a purpose; otherwise, we would not do it.

When people tell you, "Well, just stop worrying," in essence, they are saying, "Just let go of the banana." We worriers feel that if we let go of the banana, we are giving up something we have come to believe is helpful, just as the monkey believes holding on to the banana is his source of survival when it actually ensures his entrapment.

By 2010, I knew that I was burned out and I needed to leave the medical profession—but I couldn't bring myself to do it. For me, being a doctor was like holding on to the banana. Some part of me thought it was serving me when in reality it was entrapping me.

Being a doctor is one of those jobs where they brand the title into your identity by making it part of your name. Instantly upon graduating med school, I became "Doctor Russell Kennedy." I was inDOCtrinated, you might say. For some reason, they don't do this with other jobs. You don't become "Plumber Jones" or "Jack Hammer Johnson." (Actually, I think Jack Hammer Johnson is the name of an adult film actor, but I digress.)

My point is that once you're holding that banana in the form of a medical degree and title—much like our anxious and worrisome thoughts—it's very hard to let go of, even though you can clearly see the ways it is hurting you.

Sometimes it requires being forced—I mean, given the opportunity to see it from a different perspective.

On February 8, 2013, I fully ruptured my left Achilles tendon because, like the arrogant doctor I was, I injected it (myself) with cortisone and lidocaine. But, as any doctor will tell you, although the relief from Achilles tendinitis is virtually immediate from the anesthetic (and it was), the tendon is weakened by the cortisone part of the shot and there is a serious risk of rupture (which mine did).

That was the shot that broke the doctor's back. I was out, and I knew it. I haven't practiced medicine as a traditional allopathic doctor since that day, not because of my Achilles rupture (although it never fully healed), but because I finally let go of the banana and admitted that my mental health couldn't take practicing medicine anymore. I told myself it was because I was practicing in a broken medical system that relied heavily on treating everything with pharmaceuticals, which was partly true, but I was the one who felt broken. I was trapped in a feedback loop of overthinking and over-feeling, each feeding the other in an endless cycle.

Have you ever heard the saying "You can't see the label from inside the bottle"? I was so overwhelmed that I was unable to see I was trapped in my own compulsion to help others at the expense of looking after myself. If you'd asked me back then, I would have told you I was a good doctor and helping others was my life's work. But my body was in a constant state of fight-or-flight alarm, and my mind had become very adept at worrying.

In short, I had awareness of the pain but no awareness of its true source (consciously, at least).

Once again, I was a mess. As I faced the idea of giving up being a doctor, I had flashbacks to those dismal days where it was a very real possibility I would never get into medical school. I remember thinking I wasn't a doctor back then and really wanted to be, and now I *was* a doctor but really *didn't* want to be. However, being Dr. Russell Kennedy was so much a part of my identity that I felt I'd be lost without this title I didn't even want anymore. Remember that concept I brought up earlier of being torn between opposing paths?

I know now my Achilles rupture was a gift because it finally gave me the excuse I needed to look after myself. It was time to find the answer for myself and share that with people. The mandate was clear: "Physician, heal thyself." (And then help others with that knowledge ... See? I can't stop!)

The first stage of my escape from this vicious cycle involved developing a sense of awareness—a sense that I could witness what was really happening inside of me rather than suppressing and hiding from the painful feelings from my past. Much of relieving anxious thoughts and worry is making the unconscious conscious. It is your unconscious mind that runs your life, and it is the unconscious mind that drives your worry—but you don't even see it until you develop awareness.

5
What Is Awareness?

In my own healing journey from anxiety, one of my greatest weapons wasn't a technique or a doctor or a therapy or a pharmaceutical medication. It was a sense of awareness. Ironically, some of the most valuable "medications" that raised my sense of awareness were the psychedelics, a group of medications that aren't typically available to medical doctors.

Entire books have been written on awareness, but in this book, I'd like to cover the aspects of awareness that have helped me the most in my search for relief from anxiety.

So what is awareness?

We all have an awareness of the taste of our food, the touch of the steering wheel on our hands, and the sound of someone calling our name. This is the basic level of awareness that we use to experience the world. What I mean by awareness is a deeper level of awareness, typically called conscious awareness.

There is a major difference between *unconscious* awareness, which is rapid and automatic and directs attention in a reactive way, and *conscious* awareness. Unconscious awareness is feeling something, like the sensation of water as you are swallowing it. Conscious awareness is specifically directing your attention to that feeling, really honing in on and savouring the specific sensations like the temperature of the water and feeling the liquid run down your esophagus. In unconscious awareness, or just plain "awareness," time just flows by. In conscious awareness, there is a sense that time stops at that moment to allow a slower, more deliberate process of focusing specifically on an experience or object. Conscious awareness is being aware that you are aware.

As another example, you are breathing right now and likely aren't conscious of it. In conscious awareness, you would deliberately say, "I'll take a conscious, focused breath." You may even close your eyes and focus on how the breath feels going in and out of your nostrils. Try it right now: take a slow, conscious breath in and out, savouring the gamut of sensation a single breath provides.

In going from unconscious to conscious awareness, you go from daydreaming to awake, from past or future to present. In fact, the hallmark of conscious awareness is that it brings you firmly into the present moment.

Awareness can be seen as a skill, a practiced way of observing with non-judgmental curiosity. With practice, meditators develop the skill of seeing their thoughts as mere expressions of the mind, without believing the thoughts or automatically giving them the weight of truth. In a state of conscious awareness, thoughts can appear and be observed simply as byproducts of the mind.

Without the objective curiosity about our thoughts that conscious awareness brings, the mind unconsciously and automatically equates our thoughts (anxious or otherwise) with who we are. Until conscious awareness showed me these thoughts were only a part of me, I was not able to separate from them. In other words, if you are not aware of your thoughts, you *are* your thoughts. Without knowing you have an option to see things another way, you assume your singular perception of the world is how the world actually is. You never think to question your perceptions because you have never seen any reason to question your own experience and your interpretations of those experiences.

The child who grows up with an abusive or neglectful parent can often see this childhood experience as the totality of who they are. After all, this is the whole world as they know it. It is not until that child gets older and sees other models of parenting that are not abusive or neglectful that they understand there is another way. With new awareness that not everyone sees the world the way they do, they understand for the first time that there are different ways to view the world, and this is the beginning of seeing they have a choice.

From this point forward, when I say *awareness* in this book, I mean conscious awareness. Conscious awareness is specifically and intentionally turning the intensity of your observation and curiosity to a singular source, as you might focus on your breath in meditation. To become aware that you are aware—that is conscious awareness, and it is the foundation of breaking free from the automatic negative thinking that has probably ruled your life for a long time.

Before I developed this delicious newfound sense of awareness, I felt like a passive victim to projections of my painful past. Just because a situation turned out a certain way in our childhood does not mean it will repeat itself. But without awareness, the mind makes an image of the future directly from the past, in a kind of unspoken "Don't let this happen again" pattern. Without conscious awareness, I couldn't see how I was reaching back to what had happened to me in the past and throwing it onto my future path. I was tripping over my projections of doom and gloom, and I felt life was living me, not the other way around.

6

Awareness of Victim Mentality

If you consistently deal with anxiety, you are likely in a victim state—meaning that you are unknowingly victimizing yourself in an attempt to protect yourself. This takes place through an unconscious habit of allowing your mind to continuously conjure up stories, which you then automatically believe without questioning. We worriers feel that this habit is protecting us; we don't see that, instead, constantly being worried about every potential occurrence is perpetually victimizing and hurting us. It is also exhausting, as our endless rumination and worry usurp mental energy we could be using to live and enjoy life.

One of the tenets of the human mind and brain is that whatever you focus on (consciously or unconsciously), you will get more of. Using your mind and thoughts to amplify the ways you're a victim not only prevents you from moving away from the chronic worry you desire to heal but actually traps you deeper in it. Instead of holding on to a banana, you are now holding a hot potato that you won't let go of because you assume it is protecting you. But it's burning you—and it's the worst kind of burn because you are doing it to yourself.

As a family doctor, I saw patterns in families. I often say that people treat and talk to *themselves* the way their parents treated and talked to them. The external messages became the internal messages. As an example, children of perfectionists often adopt that same voice and attitude and apply impossible standards to themselves. Another common pattern I saw was victimhood. If a parent was a victim, the child would adopt that mentality as well. Victim mentality ran in families, perpetuating that chronic sense that the world was a dangerous place and we need to keep our guard up. Interactions in these families displayed a perpetual sense of being oppressed in some way. And they actually were—they were oppressing *themselves* with the unrelenting belief and attitude that the world was not a safe place.

I have a friend whom I'll call Mitchell. He and I met at a personal development retreat and had an instant connection. He was in his late forties, with salt-and-pepper hair and a friendly face with an easy laugh. He laughed harder than anyone at a joke I made to the group, so at that point, I *had* to be friends with him.

We talked at length about our childhood, mostly about our dads. Mitch was physically beaten by his father from the time he was about seven years old. His father never once beat Mitchell's slightly older sister. Mitch had a poor view of himself. He had addictions to medications, marijuana, and sex. He felt like a victim and like he could never win. That must have been exactly how that little seven-year-old boy felt.

Mitch had every right to feel victimized by life. Being beaten as a child *is* victimization. But in the end, it doesn't matter how you came to be a victim. As an adult, you have a choice to continue seeing yourself (and your life and the world) that way or to develop awareness of how you continue to victimize yourself and turn it around. Do you always assume the worst? Do you do everything for others, to the detriment of yourself? Are you a people-pleaser? Many of us learned to "read" our distressed parents and give them what we felt they needed. I certainly did this. When we continue this habit in adulthood of "reading" people's signals and sacrificing our own well-being to fulfill their needs, we are victimizing ourselves.

Failing to properly care for ourselves is another way we victimize ourselves. A lack of self-care is very common in people who struggle with anxiety and alarm. We are so used to putting others first that we neglect ourselves out of practice and habit. Of course, looking after others has its rewards. It feels good to help. But are you helping others out of choice or perceived obligation? For many of us worriers, the self-imposed obligation to look after others before we were ready was a way we could feel more like grown-ups and, thus, be imbued with the perception that we were adults—and, thus, in control. But in the process of focusing on others' needs, we teach ourselves to neglect our own. I became the man of the house because my father couldn't do it. Over-functioning as a caregiver became a habit for me, reinforced by the feeling of importance that came with being in charge. In an insidious and self-reinforcing program, I looked after others to gain a sense of power and control, but as a natural byproduct, I lost the ability to see and fulfill my own needs. I became very good at looking after others—it's no wonder I became a physician—but it came at a considerable cost. As I often say at the end of my talks, "Be careful what you're good at because people will expect it of you and you will expect it of yourself."

Again, the key is *seeing* it so you no longer have to *be* it. Cultivating awareness that you are in a victim state gives you the option to see—and then act another way. True awareness not only allowed me to see how I perpetuate the victim cycle of anxiety, but it also gave me the ability to see what anxiety is and, perhaps more importantly, what it is *not*. This distinction made it so much easier to understand and treat.

7

What Is Anxiety *Not?*

I was deeply confused by my anxiety for a long time. It felt like this amorphous blob of pain that I could never isolate.

One thing I learned in medical school is that the more I knew about a particular syndrome or condition I was treating, the better my treatment would be. In other words, the more defined something was, the easier it was to treat. That is just as true of the condition we refer to as *anxiety*. In my opinion, anxiety is really poorly defined.

If I talk to ten different people and ask them "What is anxiety?" I'm going to get ten different answers—and of those ten, four of them won't know what anxiety is at all. Maybe the only thing I do like about the word *anxiety* is that if you rearrange the letters, you get "any exit." When I was in the depths of my anxiety, I would take any exit to get out of it. So maybe we should change the name to "Generalized any exit disorder" or "Social any exit disorder" because I know when I get a bit of social anxiety, I'm looking for any exit out of there.

In an effort to narrow down and make an effective definition of what anxiety is, I'm going to talk about what anxiety is not. The first thing anxiety isn't: it's not a disease. (And this is coming from a medical doctor who loves to make diseases out of everything!) Anxiety is a normal coping mechanism that has gotten out of control. It's like putting a smoke detector in a cigar lounge.

Anxiety is an early warning system that is trying to help you survive but goes rogue. It's not there to harm you, but in its constant warnings, it makes you feel unsafe. Chronic worry is a maladaptive coping strategy, not a disease.

The next thing anxiety is not: it's not a character flaw or a weakness. Many of my patients express this feeling that they are somehow inferior or defective because they worry too much. They worry that there is something wrong with them and that their worrying will stop them from doing the things they need and want to do, but most do those things despite the alarm they feel. Counter to their opinion of themselves as weak, people with anxiety are among the strongest people I know. Not only do they do the things they are afraid of, but they do it with one hundred pounds of fear on their backs. I can tell you that becoming a stand-up comedian was something I never thought I'd be able to do because of my anxiety, and I've had countless anxiety patients get on a flight, speak at their child's school, and otherwise do things they never thought they could do.

I had to point out to them (and myself) that if you have anxiety, you're actually pretty strong. You do everything everyone else does, go to work, go to school, raise your kids, go to the grocery store, but you do it while you are sandbagged by worry! If you change your perception of this, you can see having anxiety is not a flaw but a sign of your resilience under adversity. Medical school is a challenge for people in the fittest of mental health, and I made it through (and even did well) even though at times I was afraid to leave my home. So if anything, having anxiety and living your life is a sign of strength of character. Once I realized this, I started to describe my character as sensitive and powerful versus anxious and weak.

(By the way, if you're wanting to build more of this skill, I highly recommend the book *The 5 Second Rule* by Mel Robbins. It's all about conditioning yourself to do things that are difficult or instill fear but that you know you need and want to do. As soon as you have the sense to do something helpful for yourself, try counting down 5-4-3-2-1 and *immediately* taking action before your overprotective ego steps in to immobilize you. This skill, which many anxiety sufferers have already developed to some degree as a coping mechanism, will come in handy as you're working on new habits to help you "drop the banana," so keep it in the back of your mind!)

The next thing anxiety is not—and this one's really important: it's not real. Reality and anxiety get all wrapped up together, and they're really two different things. If I'm outside about to be trampled by a group of rogue elephants, *that's* real. I have to do something to protect myself right away. However, if I'm upstairs worried that I might encounter a group of rogue elephants the next day, that's anxiety. But anxiety likes to trick us into thinking it's real. Anxiety likes to tell us we must do something *right now*—and nothing could be further from the truth. When you slow down and engage your conscious awareness,

you see that nothing has to be done. In fact, doing nothing, other than holding the thoughts in non-emotional, conscious curiosity in the present moment, is actually the best reaction to worrisome thoughts.

Why? Because anxiety and worry are generated by an overactive imagination of the future. Since the future hasn't yet happened and is strictly in the realm of the imagined, anxiety is by definition about something that is *not real*.

At this point, you may be experiencing some resistance to these ideas. I'm trying to establish anxiety as clearly as I possibly can so you can see you don't have to (and in fact shouldn't) fight with it, try to overcome it, beat it, or do anything else to it. In fact, the more you fight with it or try to overcome it, the more real it appears, because the more you fight with something, the deeper your system moves into a fight-or-flight state and the less rational your mind becomes. The less rational and more impaired by worries your mind becomes, the more likely you will lose the grounding and awareness of the present moment and be transported into the future because all worry is future-based. When your mind loses its rational faculties and you are removed from the grounding of the present moment, even outlandish worries seem real. Anxiety is not reality, although it seduces us into believing it is. Remember that you always have the choice to drop the banana instead of continuing to fight to pull your hand through the hole.

The last thing I'll tell you anxiety is not—and this might blow your mind: anxiety is not a feeling. I'm going to say that again: *anxiety is not a feeling.* Look, I get it—you picked up this book because it seemed like I knew what the hell I was talking about, and now I go off and make a ridiculous statement like this. I know how you feel if you have anxiety. Or perhaps more correctly, I know how you think. Anxiety is purely mind-based thinking of projections, expectations, stories, and thoughts of the *future.* Anxiety is a thinking process, not a feeling one.

I understand it may feel counterintuitive to think that anxiety is not a feeling, especially when you have probably labelled it as such for decades. If you are asked, "What colour is a banana?" you are very likely to answer, "Yellow." Bananas are yellow. Of course, they are. But is it not equally true that some bananas are green? We don't think of bananas as green, but if I now ask you the colour of bananas, you will probably say they can be yellow *or* green. (In fact, bananas spend more time being green than they do yellow. It's odd to think of bananas "spending time," but I digress.) I have placed a concept in your mind that has changed the way you look at what you previously assumed was an incontrovertible fact. I have renewed your perception of bananas, and I will do the same about the condition called *anxiety*.

I am asking you to do the same reframing with the term *anxiety*, to see anxiety in a brand-new way: as simply the anxious thoughts or endless machinations of the mind. Your mental health depends on it. Fully accept anxiety as simply a mind-based activity, just as you have quickly reframed the colour of the banana, and we will be in great shape!

As you embrace this new perspective of anxiety as purely a thinking issue, you have taken a giant step forward in the understanding of your dis-ease.

8
Anxiety Is Not a Feeling

Before I move on and talk more about what anxiety is, let me say a bit more about what you might be thinking after that last bomb I just dropped. "You keep telling me anxiety is not a feeling. But my anxiety hurts so much." I am showing you a critical part of my own healing from anxiety—specifically, seeing that anxiety is *only* a thinking process, only a series of *thoughts*.

Think of a headache right now. Does that thought hurt? Anxious thoughts are the same: the thought itself doesn't hurt. The pain you are feeling is a sense of alarm in your body, and that *is* painful. By the end of this book, you'll fully realize where the pain you attribute to your anxiety truly comes from and what you can do about it. I'm not saying this condition we commonly refer to as anxiety isn't a painful process. I am defining anxiety and breaking it down into its component parts—anxious thoughts in the mind and alarmed feeling in the body—so we can heal it.

Before I address the pain behind what you call anxiety, I need to show you how to break your dis-ease up into manageable pieces because trying to tackle it all at once can feel impossible. So long as we see anxious thoughts of the mind upstairs and the painful alarm feelings in the body downstairs as one and the same, it is virtually impossible to penetrate their defences.

Think of having two pairs of earphones with their cables twisted together. You are not able to discern which earbuds go with which jack. The whole tangled mess is indistinguishable and therefore unusable. You must patiently pull the two pairs apart so that both become recognizable and useful. Trying to treat anxiety as a jumble of thinking and feeling is virtually impossible. Until anxious thinking and alarmed feeling are teased apart and distilled down to their essence, we have no entry point—no way of breaking the cycle. When we can fully understand, appreciate, and distinguish each component, we can see how to break the cycle by separating and neutralizing each part. Until then, we are at the mercy of the alarm-anxiety cycle—where the anxiety *thinking in the mind* feeds the alarm *feeling in the body* and the alarm feeling feeds back into more anxious thoughts.

Incidentally, I didn't become aware of this cycle until I was in my fifties. For decades before that, I was trapped in the fear that my anguish was inescapable.

9

My LSD Trip

I experienced life as a powerless victim for many years. After more than two decades of trying multiple medications, techniques, and therapies without any significant relief, I felt hopelessly frustrated and resigned myself to the assumption that I was stuck with emotional pain forever. I heard the same story from many of my patients.

It wasn't until I realized that much of my suffering was at my own hand (or mind) and that there was something I could do to break my own victim mindset that I began to feel empowered.

Teasing out the anxiety from the alarm and treating them separately has been the single biggest discovery that has allowed me to heal. It is critical to understand this theory—even if it is difficult to grasp or believe—as the rest of this book (and your healing) depends on it.

Remember that there are two distinct components to what we call anxiety: (1) a sense of alarm in the body and (2) anxious thoughts of the mind.

1. There is a sense of alarm that occurs outside of the brain. This fight-or-flight sensation is the remnant of old, unresolved trauma we suffered, typically in childhood. It is usually felt in the midline of the body around the heart. I'll talk about this alarm in great detail in Part 2.

2. There are anxious thoughts created by the mind. The mind is a meaning-making, make-sense machine. It is constantly scanning the environment and then automatically and unconsciously making thoughts that match the environment. The mind reads the alarm in the body and notes a sense of danger or threat. The mind notes the alarm is painful and draws the conclusion it is dangerous. The mind makes thoughts in the form of worries or projections that are consistent with that perceived danger. These thoughts are worries.

I didn't come by the anxiety/alarm distinction easily. In fact, it was a revelation I had while coming off a "bad trip" I had on LSD in October 2013 (not that I have had any good trips—it was my one and only experience with LSD). One trip was all I needed to gain a different perspective, a new awareness that the pain I attributed to my chronic worry had more to do with my body than my mind.

You may wonder, if I am so prone to fear and worry, wasn't I frightened of LSD? While it is true I am more than a bit of a scaredy-cat to start with and the thought of taking LSD or any mind-altering drugs did frighten me, I was at the point where life did not appear worth living if I was in such alarm day after day. I was desperate and willing to try anything.

In September 2013, I had recently come back from India, where I was assured that my anxiety would be cured by spirituality and prayer. It wasn't. My good friend, who is an Ayurvedic doctor, saw that I was in rough shape and knew I needed a complete change of perception. The best way he knew to facilitate that was through a psychedelic. I, on the other hand, was scared of "losing my mind," having flashbacks of my father's psychotic states. I also knew that a psychedelic is a risk in those with a family history of psychosis, but after thirty-plus years of conventional medical and psychological therapy with no lasting benefit, it was do or die. The parallels with my father were not lost on me. He was exceptionally intelligent and exceptionally crazy. I am both less intelligent and less crazy than he was. Many times I wondered if I was living my father's destiny, and I often thought taking my own life may be my only escape from interminable pain.

Luckily for me, LSD did what I had hoped and gave me a new awareness—an opportunity to see things in a different way when I was "out of my mind." I was so accustomed to seeing things through the lens of my training as an allopathic physician that I had lost the ability to see things any other way. I suppose you could say I lost my mind and gained a new one. This is what I want for you: to show you how you can develop awareness so you can see your pain in a new way. I will show you how to *see* your pain so you don't have to *be* your pain.

During the psychedelic experience, I didn't see the full distinction of alarm in the body and anxiety in the mind right away. My mind was completely fractured. Colours had a vibrancy I had never seen before. A still image of my father in his Air Force uniform seemed to have him move left and right like he was dancing. As soon as I tried to focus on something, it moved. Nothing was static. Most disturbing was that my thoughts "moved" too. The more I tried to hold a thought, the more it would morph into something completely unpredictable. Also, it seemed like there was no distinct "me." While this won't do it justice, the best way I can describe what I experienced is that I had no distinct boundaries. I flowed into everything and everything flowed into me. There was no me; I was everything.

As the drug wore off and the flowing and moving slowed down, some coherent thoughts began to emerge. By no means was I holding on to stable thoughts, but I was shown that my anxiety was centred in my body. I had the distinct image of an irregular, oval-shaped, purple, crystalline density that felt like an aching pressure located just to the right of my solar plexus and lower sternum. I don't know how exactly this came to me, but I was told this aching pressure was a type of energy locked in my body. Over time and through meditation, I have come to believe this purple density was the overflow of trauma that my mind was unable to contain and process as a child. Over time, I came to know this energy was the source of my alarm.

To this day, I don't know where this knowledge came from, and it certainly didn't come all at once. There were some very rough days immediately after my LSD experience. I fear how odd it might seem, a fifty-year-old traditional medical doctor taking his first trips on psychedelics. Usually, it is younger people experimenting with mind-altering chemicals. However, I was truly desperate, and had it not been for LSD, I'm not sure if I ever would have figured out the true source of my pain. To be brutally honest, without the powerful and useful knowledge given to me on LSD, I doubt I'd still be alive.

For the ensuing months after my psychedelic trip, although I still felt alarmed much of the time, I knew something had shifted. Something felt different. I started to separate the anxious thoughts from the alarm. As I became better at directing my conscious awareness, I alternated between focusing on the *thinking* of my mind and then the *feeling* in my body. More and more, I began to see that what I called *anxiety* was not one entity but two.

Before my LSD experience, I had no awareness of this separation, and the red alarming sensations and blue anxious thoughts insidiously blended together in this purple haze of blinding pain from which there seemed no escape.

Since that experience, the concept of isolating anxiety in the mind from alarm in the body has had such power in my healing from chronic worry. This framework allowed me, with the help of awareness, to break the cycle and begin my recovery from decades of pain.

10

LSD and Me

If it wasn't for LSD, this book may never have been written. I know it may be disconcerting to think of a healthcare professional who has held others' lives in his hands fracturing his mind with psychedelics, and I can assure you it's not typical medical doctor behaviour—but I am not a typical medical doctor. I had an anxiety disorder so severe that I considered suicide. I was desperate, and desperate times called for desperate measures. I am not advocating psychedelics to treat mental disorders, as I can also say my experiences on psychedelics made my emotional pain worse in many ways. I can tell you that taking LSD moved me forward in some ways and backward in others. Do not assume that because it eventually helped me that it will help everyone.

Questioning there was something other than my mind at the helm of my fear never entered my awareness until that awareness was skewed by lysergic acid diethylamide. Under LSD I could not rely on my mind because it was fractured into a million little pieces for many hours. I cannot describe to you the terror I have felt under the influence of psychedelics. I had relied on relentless worrying and compulsive thinking as a coping strategy. When a psychedelic substance took away my ability to think, I was left face to face with the pain I had spent decades avoiding.

But despite the unmitigated terror, I do believe it was my destiny to see that ethereal side I never would have seen as an academic medical doctor so I could have a shot at healing.

The biggest lesson I learned under any of the psychedelics was not some revelation that I had past lives or that I was a beautiful and inextricable part of creation or that I was one with everything (although there was a sense of all of those things in the few moments when I wasn't actively in a purple haze). The biggest and most practical lesson I learned was that my anxiety had much more to do with a storage of old trauma in my body than any thought that I ever had. LSD showed me the alarm in my body, but it did not give me a name for it or show me what I was supposed to do with it.

Psychedelics showed me that I am more than my mind. I just had to be forcibly evicted from that mind to be able to see that it was only a (noisy) part of me. Before trying psychedelics, my unresolved trauma had me holed up in my head, firmly convinced that I shouldn't venture out of it and especially not go down into feelingtown because it's pretty rough down there.

The psychedelics allowed me to see that feelingtown was where all the life was. From that revelation, I saw the key to emotional peace lay not in my mind but in my body.

I only took psychedelics a handful of times, and I don't plan to do it again. It was kind of like a science fair project in Hell. I am grateful for the insights, but I still have semi-regular nightmares flashing back to when I lost my mind. People ask me all the time if they should take psychedelics to see if that will help them understand their anxiety as it did for me. I tell them it's probably best if they study my experience and treat it as though I "took one for the team"—I did it so you don't have to.

11

The Conscious and Unconscious

We may think that what distinguishes us, as humans, from other animals is our capacity for conscious awareness and the fact that we are not driven entirely by instinct—but the truth is that humans possess both conscious and unconscious states within each of us, and many of us are still largely driven by our unconscious.

The greatest challenge of the unconscious is that it cannot be commanded directly. The conscious, almost by definition, is under volitional control. If I want to rub my cheek with my fingers, I direct that action voluntarily. But if a mosquito lands on my cheek, I will automatically (unconsciously) reach up to slap it. On some level, we can use the conscious to influence the unconscious (I can consciously decide not to slap the mosquito), but depending on the strength of unconscious learning, the conscious may have limited power. This is why talk therapy has such a challenge changing unconsciously mediated perception and behaviour, especially if that perception and behaviour are seen as helping us to survive. Although you *can* stop yourself from slapping the mosquito, you *cannot* will yourself into not loving someone anymore.

For the vast majority of human beings, the unconscious is actually in control. The more unstable the environment in which you grew up, the more your unconscious will take over and do whatever it has to do to ensure your survival. Instead of driving you forward into *growth* toward your hopes and dreams, it will keep you exactly where you are. Fixated on *protection*, it keeps you away from perceived danger that, for the most part, your unconscious is actually creating. Many of us with anxiety and alarm start to make our lives smaller and smaller, avoiding anything that could potentially cause us pain. This often occurs unconsciously, as we slowly and insidiously shy away from doing things that challenge us.

One of the primary ways the unconscious takes us over is by creating a sense of alarm in our body. A part of our brains called the amygdala, often referred to as the brain's fear centre, sounds the alarm when we get close to anything even slightly reminiscent of our old wounding. As an example, I have a friend who was laughed at by her schoolmates when she gave a presentation in class when she was twelve years old, and to this day—more than thirty years later—she gets shot into alarm at even the thought of speaking in front of people. The amygdala never forgets. When the amygdala shoots us into physiological and psychological alarm, this state impairs the mind's ability to be rational and in control.

The more the mind is impaired by alarm, the more we will act from an old, unconscious protective place and our thoughts will reflect the need for protection. In other words, we start to create what I call the 3 W's of worry—**warnings**, **what-ifs**, and **worst-case scenarios**—in a further effort to keep ourselves safe. We cease to be able to see our anxious thoughts as simply thoughts. We imagine a scary story and then frighten ourselves by forgetting that we are the ones that made up that story in the first place.

I often get asked if the thoughts of the mind create the alarm in the body or if, rather, the alarm creates the thoughts.

From my perspective, the answer is both. But for me and most of us worriers, the most important point is that the alarm stored in our bodies is the creator of the anxious thoughts. Of course, the anxious thoughts aggravate the alarm, and the alarm-anxiety cycle takes us over, but as you'll see, for those of us prone to chronic worry, the alarm stored in the body is a much bigger player in the cycle than the anxious thoughts of the mind.

There are times that the thoughts do come first, like when someone brings up my father or I'm reading a medical paper on bipolar disorder or schizophrenia. When I see the specific anxious thoughts, I can consciously pinpoint where the alarm-anxiety cycle becomes triggered in me, but for the most part, the unconscious alarm in my body will just hit me, and I won't know where it came from. That is to say, emotional trauma stored in the body usually generates the anxiety in the mind.

Chances are, your old trauma sneaks up on you in a similar way. Most of the (over)reactions of our bodies are beyond our awareness. But once we start using conscious awareness, we start seeing a connection that was previously invisible—and with that new insight, we can start to heal our old wounds.

Here is an example of trauma stored in the body unconsciously triggering an emotional response. After I finished medical school, to become eligible to practice, I first needed to work for a year in an accredited hospital as a medical intern. For my internship, I returned home to work at the same hospital where my father had frequently been admitted to psychiatric intensive care. The first time I was called to see a patient on that psych ward, I was hit with a panic attack.

I had been so busy going from surgery to cardiology to gastroenterology and then to psych that I didn't have time to think about where I was and the implications. But my body knew. The ward had a smell to it. Old memories of visiting my incapacitated, often drugged and incoherent father on so many occasions all those years ago flooded back to me. As I arrived on the floor, my body unconsciously went into alarm without engaging thought at all. Once I did consciously think about where I was, more troubling memories of that place came rushing back.

Carl Jung said, "Until you make the unconscious conscious, it will rule your life and you will call it fate." I believe he meant our drives and fears that hide in the shadows of our minds will rule our feelings and behaviours until we see them and bring them out of the shadows and into the light of conscious awareness. Until I did LSD, the alarm energy in my body—the real source of my emotional pain—remained unconscious. In making that alarm conscious, I was able to consciously take control of my own life rather than allowing the invisible alarm to rule my life.

When you create a sense of awareness, you arm yourself in such a way that you can observe your internal and external environment from a position of power. Without this, you can be blindsided by your old unconscious programming. Inevitably, there will still be some old patterning and subconscious drives you cannot see no matter how much conscious awareness you employ, but you are infinitely better off having a mindset of openness and active awareness than just living your life as a passive victim to your unconscious wounds.

When we truly focus on how and what we are feeling, we bring in conscious awareness as a brilliant tool to start seeing and disempowering the influences of the unconscious that were previously hiding in the shadows.

The unconscious part of us, which I believe has roots in both the mind and the body, holds much of who we believe ourselves to be. But if that was forged by pain, it may not be who you truly are at all—it represents who you *had* to be to survive. The more trauma you endure, especially as a child, the more your unconscious gets redirected into your protective self and away from your real self. The more we act from the protective self, the more alarm we feel. We can be in protection or in growth, but we cannot be in both—they are mutually exclusive. The more we find the real self and commit to our growth by living there, the less alarm we feel.

12
Immobility: Held Immobilized

My mother was, and still is, a very sensitive being. Being born sensitive (as I also was), coupled with the experience of heading to the bomb shelters each night as a nine-year-old in Glasgow, made it so she did not tolerate noise or activity well. I do not blame her for exquisite sensitivity, as I know her nervous system was forged at a very tumultuous time in human history.

Unfortunately, as a child, I was both noisy and active. Had I been born in 2000 instead of 1960, I likely would have been diagnosed with ADHD. I still get frustrated easily, not by people (for whom I seem to have almost infinite patience) but by things. If I have to put together an IKEA desk or a gas barbecue and it's not going well, things will start to fly. My mother showed me in no uncertain terms that being angry and active wasn't okay, so I became immobilized because I didn't feel it was safe to be my real (active and curious) self.

To this day, I hate being told what to do. I was fired from every job I had prior to med school, and my mother said that it was good that I became a doctor because I could work for myself.

Unfortunately, being quickly shut down from the time I was a toddler sent a message to me that my emotionality and intensity weren't welcome. Many of us with anxiety and alarm were made to feel that our attempts at exploring and expressing who we are were not okay. When you take a child's ability to be angry away from them, they feel helpless, move into victim mode, and progressively lose the ability to defend themselves.

How do you feel about your anger? Are you afraid of it? Do you have a temper? Many of us anxiety/alarm sufferers have a conflicted relationship with anger. One of the ways victim mentality weakens you is by paralyzing your sense of anger—as if you feel you don't have the *right* to get angry, perhaps because you felt denied the ability to protect yourself at an early age and needed to just give up and accept what was given to you. If you were already living in a chaotic environment, you may have suppressed your anger because of the fear of adding more intense emotion to the household.

Anger is a defensive emotion. It mobilizes you to protect yourself. Anger is a response to a real or perceived threat. For example, if you hear someone has said something negative or untrue about you, anger is a normal and natural reaction. The anger creates an emotional energy that mobilizes you to protect yourself.

But often, those of us who experienced emotional overwhelm as children do not express that anger energy out of a fear of repercussions. Instead of mobilizing, we often do the opposite: freeze in immobility and, instead of protecting and sticking up for ourselves, abandon ourselves. Of course, this inability to protect ourselves and express energy outward reaffirms our victim mentality. This anger energy has to go somewhere and often turns inward, making us take JABS at ourselves (remember judge, abandon, blame, and shame). I'll talk more about how we make our emotional pain worse by taking JABS at ourselves and how we can stop and, instead, redirect this into productive energy, in Part 3.

I once had a patient (whom I'll call Mary) who always *appeared* cheery and optimistic, even when she was experiencing significant health issues. I once documented forty-three different medical complaints on a single office visit. To this day, it's still a record. Yet during that visit, she was cheery and joking. Mary had adopted a mentality of helplessness. She felt like a victim to her body and mind. I can't say I blamed her. She had so many medical issues I can completely see why she would feel exasperated. Mary had chronic anxiety and alarm, and I really felt for her.

But here's the curious thing. In ten years of being her physician, I never saw Mary get angry. Not once over an entire decade. Even when a long-anticipated medical test was postponed or cancelled or her condition worsened, she always remained resigned to her fate. On another occasion, one of the specialists who saw her was quite rude to her in an offhand and insensitive comment about her weight, and she still didn't speak up or show any signs of anger.

Perhaps the worst part of scenarios like this, and countless others I've encountered, is that when we (consciously or unconsciously) choose a victim mentality as adults, we accept futility as a way of life. There is no longer a person, external force, or circumstance disempowering us, but we have taken over the role of disempowering ourselves. I saw many of my patients who were overwhelmed in childhood just abandon the fight and give up. In a way, I can't say I blamed them. When you have a history of overwhelm with no history of success or pursuit with no chance of emotional connection, it's an understandable response to retreat and just accept defeat instead of putting more energy into trying to change your situation. But when we learn to immobilize and suppress ourselves, this is a very dangerous and damaging precedent, as it fosters a victim mentality that both originates from and perpetuates alarm in the body and anxiety in the mind.

What chronic worry does over time is recreate the impotence many of us felt as children. This chronic disempowerment, over time, creates a victim mentality. One of the most troubling features of victim mentality is that it makes you believe you are protecting yourself, when in reality, seeing yourself as a victim gives you the permission to retreat from your challenges, which reinforces a sense of helplessness. In this way, victim mentality forms a self-reinforcing loop of helplessness and retreat. If you maintain a victim mentality, you can never overcome your anxiety and alarm because you are paralyzed by them. This state of affairs further chips away at your self-confidence, eroding your faith in your own abilities and holding you back from breaking free of the very victim mentality you yourself are perpetuating.

Productive anger and mobilization allow you to see aspects of your true self that you may have lost as a child and are constructive ways out of victim mentality. Healthy anger shows you are not helpless—far from it—and that you can gain confidence in and depend on yourself for self-soothing and self-care. Worriers perceive themselves as victims and don't have the confidence to soothe themselves, and that becomes a self-fulfilling prophecy.

So the key, as always, is awareness. It may take a while to notice how you disempower yourself and hold yourself immobile because you have become so numb to your own anger and helplessness that you don't even see it anymore.

If you struggle with chronic worry, there is a good chance you were a victim to a form of abuse or abandonment as a child, at a time you had little power. There is a good chance you adapted to the futility by repressing your anger and adopting a victim mentality. It was just too demoralizing to become angry or try to fight back when you had no power to change the situation, so to minimize stress, you just gave up the fight, like an animal that is cornered by a predator and has no other option but to play dead.

This is the problem with many of our childhood defence mechanisms like adopting a victim mentality: we make the assumption that because that defence worked in childhood, it will always work. That erroneous and neurotic assumption is stored in us as unconscious implicit memory, and it's frickin' powerful.

I'll return to victim mentality as a childhood defence mechanism and what you can do about it, but in the meantime, know that you are not in the powerless situation you were as a child. It's okay now to mobilize with anger (notice I did not say rage), and it is more than okay to stand up for yourself and stand up against your worries.

13

Issues in Our Tissues

Whether we are aware of it or not, we are guided every single day by our memories. The more intense the memory (good or bad), the more it influences our behaviour, perceptions, and beliefs, in both conscious and unconscious ways.

Burning your hand on the stove as a child and never needing to be told not to do it again is an example of implicit memory, or "body memory." The memory is *in* us and unconsciously guides our behaviour. The most powerful implicit memories are attached to emotion and pain. The more powerful the emotion, the more powerful the lingering effect. In yoga, we call it having "issues in our tissues." While teaching a yoga class, I would often see my students start to cry. A certain movement or posture can trigger the release of a strong memory the person hadn't thought about in years, often resulting in a strong emotional reaction. At the end of the class, I would often reassure my tearful student by telling them that some postures are likely to bring out old pain and it's completely normal that tears come, as tears are one of the ways our system heals old pain.

Some of the most powerful body memories are created in childhood when we encode painful implicit memories deep in the body and mind. These emotionally charged memories are beyond our conscious awareness but often lead to anxiety and alarm. They can run in the background of our lives for years and cause tremendous pain. If we are not aware of them, these old traumas can hold an energy of alarm in our bodies that I have created a term for: *background alarm.* (I'll explore this concept in more detail in Part 2.)

As an example, you may have been bitten by a dog when you were very young and have no conscious memory of it yet now have an inexplicable aversion to dogs as an adult. For some reason, you just don't trust them. Even though you don't consciously remember the dog bite, it's stored in your system and you are still reacting to it.

To use a more emotionally charged and personal example, I developed an unconscious implicit program that it was not safe to love. It took my focused, conscious awareness to see why I had such an inexplicable aversion to relationships. (I've been divorced ... twice.) The answer? My father's schizophrenia. I loved him dearly, and when he was sane, he was a very attentive protector and teacher, but with each catastrophic emotional collapse and hospitalization, I could see he was progressively leaving me, mentally if not physically.

Losing him was both agonizing and devastating. Throughout my early teens, he would bounce back to a level of functionality where I could still count on him. Once I felt his counsel and presence, I would give him my heart, only to have it crushed again in six to eighteen months with the inevitable next episode of psychosis. As I got into my late teens, I went from having a father *in* him to being a father *to* him. That's not how it's supposed to work, and my unconscious response was to numb myself and slowly withdraw. I stopped trusting in being his son but, at the same time, resented the loss of him. My protective instinct caused me to start numbing my feelings toward him, as loving him was just too treacherous. But two divorces have taught me that you can't numb to one person without numbing to all people, and this caused my relationships to suffer for decades.

You can't harden your heart to one person without compromising your ability to love all people. Perhaps even more importantly, when you stop trusting love for someone else, you limit that same love to yourself. I've also found when you push love out, fear moves in to take its place.

Wow, I got really philosophical there! Maybe I should get back to the science ...

What causes alarm and anxiety? Separation. Not trusting love. Lack of connection to myself and others. Extreme resistance to being and feeling vulnerable.

What is the antidote to anxiety and alarm? Trusting and expressing the love I have for myself and others. I had to learn that it was safe to trust love and be vulnerable again. I had to learn to have compassion for my dad. I had to reinstate my love for him. In doing so, I found the compassion and healing I needed for myself.

The ego's response of withdrawing trust and love, while arguably protective in your childhood, is now preventing you from fully engaging in life by avoiding anything that is perceived to be potentially painful, including the most important aspect of life itself: opening up to the vulnerability of love and to loving yourself and others.

Staying in victim mode—numb, shut down, and "protected" from vulnerability—cuts you off from the very thing you need to heal from chronic worry: love and connection.

It is not possible to numb yourself to love in one area of your life without it affecting you globally.

The unconscious pattern or program I was playing out was "To love means to get hurt," based on my implicit feeling-based memories from the pain of dealing with my father. Loving someone set off my alarm, and love was the exact thing I needed to assuage my alarm. How are you supposed to heal when your unconscious won't let you access the very thing you need to heal?

14
The Ego

Imagine something that totally fires you up. It makes you upset, scared, and frustrated, and you can't help but react. Chances are your ego is involved, and the situation is rekindling a painful episode from your past.

Entire books are written on the ego, but I am going to stick with the parts most relevant to anxiety and alarm. The ego is a part of our unconscious that protects us from harm or, perhaps more correctly, *attempts* to protect us from harm. It has other jobs too, but the protection aspect is the part that's relevant here.

Essentially, the ego tries to prevent us from making the same mistakes again or exposing ourselves to experiences that have hurt us in the past. The ego is linked to a structure in the brain called the amygdala, as I said above is commonly referred to as the fear centre of the brain. The amygdalae (we actually have two, right and left) record everything that has ever hurt us, either physically or emotionally. It is their job to never forget anything that has harmed us. The ego, in concert with information encoded by the amygdalae, sends our system into high alert when anything even remotely close to the original painful stimulus is perceived. (From this point forward, I use the singular form, amygdala, as it is more common, but know that I mean both left and right.)

Remember that dog you got bitten by as a child? Let's say it was the neighbour's Doberman Pinscher when you were five years old. Your amygdala and ego will likely sound the alarm in your system whenever you encounter a Doberman (or perhaps any dog) for the rest of your life. In fact, since the amygdala generalizes to anything even close to the original trauma, it may very well sound the alarm and make you afraid of any animal around the same size.

Even the *thought* of a Doberman might send you into alarm.

The ego reaction doesn't have to make sense, and it often doesn't. Let's say you are in a supermarket and you have a panic attack. You go outside and the panic attack subsides. Your amygdala and ego conclude that the supermarket is the cause of your fear. The next time you need to go to the supermarket, you walk on eggshells expecting the worst and, lo and behold, get another panic attack. This confirms the evil supermarket as the cause, so you avoid supermarkets. Now your amygdala has inspired you to narrow your world so you can only go to farmers markets to avoid the ego-based supermarket monster.

This is characteristic of ego protection. It protects you from a danger you made up yourself!

The ego acts automatically, often outside of our conscious awareness. One of the biggest challenges we face is actually seeing where we are creating our own pain. The ego shoots first and doesn't ask questions at all. The ego is reflexive, not reflective. It's not interested in solutions or ways of seeing more clearly. It is primarily interested in protecting you from harm, oblivious to the mounting list of dangers (supermarkets, buses, doorknobs, open spaces, confined spaces, dogs, cats, trees, wombats) the ego itself is creating. The more emotional and physical trauma you experienced as a child, the stronger the instinct of your ego to protect you.

In us worriers, the ego is particularly active, ready to act in an instant. When the ego has its way, we are chronically in an alarmed, defensive state. We may not be overtly aware of it as we become used to its presence in the background, but make no mistake: the anxious person's nervous system is prepared to jump into action much faster than that of someone who does not struggle with chronic worry.

The ego has no life in the moment. It depends on destabilizing you by remembering traumas of the past and scary predictions of the future. Even though we may be safe in the moment, the ego needs you to be on the constant lookout for danger. Allowing you to feel safe is not in the ego's best interest, even though it is in *your* best interest. Because the ego thrives in the shadows of old fears and unresolved traumas buried in the unconscious (as well as creating new worries of the future), conscious awareness and grounding ourselves in the present moment are our most effective tools to disarm the out-of-control ego.

It is up to our conscious awareness to ask questions. If we never question why we do what we do, think what we think, or act the way we act, chances are we will stay under the ego's relentlessly protective umbrella, and our emotional and physical lives will become narrower and narrower in a futile attempt to avoid danger that is only real in the ego's warped perception.

The ego is like an overprotective mother in the extreme. Just as this hyper-vigilant mother will not let her child explore and have fun playing on the jungle gym for fear of getting hurt, your ego will not let you explore and have fun with life because of the perceived danger.

The ego is not inherently bad. It's simply misguided and relentless—much like the Japanese World War II soldier Hiroo Onoda, who hid in the jungle and kept fighting for 29 years after the Japanese surrendered in 1945. He had orders to fight to the death and, not allowing himself to believe the war was over, kept himself in constant battle. The ego is just as tenacious (if not more so). It believes the war we fought so many years ago as children is still going strong, and so it keeps up the fight.

The ego is at its most influential and believable when it takes us out of the present. The ego knows it has no power in the now. It only remembers the past and maps it onto an imagined future. When you bring yourself into the present moment of conscious awareness, the ego is a deer in headlights. Feeling pow-erless, the ego will try to scare you out of your present moment state by getting you to emotionally time travel to past traumas or future worries. Later on, I'll show you how to see your ego with compassion and the knowledge that it's only trying to keep you safe so you will have the option not to do everything it says.

15
The Fear Bias

Our brains have a bias toward survival, which means they also have a bias to worry and overestimate threat.

On an evolutionary basis, those who were more fearful or assumed the worst were more likely to survive. Thousands of years ago, if you saw a bush move and you assumed it was a predator and made your way to a safe place, you would live to mate and pass on your genes. However, if you assumed it was just the wind that moved the bush, you might become something to eat, and no mating for you. In a very real way, we were rewarded for being fearful, and parents with a bias towards fear made fearful offspring. Fear became a factor in natural selection, and the fear bias was passed on.

Back then, the main threats were physical, but in modern times, our threats are much more mental and come from inside of us more than from the outside. You could say that primitive man feared his predators and modern man fears his creditors, but the "modern" human brain and body react the same way to both.

While that cautious mindset was likely to help us survive the hostile environment thousands of years ago, chronic worry itself has now become a modern hostile environment. In trying to keep us safe with worrisome thoughts, worry has become a threat to the very survival it so desperately tries to preserve!

The *fear* bias, designed to protect us from real threat, is now the *worry* bias designed to protect us from imagined threats. By and large, we have come to be more of a threat to our own well-being than anything or anyone else.

It's like a dog biting his own tail, thinking he is fighting an opponent: as the dog feels more pain from the imaginary combatant, he bites harder, trapped in a cycle that keeps escalating. The good news is that once we realize we are biting our own tail, we can let go. This book will show you how you are unwittingly biting your own tail, like the self-fulfilling ego causing you pain in an attempt to keep you from pain. Most importantly, it will also show you how you can stop. But again, you have to start *seeing* it so you can stop *being* it.

16
The Compulsive Need to Think

Anxiety is essentially thinking that can't control itself.

The mind thinks. It's what the mind does. From the time we are toddlers, we explore and use trial and error to figure out how the world works. From the time we start to speak, feeling begins to take a backseat to thinking, as the language of words replaces the "language" of feelings.

Since we've been using the mind since we were toddlers, we worship it. We see it create amazing things like space travel and Candy Crush and assume it has all the answers. It reminds me of a joke by a comedian I once shared the stage with named Emo Phillips. He said: "I used to think that the brain was the most wonderful organ in my body. Then I realized who was telling me this."

In anxious people, the mind goes faster than the body. The body has a regulating influence on the nervous system, but if we are bypassing the slow and grounding, present-moment wisdom of the body by constantly thinking speedy, future-based, anxious thoughts, how are we supposed to tap into the calming effect of the body?

If we struggle with anxiety, we speed up our thoughts as a coping mechanism in the false belief that we can *think* our way into *feeling* safer. This is like saying "eat yourself skinny" or "drink yourself sober." Instead of slowing the mind down and allowing the body to catch up and support us, the mind just goes faster and faster. Unless we stop to *feel* (versus stop to *think*), the mind will always take the lead by default, and we'll keep biting our tail harder and harder in a misguided effort to stop the pain.

I once had a patient who had just lost his wife to cancer. He was clearly distraught and was endlessly ruminating on things he should have done differently. He said to me, "Dr. Kennedy, I'm so depressed and anxious. I just have to find a way to dig myself out of this hole." I told him in the most compassionate way possible, "You can't dig yourself out of a hole. When you see you are in a hole, you need to stop digging."

Trying to think your way out of anxiety is like trying to dig your way out of a hole. You literally can't do it! If you find yourself in a hole with a shovel, you might try using the tool you have at your disposal—and you might feel you are accomplishing something if you keep on digging. But in reality, you are getting farther away from a solution as your hole gets deeper and deeper. You would be better off if you just stopped digging.

This is exactly what we are doing when we try to use our thoughts to find our way out of anxiety. The thoughts make the alarm worse, and we move deeper into the cycle—yet we feel we are doing something productive by using the only tool we see at our disposal, our thoughts.

The trick is to learn how to stay more with the feeling and escape less into thinking. This is best done gradually. You can't stop thinking all at once, since it serves as a protective coping mechanism. But little by little, you can learn to stop digging in deeper.

When you try to think your way out of a feeling problem, over time, the ever-increasing speed of the mind results in the body and mind becoming progressively more out of sync. Instead of trying to think our way out of it, we need to slow down our mind *and* body if we are going to get some relief. But many of us are afraid to slow our thinking because we have been unconsciously convinced by our egos that thinking will make us safe and we become unsafe when we stop thinking. Indeed, one of the most powerful ways we teach ourselves to make our anxiety worse is to believe that if we just keep thinking the answer will come. It's biting your own tail harder and harder and being genuinely confused as to why it's hurting more.

It is akin to this riddle: a man says, "Everything I say is a lie." Having established that, he then says, "I am telling the truth." You end up going in circles because you cannot make this make sense by thinking. The same is true for worry: it is an endless loop, and the only way to escape is to stop thinking (and drop the banana). But the ego tells you the only way out of worry is more worry—and we believe it. We trap ourselves in a "cycle" of thinking and just keep pedalling faster, believing this will slow us down.

Like your ego, your anxiety is not here to punish you or hurt you or persecute you, although it may feel that way sometimes. The anxious thoughts and worries are the ego's attempt to keep you safe, but they never truly provide any safety. However, as long as you stay unaware, you are seduced into the never-ending loop of worry.

The late, great comedian George Carlin wrote a book in which he calls his incessant and compulsive thoughts "brain droppings." That is a brilliant way of looking at thoughts—as little droppings the brain poops out like a deer as it walks along—except that unlike the deer, we humans fail to just move on. As we consciously or unconsciously stay stuck in those worrisome thoughts, our lives get shitty.

17

Ninja Worries

We must be conscious of our thoughts in order to see that the only power they hold is the power we bestow on them. It reminds me of the saying by Robin Sharma, "The mind is a wonderful servant but a terrible master." If we believe everything we think, we are the servant. If we see the thoughts as brain droppings, with only the power we give them, we are the master.

Like a ninja, worries gain their power by not being seen. Worrisome thoughts are often habitual and slip beneath our awareness. As a result, we believe everything we think and fail to see intrusive thoughts like "I have a fatal disease," "I'm going to lose all my money," and "My family will leave me" as mere thoughts that we ourselves have made up. The trouble starts when, instead of seeing our worries as merely intrusive thoughts, we unconsciously accept them as true. We create these imaginings of the future, then magically believe and act as if they are real in the now. Our worries seem to have some sort of diplomatic immunity where they can cause all sorts of damage but not be held accountable. We do not critically appraise them; we just accept them as true. A worry accepted as true, without due process, creates painful alarm in the body. That alarm both creates more worries and lowers our ability to see those worries as false, imaginary projections of the future. In other words, when we are alarmed, we are likely to believe everything we think—and that is disastrous to our mental and physical health.

Bringing the thoughts of the mind into conscious awareness (along with bringing the alarm in the body into conscious awareness, which you'll learn more about in Part 2) reinstates the full ability of the mind to see worries as only a function of imagination. An unbelieved thought or worry has no power to create alarm in the body, and we can break the alarm-anxiety cycle and let go of our own tail.

Of course, if it were as simple as being completely conscious of our worrisome thoughts and divorcing them from belief, we could erase anxiety easily. Some relatively superficial worries are easily recognized for what they are in the light of conscious awareness, while other, deeper, more emotionally charged ones are so familiar they are allowed to stay because they hide in plain sight, masquerading as part of our neural furniture.

The deeper worries that are linked to self-worth (or lack thereof) or guilt or shame are often the most damaging, creating alarm in our bodies before we even know they are there. They are like ninja worries, dressed in the black of the unconscious mind, sliding past the gate of our awareness to do their dirty work.

The ego doesn't see the pain it is causing you, with these ninja worries transporting you to a painful future. The future is not real by virtue of the fact it has not happened. Therefore, worry by its very nature is imaginary, since all worries are about the future—and the only place worries have any power is in our automatic belief of them. Once we bring worries into conscious awareness, often simply by labelling them by saying "This is an intrusive worry," they lose much of their power to control us.

To paraphrase one of the Dalai Lama's sayings, "If there is nothing you can do about your worry, you need not worry—and if there is something you can do about your worry, you need not worry either."

18
Where Are You?

When you are in a state of chronic worry, you may think you are worried about something specific that is about to happen, like an examination, a public speech, or a medical test. Even though your mind may be in the future, your body is living in an alarm state *re*created from your past that is being *re*membered and *re*energized through your anxious thoughts.

You might say, "I thought you said worries are always about the future. Now it seems you are saying that your worries also come from the past?" You might also say, "Which is it, Dr. Kennedy, if that is your *real* name?" Well, you don't have to get so angry about it, but I'm glad to see you sticking up for yourself instead of being a victim!

All worries *are* about the future, but in a way, worries are a way of preparing and protecting you from something that has happened in the past. If you were bitten by a dog when you were a child and you see a dog that resembles the one that bit you, you may have the worrisome thought: "I hope that dog doesn't bite me." But *you* don't worry about the past dog bite. You can't. It's over. You can't worry about something that has already happened. You can be sad or frustrated or angry, but *worry* is always anticipatory.

Worry, the way I define it (and it's *my* book), is always about the future, and that gives us a conscious way to separate from it. Although the feeling of alarm may be present in the moment, the worry itself is always about what *might* happen in the *future*. When I say all worries are about the future, I find it is a useful construct to help us disarm the charge of our imagination by bringing ourselves into the real and present moment where the future-based worry is not, well, present. If you are worried about something, by definition it is not happening now.

When we bring our worries into conscious awareness, we also slow them down and bring them squarely into the present moment, and as those worries need to transport you to the future to have any impact, being in the present suspends their power.

Perhaps a better way of saying this is *all worry is dependent on your belief in how well you can transport yourself into the future.*

Let's say I told you: "Tomorrow, I am going to give you a wrogglebot." You would meet that statement with some curiosity, but it's likely you wouldn't be too upset about it because you have no past history with wrogglebots.

Now, if I told you a wrogglebot is a medical examination that looks for disease, then you might worry if you have a frame of reference to draw on from your past concerning illness or disease. In other words, when we worry, we draw from our past and toss it into the future, and in that process of worry, we totally bypass the present.

In case you were worried, a wrogglebot is just a word I made up for fun so we can have a little laugh in the present moment.

We do this all the time with worry. We split ourselves from the inside, with our body automatically jumping into the memory of past events and our mind leapfrogging into the future prognostications. In this split, there is no wholeness or grounding, so we have no place from which to soothe ourselves.

When you catch yourself worrying, it's a great time to ask yourself, "Where am I right now?" Worrying about something is mental time travel into the future and then recreating the pain of the past, in your body, when you get there and *then* believing the story you are telling yourself. Bringing yourself into the present moment neutralizes the worry, pulling you out of the ego's time-machine, helping you realize you are safe in your body in the present—

even if the safety is just for this very moment or the next five minutes or the next day or week.

Consciously bringing yourself to the present moment and affirming that you are safe and actually feeling safe is a revelation for many (I know it was for me). I had told myself for years that I wasn't safe, or at least I had never explicitly told myself that I *was* safe. This is true for many of us with anxiety. So choose the moment and see your safety. It is always there if you look for it. Peace is an available choice in every moment. I'll talk more about this in Part 3, but note that you can always consciously choose your own peace, in the moment, or run the risk of your overprotective ego unconsciously defaulting to fear and worry.

If you would have asked me ten years ago, "When did you last feel safe?" I would have told you that I had never felt safe. For many others who have never felt safe, just to open up to the possibility that in this present moment, this *right now*, you are completely safe can be a revelation. For many of my patients (and me too!), asking themselves "Am I safe in this moment?" and realizing the answer is "yes" has been the first time in their lives that they've actually acknowledged they *were* safe.

How about you? Can you see and feel that you are safe in this moment? Even if you are facing impending doom five minutes from now, you are still completely safe *in this moment*. Many of us worriers as children never allowed ourselves to feel safe, even for a second. We just assumed the next trauma was coming and didn't stop to see that for much of the time we *were* actually safe.

Perhaps you never knew when your father would get drunk, or your mother would be abusive, a family member would become sick or incapacitated, or if your caregivers would even be home to look after your needs. When you have to stay in a constant state of vigilance, the human mind and body adopt a strategy that it is best to stay ready for trouble. In my early teens, I would let down my guard with my father and believe he was going to return to normal and then get blindsided when he would inevitably become psychotic again. Over time, I adopted the coping strategy of hypervigilance and self-protection—an attitude that by its very nature assumes danger as its default position.

As children with little understanding of, or power over, our stressors, it made sense to stay vigilant and assume trouble was just around the corner. But now as an adult, when you make the unconscious conscious and affirm to yourself in conscious awareness that you *are* safe, even if it is only for the next five seconds, you are interrupting that unconscious vigilance. You are breaking the spell.

Many of my anxiety patients unwittingly lived with this sense that they were constantly in danger, often decades after their trauma had ceased. Even though the events of their trauma were well behind them, they retained that childhood framework that they could face danger at any moment and must stay vigilant.

For many, asking themselves "Am I safe in this moment?" and consciously seeing that they were, broke an unconscious habit of assumed danger they had maintained since childhood.

19

Wired to Worry

If I could find the guy that invented worry, I would punch him in the balls. Worry has cost me so much and limited my enjoyment of life more than I can express. I imagine you might feel the same way.

So then why in the world do we do it? Well, let's start by looking at the different types of worry.

Remember the three W's of worry: warnings, what-ifs, and worst-case scenarios? I see all worries falling into these three categories, which are progressive in terms of severity.

Let's say you have an upcoming doctor's appointment for your yearly checkup. A warning thought might be: "My blood sugar was borderline last year. I hope it's not worse this year." The second level of worry (the what-if) might be: "What if I have diabetes?" The third level of worry (the worst-case scenario) goes all the way to the extreme: "Diabetes is genetic. My dad had it and it killed him. I bet it will kill me too."

Sometimes it is easier to see worries for what they are, by identifying which of the three categories your anxious thought fits into. Being able to look at it more closely helps you bring it into awareness and then see it for the figment of your imagination it truly is.

Chronic worries hold a tremendous amount of inertia. In physics, the concept of inertia states that an object at rest tends to stay at rest and an object in motion tends to stay in motion. This is equally true with anxiety: The more you worry, the more likely you are to keep worrying. The opposite is also true: The less you worry, the less you *will* worry.

Once we start worrying and there is inertia behind our worries, next comes resistance. This is the hallmark of the ego. Remember when I said we worriers do not take well to uncertainty? Resistance is the result of objecting to the change we need to adopt in the face of uncertainty. Resistance keeps us frozen in a form of ego-based protection and blocks us from growth. And moving away from protection and toward growth is exactly what we need to move past chronic worry.

When we have bonded or imprinted to worry as a form of safety and practiced worry so much that it's gained inertia, we have tremendous resistance to letting it go. Much like the monkey that refuses to let go of the banana and escape, we worriers are resistant to letting go of our worries and escaping our minds. Instead, we have become WIRED for **worry**, **inertia**, and **resistance** as a form of **ego defence**.

What exactly is the ego protecting us against?

Feeling.

In essence, we become afraid to feel, and worry becomes a convenient substitute. Worrisome *thinking* is a distraction from painful *feeling*.

Remember the concept of background alarm, that excess, chaotic energy that spilled over when our minds were overwhelmed and was stored in our bodies as unresolved trauma? This state of uneasiness, this uncomfortable energy sits vigilantly in the background, waiting for any reason to rise up. If you've been sitting in a movie theatre or at a family dinner or driving to work and you've felt a sense of impending doom when there's no actual danger in sight, you are sensing your background alarm.

For our younger selves, the feeling of background alarm in our bodies was too much to bear. We developed resistance to feeling our bodies because in connecting to our bodies we would need to face the old trauma stored there. If you've ever been told "Get out of your head!" there is a good chance you've experienced this.

As the lesser of two evils, the ego decides that the body is not safe to inhabit and retreats or detours into the mind to avoid pain. The ego-created worries keep us *in* our minds as a way of keeping us *out* of the background alarm stored in our bodies. Just as the person with obsessive-compulsive disorder (OCD) counts stairs or turns three times before going through a doorway as a form of distraction from their inner pain of alarm, we worriers obsess with worrisome thoughts as a form of distraction.

The more dramatic the thoughts, the more effective the distraction from feeling. This explains why worries tend to get more and more intense over time. Compounding matters, I have often noticed that worriers seem to be quite intelligent and artistic with hyperactive imaginations, so we can conjure up very elaborate and complex worries! Basic worries like fear of flying are for amateurs; we elite class worriers can make a nine-headed, flying, fire-breathing hydra that sweats acid and has cobra venom for blood and still have some imagination left over for something *really* scary. I'm not saying fear of flying can't be debilitating; I am saying that the worries we can come up with are often much more elaborate and complex. The reason why our worries are so scary to us is that they have to be really frightening to keep us in our heads. If they weren't so scary, we might venture back down into our bodies and revisit the background alarm of our past. As scary as the worries are, that childhood pain looms as infinitely more frightening.

So our worries do serve a purpose in distracting us from the background alarm in our bodies, but they have a devastating side effect. As the worries become more intense and pressing, they begin to increase the alarm in our bodies. Because the body has difficulty distinguishing a thought from reality, the thought in question ("Am I having a heart attack?") is read by the body as a declarative statement of truth ("I *am* having a heart attack!"). It's like the game show *Jeopardy!* Even if you phrase the thought in the form of a question, your body reacts with an activation of your fight-or-flight, or sympathetic nervous system—just as a normal body would when faced with a threat it accepts as real.

Eventually, our coping strategy of worry to distract us from the alarm in our bodies intensifies the very thing we are trying to ignore.

It is sort of like drinking beer to quench your thirst. Initially, there is a sense of satisfaction, but ultimately, the ethanol in the beer makes you excrete more water than you are taking in. You are becoming more dehydrated by the very thing you are using to slake your thirst. In the same way, the mind has learned to distract with worry to alleviate the pain of uncertainty we feel in the body. The choice to believe an anxious thought comes from the mind of our wounded inner child, the psyche of our younger self for whom accepting a worrisome thought as true is preferable to simply leaving the whole situation uncertain. As uncertainty was so painful in childhood, it is a place our younger selves never want to visit again.

20

Making the Uncertain Certain

When I was a teenager, my mother (in addition to taking care of two sons and a husband who was frequently incapacitated with psychotic depression or manically talking for seventy-two hours straight) worked a lot of evening shifts at a local hospital as a full-time registered nurse. We lived fairly close to the hospital, and she would almost always be home ten minutes after her shift ended at eleven o'clock.

By five past the hour, I was usually starting to get excited to see her and would wait for her anxiously. On the rare occasions that it would be 11:10 and she wasn't home, I would start to get agitated. This was in the days before a quick call or text via cell phone could have reassured me. I simply had to wait … and then I would return to my coping strategy: worry.

I'd start out telling myself that one of her patients was sick or she had to do overtime. But with each minute that passed, the scenario became direr. Perhaps she had fallen? Maybe she was in a car accident? It's dark outside—what if she got attacked or got hit by a bus? As my body would react to the worrisome, painful projection as though the scenario were indeed real, I would be activating a state of alarm in my body.

Then I'd hear the key in the lock. She was home! My body and mind would get a tremendous rush of relief.

Worry releases dopamine, a neurotransmitter that is part of our brain's reward system and is part of what makes drugs like cocaine pleasurable—and addictive. The worry itself becomes an addiction—and to further reinforce this habit, when I would worry about my mother's safety, other highly pleasurable substances would rush in when my worry turned out to be false. So this habit was doubly addictive.

Especially if your youth had more than its share of pain, can you see how you might have adopted worry as, paradoxically, a source of comfort when surrounded by a sea of uncertainty and pain? When the thing you worry about does not come to pass (as is usually the case), the rush of feel-good chemicals can be a welcome change from a chronically hypervigilant, protective state. I know this sounds counterintuitive, but much of anxiety and alarm *is* counterintuitive. As you'll see as you go through this book, much of *healing* from anxiety and alarm is also counterintuitive.

Here's an even more counterintuitive consideration. What if, on some unconscious level, you believe the worrisome thing did *not* happen *because* you worried? Consciously, we know worry has no positive effect, but unconsciously there is an unwritten belief that worry not only can make you feel good but that it has the power of magically changing events in your favour! Can you see how anxious thoughts and worries become a part of your toolkit?

Again, *consciously* we know that worrying about the results of a biopsy makes no difference to the pathologist's report. But if the biopsy comes back benign, we expert worriers use that positive result and the ensuing joy of relief as unconscious "evidence" that our worry (1) did something and (2) magically changed the results in our favour. Again, this is not rational, but your unconscious mind is not rational. Furthermore, many of us started to worry as children, and the magical thinking of a child is not too far away from assuming worry had a protective effect. For many of us, worry was seen as a childhood friend and one we are resistant to let go of, even decades later.

In addition to being a familiar friend, worry is a childlike attempt to control the uncontrollable. Although we are not consciously aware of it, we worriers trick ourselves into believing in our self-created, worrisome stories because they provide a sense of control, a magical way of predicting the future. When we buy into our own illusions of the future, it creates a sense that we can prepare for what is going to happen.

For example, I would often focus on my father and see if I could predict if he was going to need hospitalization. When he would become what I perceived as overly happy or overly sad, I would begin to prepare myself and worry that he was indeed heading for a stay on the psych ward. I would focus on the possibility of him being admitted to hospital and worry about it so much that it seemed like a certainty. As painful as that was, it seemed less painful than being in limbo as to whether he was truly heading for hospital admission or not. The odd thing was that most times I worried and convinced myself he was heading for a tour of duty on the psych ward, he would improve. It was only on rare occasions that my worrying turned out to be an accurate prediction. Even though I was wrong most of the time, I couldn't seem to stop doing it. Crazy, huh?

All human beings have a drive for certainty, but for worriers, that drive becomes an obsession. If you had trauma in your childhood, your drive for certainty becomes exaggerated, and creating a worrisome story is a way of creating a semblance of order where there is none. OCD is, at its root, a drive to make things certain. Typically, the obsessions become more elaborate over time in a fruitless attempt to create certainty where none exists. For the OCD sufferer, the obsessions provide a little patch of certainty in a frighteningly uncertain world. But the obsessions become the problem as the person becomes overtaken by them, just as we worriers are overtaken by our worries. Just as the OCD sufferer becomes afraid *not* to count stairs or tap the doorknob six times, we worriers become afraid not to worry.

That worry is a source of both pleasure and pain is one of the paradoxes of anxiety. Given the massive amount of pain, uncertainty caused me, I can completely understand why I created a worrisome story to make a scenario appear less vague and uncertain. But, just like drinking beer to relieve thirst, my worry was compounding the problem my child mind perceived those worries would solve. In other words, to my inner child, uncertainty needed to be avoided at all costs, so it was worth it to bear the cost of accepting the painful worry as true. In an effort to avoid the familiar, intolerable alarm of uncertainty and not knowing what was going to happen, I created a story of worry that gave me the illusion of knowing what was going to happen. By creating a worrisome story, I was fooling myself into creating a fable of what was going to occur because simply leaving the situation to uncertainty was an excruciating reminder of a time when I truly did not know. Imagining the worst was actually preferable to not knowing, and that is one of the most devastating aspects of the anxious mind.

When you experience trauma in childhood that is not resolved, you lose faith in the world—yet faith is exactly what you need to endure, and even embrace, uncertainty. I'll show you in Part 3 how to embrace uncertainty so it no longer backs you into a corner.

It wasn't until I saw worry for what it really was—a magical attempt to make the uncertain certain—that I ultimately learned how to manage worry. Having faith amid uncertainty, and even embracing uncertainty as the spice of life, is worry's undoing. Awareness is the antidote to both uncertainty and worry. Being aware of your power and your access to choice, along with calming the alarm in your body, will help you relish and embrace uncertainty, for it is the uncertainty of life that provides the true fun and joy. Developing a sense of awareness is a critical step to learn, and eventually, the space taken up by the negative habit of worry will be filled with this new positive skill of being present in the moment, no matter how uncertain.

Old habits die hard. I still get caught up in worrying sometimes. But with the keen sense of awareness I possess now, I know that I have the choice to worry or not, and it is much less of a problem in my life.

21
Stronger Than You Think

It's worth repeating here: chronic worry and anxiety are a dangerous combination of overestimating threats and underestimating our courage to deal with them—and this programming usually starts in childhood.

One thing about childhood trauma is that it forces you to be tough before you are ready. Ironically, the trauma makes you tougher than you believe yourself to be, not in spite of the trauma you endured but *because* of it. You are both strengthened and weakened by your traumas.

There have been many times in my life I thought I would collapse if something bad happened. If worrying were an Olympic sport, I'd be the silver medalist (my mother would probably edge me out for the gold). The keyword here is *if* something bad happened—but *when* that something did happen (which was very rare), not only did I not collapse, I showed what I was truly made of. So often, we worriers adopt a victim mentality and underestimate our true abilities. Take a second to look back at the challenges you thought you could never handle and see that you are still here. Do not fall into the trap of overestimating the threats and underestimating your abilities. In many ways, your anxiety makes you stronger, not weaker—but the alarm in your system does not allow you to see this power in you.

Moving across the country with a new wife and child and starting medical school only months after my father's death seemed impossible to me. I came seriously close to quitting at least four times in the first year. Halfway through the year, I signed the paperwork to quit. I went to the university to hand it in, but as I got to the door of the medical school office, something told me I should stay one more day. By midway through the second year, I had finally shown myself I could do it, and even though I struggled right through the four years, knowing I had survived the toughest part of med school (the first eighteen months) gave me the confidence to see it through.

I was a total mess for that first year, but I was very good at hiding my suffering (as most of us worriers are). I didn't know it back then, but my anxious thoughts and wanting to quit were a way of protecting me, even as they were crushing my belief in myself. In anxiety's typical shortsighted way, my anxious thoughts slowly destroyed my self-confidence and made me doubt myself more and more.

But I had, indeed, underestimated my abilities (as most worriers do). I finished my MD degree as class president and even won a few academic awards and distinctions at graduation. Not bad for a guy who was a complete mess for the first eighteen months of med school and came very close to dropping out.

I had hoped that once I had shown myself I could do it and graduated medical school, my chronic alarm and anxiety would resolve. It did improve, but even after becoming a doctor, at points, I was so paralyzed by fear that I didn't leave my apartment for days at a time, and just getting into the shower seemed like a monumental achievement. I felt paralyzed and persecuted by my anxiety. But just like making it through the dark days of med school, I did what I had to do when I had to do it. Even though I felt like a weak victim of my mental state, I always found a way to do what I had to do. In my decades of practicing medicine, I never called in sick until my last day of practice after I ruptured my Achilles tendon.

And then I *really* called in sick. I never went back.

Anxiety, in its relentless pursuit to shield and protect you, makes you shy away from challenges and tries to convince you to quit, or worse, not even start. It harkens back to the time in childhood when you were unprepared and weren't able to handle the pressure and assumes you are in the same place now. Anxiety tells you, "You shouldn't try. It'll be easier if you just avoid this." But as I have seen with many of my patients, once you start to narrow your experience of life in an attempt to avoid pain, it becomes a slippery slope. Your toboggan gains momentum sliding down the hill, and your life becomes less about experiencing new fun and more about avoiding old pain.

So often I have given in to it, but just as often I have risen to the challenge—and if you are reading this book, I am sure you have too. You might look at what I've done—doctor, speaker, yoga teacher, stand-up comic—and think, "How can he have an anxiety problem if he's done all that?"

It's because I am much stronger than my anxiety would have me think.

And so are you.

Again, look back on the times when things really did go bad. Did you handle it? Are you still here?

I thought so.

Here is one of the secrets anxiety doesn't want you to know: On the rare occasion that it does go bad, you will handle it. There is this illusion that you're going to collapse if your worries come true. You won't. In many ways, living and coping with anxiety has made you *much* more resilient than you give yourself credit for. I can't emphasize this enough. In decades of working with anxiety patients, I have seen them rise to the occasion of adversity with faith and courage they never believed they had. You are infinitely stronger than you believe you are. Please read this paragraph over and over until you really absorb its message. I guarantee you that it is true.

Not only are *you* much more capable than anxiety would have you believe, but you'll have help. The child in us may have felt that there was no hope and no help was coming. But that is also a misperception. Think of your biggest past challenges. Now, notice (1) how you clearly made it through and (2) where the universe helped you. There is no reason to believe that is not going to be the case in the future. Don't abandon your faith in yourself and reject the uncertainty of life for the illusory certainty of worry. It's a bad deal every time. But you can't change it until you turn up your awareness and understand that you have a choice. In Part 3, I'll show you specifically how to choose wonder over worry.

The big lie of anxiety and alarm is "You can't do it." Even after you've done it many times before, it *still* tells you *this* is going to be the time you fail. For my first five years of doing stand-up, every set I did I was convinced would be a catastrophe. No matter how many times I did well, my child self was convinced that the next set would be a disaster. Your child self is also likely to believe your catastrophic predictions because they are based on your real experiences. But you're not a powerless child anymore, and once you see yourself as a powerful adult, you can break anxiety's hold on your thoughts. You can retreat into the servant to your worries or you can expand into the master of your mind. In the former, you have constricted and regressed into your fearful child from your past and see the world that way. In the latter, you expand into your wise and resilient adult in the present and see the world that way. Awareness gives you the choice to live in your adult now or your child then.

"If you are not living this moment, you are not really living." – Eckhart Tolle

Anxiety and alarm hit us with a double whammy. Our anxious thoughts make us think we are much smaller than we truly are and the alarm in our bodies makes our challenges feel much bigger than they truly are because we are perceiving through the eyes of our anxious and alarmed child from the distant past. As an adult, committed to being grounded in the present, you become a powerful force and are much tougher than anxiety would have you believe. And your challenges are there to expose your beliefs. Your child, who lives in the past, believes he or she can't handle it, but I can assure you from personal experience, your adult who chooses to live in the faith of the present moment can handle anything.

It really comes down to committing to awareness of the present moment and seeing at any moment you have a conscious choice to be your present-moment adult self. Alternatively, if you do not see the choice of engaging your empowered adult self, by default you will regress into the victimhood of your child self. If we can stay in the present moment and choose faith and courage, we become the master. If we are swept away by our old alarm, we become the servant and fail to even see the choice of staying present. We default back to the anxiety and alarm that characterized our childhood, and we may even regress into a form of our child self. If you have fallen into the mindset of a child, how are you supposed to manage the life of an adult?

Even when we've been practicing awareness for a while, challenges have a way of knocking us back into our old destructive habit of believing every worry we think. Before we are aware of it, our bodies get alarmed, and we are back in that hole of our childhood wounding. The only way out is to commit to seeing our "tells" of anxiety and, in that awareness, taking a few breaths and seeing that we have the power to choose to stay present in our adult selves or fall into the hole of our old childhood wounds. This is a learning process, and I have fallen back into my childhood wounding thousands of times. But when you see the choice is always there and you practice staying present in your adult self, the path of the adult becomes wider and easier to take. Then we can consistently use our adult selves to pick up our scared child and move to courage and faith together

When you say, "I can't go out today because of XYZ," that is a belief that is not necessarily true. It is the belief of your child self, and that belief needs anonymity to survive and exert its influence. Bringing your beliefs into the present moment light of awareness takes away much of their power. Then your present moment adult self can take over and reassure that worried and alarmed child in a way they never received back when they needed it most.

There is no worry-based belief you can have that is true. How do I know? Because worry is always about the future, and since the future is unknown, anything that claims to know the unknown cannot be true. Worries are predictions we accept as fact in order to avoid the pain of uncertainty, and then we suffer, believing to be real what is only an imagining of the anxious mind. Once you see the worries are merely illusions, you break the cycle of worries aggravating alarm in the body and alarm aggravating the worries of the mind. The cycle needs your unconscious belief to operate. Once you make the unconscious conscious, you learn to objectively *see* your worries so you no longer have to subjectively *be* your worries.

22
The Feeling/Thought Cycle

I clearly remember getting home from India at the end of September 2013 and feeling paralyzed in my bed under the crushing weight of anxiety and alarm.

I was biting my own tail and then biting it even harder to try to get the pain to stop. I was caught in a vicious cycle to the point I considered suicide because not only did I not see a way out, but the anxiety and alarm were continuing to worsen. I felt like I was losing my mind (and my body) along with my hold on

reality—there was no safe place. Suicide is not so much that you want to die as you just see no other option for the pain to end.

I used to do a joke about this. In a down-south, evangelical Georgia accent, I would say "Gawd, I say, Gawd, will never give you ... more ... than you ... can handle!" I would pause and then say "Does God meet suicide victims at the pearly gates and say "ah ... sorry ... um dude, my bad, I really thought you could handle it."

When I look back now, part of me was glad it got this bad, as I don't think I would have taken my transformative trip on LSD, had I not had my back squarely up against the wall. Even though I was on my knees, I was strong enough to go deeper, and that is my point when I say we worriers are much stronger than we think when we are actually faced with what we worry about. As much as I was absolutely terrified of LSD and was already in a desperate state, I knew I had to do it, so I did. As I alluded to earlier, on my father's birthday, October 5th, in 2013, under the supervision of my guide, I took my first hit of acid. I did not know what to make of the massive change in perception, I experienced under the influence of the psychedelic, right away. Over time, seeing the alarm trapped in my body as different (and separable) from the anxious thoughts of the mind allowed me to see I was trapped in a feedback loop of thought (worry) and feeling (alarm).

Although I didn't immediately know how to feel and think better, after the LSD trip I was no longer dealing with a ghost. I had two distinct elements of thought and feeling that I had assumed were one and the same. Not only were these elements different, but they were separable from each other. For the first time, I had the very real sense that I was dealing with a process that could be broken down by separating the component parts.

When we are not aware of how the alarm-anxiety cycle works and are not consciously aware of its tricks, a thought leads to a feeling and that feeling creates more thoughts that are congruent with the feeling. In that state, negative thoughts that are consistent with the negative feeling are accentuated, encouraged, and magnified, while thoughts that are inconsistent with our present feeling state are discounted, discouraged, and diminished.

Simply put, the feeling-thought cycle states that how you feel dictates how you think. It is also true that how you think is how you are going to feel, but feeling influences thinking much more than thinking influences feeling.

How do I know? Personally, I find it extremely difficult to try and think in opposition to how I feel. Furthermore, with both myself and my patients, I've seen it is much more effective to change your thinking state by changing your feeling state than the reverse. Thoughts and thinking states can be reversed in a matter of seconds by simply consciously focusing on the exact opposite of the thought. Whatever you are thinking right now, I can guarantee you the exact opposite of that thought has some truth to it. In this way, thoughts are more changeable than feelings but have less momentum. You can change your thoughts, but unless your state of feeling changes to support them, those thoughts don't tend to "stick," and they will default back to mirror your feeling state. Feelings are denser and carry more energy to create long-lasting change and, thus, are a better focus for our interventions.

This example may sound trivial, but it makes a point. Let's say you believe that Toronto is the capital city of Canada. You call me and it comes up in conversation, and I correct you by saying it is actually Ottawa that is the capital of Canada. From that point on, you have switched the erroneous thought of Toronto for Ottawa.

Simple.

Now say you are feeling down because your pet has passed away. Does telling yourself "don't be sad" significantly change your emotion? No, because emotions have more power and momentum than thoughts do.

So contrary to what most "positive psychology" advocates will tell you, simply having people change their thoughts is not likely to carry much power to change their feelings. I'm not saying it is not helpful to change thoughts of the mind, but changing feelings in the body is a much more effective way of making long-term change. Typically, it is hard work to stay aware enough to consistently try to think thoughts in your mind that are in contradiction to the feeling in your body. Not saying it can't be done, but I have found adopting the approach recommended by positive psychology required tremendous commitment and perseverance, and I simply can't keep it up. People who are chronic worriers have an immense amount of alarm in their bodies, and relentlessly trying to think positively while feeling a panic state in the body is an exercise in futility. Personally, I have found it much more beneficial to devote the energy I was supposed to use to change the direction of my thoughts, to change the feeling state in my body instead—but more on that soon.

I remember being in Las Vegas with my daughter, Leandra, when she was about ten. (I'm not an irresponsible father. In 1996, Vegas was really focusing on family fun, with waterparks and kids' shows.) Leandra has never been comfortable in hot weather. She likes *warm* weather, but she hates it when it gets *hot*. We were on an open-air shuttle bus going down the Las Vegas strip in August. Did I mention it was noon, in August, in the Nevada desert?

Lea was not happy.

She was sitting on a bench on the little shuttle bus and I was standing above her holding the grabrail. I can still remember the tilt of her head, looking up at me with those big brown eyes, with the "What the he** did you get us into here?" look on her face. If you don't think an otherwise genteel ten-year-old girl can gun you off with a look, you are dead wrong. As we were going to be on this shuttle for another twenty minutes, I told her to imagine she was in an ice-cold swimming pool. That bought me a little time, but in another three minutes she "convinced" me to get off the bus, and we found an air-conditioned taxi to take us the rest of the way.

Leandra has always been a happy-go-lucky kid, so to see her mad like that was atypical for sure. As soon as we got into the cool cab, Leandra's sunny disposition returned. That is to say, once she *felt* better, she *thought* better.

Although both influence each other and changing both feeling and thinking is beneficial, our feeling has more of an influence on our thinking than the opposite. As you'll see as you move through this book (and although I'll absolutely show you how to do both), you'll get the most bang for your emotional buck by directing your energies into improving how you feel rather than improving how you think.

It is an uphill battle on the scale of Mount Everest to think in a way that opposes the way you feel. This is not to say that consciously changing your thought processes is not helpful, but trying to think in constant opposition to how you feel is exhausting and demoralizing. Unless you are hypervigilant about thinking more positively, simply changing your thinking will give you only short-term relief. Feeling states like alarm, anger, and frustration have much more inertia and take more time to turn around. I often think of thoughts as a speedboat and feelings as a freighter. Once a feeling gets a hold, especially the feeling of alarm, it's like trying to get a thousand-ton ship to turn on a dime.

Here's another way to look at it: The heart exerts an electrical field five thousand times stronger that of the brain. Given that biological reality, it feels rather futile to try to use thoughts to strongarm our feelings into submission, doesn't it?

Now, here is where it gets more complicated: thinking positively does tend to have a positive effect on how you feel, but typically the effect is not that powerful. However, thinking negatively has a much more robust effect on how you feel, probably due to energizing the inherent fear bias of the brain. In other words, a positive thought tends to make you feel only a little better, but a negative or scary thought can make you feel *much* worse!

So I am not saying thinking is unimportant. It is *very* important to see your negative thoughts and worries. But once you see them, it is a much more effective course of action to direct your energy into changing the way you feel than trying to address the way you think. Changing your thoughts may only last a few seconds. Changing the way you feel lasts considerably longer and addresses the issue at its root cause. When you are trapped in worry, it is a much better use of your time to abandon thinking altogether and focus on changing your feeling state. The best way to change Leandra's discomfort was to change her feeling state by getting her into an air-conditioned cab. Although having her think and imagine she was in a cool swimming pool bought me some time, changing how she felt was much more effective.

Typically, how you feel and how you think are consistent with each other. If you feel alarmed in your body, it's likely that will be reflected by anxious thoughts in your mind. In fact, without awareness, chronic worriers default to the state of alarm in the body and anxiety in the mind. This is the unconscious pattern I followed for decades before I saw another way of feeling and thinking.

Even in non-worriers, the feeling-thought cycle operates unconsciously and automatically, feelings feeding thoughts and thoughts feeding feelings, in a self-reinforcing loop. To break the cycle, we first need to be aware that it is operating. When we know we are feeling alarm, we can anticipate our mind handing us alarming thoughts. Our best defence is awareness of the cycle's existence and the knowledge that we can break it by separating the two components.

I don't mean to give the impression that thoughts don't have power. Both thoughts and feelings are powerful in their own right. Some thoughts are more disturbing and "heavier" than others, but that also depends on how much belief and subsequent feeling they are granted. At the end of the day, however, changing the feeling state is what will give us the deepest and longest-lasting form of relief from chronic worry.

When you become aware of the thoughts as simply thoughts (or brain droppings!) and separate them from their energy source of feeling, you have taken a crucial step towards healing. What you are aiming for, by practicing awareness, is to see and isolate the thoughts before you *believe* them.

Again, my goal is to show you how to *see* your thoughts so you don't have to *be* your thoughts. Seeing your thoughts (especially your worrisome thoughts) as groundless, transient, and inconsequential helps you avoid turning a painless thought in the mind into a painful feeling in the body.

Just to emphasize (and to save me putting a diagram in here), imagine the thoughts of your mind travelling down to your heart area and influencing your feeling state. Then imagine your feeling state around your heart travelling up to your mind and influencing your thoughts. There is no beginning and no end to this cycle or feedback loop, thought can create feeling and feeling can create thought. This is the feeling-thought cycle and it operates in all humans. The alarm-anxiety cycle works in the exact same way in we worriers, with anxious thoughts of the mind generating alarm feeling in the body and alarm feeling in the body generating anxious thoughts of the mind. Again, there is no beginning and no end to this cycle, or feedback loop.

As both cycles act unconsciously, awareness is the key to seeing them and breaking the feedback loop so we don't have to charge either cycle by believing in every thought we have and staying unaware of every feeling that we feel.

Even in our minds, worries have no power to hurt us until we bestow them with the power of belief. Once we see it's up to us whether we believe our worries or not, we can make real progress in breaking the cycle. But as you'll see, your energy is better spent connecting to and changing your feeling state versus simply trying to change your thinking.

23
Awareness Gives Choice

Perhaps the most powerful aspect of awareness is that, in slowing down and becoming aware of the anxious thoughts of the mind, you create the space that wasn't there when you automatically believed everything you thought. It is in that space that you create choice—and choice is power.

As Dr. Viktor Frankl said: "Between stimulus and response there is a space. In that space is our power to choose our response. In our response lies our growth and our freedom." This is the space I'm talking about, and it holds your liberation from chronic anxiety.

That space is the gift in the practice of awareness. With conscious awareness, you see options that were not available to you previously, and in those options rests the power of choice—including your power to choose to not be a victim of your old wounding.

Dr. Frankl also said, "Everything can be taken from a man but one thing: the last of human freedoms—to choose one's attitude in any given set of circumstances, to choose one's own way." When I learned I had a choice—that I had the power to see my thoughts without believing them, that I could take the energy I previously funnelled into thinking and worries and divert that energy into staying with my feelings—from that point on, I was choosing my own way, and that way was to value feeling, however painful, over thinking. My choice became to see the thoughts, with curiosity, suspending them while I focused inward on sensation. Starving anxious thoughts, of the energy of credibility, allowed me to break their spell. This took practice, but it was fuelled by a sense of agency over this condition called anxiety that had ruled my unconscious for decades. Since I could *see* my anxious thoughts and chose to focus on something else, starving them of belief, I was free from *being* my anxious thoughts.

24

Family and Liar

The vast majority of patients I see who suffer from excessive worry felt distinctly unempowered and victimized as children, as I also did—and in a nasty glitch in our wiring, whatever was familiar to us as children is what we tend to replicate in adulthood. It is built into the human brain to equate familiarity with security. This means that whatever was familiar for you as a child, there will be an unconscious push to repeat as an adult—even if you are repeating something that caused you considerable pain.

One of my own quotes that I am proud of is: "If you grew up in a dysfunctional family, the word *familiar* can be broken into two words—*family* and *liar*—because your family essentially lies to you about what is safe." As a result, we will often reproduce the negative events from our childhood in adulthood in an attempt to recapture the security that was never really there in the first place! Freud called this urge to recapitulate the past the "repetition compulsion."

If you felt disempowered as a child, part of you will unconsciously and automatically gravitate toward that victim state as an adult. In other words, we will unconsciously and compulsively select for experiences and thoughts in our adulthood that replicate that familiar victim mentality of our childhood. Thanks, brain! Add to that a felt sense of fear in our bodies, and you have the perfect environment for the alarm-anxiety cycle to form and thrive. If we do not apply conscious awareness to the alarm-anxiety cycle, it will take us over—and that is exactly what happened to me.

But it's not just me. Let's look at a patient of mine, Jane, who would tend to pick men who were abusive alcoholics. Whenever she met a man who fit that profile, she was drawn to him like a moth to the flame. Jane was on autopilot, seduced by her unconscious drive to replicate her childhood, exchanging an abusive alcoholic father for an abusive alcoholic boyfriend—endlessly trying to recapture a security with her father that was never there in the first place. I always felt Jane was hoping the new boyfriend would take care of her in a way her father never did.

Of course, it always ended badly. Yet for many years she persisted in attracting alcoholic after alcoholic, with no awareness of why she repeatedly put herself in harm's way. Since you can't change what you can't (or refuse to) see, the unconscious and destructive pattern of victimizing herself continued for as long as I knew her, although in the latter stages of our doctor-patient relationship she did start seeing her behaviour with more awareness.

Many of us worriers became familiar (aka secure) with worry when we were young. Just like Jane embraced alcoholics and replicated that pattern, we worriers embrace worry (even though it is toxic) in part because it is familiar to us. Perhaps, like me, you had a parent or caregiver who was a chronic worrier and modelled that behaviour for you. When we worry, we get an odd sense of security from the sense of familiarity it provides. In my case, I saw my mother worry a great deal, and it became a familiar ally of mine. In times of stress, I will still replicate that old pattern, and in search of security that was never actually there, I will mindlessly accept worry as an old friend. Then I bring myself into conscious awareness and realize I can see worry for the toxic influence it truly is. In the choice that awareness provides, I choose to release it, move into sensation, and stop feeding the worry with my attention. When my conscious focus shifts to sensation in my body, the energy that was previously feeding my belief of my worries is redirected into sensation and feeling and away from thinking and worrying. In awareness, I direct my attention to physical sensation in my body. Without the energy of my attention, the worries atrophy and fade, as there is no longer any belief to sustain them.

It's time to take your power back. There's an old saying that goes: "If you do things the way you've always done them, you'll get what you've always gotten." If you aren't aware of your actions and don't see that you have the power to consciously and objectively observe your impulses and desires, you'll never be able to change them. Without awareness, we just repeat the same old patterns, and if those patterns involve you being a helpless and unwitting victim, your anxiety and alarm will never resolve.

25
Is It a Belief Problem or a Problem of Belief?

Did I mention that I went to medical school? Did I also mention that I am an anxious hypochondriac? Do you see the potential problem here?

Let's count this out. (1) I am a hypochondriac, (2) I am afraid of illness, and (3) I am in a professional program that is predicated on studying illness. Being a doctor and a hypochondriac is like being a tree surgeon who is afraid of sap. There is a well-known phenomenon called "medical students' disease," in which medical students start convincing themselves they actually have the diseases they are studying.

During medical school, I would create an anxious thought about having a fatal disease and then try to argue with it, attempting to reassure myself that I didn't have to believe it. But here's the rub: the more energy and attention I gave to arguing with the thought, the more credibility I gave it. In trying to convince myself that I didn't have to believe the thought, I was unconsciously paying more attention to the possibility that I could have the disease!

It's like telling yourself not to think of a pink elephant. Pink elephants are not real; everyone knows that. Who thought of the idea of a pink elephant anyway? Ridiculous. There is no such thing. Pink elephants do not exist. I should just stop thinking about it. Unless I guess, you sprayed an elephant with pink paint, but why would you do that? In that respect, you could paint an elephant pink and create a pink elephant, but in that case, it's artificial, not real. Though I guess it *would* be real to someone who saw it and didn't *know* that it was painted. Or a child, a child would definitely believe it was real ...

I think you get the picture. The more I tried to tell myself my thoughts were not to be believed, the more real and believable they became.

During the stress of medical school, my muscles began to twitch involuntarily. The medical term is fasciculation. They twitched all over, even in the muscles of my tongue. Of course, I looked up fasciculation in a medical text and it told of a horrendous disease called amyotrophic lateral sclerosis, or ALS (also known as Lou Gehrig's disease), where literally your muscles waste away until you die.

And one of the early signs? Fasciculations.

So I was off! I completely freaked out.

One of the cardinal signs of ALS is weakness or discoordination in the hands. Guess what—I became fixated on my hands. Anytime I did something clumsy I convinced myself that this was the beginning of the end.

It. Was. Awful. The more I tried to convince myself that I was okay, the more worried I got. It was the pink elephant situation all over again. I cannot tell you how terrified I was and how I pestered my wife every day asking her if she could see changes in my hands.

Luckily, I got to see one of the most caring doctors I have ever had the good fortune to meet. Dr. John Noseworthy was a staff neurologist at the University of Western Ontario Medical School and went on to be CEO of the world-renowned Mayo Clinic. Dr. Noseworthy gave me a thorough exam and reassured me that he had seen many cases of ALS, and although he could not tell me one hundred percent, he was 99.9 percent sure I had a condition called benign fasciculations.

Do you think that ended it?

Although I felt immeasurably reassured, that 0.1 percent still haunted me. It's like the old joke about the man who asks a prospective mate on a date by saying, "What are the chances you'd go out with me?" The response comes: "Ha! One chance in a million!" And he answers, "So you're telling me there's a chance."

Despite the reassurance of a world-class neurologist and additional tests that showed no sign of degenerative disease, I held on to that fear for another year. After twelve more months of no additional symptoms other than the fasciculations (which I still have thirty-plus years later), I was finally able to acknowledge that I *probably* wasn't dying.

At the time, I had no awareness of what was going on. I was deep in alarm, and as I'll show you soon, an alarmed brain is one that defaults to survival mode and redirects its energy toward avoiding danger and potential threats and away from rational thought. As a result of being in survival mode, my threat-focused brain was unable to see and accept the overwhelming evidence that I was fine.

The critical error people with anxiety make is attributing their pain to the thoughts of the mind, since the fight-or-flight alarm reaction occurs immediately after the thought. The thing is, the alarm reaction is not a thought problem—it is a *belief* problem.

Don't believe me? Let's say you are a female who does not want to be pregnant. Let's also say you have the thought, "I might be pregnant." Your body will go into a fight-or-flight alarm reaction when you believe that thought. It is not the thought but, rather, the belief of the thought that creates the alarm and the subsequent pain and discomfort.

Still don't believe me? Okay, let's say you are male and you have the thought, "I might be pregnant." Your male body will not go into alarm because you simply do not believe the thought (because it is impossible). Same exact thought—"I might be pregnant"—but no belief, so no body reaction. It is therefore not the thought that causes your pain. Thoughts and worries are collections of words in a particular order. Thoughts themselves are painless brain droppings—until we believe them.

Incidentally, I once had a psychiatrist tell me in reference to my hypochondriac tendencies, "It seems to me you're not afraid of dying—you're afraid of living." He told me that more than thirty years ago and it still sticks with me. With hypochondria and other phobias, fear of death can be a convenient scapegoat that obscures the fact that our fear is actually preventing us from feeling and enjoying life. When we *fear* life, we are unable to *feel* life—and as you'll see, that is the whole point of the fear. The phobia is there to block us from feeling—and from living—because feeling life in the present opens us up to the reminder of what feeling life meant in our painful past.

26
The Alarm/Anxiety Cycle

In my book, anxiety, anxious thoughts, and chronic worry are synonymous. They are all activities of the mind, and none have any feeling attached to them—until we believe their content. When we believe the content of the worries, our bodies react with a form of alarm. As I will show you in Part 2, that alarm comes from your sympathetic (fight-or-flight) nervous system—which I call *foreground alarm*—or an activation of the old unresolved traumas that you still hold in your body—which I call *background alarm*. We'll explore these in greater depth later, but, for now, just know that alarm has two components—one reactionary and new, *foreground alarm*, the other anticipatory and old, *background alarm*—and each acts to energize the other.

It is the alarm that we experience as painful, but again, since the thoughts immediately preceded the alarm sensation, the mind assumes the thoughts are what causes the pain. As you'll see in Part 2, you do not need conscious thoughts to create alarm in your system. The background alarm stored in your body—the energy of your old, unresolved childhood wounds—can flare up at any time. You may encounter a person or event that reminds you of a painful experience from your past, and even if you are not aware of it, it can unconsciously send you into a state of alarm.

I remember being at a big-band style concert many years ago, the type of music popular in the 1940s, and really enjoying it. Then, seemingly out of nowhere, I got really angry and stopped enjoying the concert. Not only did I stop enjoying the concert, but I wanted to leave—pronto.

It was the strangest feeling to be enjoying something and then, in a matter of seconds, almost hating it. I was stunned by this sudden turn of events and just stood there in frustration, thinking the music was too damn loud and there were too many people there and I should go. Then the trumpet player stood up to play another solo, and I had an immediate flashback to my father, playing that same solo in that same song, many years ago.

My father was a trumpet player and he would practice in the house, often playing the same phrase fifty times in a row. The trumpet is not the most soothing (or quiet!) instrument, and it has always been an irritant to me. Okay, my apologies to all you trumpet players out there, but I hate the trumpet. Not for the musical instrument it is but for what hearing the trumpet does to me. It always takes me back to my father imposing himself on the rest of the family.

The trumpet is an instrument you can't just practice unobtrusively in your own room; the sound penetrates the entire house. Played well, it can be tolerated, but when the same phrase is played (poorly) over and over and over again, it's a form of torture. When my father was alive, I often thought the FBI should make him play outside of a hostage-taking (behind a bulletproof barricade of course). The perpetrators would give up within fifteen minutes.

Let's get back to the sound of the trumpet triggering my old background alarm. Even though it had been twenty years since I heard that same phrase, it fired me right back to the same frustration I had felt with my father years before. In other words, it triggered the old background alarm, flaring me into a full-body reaction.

After the fact, I figured out it was the sound of the trumpet that had triggered me. However, it was not the thought "Oh, this is the same phrase my father used to play" that sent me into alarm. Rather, it was the sensation that alarmed me, before I recognized the phrase. I had an implicit memory (aka a "body memory") of background alarm that was reignited, and even decades later generated a significant alarm reaction in my body and mind.

So, I do not agree that *all* stress comes from thoughts. There are old wounds that become activated in us that have nothing to do with conscious thinking but still cause considerable alarm—and they often occur well before the brain has time to process what's happening into a coherent thought. Many of my patients who had trauma before they could speak well (before the age of seven) can be triggered by a feeling or a smell or a touch that had nothing to do with thought. Cognitive, or talk, therapy has little benefit for these people as their trauma is in the "feeling" more than the "thinking." These patients respond much better to feeling therapies like therapeutic touch than they do to cognitive therapies.

People with a fear of spiders have a full-body reaction of alarm to the sight of a spider, or even anything that resembles a spider, and their body will recoil instantly—much faster than the brain can process the thought, "This is a spider." Neurologically, this recoil reaction occurs almost instantly, well before the conscious thought has had a chance to form.

There are at least two parallel pathways for alarm to be activated, one conscious and one unconscious, and the latter has very little to do with thinking and everything to do with feeling. So while stress and alarm can absolutely be made worse by our thoughts and worries, thoughts are not always a prerequisite to the creation of stress. All stress does not come from a thought. I did not create my reaction of getting upset by thinking to myself, "Oh, this is a trumpet solo." I *felt* it. Anyone who has had an intense panic attack seemingly out of nowhere can tell you this is how it works.

Often, though—and especially where chronic worry is involved—we *do* have a thought or worry that perpetuates the alarm-anxiety cycle. How we feel reflects and perpetuates what we think and vice versa. As I said earlier, the feeling-thought cycle is directly analogous to this alarm-anxiety cycle, and you will soon know both like the back of your hand. The two cycles are so similar as to be virtually interchangeable. Just like the feeling-thought cycle, the alarm-anxiety cycle also runs on a type of autopilot, automatically operating outside of our conscious awareness. To break the cycle, we must first be intimately aware of how it operates beneath our awareness, with the cycle insidiously becoming our master. When we adopt an attitude of non-emotional, nonjudgmental awareness, we can return to a place where we are in control of our minds, as opposed to our minds being in control of us. As Dr. Frankl shows us, awareness creates a space between stimulus and response, and that space is an omnipotent place of power and choice. Seeing the space between anxious thoughts and the alarm in the body, and in turn between the alarm in the body and the anxious thoughts of the mind, was crucial in my own healing from the cycle.

When we unconsciously assume the anxiety of the mind and the alarm of the body are inextricably linked, or one and the same, we see them as one impregnable and invincible enemy. I know that over many years of conventional therapy, I felt extreme frustration with my lack of progress, like I was fighting an indomitable giant. After my LSD experience, where I visualized my anxiety as a state of alarm in my solar plexus, I knew that thinking and feeling could be separated. Once I sat in awareness and saw that space between emotion and thought, I knew I had a way to break the alarm-anxiety cycle. Awareness of that space between the alarm in my body and the anxious thoughts of my mind showed a vulnerability in the loop that was previously invisible to me. I surmised that if there was a space between anxiety of the mind and the alarm in the body, they must be separate and separable—and separating the components of the cycle might very well be the Achilles' heel of the previously indomitable giant.

If we do not see alarm and anxiety as distinct, we have no entry point—no place to "break in"—and we are victims to the effect of the cycle's destructive power. You can't change what you can't see, and when we use awareness to see them as separate and distinct entities, we are able to divide and conquer. Seeing how the anxious thoughts of the mind need the alarm feeling of the body for fuel and vice versa allows us to disarm the cycle. We are now the victor and master and no longer the victim and servant.

In Part 3, I'll show you specific ways to break the cycle and use the space to your advantage, but I will give you a little foreshadowing. The best way is to use the space as a marker to divert your attention away from thinking and into feeling, and when you do that, you starve the anxious thoughts of energy.

Once we have awareness that we can use the space to choose to redirect our attention away from thinking of our mind and into the feeling of our body, we see a chink in the armour that was previously invisible.

Unconsciously, we give our thoughts an omnipotent status they do not deserve. I'll show you that in using your awareness you will see there is no anxious thought that is worth having. It is time to consciously use awareness to take that power back and break the alarm-anxiety cycle apart.

27
You Are Not Your Thoughts

The common saying, "You are not your thoughts," captures the idea that when you can *see* your thoughts, you don't have to *be* your thoughts. So many of us go through life identifying with our thoughts, but when you can learn to see them as mere machinations of the mind that you can observe with curiosity—and without reacting—that's when the realization dawns; while you are the entity that thinks the thoughts, those thoughts are separate from your essence. They are just thoughts—just brain droppings.

Seeing yourself as separate from the thoughts you think is crucial—but this is often easier said than done and is virtually impossible if you don't employ the power of awareness. With awareness, we apply a nonjudgmental air of curiosity to our thoughts. If we are in alarm or intense emotion, we may lose the ability to engage our awareness, as our emotionality drives us into survival brain and away from the rational brain we need to employ awareness in the first place. Adopting a framework of curiosity in our awareness can strip the emotionality from a thought, since curiosity engages a rational, non-emotional part of our brain.

For me, conscious awareness is curiosity, openness, and a calm and rational place where I have the ability to slow down and stay focused and discerning without being judgmental. It is a place where I can see my anxious thoughts from some distance and don't have to be taken over by them. The catch here is the thoughts I need to see with the most curiosity and rational, nonjudgmental awareness are the very same worries that send my system into a state of alarm and rob me of the rational brain I need to practice awareness. The emotionality of some thoughts puts me in a place where I lose my rational mind and therefore have less access to my non-judgmental awareness. It's much easier for me to be a curious observer of the thought, "I need to eat less sugar," than of the thought, "I'm going to die from diabetes," because in the former I am not as emotionally triggered and I can stay in my rational mind. Coming up, we'll explore some ways to stay present in awareness so you don't get swept away by worries (which, remember, you yourself create).

Conscious awareness is being aware that you are aware. It is a sense that you are a curious, conscious observer of the events of your life, not a hapless, unconscious victim of circumstance. With this non-attachment, as Buddhists call it, you can be the observer of both the anxious thoughts of your mind and the alarm feeling in the body, and in deciding to be the observer, you gain a degree of separation from that automatic thought and feeling. From that separation and detachment, you can literally catch your breath and stop short of activating the alarm in your body. As the alarm is diffused, you also do not need to protect yourself by descending into survival brain, allowing you to stay present in your rational brain.

With practice, as your rational brain increasingly sees you as separate from your worrisome thoughts, that space creates an atmosphere of choice. Awareness and presence allow you to stay in your rational brain so you no longer automatically believe your worries. Without conscious awareness, we unconsciously believe everything we think, especially our scary predictions of the future. This unfortunate and automatic belief of our worries is a major player in activating our alarm, which impedes the rational mind so needed for conscious awareness. Without our conscious awareness, we stay unconscious and fail to see our worries as simply scary prognostications of the future that we ourselves have created. When we automatically believe our worries we energize the alarm-anxiety cycle. When we commit to curious, objective awareness, we see those worries as something that is not an integral part of who we are but just objects that mind has created. When we become less attached to our worries in this way, those worries lose much of their power to hurt us by aggravating the alarm in our system.

With the core tenet of non-attachment, Buddhists are very skilled at detaching from their discomfort. When I visited a Buddhist monastery in India in 2013, I noticed there was dirt in the corners of their temple. I asked one of the monks, "Why don't you vacuum in the corners?" and he said, "Because we are Buddhists. Even our vacuums don't have attachments."

(Sorry, all this talk of alarm was getting a bit heavy, so I had to lighten the mood.)

28

Power of Belief

Why would we do such a thing as believing alarming thoughts? Why would we make ourselves sick with worry? Why would we accept thoughts we hate as true?

Remember that if we've had a lot of trauma and uncertainty in childhood, believing our scary thoughts seems like the lesser of two evils. Given the choice of believing a scary thought and bestowing it with credibility or living with complete uncertainty, our automatic, protective reaction as worriers is to believe the thought because we hate the uncertainty of not knowing more than we hate the anxious thoughts.

Here's one more example. You are supposed to have a coffee with a new friend and she doesn't show up. You have no idea why. Let's say you see her out with someone else at the same time you were to meet. The pain is unavoidable and a consequence of being human. But in an attempt to make the uncertain certain, your mind makes sense of the situation by telling you that your new friend probably thinks you are unworthy and boring. You go on to tell yourself that you'll never find a good friend and you'll end up alone for the rest of your life.

Now let's back up. Looking at that situation with conscious awareness, she missed your coffee meeting. That's it. You can be curious as to a potential reason why without adding all sorts of emotionality that only creates suffering.

This is how anxious thoughts work. We allow thoughts to snowball into massive amounts of emotionality and suffering simply because we fail to see that we can create a space, and therefore, we have a choice about whether or not to believe those thoughts. When we unconsciously and automatically accept and believe everything we think (especially our anxious thoughts), we suffer. We take what are only alarm-created *suggestions* of the mind and elevate them to the level of truth.

If you can become aware of the space between stimulus (getting stood up) and response (I must be a boring person), in that space you can bring in "Don't believe everything you think." Here's a non-fun fact about your mind. Your mind is a compulsive meaning-making machine, and in us worriers, the mind strives to make sense (and limit uncertainty) more than it strives to make you feel better. For worriers, the mind's mandate is to limit uncertainty, even at the cost of accepting a painful thought or worry as truth. In other words, the anxious mind places making sense first and foremost, and if it creates collateral damage to you in the process, it accepts that as the price of doing business. In this case, telling ourselves we were stood up because we were boring and/ or unworthy is yet another way we use our mind to victimize ourselves. We do this to ourselves but while we are unconscious it's not our fault. Now that you know about developing conscious awareness, if you victimize yourself by compulsively and automatically allowing yourself to believe your worries, it *is* your fault.

That may sound harsh, but I genuinely don't mean it to be. On my YouTube channel called "The Anxiety MD," I end all my videos by saying, "Don't believe everything you think." I know how challenging it is to not believe your own mind and its compulsive warnings, what-ifs, and worst-case scenarios. If you are a worrier, at some level you've convinced yourself that your worries are keeping you safe. I am telling you the complete opposite. To paraphrase Maya Angelou, " When you know better, you do better." Doing better is a gradual process, but the first step is seeing that your mind is not always accurate and it's not always your friend. Sometimes it craps on you (remember, brain droppings).

Let me remind you that you are not abnormal in your tendency to worry, and in fact, your mind is operating exactly as expected if you have unresolved trauma. What you have is a compulsive habit of believing (and being) your thoughts in a misguided attempt to protect yourself.

Another way of saying this is: Your mind avoids pain by creating pain. It sounds ridiculous, right? But until I saw what I was doing, I could not change it. Until I saw the choice and space in my commitment to awareness, I unconsciously just kept going with my childhood coping strategy of worry and believing everything I thought. Until I saw the space between the alarm I felt in my body and the thoughts I created in my mind, I had no way to change it.

I am here to show you the way out of chronic worry. Are you ready to learn? The way to break the alarm-anxiety cycle is to learn how to detach from your thoughts. Learn how to see your worrisome thoughts as simply thoughts, or better yet, brain droppings. Learn that you do not have to believe everything you think. Learn how to be the master of your mind and not its servant. Learn that your anxious thoughts are not protecting you or making things more certain. Learn that when you are in alarm, your brain is in survival mode and those thoughts are poisoned by fear and should not be consumed. Learn that when you are feeling alarmed, you can create space to move into the sensation of the body and away from the thoughts of the mind. Learn to create a pattern of awareness so you avoid continuing on with the old coping strategy of worry and pain. Stop blindly making sense of the feeling of alarm by automatically and unwittingly turning it into the thoughts of anxiety. Learn that between stimulus (alarm in the body) and response (anxious thoughts) there is a space, and in that space there is a choice to make a new reality, breaking the unconscious and maladaptive habit of the alarm-anxiety cycle.

Jerry Seinfeld has a joke about the use of helmets relating to why humans want to carry on with old habits even though we know they are bad for us. He asks: "Now why did we invent the helmet? Well, because we were participating in activities that were crackin' our heads. We looked at the situation, and we chose not to avoid these activities but to just make little plastic hats so we could continue with our head-crackin' lifestyles."

You do not have to carry on with your alarm-anxiety lifestyle. Your coping strategy of chronic worry had some adaptive advantage when you were a child, but you don't have to ride it till the wheels fall off.

I'll talk more about this in Part 3, but many therapists suggest to critically and rationally appraise your anxious thoughts on the spot so you can show yourself they aren't true. I do not agree. I've learned the hard way that trying to access my worries while I am alarmed, just gives more credibility to those worries. When I am alarmed, my survival brain takes over and I lose my rational brain, so why would I try to rationally look at my worries if the rational part of my brain was offline?

I've found the best way to deal with anxious thoughts is to immediately redirect the energy that was going into believing or analyzing the worry, into a focus of grounding a safety in the body. In this grounding, we can focus on faith and a knowing of the inherent safety of life. Once we have grounded ourselves and our rational brain is back online *then* we can critically appraise our worries, if we feel we still need to do that.

I've lived well over twenty thousand days, and I can honestly say that at least one thousand of those days I was absolutely convinced I was dying. This is not a joke or trying to make a substantive, literary point. I have spent months convinced that I had some neurological, psychological, or cardiac condition (among many other organ system disorders) and truly believing it might kill me. I have the journal entries to prove it.

And I am still here, still healthy.

We can use belief for us or against us. We get to choose what we believe, but only if we see the space that allows that choice to take place. Seeing that space between thought and alarm, between stimulus and response, is invaluable in healing from chronic worry.

29

Awareness Versus Autopilot

Many of my patients describe a powerless, helpless state of being tortured by their own minds. Perhaps this resonates with you? I, too, have spent much of my life in this unconscious, unaware autopilot state where my mind believed scary thoughts created by my emotions and my emotions, in turn, created yet more scary thoughts.

I had awareness, as all humans do, of the pain I was in. It was an ill-defined pain that seemed to go all the way up, down, backward, forward, and through me—but not all the way through. It got stuck. Because I kept believing my anxious thoughts, there was no chance for the pain of alarm in my body to release or pass through me. I kept holding on to it by generating and believing my scary predictions.

When we separate thoughts from belief, we see a viable path to our ability to control the feeling-thought and alarm-anxiety cycles, versus the unconscious autopilot state where those cycles control us. Notice I say *separate* thoughts from belief and not *analyze* thoughts for accuracy! You need only use your awareness to see your anxious thoughts and then make a conscious choice to separate from them and find the grounding in your body. Again there is no point in trying to wrestle a thought while you are in survival brain, it will pin you every time. Remember the Pink Elephant going from ludicrous to plausible?

We worriers have a tendency to automatically believe our thoughts, and this unconsciously triggers our alarm, putting us into survival brain and by definition, making us less rational. From an evolutionary, protective standpoint, when we become alarmed, we direct our energies *toward* survival and direct those energies *away* from rational thinking. The more we wrestle with our worries the more we go into survival physiology, and the more rational brain we lose. As our reasoning function decreases, our worries seem more real to us, and this increases our alarm, further disabling our reason. As alarm increases and reason vanishes, worries that seemed ridiculous now seem inevitable. This sequence of increasing alarm and losing rationality is exactly why trying to think you way out of your worries is a trap! Once you recognize you are stuck in your worries, you must get out of your mind and go to a grounded place in your body.

When people tell you to get out of your head, believe them! (Don't worry! I will show you exactly how to do this in Part 3).

30

In Survival, We Lose Our Minds

When the body is in alarm and the mind goes into survival mode, we literally lose blood flow to the more cognitively oriented "thriving" parts of the brain. When you are being chased by a lion, you don't need to know where the lion came from or if the lion is hungry or scared or what his motivation might be. You just need to get the heck out of there.

This descent from our "newer" (evolutionarily speaking) brain, called the neocortex or rational brain, into the older, more primitive lower brain areas, called the limbic or emotional brain, is a remnant of a time when our thoughts were more likely to be about predators or mortal threat. In that world, we did not need reason as much as we needed to escape a clear and present danger. The reaction to thoughts of threat became hard-wired: channel energy into focusing on immediate danger and deciding to flee or stay and fight. This fear is real and must be acted upon immediately. But in modern times, most of our thoughts are of delayed and/or imagined danger, like running out of money or potential sickness. This is not actually fear but anxiety and does not need immediate attention, although your impaired mind will make you feel that it does. If you ever question whether you are dealing with fear or anxiety, ask yourself if you can wait five seconds. Often what we call fear is really anxiety and nothing needs to be done right away. However, our brains still react to thoughts of perceived threat by acting much as they did fifty thousand years ago. In other words, the brain reacts to non-urgent imaginings in the same way it would to urgent realities. One of those reactions is to limit our ability to stay in awareness by squeezing out the feeling of space and making us feel we must act immediately, on limited information—on a mere perception from an alarm-impaired brain that is fixated on seeing threat.

Sound like trouble?

By shunting energy from our rational brain into our survival brain, we lose access to our reasoning minds. In this process of losing our minds, the worrisome thoughts appear more real than they really are, and this overestimation of danger creates an even greater alarm reaction in the body, triggering the alarm-anxiety cycle all over again.

From this survival-focused state of alarm, it can be very difficult to become aware of the possibility of engaging a more cognitive strategy, such as seeing the worries and making a conscious choice to move away from the thinking of your mind and into the sensation in your body. Without awareness you don't see the choice to change the direction of your energy, you redouble your efforts to try to think your way out, even though *your mind isn't rational enough to realize that you aren't rational.* You increase both your anxiety and your alarm as you become more frustrated at your inability to think your way out of a feeling problem.

This is why cognitive and talk-based therapies are limited in their effectiveness. They try to use the mind prematurely, assuming the mind is in a capable state to immediately grasp cognitive solutions.

When you are in an alarm state, your mind is far from capable—it's downright impaired. A more effective approach is to move away from thoughts altogether and focus your energy on grounding yourself in your body. Once you have moved out of alarm and your rational brain has returned, then and only then is it safe to go back into the land of thoughts.

31
There's a Hole in Your Boat

Most traditional therapies go after thoughts, believing that all stress comes from our thoughts and that if the thoughts are fixed, the condition will resolve. That has not been my experience personally or professionally. While cognitive or talk therapies may help for a while, the research shows the effects of talk therapy fade over time. If the alarm in the body is not addressed directly, it is only a matter of time until that alarm rises up and begins skewing your perception (and your subsequent thoughts) back to worry.

If there is a hole in the floor of your boat and you learn better techniques of bailing water, things will appear to get better, *but you still have a hole in your boat.* Trying to fix the anxious thinking alone is like bailing out the water with a hole in your boat. The underlying cause and main source of emotional pain is the alarm *feeling* in the body. Fixing the thoughts will not fix the problem. The alarm must be "repaired" before any thinking strategies will be able to "hold water."

Diffusing anxious thoughts will help a person feel better and reduce alarm in the short term, but the alarm needs more than a cognitive intervention to resolve. The thoughts are just a symptom of the underlying condition, which is still there if the thoughts are changed. Remember, the body's activated alarm state comes from unresolved childhood trauma, and the mind makes up scary thoughts to bring itself into congruence with the alarmed feeling in the body. Thoughts aggravate the alarm, but they are not the ultimate cause of our pain.

While talk therapy and learning to not believe everything you think are still valuable, focusing on the feeling/alarm component of the alarm-anxiety cycle holds the most promise in overall healing. I am not saying you just need to do yoga and stand on your left ovary twelve hours a day and that will heal you. You do need to have some ability to "tell your story" in a way that makes sense to you, what interpersonal neurobiologist and child psychiatrist Dr. Dan Siegel calls having a "coherent narrative" of your life. In my own journey to relief from anxiety and alarm, I needed a combination of a visceral/feeling/body strategy and a cognitive/mind/thinking strategy to make sense of what happened with my father, but ultimately, it was addressing the alarm in the body that made the most difference.

My approach goes against the current dogma, suggesting that cognitive therapies are the most effective for anxiety disorders. I spent over twenty years operating under that assumption and did not experience lasting relief until I embraced the critical role of my body in the healing of my mind. This book's perspective is one of "physician, heal thyself." After decades of limited success with conventional therapy, I had to go outside of my own profession to heal. I want others to have access to the perspective that ultimately helped me heal.

Skeptical that alarm in the body is at the root of your pain? Consider this. There is a procedure called a stellate ganglion block (SGB) in which local anesthetic is injected into the stellate ganglion, a mass of nervous tissue in the neck. This ganglion transmits information from the body to the brain, and the SGB is typically used to reduce the sensation of pain. When this procedure is done on combat veterans with post-traumatic stress disorder (PTSD), between seventy and eighty percent of them report *immediate* improvement of their PTSD symptoms. They state it is like having a weight lifted off them and they can think calmly and clearly again. Their families say it is like witnessing a miracle. The vets are able to experience a state of calm in their minds once the constant alarm signals from the body have been blocked. From this uncluttered place, they are better able to engage with the talk therapy they do receive.

It seems that the talk therapy these vets receive "sticks" better post-SGB because the deafening "noise" from the body has been silenced (or at least turned way down). They are now able to move out of survival brain into thriving brain and actually integrate the good information that talk therapy provides. This highlights the overpowering force the body exerts on the mind. Once the body's influence is taken out of the equation, the mind can think clearly again and absorb the cognitive strategies that calm the worrisome thinking.

This is one of the reasons I believe what we have come to call *anxiety* has more to do with the state of the body than the machinations of the mind.

However, since feelings are much less tangible than thoughts and since thoughts are much more easily identified and described, we are seduced into believing that the thoughts are the cause and therefore that fixing the thoughts will fix the problem.

We are missing the (hole in the) boat.

32
The Body Trumps the Mind

For us worriers, our minds know it is okay to relax and let our guard down, but our bodies won't let us, just like the monkey who can't release the banana. When our bodies have learned to stay alert regardless of what our minds are saying, talking about our stresses won't release them. Since the body has learned to reproduce the alarm, the body is the better place to focus our energy because it carries more "weight" than the mind in the calming process. The alarm in the body is more tenacious than the anxious thoughts of the mind and that alarm must be released at the level it is encoded, at the level of the body.

To use a computer analogy, imagine the operating system that runs the mind is Windows and the body is a Mac. You can get complicated programs that will convert the information from one into the other, but a Mac computer runs best on Mac programs and a PC works best with Windows programs. In other words, it's a lot more complicated to calm down the body by starting with the mind than to just start with the body itself.

Changes to the mind alone cannot heal our alarm, but the power and intention of the mind are used to direct the calming of the body. We use the mind to start the process—for example, by directing the breathing or by focusing our attention on calming and relaxing the body. Once the body moves into calm, the mind follows, moving out of resistant, survival mode. That's when we can start using the more complex, mind-based approaches. Trying to reason with a mind in alarm-based survival mode is like trying to use objective reasoning with an upset five-year-old at the mall who has just been told they cannot have an ice cream cone as it will spoil their dinner. (Or explain to an overheated ten-year-old in the middle of the desert she should think of a cold swimming pool).

33
On Alarm in the Body

Our alarm is activated as a learned response. In essence, the body has learned how to activate the alarm in itself without the input of the mind and actually does it more automatically and smoothly than the mind. Like the groove the body falls into when we drive our car, the body has learned to launch a fight-or-flight alarm response without much input from the mind. Once memorized by the body, through countless repetitions, this pattern can be activated virtually instantly, sending the body into alarm faster than the mind has time to process.

When I heard that trumpet solo, my body went into instant alarm; it was only a few minutes later that my mind figured out why. This pre-loaded, firing pattern is a form of implicit memory, also called *body memory*—a pattern or framework that is automatic, repetitive, and unconscious. The alarm is then replicated when we are triggered and taken back to a time in our lives where we felt helpless and hopeless—and alarmed. When I heard that trumpet solo, I regressed to a powerless, angry, and frustrated thirteen-year-old boy who was frustrated by a father who seemingly paid more attention to a brass instrument than to his son.

When we experience trauma as children, we develop a hypersensitive alarm system. It doesn't take much to fire it back up. And because many of us are in a state of hypervigilance (never letting our guard down and always looking for potential threats) the alarm setting is quick to fire up and slow to calm down. This hypersensitivity is the legacy of childhood trauma and cannot be healed by just talking about it.

Upon examination of my own alarm, in times of stress, my body replicates the same alarm state I felt as a teenager watching my father lose his mind. It is the same pressure and pain I feel in my solar plexus to this day.

Alarm in the body becomes automatic, without conscious input. Like riding a bike, the body learns how to do it with minimal input from the mind. This is not to say the alarm state operates completely outside of the conscious mind, as worrisome thoughts can absolutely make the alarm more intense, but certain patterns and programs are run unconsciously, and the alarm state in the body is one of them. To illustrate this point, I remember hearing Joe Dispenza, DC, talking about what I refer to as alarm, and what he said so poignantly has always stuck with me: "The body has learned to do it better than the mind."

For many years, I woke up with an alarm. Not an alarm clock or an alarm on my phone; it was an alarm in my body. It felt the same way every single day. Just the stimulus of waking up at an hour when, as a child, I had been woken by a stressed-out mother who needed to get to work, would send me into a state of alarm. My wake-up alarm (forgive the double entendre) is a form of implicit memory and a throwback to my childhood. My body did it every day for many years—it did not need the mind.

I started to consciously bring my mind into my morning alarm. I saw that by playing with believing scary thoughts, I could consciously increase the intensity of the alarm sensation in my solar plexus. I also observed that as the alarm would increase, I had a tremendous desire to explain it with more thought. In other words, there was a compulsion to attach *thinking* to the painful *feeling*.

In conscious, pointed awareness, I observed that if I separated the alarm in my solar plexus from the thoughts in my mind, by putting my hand on my chest, focusing on my breath, and generally directing all my attention to the feeling in my body, I became less aware of my scary thoughts. When I consciously directed my focus of attention into my body and breath, there was not enough mental energy left over to pay attention to or create more negative thoughts.

I also observed that the longer I focused on the present moment sensation in my body, the more it seemed to starve the thoughts of energy, and as a result, those thoughts tried to get louder. It was as if the pain of alarm in my body needed an explanation, dammit! But I intuitively knew I needed to stay the course, and I would redouble my efforts on focusing on the pure sensation of the alarm. With practice, the more I focused on the sensation of my body in the moment, like putting my hand on my chest and focusing on the pleasant sensation of my breath going in and out, the more distant (and less powerful) the thoughts would become. It was almost like when the thoughts finally saw they wouldn't be believed, they gave up. In conscious awareness and by making this unconscious alarm-anxiety cycle conscious, I was shown how to break the cycle.

I want to show you the same thing—how to break the cycle and stop feeding the alarm with anxious thoughts but, instead, stay in the moment by focusing on sensation.

34
Intention and the Power of It

So many times, I felt like giving up. The fight with anxiety and alarm seemed never-ending. My hopes and promises of relief were repeatedly dashed. I tried so many medications (legal and not), therapies, retreats, and processes of all kinds. You name it, I probably tried it. When nothing really helped and I woke up every single day with unbearable alarm, I lost hope that I would ever recover.

The tide started to turn when LSD showed me there was a source of pain in my body that was distinct and separate from my mind. Then, a year later, I learned of the concept of alarm from Dr. Neufeld, and my anxiety started to make sense to me for the first time in my life. The pain I felt in my solar plexus was alarm, and I honed the concept of alarm as it related to the condition doctors refer to as *anxiety*. Although it was aggravated by my worrisome thoughts, the alarm in my body could be separated from those thoughts in my mind, with the application of my specific intention to do so in awareness. Learning to set an intention, to allow the alarm to just sit in awareness without having to respond to it in any way, was invaluable.

I now realize, as a physician, I had an urge to be proactive and initiate treatment or prescribe medication, but what I really needed was patience. One of my medical school professors actually gave us some very sage advice on this topic: "Outside of life-threatening events," he said, "often the best response, when you are confused, is to just watch and wait." We doctors pride ourselves on being able to respond when someone says "Don't just stand there, do something!" But according to him, unless it's an emergency, the better advice is, "Don't just do something, stand there!" In other words, wait and watch—in curious, non-judgmental awareness that will allow you to gather more information, rather than grasping at a treatment that could potentially make things worse. Just as the physician can "sit with" his desire to take action and exercise patience to gather more information, each of us can "sit with" our alarm and observe it without reacting by adding worries or thoughts to it. We can commit to feeling the sensation without compulsively needing to give it an explanation.

For me, learning to be present with a feeling, without succumbing to the compulsive urge to add thoughts to it, was one of the keys to breaking anxiety's grip on me. When I saw I could separate the alarm in my body from the thoughts of my mind, I gained a decisive advantage. If I could sit with the *feeling* of alarm and not allow myself to add mind-based *thinking*, in an attempt to explain or relieve the body-based *feeling*, then I could separate them from each other and break their self-propagating feedback loop.

You cannot change what you cannot see, and awareness makes the invisible visible. Once you see the issue clearly, you can create a conscious intention—in the form of a commitment to adopt a specific program or pattern—designed to create a change in focus and behaviour. Where awareness goes, energy flows. We can use that energy as power to start to make real changes to unconscious patterns that were previously both destructive and invisible. When you find yourself in the alarm-anxiety cycle, you'll set the intention to focus your awareness and attention on the feeling of alarm in your body and deliberately ignore the incessant propositions of your mind to add thoughts to the alarm.

You can't think your way out of a feeling problem. You must feel your way out. I know the way and I'll show it to you.

35
You Can't Think Your Way Out of a Feeling Problem

If you've ever been super tense and had someone say to you, "Hey, relax," did it help? Probably not, because you cannot effectively calm a fight-or-flight feeling with words.

Learning coping strategies in our higher brain centres during psychotherapy is valuable, no question. But we must learn techniques not only with our thinking minds but also with our feeling bodies. We cannot fight a *feeling* armed only with *thinking*.

I'm very close with my ten-year-old eighty-five-pound blond labradoodle, Buddha. I estimate that I have given "BooBoo" close to half a million kisses on his snout. In contrast, he's not one for displays of affection, public or private. Buddha's internal ranking of things is: (1) breakfast; (2) dinner; (3) snacks; (4) any ball; (5) my wife, Cynthia, and my daughter, Leandra (it's a tie); (6) swimming; and (7) me. I got Boo as a three-month-old puppy on my birthday in 2009, and he has seen me through a lot of transitions and changes. Some days, I felt so alarmed, the only reason I would get up was that I needed to take him out.

He started to have seizures when he was eight years old. Now, as a doctor for humans, I know the onset of seizures in an adult has a good chance of being a tumour. I would tell myself it could just be epilepsy and then I would argue with myself and say it's probably a tumour. Then it would be a benign tumour, then a malignant tumour. (As a fellow worrier, you know how it goes.) The more I believed my catastrophic predictions, the more alarm I felt in my body, which activated my survival-focused brain. I was challenged to reassure myself because *thinking* Boo was going to be okay was not consistent with the *feeling* of alarm in my body.

So, in the days leading up to his MRI scan, whenever I caught myself thinking dogastrophic (as opposed to *cat*astrophic) thoughts, I would put my hand on my solar plexus area, focus deeply on connecting to myself, and visualize breathing into the area of alarm, only allowing myself to focus on the sensation in my body. I had to make a concerted effort not to be seduced back into thinking and to focus completely on the feeling, even if the feeling was uncomfortable. Focusing on the uncomfortable sensation of alarm in my body and then putting my hand on my chest, or breathing into the feeling with an attitude of compassion for myself, shifted my perception from a projected painful future to a consciously connected present. It also gave me a sense of control, in a milieu of uncertainty, about what was going to happen to my beloved BooBoo.

Whatever you focus on, you get more of. When I focused on connection to myself, I got more of that. When I focused on the worries about my dog, I got more worries about my dog. Your attention will fall into a groove, and the groove it falls into can be conscious, willful, and constructive, or it can be unconscious, chaotic, and destructive.

If you aren't paying attention, and the feeling in your body is one of alarm, the groove of your attention will fall into seeing things that are completely consistent with that feeling of alarm. To use a different metaphor, if you don't direct your focus consciously to something productive, when you are in a state of alarm, your attention will be hijacked to what they refer to in *Star Wars* as the "dark side." When you have been hijacked by alarm and are taken over by the dark side, your perception will follow. You will actually start to see negativity when none is really there. That is the power of perception.

When I consciously chose to break the hold that worry had on me and, instead, focus on connecting—putting my hand on my chest, concentrating on my breathing, and moving from a focus on worries to a focus on the pleasant sensation of self-connection and self-care in the moment—my worries fell into the background. It is not that they disappeared completely, but I was in charge of my worries, not the other way around. By disconnecting the scary thoughts from the alarm sensation, I broke the unconscious cycle and stopped the runaway train. I felt like I could consciously and deliberately direct my thoughts, as opposed to my thoughts unconsciously and automatically directing me. I was learning to be the master and not the servant.

You cannot beat thoughts on their own turf. If your mind has been seduced into worrying and the subsequent yea-or-nay back and forth that ensues, you've already lost. You can't find your way out of worrying by thinking; you must learn how to feel your way out.

I am a little hard on talk therapy (mostly out of frustration with my own lack of progress with it) but it's not so much that talk therapy isn't effective; it's that it's not effective when the patient has significant alarm in the body. This is why we need to calm the body first and *then*—when the brain is receptive, open, and fully available to absorb information—work with the cognitive tools.

There is little point trying to learn rational concepts when your alarm has taken you out of your rational mind! Once we have grounded ourselves in sensation, we can go back to thinking within a calm body. (Contributing to my calm body, a healthy Buddha is lying beside me as I write this.)

As I've already noted, you can't think your way out of a feeling problem. You must first meet the scary feeling on its own level. To do that, you must get to know your alarm.

36

When It's Not Safe in the Body, We Retreat Into the Mind

When the energy of our old childhood wounds became too much for our mind to bear and was exiled into our bodies, that painful energy did not disappear. It was just changed into a form that is less acute and more chronic. That chronic energy, hidden in our bodies, is what I've been referring to as background alarm.

From an early age, many of us retreated from our bodies. It was just too painful to be in our bodies, where the exiled pain resides. Instead, we retreated into the endless, worried thoughts of our minds.

When there is trauma in your home and you don't feel safe, you overthink and worry, which keeps you in your head, and that keeps you conveniently away from the discomfort in your body. When trauma makes us move away from being grounded in the present moment in our body and into the fractured and compromised future-based mind, this is called *dissociation*. We will explore this concept in greater depth later, but for now, know that it is akin to a daydreaming state where you are not in your mind *or* your body. The bigger the trauma experienced, the more likely a person is to dissociate. Worry could be explained as a mild form of dissociation, while being held against your will and assaulted would require a higher level of detaching from reality and would be a form of severe dissociation. Survivors of major trauma often have little memory of the incident because they dissociated and left their bodies as a form of self-protection.

So why am I telling you about dissociation? Because worrying is a mild form of dissociation, and it's critical to recognize when you start to dissociate and lose touch with yourself. Your worries are like daydreams hovering just outside of your conscious awareness. The alarm in your body impairs your mind and drives you into survival brain. The worries feel perpetually out of reach, as your impaired mind does not want you to be able to grasp them in conscious awareness—because if you committed to seeing them by bringing them into the light of your focused attention, you could see those worries were false and they'd lose their power to distract from the pain in your body. When you see your signs of dissociation, daydreaming in worry, being unavailable to others, absent-mindedness, you can use that as a "tell" to use your awareness and get into the present moment sensation of your body. My wife says when I get anxious (alarmed dammit!) I am all of those things and she says I am in "my own little world."

Maybe you can relate? I love the T-shirt that says "I'm in my own little world, but it's ok ... they know me here."

Growing up, I felt safe physically, but I didn't feel safe emotionally. I didn't know when my father was going to lapse into a deep depressive state or stay awake for days in a manic state. This had the effect of keeping my body in a state of alarm, waiting for the other shoe to drop. As a coping strategy, I began to overthink and worry. Some part of me felt that if I stayed vigilant with worry, I would be emotionally prepared for my father's next trip to crazytown.

Worrisome thoughts acted as a temporary distraction. Worry diffused some of the uncertainty energy, by giving me something to do. Also, ruminating on what could go wrong, kept my focus in the machinations of my mind and away from the alarm, I couldn't bear to feel, in my body. I would think things like, "He seems a bit down today, he must be heading for depression," or "He seems in a good mood, I wonder if he is heading into a manic phase?" But I was essentially robbing Peter to pay Paul. Although those worrisome thoughts initially distracted me from the feeling of alarm, over time they created *more* alarm as I invariably and unconsciously believed them.

Worries are like a drug we develop a tolerance to. Over time, my anxious, ruminative thoughts had to become more frequent and more intense, to maintain their ability to distract me and keep me in my head. This is why worries tend to get more and more intense over time, as they need to keep you in your head and out of the alarm in your body.

Because of my trauma, I had retreated into my head and lost the grounding potential of my body. When you perceive your mind is your only safe place or, at the very least, the safest place available, you try your best to stay there. I had lost faith that my body was a safe place, and that left me with my mind as the only port in my (childhood) storm.

This overidentification with the mind (believing your thoughts and believing that you *are* your thoughts) is one reason, I believe, people ascribe anxiety solely to their anxious thoughts. Perhaps, on some level, we don't even feel like we have a body. As an aside, for a long time, I didn't feel hunger or the need to go to the bathroom until it was urgent. I postulate that is because I had denied my body for so long that I was numb to the messages it sent me. Now that I have done a lot of work to re-establish a connection with my body, I can feel its nuances. I can feel "a little" hungry, or get the message I'll have to pee in the next hour or so. I've also learned that many of my anxious patients were bedwetters as children, which may be a sign of this same dissociation from the body and its signals.

I find anxious people, as a rule, quite smart. A possible reason for this is when mind-based thinking is your only option (because body-based feeling is too painful), you get very good at it. When thinking (and worrying) become a coping strategy, you get more practice, and you get better at it. But you fall under the illusion that rumination and excessive thinking are productive. Nothing could be further from the truth. This habit does distract us from the pain and alarm in our bodies; with practice, it becomes a familiar groove, and we tend to go there when we are stressed. It gives us a sense of control and power and, therefore, a respite from the pain. This is how many of us get trapped in our minds.

As we prepare to move on from the mind to the body, let's look one last time at how important your thinking truly is. I have stated, as the premise of my theory on chronic anxiety, that it is more of a body-based issue than a mind-based issue. That is absolutely true, but let's not forget the powerful role thoughts can play by pulling us out of our bodies and thus away from our healing.

It's analogous to a scab on a cut. Thinking worrisome thoughts is like picking the scab. When you pick at it, the wound can't heal. When we starve the worrisome thoughts of our attention, we are leaving the scab alone to let it heal.

You might ask, "What if my thoughts are positive?" Know that *any* thinking when you are in an alarm state is likely to be hijacked to the dark side. You may start off positive, but as soon as you focus on thought of any kind, the ego is very slippery and before you are aware of it, your intent to think positively has been hijacked into worry. You are much better off focusing your energy and attention on calming the alarm feeling in the body and, once your body is out of alarm, *then* moving back into the realm of thought. In the cartoon strip "Peanuts," Charlie Brown is constantly being seduced into thinking he is finally going to get to kick the football, and he invariably winds up exasperated when Lucy pulls it away once again. You are being seduced by your anxious thinking. Unless you *see* it, you are doomed to *be* it.

My thoughts had me think they were the problem. I thought (haha) if I could just get rid of the anxious thoughts my dis-ease would go away. This is also the rationale for traditional therapies: tame the thoughts and the system just returns to peace. While developing ways to manage thoughts and think differently may help, this does not solve the problem, because the thoughts are only a symptom. Treating the thoughts, to cure anxiety, is like bailing the water out of a flooded boat. It helps, but unless you find and seal the crack in the hull underneath, the problem is just going to come back. The underlying dis-ease originates from background alarm from old trauma stored in the body. Removing the aggravating aspect of worrisome thoughts will not erase the imprint of the old trauma. We need to isolate the background alarm and work on it specifically as a separate entity if we are going to heal. We need to fix the hole in the boat by resolving the alarm in the body, then the thoughts will disappear, just as the boat stops sinking when you seal the crack.

The more you can see why you worry, the less you'll be tricked and trapped by it. Before we move on, let's take one more look at worry and what purpose it serves.

Anxiety/worry is a way of keeping you safe. The worry is there as an attempt to warn you and prepare you for potential danger. In constantly warning you, it feeds the alarm in your body. Once you see and feel you no longer need to worry to stay safe, you can begin to release it.

Anxiety/worry is always about the future. This is where you can unmask worry. When you know it depends on you being mentally transported into the future, you can neutralize it by focusing on, and staying in, the present moment.

Anxiety/worry is a way of avoiding uncertainty and creating a sense of control. When we worry, we are creating a story of the future that makes the uncertain appear certain. There is nothing worse to a worrier than uncertainty because of what uncertainty meant in our childhood. When we can start to accept and, I dare say, even embrace uncertainty as the spice of life, we can release the worry.

Anxiety/worry is a way of explaining the alarm felt in the body. When we feel alarm in the body and there is no obvious cause for it, this creates *dissonance*—a state of conflict between thinking and feeling. If you are standing at the edge of a cliff and your body goes into fight-or-flight mode, that makes sense to you and there is no dissonance. However, when your body is reacting like you are standing at the edge of a cliff while you are lying safely in your bed, that dissonance only adds to your uncertainty and consequently to your alarm. When we feel alarm in the body, worrying is a way of creating congruence in mind and body. That worry, although it makes things more congruent in the short term, is only adding to the alarm in the long term.

Anxiety/worry distracts us from the painful alarm in the body. There is a misdirection to worry. On one hand, it redirects the painful alarm energy by distracting us into thinking, with a very temporary reduction in the perception of alarm. But ultimately, on the other hand, the worry creates more alarm and we get trapped in the alarm-anxiety cycle.

To recap, the worries of the mind aggravate anxiety, but the painful part comes from a sense of fight-or-flight alarm in the body. By all means, we should understand why we worry and neutralize those worries to the best of our ability, but our ultimate relief lies in healing the alarm stored in the body. I will show you the means of doing both.

Now let's turn to the true cause of our pain: the alarm that flowed into our bodies when our minds were overwhelmed by trauma.

PART 2

AWARENESS OF BODY

37
The Source of Your Pain: Waking the Tiger

I was trapped in my worried mind for many years. I also believed, because my worries were so easy to see ("I sure hope _____ does not happen!"), that my worries were the source of my pain. *To heal anxiety, you must focus on the worries of the mind* was, and still is, the predominant narrative in psychiatry and psychology, so in a professional sense as well as my lived experience, I was just going with the flow. I had been trained in this worry-centric view that anxiety could and should be treated by talking about and modifying our way of thinking.

It's just that decades of therapy focusing on changing my thoughts did very little to help me. Perhaps assuming my mind was the source of my pain was the reason I wasn't improving. What if the pain I felt was a sleeping tiger rooted in my body and no therapist had thought to wake that tiger up so we could examine it? What if, in being hyper-focused on thinking in the therapy of anxiety, we completely missed the aspect of feeling?

Remember the male who thinks "I might be pregnant." Thoughts are just collections of words that are painless until they are believed to be true. Worry, in and of itself, is painless. The pain we attribute to it is in reality coming from a state of activation or alarm in the body. This is where we should be directing more of our energies in treatment, as it is the ultimate cause of the pain we feel.

A body-centred focus, in treatment, tackles the root of the issue, essentially cutting off worries' power supply. With body-centred approaches, I finally got somewhere because I went back into my body and faced the alarm that had been stored there for decades.

I had to feel it to heal it.

To understand where our pain truly comes from and start to heal from the source, let's learn more about this entity I call alarm.

38
The Two Types of Alarm

Recall that there are two types of alarm: foreground alarm and background alarm.

Foreground alarm is a function of the sympathetic wing of the *autonomic nervous system* (see diagram below). The autonomic nervous system is the "automatic" nervous system of the body, governing functions that happen automatically and don't require conscious awareness, like heartbeat and digestion. It comprises two wings with opposite functions: the *sympathetic* (fight or flight, for shorthand) and the *parasympathetic* (rest and digest). *Foreground alarm* is a term I invented to describe the activating fight-or-flight reaction of the sympathetic nervous system that all humans have.

The job of the sympathetic wing of the system is to activate in times of threat by increasing heart rate and blood pressure, tensing our muscles in preparation for action, stopping our gut motility and salivation, and making our breathing fast and shallow. It is an ancient and evolutionarily, hard-wired part of all humans, designed to protect us by mobilizing our entire system to react to physical danger either by fighting or fleeing, hence the term "fight or flight."

Let's say you are driving and a child on a bike shoots out in front of you between parked cars. You slam on the brakes to avoid hitting the child. In the aftermath, as your system relaxed and flooded with relief over not getting in an accident, perhaps you noticed your rapid heartbeat and hands clenching the steering wheel. Maybe you observed your dry mouth or felt your stomach cramping up. As you sat in relief, you might have been aware of the signals of your sympathetic nervous system doing its job. I call this *foreground alarm* because it is relatively easy to observe as a predictable response to a *perceived* danger. The operative word here is perceived, because this fight-or-flight re-action of foreground alarm will be activated in modern times just as it would have been in our ancestors, had they been faced with an unexpected threat. This type of alarm would suit its original purpose of protection from threats that are real, external, and physical (such as an actual impending collision or accident), but it will also fire the alarm for threats that are also only imagined, internal, and emotional (such as the speech we fear we may be asked to give at an upcoming business meeting). In other words, foreground alarm responds not only to actual danger but to our worries as well.

AUTONOMIC NERVOUS SYSTEM

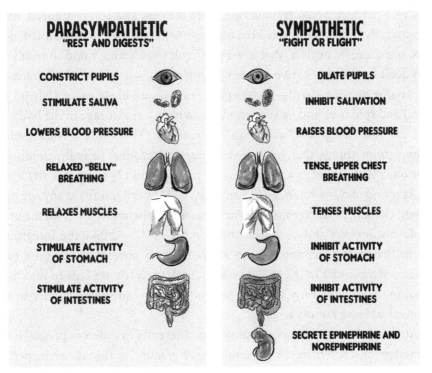

In contrast, **background alarm** is a chronic energy. It is a remnant of old, unresolved trauma, typically from childhood, that was too much for the mind to process and became stored away as an energy in the body.

We all experience trauma as children; it is unavoidable—it is just a fact of life. We all have trauma, but the manner of dealing with the trauma makes a critical difference. If you had a securely attached, attentive parent, that parent's comfort and reassurance may have been enough to assist you in successfully processing whatever trauma you experienced. The trauma energy would be resolved by a secure attachment to a loving parent. However, if you did not have an available and supportive parent, that trauma energy would not be processed and resolved. As energy cannot be created or destroyed, that energy is changed in form, deposited in the body in the form of background alarm.

Complicating matters, some children are more sensitive than others, and what is traumatic to one may not be so to another. I have seen a child with a connected parent work through the loss of a close family member in a matter of weeks, and I have seen another child unravel for many months over the loss of a pet fish. Some traumas are more serious, and some children, more sensitive. But, in general, when the trauma involves abuse, abandonment, deep loss, rejection, or neglect, that is very difficult for a young mind to resolve. If you don't have a supportive and reassuring parent—or worse, if the parent is the source of your alarm—the energy is even more likely to overwhelm the mind and spill over and be sequestered into long-term storage in the body.

I call this *background alarm* for two reasons: (1) because it is unresolved energy from things that happened in our background (usually childhood) that our minds could not metabolize or process and (2) because it sits in the background of our awareness. (As an aside, PTSD from trauma at any age has a strong element of background alarm because it is also an overwhelm the mind could not process and becomes stored in the body). Unlike the foreground alarm that is obvious and easy to attribute to an obvious precipitant, background alarm hides in the background. It took me a trip on LSD to find mine. Finding the source of my alarm in my body was an indispensable insight and an invaluable part of my healing.

Although background alarm shows up differently in different people, it has consistent characteristics or an "emotional signature" within the same person. For example, the background alarm shown to me on LSD is a fist-sized, hot, sharp, irregular, purple crystalline structure located in my right solar plexus area that exerts pressure up into my heart. I have shown many of my patients how to find their alarm and they often have exquisite descriptions of their own background alarm. Soon, I'll show you how to find your background alarm, and you won't have to drop acid to do it. (How's that for an incentive to keep reading?)

While everyone has foreground alarm, the normal fight-or-flight aspect of the nervous system, background alarm only appears in those of us with deep, unresolved emotional wounds or PTSD. That being said, if you are reading this book to help yourself heal from chronic, nervous system hyperactivation and worry, I can pretty much guarantee you do have background alarm in your system. I can also guarantee I can help you with it, but you first need to see it.

Because you can't change what you don't know is there—and most doctors don't know it's there—most doctors and counsellors will, instead, try to treat the worry they can easily see, namely the thoughts of the mind. But the worries you can see are only the tip of the iceberg, and by directing your efforts at the surface, you'll only get superficial results. We must address the alarm underneath the surface, and when we melt that, you'll get long-lasting relief. By the time you finish this book, you will know more about anxiety and its effective treatment than most doctors do.

Foreground alarm is normal sympathetic nervous system activity that is in everyone; background alarm is abnormal and only found in those of us with significant unresolved trauma. Background and foreground alarm are both processes that activate an energy in the body, and each one tends to activate the other. Panic attacks are one example of how foreground alarm and background alarm can combine to create a massive reaction by escalating each other. Panic attacks come from background alarm that is bubbling to the surface and activating foreground alarm. Once this happens, the two alarms energize each other in an explosion of nervous system hyperactivity. Panic attacks are an extreme example of acute activity, but background and foreground alarm can also activate each other chronically in more subtle ways that can still create significant pain and discomfort.

foreground alarm + background alarm = chronic alarm

Together, background alarm and foreground alarm resonate with each other to form a state of *chronic alarm*. This is often what we feel when we are having a "normal" day with no acute stressors, yet we feel this sense of uncomfortable activation or energy in us. Some of my patients call it a sense of impending doom. This chronic alarm is not present in people who do not have background alarm. Without background alarm, foreground alarm works as it should, the fight-or-flight response arising quickly in the presence of a threat and fades quickly once the threat is gone. But for those of us who do have alarm constantly simmering in the background, this maintains a little chronic alarm in our system at all times, although it may fall below our awareness. However, it doesn't take much to fire it up, as anything even remotely reminiscent of our old trauma will set it off, and once activated, it takes a long time to settle.

When we learn to separate background alarm from foreground alarm or to decrease them independently, we decrease our general chronic alarm. As chronic alarm decreases, we feel better and calmer at our core. With less alarm in our system, there is less energy to create anxious thoughts, and we are no longer blocked from engaging in both thinking- and feeling-based approaches to prevent the alarm from coming back. It's a win-win.

39
The Source of Background Alarm

You may be wondering: if you didn't have unresolved trauma from childhood, but you suffer from anxiety, can you still have background alarm? The answer is yes.

Not everyone reading this book will have obvious unresolved trauma. Clearly, growing up with a schizophrenic father was traumatic. Many of my patients endured trauma that was clear and easy to see in the form of abuse, abandonment, neglect, or great loss. Again, it's often not so much the trauma itself but how that trauma was handled by parents and caregivers that would determine if the energy was successfully resolved and metabolized (by a loving parent as an example) or if (in the absence of a supportive figure) that trauma energy overwhelmed the system and was therefore deposited in the body.

For some people, their trauma may be more subtle, or they may not even view it as trauma. Some people are highly sensitive, so they require less trauma to activate their background alarm. Other people are more stoic and appear to handle what most people would consider very traumatic. Some war vets suffer PTSD and others do not. Warfare aside, you don't have to have a significant and obvious trauma history to suffer from chronic worry, but if you suffer from chronic anxiety, it has to be coming from somewhere. You almost certainly have background alarm that is feeding your chronic worrying, even if you can't find an obvious source of trauma from your childhood. I have had many patients who told me their parents were loving and supportive, but when we really looked back, they were neither. If you have chronic anxiety and it's not from something obvious like PTSD, your childhood may not have been the securely attached experience you may have told yourself it was.

I am not one of those people who wants you to go back and find blame for your parents. The truth is, we parent the way we were parented, and for the most part, our mothers and fathers did the best they could with one of the most difficult undertakings in life—parenting.

New information is showing that trauma can be transmitted from parent to child through non-coding genetic material. (In other words, it operates not on the genes themselves but on their packaging, which affects how they are expressed.) Of course, there is another mode of transmission of trauma—namely, behaviours that are repeated from generation to generation without awareness that they're dysfunctional. Even if you can't specifically point to trauma in your childhood, you may very well still carry it. And that means you have an inherent susceptibility to anxiety—which ultimately means you are carrying background alarm in your body.

In recent years, I have seen a trend in young people toward sensitivity and nervousness. I believe this is also due to a form of background alarm. One common source of background alarm is a feeling of disconnection from your family. While I do think the parents today are under considerable stress and are busier and have to work more than ever, I've seen the rate of anxiety in young people skyrocket in the last ten to twenty years, and I think their lack of connection comes from one major factor: screens (computers, tablets, smartphones, and the like).

Humans have a mind-body system called the social engagement system (SES). We use it to feel truly safe and connected to each other and ourselves. The system uses elements like tone of voice, body language, and facial expressions to relate the experience of one human being to another. In short, our SES is hard-wired in all of us to relax when we are engaged in the presence of people we care about. If you've had the experience of having an "anxious day" and then going out with your friends that night and laughing and connecting, it is your SES activation that saved the day. The SES not only soothed your feeling of alarm but actually helped you feel *good* by the time you got home.

SES engagement is what I lacked as a teenager. There was simply too much stress in the house for my family to feel relaxed enough to engage my social connection, and my SES did not mature well in me. An engaged, high-functioning, often-used SES is what helps metabolize our traumas, especially as children. But we need frequent and positive personal connections to engage and mature the system. The SES learns best by dealing with others *face to face* who are happy, sad, excited, loving, hurt, lonely, or frightened. It need not be an interaction with love to mature it, but love is probably the best maturation factor. We use our SES to read emotions and connect to other people, and it is in observing others that we learn to read ourselves. And when our social interactions are coming through a screen (and perhaps not even with real people on the other side of the device), it impairs our ability to develop this system and to benefit from its healing power. Face to face interactions are being replaced by face to screen interactions and anxiety and alarm in our children is increasing, while at the same time, empathy in our children is decreasing. It is no coincidence that the lack of activities that mature the SES is corresponding to a jump in anxiety and alarm in our children.

I wrote this book to explain where my own anxiety comes from in the hope that I am not some mutant and that you will find elements of your experience in mine. I hope that my theory—that a lack of connection in childhood (for whatever reason) led to background alarm, which is the *real* cause of what you have been told to call anxiety by modern medicine—will point you toward your own healing.

When I say that unresolved trauma is the cause of background alarm, know that your trauma could be from something as obvious as being abandoned or abused as a child or it could come from spending much of your life in front of a screen or smartphone. Although it may not seem traumatic, in the sense you've understood the word before, know that your system views a lack of connection (whatever the source) as traumatic and develops background alarm as a result.

40
How Background Alarm Takes Root in the Body

It's been said that it is not so much the specific childhood traumas we experience but how those traumas are handled by our caregivers that determines the long-term effects. In my case, the trauma of my father's illness was both acute and chronic, and there was nobody skilled enough to mediate it for me or help me process and metabolize it. As a result, I developed a state of energy in my body that you now know as background alarm—a state of activation stored in my body that I have carried since my youth because of the unresolved events in my background. Although that energy significantly affected me, it stayed in the background outside my awareness until my LSD experience. Until then, I blamed my pain on the worries of my mind. I want to save you the trouble of taking a psychedelic and suggest to you that the "engine" of your emotional pain is not your worries per se but, rather, your background alarm that may be hiding in plain sight. I'll show you both how to find it and what to do about it.

Background alarm develops when there is trauma, usually starting in childhood, that is not mediated by a secure attachment figure, usually a parent. My brother and I needed loving reassurance, and my mother—while being a very organized and efficient registered nurse, good at caring for other people—had no real idea of how to reassure us over my dad's craziness. To be fair, my mother was the sole breadwinner in the family. She was also responsible for all of the household duties, so she simply did not have the time to help us handle the destabilizing, emotional vortex that was our family. My mother loved my brother and me very much, but she simply was too overwhelmed to be able to consistently connect with us in a way that would provide the emotional reassurance we would require to feel safe in that chaotic environment.

My mother was a product of her very reserved and emotionally cool Scottish family. As is often the case in British families, you were expected to know you were loved by default. I have heard from many children of British parents the fact you were fed and clothed implied love and negated any further need for those parents to actually say the words "I love you."

Since my mother received little in the way of loving reassurance from her own family of origin, I am not surprised she wasn't really able to give that to my brother and me. She was not cold or distant; I just don't think she had an experience of loving closeness. Her background alarm is still active to this day, and she is eighty-seven years old! My mother loves coming to family gatherings, especially now that she has two great-grandchildren, but to this day, if she is surrounded by our connected and loving family, it often makes her uncomfortable, and she wants to go back home early. I do believe a loving connection can be hard for her to settle into because she didn't have that in her own childhood.

You can't give what you didn't get, and you can't teach what you never learned. I do believe that background alarm can be ameliorated if you are seen, heard, and loved by a secure attachment figure. As you'll learn in Part 3 of this book, one of the ways of neutralizing your own background alarm is creating a real connection with yourself, in essence *becoming* the attachment figure now that you needed back then.

As my mother did her best but couldn't give me the love she did not get herself, the trauma of my father's illness had nothing to ameliorate it, so year over year, my background alarm grew and with it my habit of worrying. This habit, I now know, was a way of staying out of my body, which was full of background alarm. As an adult, I began getting therapy from doctors and psychologists, but as they had no idea of what background alarm was (nor did I at the time!) or how to treat it, they focused on treating the anxiety of my mind, while the real source of my pain went unaddressed as background alarm in my body.

Traditionally, psychiatry and psychology have attributed the lion's share of chronic worry to the mind, assuming the body has only a passive role. It is only recently that traditional disciplines have even begun to consider that the body may play a significant role in the propagation and treatment of the condition commonly referred to as chronic anxiety.

Prior to my LSD experience, I was of the same mind. I was a classically trained Western doctor, and the prevailing theory was that anxiety was a function of the mind. It's been said there are some trips you come back from as a different person, and that's how LSD was for me. That trip showed me my unresolved trauma created and stored an uncomfortable energy state in my solar plexus, a deep source of my emotional and physical pain that is still there (in a much less intense form) to this day. It wasn't until I started addressing this stored emotional energy in my body that my anxiety started to shift. For many years, I kept trying talk-type therapies that would address the conscious mind. I know now why these cognitive therapies weren't that effective: Remedies that focus on the mental, conscious mind are going to be of limited help when the problem is background alarm stored in the physical, unconscious body.

My background alarm was added to by my father's many bouts of mental illness and frightening psychotic breaks. He was never violent or physically abusive, but seeing the person I regarded as my teacher and protector turn into a wide-eyed, up-all-night psychotic was emotionally devastating to a boy in his early teens. As a result, because the trauma was too difficult for my child mind to bear, the trauma energy went underground into my unconscious mind, and from there it was a short hop to lodge into long-term storage in my body as background alarm.

Let me explain. When something new or frightening happens, we look to our past for ways we dealt with it, and that familiarity gives us a sense of power or control. That sense of power or control allows us to stay in our conscious and rational mind. But what if you have no previous experience to draw on? What if you are a thirteen-year-old boy and your father has clearly lost touch with reality and is accusing you of stealing fuel from the gas station down the road? There was nothing in my memory that I could have drawn from to empower me in the conversation with my clearly deranged father.

My mind would have searched for a previous cognitive solution to this novel situation, and I would have told him the truth—that I wasn't stealing anything. He would then insist I was lying and that the CIA was encouraging me to take the gasoline to fuel a secret project. I might try to continue to reassure him, but I would eventually realize there was no resolution to his psychotic accusations.

My mind was overwhelmed, with no way to resolve the conflict, so it froze. I was trapped in my mind with a thousand possibilities. Do I continue to plead my case even though it is clearly going nowhere? Also running through my mind was "This guy is crazy!" and being the problem solver and oldest son, I felt a sense of obligation to protect the rest of the family from this man. When the mind is frozen, or given two equally abhorrent choices, those are places the mind cannot stay for long.

In that moment, the trauma overwhelmed my conscious mind's ability to deal with it, and the energy spilled over into my unconscious mind as a way of protecting me from a vulnerability too great for my thirteen-year-old self to bear. From my unconscious, it was a short trip to find its long-term storage in my body, and I still hold some of it in my solar plexus as background alarm. The body acts as a reservoir where the mind can sequester painful energy away from everyday awareness to both protect us and allow our minds to be less encumbered by the clutter of the old trauma. In his brilliant book, *The Body Keeps the Score*, psychiatrist Dr. Bessel van der Kolk shows how the body plays a big role in emotional trauma. It may be out of mind, but it is by no means gone. (Freud called this repression.) That trauma may well have stayed there undetected had it not been for my revelation on LSD.

With every new trauma that overwhelmed my mind's ability to process (like going through medical school, moving across the country, and getting divorced—twice), the body stored it in my solar plexus reservoir of repressed alarm, throwing it on top of the pile of all the other old unresolved traumas. (After two divorces, it was getting pretty crowded in there.) It was like one of those dated, neon signs that had a flashing arrow pointing to my solar plexus saying, WE NEVER CLOSE! COME ON IN! (Incidentally, I've always thought the "Come On Inn" would be a great name for a brothel. For added effect, you could have Jack Hammer Johnson on the sign too.)

Jokes aside, not knowing how to metabolize and release these unresolved traumas from my body, the background alarm grew more and more intense as new trauma was added to it. Despite my best efforts using therapies of the mind, those old traumas weren't cognitively processed and released because they weren't centred in my mind—they were in my body.

41
Is This Plane Crashing, or Can I Get a Snack?

Have you ever wondered why some people have a more prolonged response to traumatic or anxiety-inducing situations than others do? I believe that in many cases, this is because of background alarm.

For example, if you are in an aircraft experiencing severe turbulence, your foreground alarm will activate. This is natural and healthy.

Let's say the plane has two passengers sitting beside each other, Restless Rusty and Stable Shirley. When the plane starts to bounce around violently, both of them experience activation of their sympathetic nervous systems. Their heart rates and blood pressure increase, their muscles and guts tense up, and their breathing becomes rapid and shallow.

Then the plane stabilizes. The pilot comes on and says, "Sorry about that, folks. We're through the rough air and it should be smooth sailing from here." About ten minutes later, Shirley's foreground alarm has fully resolved she is enjoying pretzels and a coke. Rusty, on the other hand, will feel "on edge" and have no appetite until a few hours after the plane lands. Why?

Rusty is me, with all my old background alarm, and Shirley has no background alarm because she was raised in a securely attached home.

Background alarm can contribute to a sense of difficulty in "winding down" from stressful experiences or in worries and anxiety coming on seemingly out of nowhere at times when our physical safety is not in danger.

Perhaps you, too, have been safe and sound in a fancy hotel room, comfortable and peaceful in your bed—when out of nowhere the worries come. For me, it's usually something like "Your talk at the conference tomorrow is going to go badly." From there I start envisioning all the times I bombed onstage as a comedian and my background and foreground alarm flares up, until it feels absolutely inevitable that the next day's talk will be a disaster.

In that comfy hotel bed, there is nothing in my environment that is in any way threatening—yet my background alarm is still with me, so my mind needs to invent a story to match. This, in turn, starts up the foreground alarm—the sympathetic, fight-or-flight reaction that was in high gear earlier on my flight to get to the hotel. (Just when I was finally able to eat something!)

This is also what happens with PTSD. A soldier's mind knows he is back home, but his body maintains the alarm as if he is still in an active combat zone. His mind knows he is not in danger, but his body doesn't, and the body keeps the score.

Foreground alarm serves a definite purpose. If your house is on fire, you are better off getting out of the house immediately versus waiting until you've calmly finished going through your credit card bill and trying to figure out this strange charge for the "Come On Inn."

But when our foreground alarm is being activated by our background alarm and not by a threat in the environment, we're trapped in the alarm-anxiety cycle with no way out. This was my life for many years.

But I know the way out now. Read on. And pass the pretzels.

42

Fix the Hole in the Boat

Have you ever had a thought that caused you distress and yet that very same thought hours later seemed like no threat at all, or even provoked the opposite reaction? It is very likely that in the first instance, your sense of alarm was active and by the latter, it had eased.

For many years, I was doctor by day, stand-up comedian by night. I can't tell you the number of times I would wake up in the morning in a panic, knowing I had a show that night and fearing I wouldn't be able to perform because I was too alarmed (although back then I would have told myself I was too *anxious*). All the way to work and all morning, I would be dreading this event, imagining the worst, and trying to come up with a plausible excuse to get out of it. However, by three that afternoon, I would often start looking forward to going and doing the show!

What was the difference? In the morning, my sense of alarm was up. I was in survival brain, and *everything* looked scary. By the afternoon, my alarm had settled and I had my rational brain back. By the time I got to the venue and was ready to go onstage, I was psyched and so grateful I was able to get up there and entertain. It was a true gift.

But the next morning, I would go through the exact same process!

Chances are you've had a similar Jekyll-and-Hyde experience with your thoughts, and it was your state (alarmed or not) that determined your perception. Contrary to popular belief, it wasn't the thought itself that disturbed you; it was the state of your nervous system. Simply put, in a state of alarm, thoughts are perceived as dangerous when they are not. You can have the same thought and have two entirely different perceptions of that thought depending on the alarm state in your body. Given this fact, the thought itself cannot be painful. It's the state and degree of alarm in your body that makes it so.

Remember—trying to fix anxious thoughts of the mind without regulating the alarm feeling in the body is like bailing water out of a boat with a hole in the hull. Relentlessly trying to "think positive" and moderate the anxious thoughts is just bailing water. It may help you stay afloat, but unless you fix the source of the problem, you'll be bailing forever. Furthermore, it's exhausting to think in opposition to how you feel. If you feel alarmed, trying to think happy thoughts requires a tremendous amount of energy, attention, and effort.

Anxious thoughts are like the water in the boat. They are the obvious sign of danger, but not the ultimate cause of the problem. The cause—the hole in the hull—is the alarm. Fix the hole and you solve the problem at its source.

It was no wonder the mind-based strategies offered by my therapists had limited effect, as I was trying to fix the problem of the sinking boat by bailing water while the hole in the hull was being ignored.

The take-home message is this: A worrisome thought is infinitely more likely to be believed habitually, automatically, and unconsciously when there is alarm in the system. When there is alarm in the system, the mind goes into survival mode. It is just how we've been wired for thousands and thousands of years. If there is no threat, the mind makes one up. This is the origin of worry.

There is a story, I heard, about how they train military pilots. They put them in a room and gradually start to decrease the oxygen in the room. They will often have them sort cards into piles of black and red. As the oxygen drops lower and lower, the pilots experience different symptoms. Some will get a tingling in their hands, others will get a headache, and others will become nauseated.

They were told to be keenly aware of their symptoms, and once they set on, to automatically, without thinking, flip their oxygen mask over their face. It had to be instantaneous and automatic, since if the oxygen dropped any lower they would lose the ability to "see" that they were losing oxygen and could easily go unconscious—and indeed, this has happened. Sometimes pilots, instead of flipping their O2 masks on, try to figure out what the problem is and become so hypoxic they fall unconscious.

In a way, we worriers do the same thing. Failing to understand that the worries themselves are not the problem, we try to fix them, while all the while the alarm builds in our systems and zaps our ability to see and fix the real problem: the increasing alarm in our bodies. If you take nothing else from this book, know that your worries are not the cause of your pain. The worries aggravate the background alarm in your body, and *that* is the true source of your pain.

When we decrease our alarm, the mind moves out of the *surviving* brain and into the *thriving* brain. When the alarm is removed from the system, we move back into the rational prefrontal cortex and increase the mind's ability to critically appraise thoughts.

In the morning of my shift at my medical clinic, I was in alarm and my thoughts about the gig after work were negative (*What if I am so anxious I can't think and I blank onstage?*), created and directed by that alarm I was experiencing *at that moment*. Once the alarm dissipated, I got my rational mind back and I could see the positive aspects of performing, I knew it would probably be fun, and it (almost) always was!

Imagine I am going to teach you how to ride a unicycle. You'll need a clear, unimpaired mind to learn this new skill. Now imagine I give you five shots of tequila and try to teach you how to ride that unicycle. While you may retain some of the skill of riding the one-wheeler, you would be able to perform much better if your mind was unimpaired by the alcohol. You would be better off going home, sobering up, and trying again tomorrow without the bug-juice.

In the same way, you are better off clearing the impairment (alarm) from your system first before working on the skill of dealing with your thoughts. When your system is hijacked by alarm (just like with alcohol or low oxygen), you lose the ability to rationally examine your thoughts because the rational part of your brain has been taken offline. The first goal is to clear the impairment in your body (the alarm). Then we can go after the thoughts.

43
Alarm Is the New Anxiety

We all know that forty is the new thirty and orange is the new black. Well, I have a new one for you: alarm is the new anxiety.

At that 2015 anxiety conference in Vancouver, British Columbia, (a bunch of nervous people in a room, remember?), where I first heard Dr. Neufeld say that all anxiety is separation anxiety, it was the first time I heard the term *alarm* used to refer to the state associated with anxiety.

Like that moment where, under the influence of psychedelics, I'd been able to see the separation between thought/feeling and mind/body, this was also a moment that changed my worldview completely. When I heard the word *alarm* used that way, it felt like something clicked into place.

What if this painful sensation I had in my solar plexus was the manifestation of alarm? What if this alarm held emotional energy that could not be contained upstairs in the mind? What if the anxious thoughts of the mind were

adding to or aggravating the alarm in the body? What if the alarm in the body somehow created worrisome thoughts of the mind, to be consistent with the uncomfortable feeling of alarm in the body? What if each charged the other? If the anxious thoughts of the mind and the alarm in the body could be separated, would that break the cycle?

I had so many questions—and, maybe by now, you can see in that moment the entire premise of this book began to take shape. The shift in seeing that my pain was more a function of my body than my mind was an absolute revelation that had me start thinking about my condition in a brand-new way.

I've come to understand that alarm and its byproduct, anxiety, almost always result from a break in the perception of safety during childhood—from a deep experience of being isolated or separate, specifically from our parents or caregivers. When we are separated from our attachment figures, either physically or emotionally, our bodies go into a state of alarm.

Dr. Neufeld has been one of my greatest influences and mentors. While the alarm-anxiety theory is my own, I could not have come up with it without the information I obtained from his teachings. Since that conference, I have come to see clearly that virtually all mental illness has its roots in childhood, and understanding a child's psychological development (or lack thereof) holds the clues to treatment and recovery.

In those of us without childhood wounding, there is only foreground alarm, the natural reaction of the sympathetic nervous system. In those of us with unresolved trauma from childhood, we have both the regular, acute, fight-or-flight foreground alarm and chronic, background alarm. As a result, our alarm reaction is likely to come up twice as fast and resolve twice as slowly. This is why it took Rusty hours to calm from the turbulence experience while Shirley was enjoying Coke and pretzels ten minutes later.

Remember, foreground alarm is logical and functional in the sense that it responds to an identifiable cause. But what if we start feeling a tense gut, dry mouth, muscular tension, and a flushed sensation when there is no obvious danger? What if your body is reacting as if you're facing a dragon when you're just lying in bed or heading out to watch a movie with your partner? The background alarm in your body is the likely culprit, as it can activate the foreground alarm at random times. This is why we can feel alarmed when there is no obvious precipitating cause.

Panic attacks are a classic example of background alarm, that we are not consciously aware of, suddenly and violently activating the fight-or-flight reaction of foreground alarm. Panic attacks feel exquisitely more frightening and disorienting *because* there is no obvious reason. It is excruciating when you are in an extreme state of foreground alarm completely out of the blue.

The mind's response, to this acute state of alarm, is to make up a story that is consistent with the intensity of the alarm you feel. In a panic attack, your thoughts jump very suddenly from being nervous about going to a party where you won't know anyone to thoughts like "What if I'm having a heart attack?" or "What if I'm having a stroke?"

But it gets worse.

Because we are in a state of alarm and our brains are in survival mode, we've lost access to our rational mind. Since we can't reassure ourselves that we are probably not having a heart attack or a stroke, we believe the thoughts, and this plunges our bodies deeper into alarm. As we lose whatever ability for rational thought we had, the mind creates horror stories that the body believes and reacts to. Panic attacks are devastating at the time they occur, and what is almost worse is the fear of having another. Until ayahuasca and LSD, the fear of panic attacks was the worst fear I had ever experienced.

(As an aside, and this may sound ludicrous to you, I actually enjoy panic attacks now. I embrace the rush and don't get caught in the victim mentality that allows panic attacks to escalate. Although I don't have the space in this book to specifically go into how to approach panic attacks, if they are something that afflicts you, I do have a video on my YouTube channel that addresses this, which you can find a link to on the resources page.)

When we have childhood trauma, the mind will pick certainty over pain. So using the panic attack example, given the choice, the mind will make you believe that you are dying of a heart attack or stroke, rather than just leaving the reason for the extreme reaction in your body uncertain. Said another way, the mind creates (and needs) worry to explain alarm.

Everyone's mind makes up stories to make sense of feelings. But we worriers have scaring ourselves down to an art form.

Although we typically describe foreground alarm as a fight-or-flight reaction (i.e., the impulse to run *away*), I return to Dr. Neufeld's concept of pursuit. I believe the sympathetic nervous system's activation of foreground alarm is to provide energy for a state of *pursuit* to reconnect to a safe attachment figure. If we look back to early childhood, any type of danger that would have caused foreground alarm would cause us to retreat not just *away* from the barking dog or the hot stove but *toward* our caregiver in search of protection and connection. Recall how my alarm in childhood stemmed from a desire to reconnect with my dad when he was lost in his illness—so it was motivated by pursuit.

Alarm-based pursuit, as a reaction to real or perceived separation, is an automatic protective response that seeks to reconnect us with our attachment figures. The example of a child who loses his parents in a store illustrates this principle. Rather than running away from anything specific, the child directs his foreground alarm energy into desperately trying to find his parents and reconnect with his secure attachment figures. If the pursuit fails and despite his best efforts he remains separate from his source of security, he eventually gives up. The acute foreground alarm energy becomes a trauma that is stored in the body as background alarm.

This pursuit scenario played out in a less direct way between my father and me, when I was young. Up to age twelve, I was very close to my father. Through my early teens, he would get sick and I would experience threat that would trigger my foreground alarm. But instead of fight or flight, I would move into pursuit in an attempt to connect with him. As his episodes of mental instability were time-limited, as he started to become more lucid and we reattached, my pursuit would eventually be rewarded. I would reconnect with him and my foreground alarm would fade.

However, as I got into my middle to late teen years, he would plunge deeper into mental illness and stay there longer. My pursuit would still activate, but as my father became more incapacitated and the episodes lasted longer, he would stay unreachable and there came a point when I felt pursuit was futile.

I understand now that when pursuit did not end up in reattachment—when my efforts to reconnect were thwarted—without a way to resolve this uncertainty, my mind became overwhelmed and my acute foreground alarm morphed into background alarm. When the connection was lost and I could find no way of getting it back, it became too much for my mind to bear, so the energy was packaged up and shipped off to my body, where it was stored "out of sight, out of mind" as background alarm.

My father was ill, off and on, from the time I was a teen until he died when I was twenty-six. As I got older and more jaded, with every bipolar or schizophrenic episode, my system would abandon the futile pursuit more quickly and just pour the trauma directly into my body, adding to the reservoir of background alarm that I held in my solar plexus.

Your foreground alarm would be activated and you too may have tried to connect with your parent until you saw it was futile, as I did. As children, if our foreground alarm was activated and our pursuit reaction failed to resolve the disconnection, the emotional trauma would likely spill over into your body and get stored as a background alarm. The more times pursuit was futile, the more background alarm was added.

Returning to Freud's concept of repression, the pain of the trauma of being unable to connect to a pursued parent would be too much for the child's mind to bear. As a result, the energy would be exiled from the mind and buried in the body as background alarm.

Remember Jane, my patient who repeatedly picked abusive alcoholics as partners? Of course, I can't know for sure, but it is very likely that when Jane was a little girl she felt pursuit energy and tried to connect with her alcoholic father when he was drunk. There probably came a point when Jane felt that pursuing him was futile and stored the pain of that disconnection as background alarm. As an adult, Jane's choice of partners helped her mind make sense of her body's background alarm by replicating the familiar dynamics from her childhood—including the pursuit energy of trying and failing to connect with her alcoholic father.

Perhaps you had a similar story with one or both of your parents? A perception that you were no longer connected? Perhaps your parent was the cause of your feeling that you weren't safe? Maybe your parent was an addict and you would "lose" them to alcohol or some other addiction.

If you struggle with anxiety, it is highly likely that you have a version of this background alarm state smouldering in your system—and it's likely to be from a time in your life when you felt emotional pain and were separated from your attachment figures.

Unresolved trauma does not have to be chronic to generate background alarm. Acute episodes of overwhelm, especially in childhood, can most certainly create background alarm. I have had many patients ask me if a discrete incident can create background alarm, and the answer is an emphatic yes.

Acute trauma that is too much for the mind to bear, like an episode of emotional, physical, or sexual abuse; the death of someone important to us; or an episode of abandonment or rejection by someone we love, can also overwhelm the mind and deposit background alarm in the body. My own experience of unresolvable trauma was chronic, but any trauma, acute or chronic, that overwhelms the mind will deposit as background alarm in the body.

44

The Tuna Lady

When I was a med student on my psych rotation, circa 1990, I had a patient I called the Tuna Lady. She was a little older than me, at the time about 35, and she reminded me of a young Sally Field. She was admitted to hospital for severe anxiety. She was experiencing mild swelling around her ankles and had read (there was no Google back then) that ankle swelling was a sign of protein deficiency. She decided that protein deficiency was also the cause of her anxiety, and it became all she could talk about. In a five-minute conversation, she used the word protein about a hundred times. Every time I saw her, she asked me how she could get more protein. She was not psychotic, but she was fixated and clearly alarmed.

In an attempt to reassure her, I did a blood test that showed her serum protein (albumin) was actually in the high normal range. I showed her the results, but it made no difference to her. She insisted that when her blood had been drawn for the test, she had just finished eating a full can of tuna, and that is why the level had come out okay. I told her that protein levels are stable over days to weeks and do not change quickly and that she could eat twelve cans of tuna and it wouldn't alter the results of the test.

In hindsight, this was the wrong thing to say to the Tuna Lady. She had been having her friends bring in cans of tuna and she was eating about three cans a day, so saying she could eat twelve cans a day and it still wouldn't make much difference was probably one of the dumbest things I have ever said to a patient. She even asked the nurses if they could mix the tuna with cream in a blender, if her friends brought one in for her. (The blender request is when she got the official designation as the Tuna Lady.)

She was alarmed, and her mind looked for why. Since nothing was obviously wrong with her, other than some very mild ankle swelling, she drew the false conclusion that she was protein deficient and the lack of protein was making her anxious. With this conclusion, her mind had a "good" reason to explain her emotional state. But the more she worried about her protein intake, the more alarmed she got, which made her eat tuna in quantities comparable to an elephant seal. She was caught in a loop of creating a story in her mind to explain the alarm she felt in her body. It may seem like an extreme example, but I can relate. My own mind, on multiple occasions, comes up with its own hypochondriacal and irrational fixations that would rival the Tuna Lady's obsession with her protein levels.

Why are we so irrational? Why couldn't the Tuna Lady understand her protein level was completely normal and not in any way responsible for her alarm and anxiety?

Because worry has a purpose. When people say worry is useless, I disagree. Worry distracts us away from the background alarm we store in our bodies. This is what I believe happened to me and why I worried for so long. Perhaps you can relate.

If you have unresolved emotional traumas you probably have chronic alarm, although you may not be consciously aware of an alarm reaction in your body. What you may be more aware of is chronic irritability or worry. I know that for many years, I wasn't aware of the background alarm in my chest, but I was definitely aware of the chronically anxious thoughts.

Because the activation in my youth was chronic and perpetually anticipatory (I worried more about my father *going* crazy for much more time than he actually *was* crazy), a general feeling of *always* being unsafe was created, and that added to my background alarm.

Background alarm, for the most part, stays in the background, but that is not to say it is silent. On the contrary, it gives us a sense of impending doom or uneasiness, but unless you know where to look for it, it can easily stay out of sight. My own background alarm did not become apparent until my LSD experience. One of background alarm's favourite tricks is to hide behind worry. If the worry is powerful enough, we don't even consider looking anywhere else for the source of our pain.

By the way, I know exactly where to find mine now. If you'd like to contact it, you'll find it here:

the other driver's lack of skills or manners. But with background alarm, we get stuck in a feedback loop because of the illusion that worrying protects us.

This is where background alarm becomes really insidious. One of the greatest barriers to healing is the unconscious assumption that the familiar alarm we carry is the source of our safety and not the source of our pain.

As I got into my late teens and early twenties, whenever my alarm faded and I let down my guard and stopped worrying so much, the old fear of being blindsided came up and snapped me right back into alarm. This is why it's common to have an anxiety attack just when we start to feel safe—because feeling safe as children was not safe. Feeling safe and relaxed reminds us of a time before when we felt safe but it turned out we weren't. It leaves us vulnerable. When I let down my guard in October and my dad got sick in November, I would feel blindsided. So I stayed with the certainty of maintaining my background alarm, because part of me perceived it was protecting me. Like the woman who shouted "I told you so!" to her doctor, I used my father's (anticipated) illness as a reason to maintain my constant alarm.

In a similar fashion, the Tuna Lady was in a deep state of background alarm that her unconscious mind used as evidence that she needed more tuna, to avoid the very alarm that was causing her to believe the tuna was saving her.

Returning for a moment to my hyperreactive smoke detector, you might wonder why I didn't just replace it. (1) I am lazy. (2) I grew attached to my little smoke detector. I had a kinship with it. I understood it. I knew what it was like to have a hair trigger and to react to little things like they were big things. I also knew what it was like to wake up in a panic in the middle of the night. I wasn't going to toss it away; I was going to care for it.

There's a reason I'm telling you this. Taking care of the smoke detector instead of tossing it is a metaphor for how to relate to our background alarm. Keep reading and you'll see what I mean.

45

When Making Sense Doesn't Make Sense

When I tell people I'm a doctor and anxiety specialist, just about everyone tells me they have a child, partner, parent, close friend, relative, or pet rabbit who struggles with it. They will often tell me they don't know how to support them, and they have a hard time understanding what they are going through.

I remember my dentist, Angela, asking me about her daughter, Jenny, as Jenny had recently shown signs of what Angela called anxiety. Angela had very amicably divorced from Jenny's father three years earlier, and Jenny seemed okay for the first couple of years. Angela and her ex agreed to have Jenny and her brother stay at the family home, while the parents would take turns looking after the kids, with each parent spending one week living at the house and then one week staying elsewhere. It seemed to be going okay, until, about two years into this arrangement, Jenny, now sixteen, began having panic attacks, disordered eating, insomnia, and mood swings. Angela had never really experienced anxiety and told me she could see Jenny was suffering but didn't understand what anxiety was. Angela had said she wanted to understand what Jenny was going through but felt lost.

I asked Angela if she had ever been frightened for her life. She confided in me: years earlier she had undergone a biopsy for breast cancer. Her family doctor had told her that the tissue he could palpate was suspicious for cancer and the biopsy results would take five days to come back. She told me for those five days, she couldn't eat or sleep and was "full of anxiety."

I told her, instead of calling it anxiety, she should more correctly say she was full of *alarm* for those five days. Angela told me that referring to what she felt as *alarm* felt more resonant to her. (Indeed, people generally tell me when they start calling their emotional pain *alarm* instead of *anxiety*, it feels much more descriptive and authentic.) Angela asked me if the alarmed feeling she had experienced in those five days was what her daughter was experiencing now.

It was a light-bulb moment for Angela, as for the first time she had a real sense of what her daughter was feeling. For the first time, Angela wasn't dealing with the concept of anxiety as a label with little resonance or meaning. She could relate to the feeling sense of the alarmed state she had experienced in her own body while waiting for her biopsy results. As I told Angela, although many people don't experience anxiety, *everyone* has experienced alarm.

Once Angela could relate her daughter's experience to her own, she had a better understanding, but there were some specific differences. Using the terms we've gone over in this book, we can say that Angela was experiencing foreground alarm because she had a distinct and direct cause for her alarm—the biopsy results. In contrast, what her daughter was experiencing was likely originating from background alarm because Jenny had trouble pinpointing the source of her pain. Jenny had convinced herself that she was "fine" with her week-on, week-off parents and was even proud of the way the family was "staying connected."

Because Jenny's background alarm did not have an obvious cause, it, therefore, did not have an endpoint. It became chronic, bringing with it worry, disordered eating, and panic attacks—and a great deal of uncertainty.

One of the most alarming (forgive the pun) things about background alarm is that we are alarmed without an obvious reason. We feel distinctly unsafe, but there is nothing supporting that threat in our environment. I have heard anxiety described as "fear without eyes," and that makes sense to me. This is why panic attacks can be so difficult. If we were looking over the rail of a balcony on the 49th floor of a high-rise and our body went into alarm, that would make sense, and it would be an appropriate reaction. Our body and our mind would be in sync at the potential threat of falling, so there would be no confusion or dissonance. We would know and accept that our body was in alarm because we were truly in a potentially life-threatening situation.

But with anxiety and panic attacks, our bodies are acting like we are in mortal danger when we are just sitting in a coffee shop, waiting in line at the bank, or feeding our nervous rabbit. (Except if you're waiting in line at the bank with the intention to rob it. Then you *would* have a good reason for the alarm in your body. But most of you reading this book aren't likely to be bank robbers. And if you *are* a bank robber, that's probably because you experienced trauma as a child that is still alive in you and creating background alarm—so please keep reading this book, and maybe once you get out of prison you can live a productive life without chronic worry.)

The Tuna Lady, whom you met in the last chapter, existed in this state of dissonance, where her internal state was out of sync with the external environment. In her admission history, she had told me her parents had split when she was eight years old. Her father disappeared and she had to live with her abusive mother. It is no wonder, with that degree of childhood trauma, that she had significant bouts of becoming alarmed and irrationally fixated on elaborate worries, with some episodes requiring hospitalization. I saw a woman in her prime, with mental illness robbing her of her life. But because her body held the alarm of a traumatized eight-year-old, her mind believed eating tuna like a great barracuda was going to cure a protein deficiency she did not have.

The Tuna Lady's fixation on a lack of protein as the cause of her distress actually made sense to me in a way because of how I fixate on my own health concerns and make up paranoid stories. She and I were not so different, and seeing her oddball fears exacerbated my own hypochondria. (Which reminds me this is the time of year I usually get my pap smear.)

What makes the Tuna Lady even more memorable is that she was one of my first patients on my psych rotation. I cannot even begin to describe the alarm (both background and foreground) that psych wards flare up in me, even to this day. It is in me. When someone tells you they have a "body memory" of something painful, that is just another way of saying background alarm. For me, the experience of walking onto a psych ward is a body memory that brings up that same state of impotent alarm I felt as a teen and young adult.

When people experience a similar environment to what created their back-ground alarm, they often dissociate and regress to a confused and irrational younger state. When triggered, we regress to the "emotional age" and coping skills we had at the time of the original trauma. This happens to me when I step onto a psych ward and also when I feel there is nothing I can do to help one of my patients. How ironic that I spent ten years working to become a doctor so that I would have power over illness and would never have to feel helpless again—only to find myself faced with patients I could not help on a very frequent basis.

I think this is why the Tuna Lady sticks so poignantly in my mind, and I vividly remember her to this day. Although I don't remember this specifically, I must have seen my father in her. She activated the alarm I felt when I couldn't fix my dad.

When our background alarm is feeding into worries that then feed into more alarm, we can say that "making sense doesn't make sense." There's a mismatch between our internal state and what we see around us. Irrational worries and panic attacks are our minds' attempt to resolve this dissonance, but they just wind up making the situation so much worse.

Imagine that one afternoon you see your partner's car parked in an unfamiliar neighbourhood by the ocean. Your partner has told you they have a dentist's appointment, and you know their dental office is actually very close to your house, on the other side of town from where you're seeing the car. Now there is incongruity and dissonance in their story, and dissonance creates alarm. Until now you have felt perfectly safe with them and they have never given you any cause to think they may be unfaithful, but nevertheless your mind resolves the dissonance with a painful thought/worry: "What if they are having an affair?"

You call them and get no answer, which is odd. Your alarm increases, and your mind starts wondering if you've missed something. You wonder about their "friend" that they seem to be talking a lot about lately and if, maybe, that friend lives in the area of the parked car. Your mind can't seem to stop itself. You imagine them together, going for a romantic walk along the ocean. It doesn't take long for you to be convinced that your previously trustworthy partner has fooled you and may very well be a cheater!

This worry-alarm cycle goes on for a while until they call you back. You say, "Where are you? You didn't answer!" And they say, "I just got out of the dentist's chair and I'm now walking home." Then you say, in as innocent a tone as you can muster, "Hey, I saw your car parked by the ocean." You're keeping it casual, trying your best not to sound too confrontational and let your voice betray how alarmed you truly are.

When they say, "Oh, I loaned my car to Terry for the day because I knew I could just walk to the dentist," your alarm drops precipitously and takes your anxious thoughts with it. Then you wonder how you could have doubted your partner and been sucked into thinking such a preposterous scenario.

Notice how as your alarm rises, the implausible becomes possible and then probable and then true. This is because your mind is impaired. When you are in alarm, you literally cannot think straight. This is true in the "car at the beach" scenario, and it was true for the Tuna Lady. To paraphrase Dr. Bruce Lipton, author of *The Biology of Belief*, the conscious mind is only at the helm five percent of the time. The dilemma is that the mind is impaired by the alarm in the body and further impaired by its own faulty assessment.

When we have alarm in our system, if our minds cannot find a good reason for that alarm, they will simply make one up. It is amazing what we can convince ourselves to believe. But (and this is some *major* foreshadowing of Part 3!) instead of using worries in an attempt to make sense of the feeling of alarm, we should, instead, direct our energy into reducing alarm in the body.

When we focus on resolving the alarm in the body, we don't need to create elaborate fears of disapproving audiences, cheating partners, or protein deficiencies that can only be resolved with three tuna milkshakes per day. This is how we resolve the dissonance so that making sense once again makes sense.

At the end of her three-week stay on the psych ward, with her alarm significantly calmed, the Tuna Lady told me she was embarrassed by her tuna fixation and by her invention of the tuna milkshake. If I could talk to the Tuna Lady today, I'd tell her not to be embarrassed, as her mind was profoundly impaired by revisiting a deep state of background alarm that began when she was an abandoned and frightened eight-year-old. So, dear Tuna Lady, if you are reading this book, thirty years after your admission to St. Joseph's Hospital in London, know that you made a profound impression on me, and I sincerely hope you're okay.

46
Foreground and Background Alarm

Foreground alarm and background alarm are man-made inventions (made by me, a man) and as such, they cannot explain everything perfectly, especially since feelings, by their very nature, are difficult to capture in words.

Still, they explain quite a lot about anxiety and how to heal it, and thus it's worth understanding them in more depth.

A few key points in review:

- **Background alarm can be localized in one area, while foreground alarm is a body-wide activation.**
- **Background alarm isn't in everyone, but it is in those of us with unresolved trauma.**
- **Foreground alarm is a response to a consciously observable event, while background alarm is triggered unconsciously and often not obvious to us.**
- **Background alarm and foreground alarm form a feedback loop.** The

more the two systems are activated together, the more likely they are to "wire" together and continue activating together in the future—and if you had a particularly traumatic childhood, your foreground alarm and your background alarm were frequent table tennis opponents. Think of two tuning forks that vibrate at the same frequency. If you hit one and put it beside the other, they both will start to vibrate, even though one wasn't even touched.

- **Background alarm can be triggered by experiences similar to the ones that first created it.**
- **Background alarm generates a survival state in the mind, and that state creates worries.**

If you've read any of Eckhart Tolle's books, he refers to something called the *pain body*, a kind of amalgamation of pain and trauma that human beings carry within them, both from their own life experience and the traumas of our close and distant ancestors. What I call background alarm is directly analogous to what Tolle calls the pain body, but my definition is more personal. While we all carry trauma from our ancestors, background alarm is more unique to our own personal experience. This is not to say that we can't absorb some of it from our parents and ancestors (I believe I carry alarm from both my mother and my father), but the more trauma we do not neutralize in this lifetime, the more it contributes and accumulates in our (pain) body.

One thing to note about background alarm is individual levels vary not just based on one's experiences but based on one's temperament or personality. Some children seem to experience trauma and metabolize it without moving it into long-term storage in the body as background alarm. This has to do with the severity and frequency of trauma and with the presence (or absence) of adults to help them process it but also with the child's own disposition—sensitive or less sensitive. This is one of the reasons we shouldn't compare our trauma to others' and assume because we had it "easier" we should be less affected. Your feelings are real and valid. There is not some arbitrary amount of background alarm you "should" have based on what you have experienced. The amount you have is what is there—and it can be healed.

As I came to understand more about background alarm, I looked back on my relationship with a woman named Katerina and a lot of things started to make sense.

Kat was one of the most driven people, if not *the* most driven person, I have ever known. She was as beautiful as she was intense. (Picture Michelle Pfeiffer's Catwoman with dark hair.) To say that she was a perfectionist would be an understatement. Kat woke up every morning at five for a rigorous exercise session. I remember one particular adventure in perfectionism when she had the flu. She was practically hallucinating with a temperature of 103, and she still got up with her alarm clock and staggered to the living room to do her exercises. When she fell over, I put her back to bed. Believe it or not, she kept getting up and trying to get back to her workout, and I kept having to put her back to bed when she passed out again. It was like trying to contain a honey badger once it made up its mind. It wasn't funny at the time, but once she recovered, we could laugh about it (or perhaps more correctly, *I* could laugh about it.)

I'm pretty sure I know where Kat's drivenness came from. She grew up with a father who only praised her when she got a perfect score on a test or won the race or was the fittest or best on the figure-skating team. Katerina had a tremendous amount of background alarm stored in her, and I believe the trauma of her father's love being conditional on her performance contributed.

When I look back, I have a lot of compassion for Katerina. I always knew her to be a very intense person, but I now know it's very likely she carried considerable background alarm. She had a hair-trigger temper, and although she never seemed to be what I would call classically anxious, she was almost always on edge. This is a topic for another book, but I believe background alarm that settles in our bodies from old, unresolved traumas can manifest in many ways other than chronic worry. Specifically, OCD, depression, eating disorders, and chronic irritability and anger, just to name a few. As I will show you in Part 3, the treatment of background alarm is the same no matter how it looks from the outside. Healing depends on developing a new relationship with the activation in your body and creating the environment you wished you had when the background alarm started.

But back to Kat and her temper. One day before Christmas, while in the car with her (she was driving), I made the mistake of telling her, in what I thought was a fairly humorous tone, that she should consider calming down when she was driving. I think I said something like, "If there was a TV show called *The Road's Ragiest Driver*, you could win it."

Bad idea. In an instant, she turned the rage previously directed at the guy who went too slow and made her miss the light, on me. She lost her sh** on me and was getting angrier by the second. Luckily, we had missed the light and were stopped, so I simply got out of the car, closed the door, walked away, and hailed a cab home. As I walked away, through the closed car doors I could *still* hear her screaming.

This wasn't the first tongue-lashing I had received from her, but it was the last. As my daughter, Leandra, would say, "The juice wasn't worth the squeeze." Once I got home, I knew that was the end of our relationship. And it was. We haven't communicated since, and that was more than ten years ago.

When I had the audacity to imply to Kat that she might consider calming down when driving, in that moment she probably felt the same way she had when her father scolded her for some mistake or imperfection. I remember she looked and acted just like a child having a tantrum. The rage she showed was childlike and irrational and way out of proportion for the situation.

A *hyperreaction* is a term I have created to describe a response well in excess of what would be appropriate. When we have an emotional hyperreaction like Kat did when I urged her to calm down when driving, we are almost certainly in an age regression. When I look back, it must have been so hard for Katerina since she was expecting me to be a support figure, but instead, I mirrored her father by pointing out her imperfections. Although I was not trying to hurt her, she lashed out at me as the creator of her pain because she couldn't see that I was only touching an old wound that still hurt.

In her background alarm-driven reaction, Kat was using a concept called *transference*, where the critical nature of her father got transferred on to me. When Kat perceived I was being overly critical of her, it reminded her of how her father was the same way. Just as she had relied on her father to be support-ive and he was the source of her pain, she saw me as doing the same thing. As I was someone who was supposed to be a safe person for her but, instead, turned into a threat, this inflamed her old childhood wounding. The true source of her hyperreaction was the pain she felt from her dad's criticism and the flare of background alarm linked to it. When I commented on her tendency to rage at other drivers (albeit in a joking way), her amygdala picked up on the similarity of the "not perfect" program that was put into her as a child. Her background alarm flared, followed quickly by her foreground alarm, and she started to yell at me.

Of course, that brought up my old background alarm of being shut down from expressing myself, and I had a hyperreaction of my own. But instead of turning outward and yelling back, I turned inward and withdrew. I left her screaming in that car over ten years ago, and I haven't seen her since.

Anything new that causes us to remember our old pain triggers our background alarm, and that reaction shows up in both the body and the mind. In Katerina's case, at the suggestion she was somehow imperfect, her old background alarm flared up and her mind hyperreacted, triggering her fight-or-flight foreground alarm. This triggered the full-blown nuclear meltdown I witnessed before I ejected myself from the car and got clear of the fallout zone.

When Katerina's background alarm was flared up, she reacted with anger, and it was directed outward. In contrast, when my own background alarm gets activated, typically my reaction is to direct it inward and create worry. People who have anxiety tend to have a victim mentality and direct their pain inward and have a reaction to background alarm similar to mine.

Back then, if you asked Kat what her problem was (after she calmed down, of course), she might have told you she was too quick to anger. If you asked me what my problem was, I would have said I worry too much.

But really, we were two sides of the same coin—and both of us were wrong.

If Kat goes to anger management classes and I go to worry management classes, that may help for a while, but because the problem, at its source, is the background alarm stored in our bodies, any benefits we receive from treating the mind-based effects instead of the body-based cause will only be temporary.

(One interesting note: it may be that the people who respond by lashing out instead of turning inward and ruminating have stronger activation of foreground alarm. The degree of fight-or-flight activation in response to background alarm may determine whether someone's response is oriented outward or inward. In any event, once you are triggered, your background alarm is driving the car.)

I once had a patient, Brian, who was what we sometimes call an alpha male, an athletic and muscular lawyer in his late thirties. On vacation, he met Marta, a vivacious and beautiful redhead, who was almost fifteen years his junior. It was love at first sight. They had a long-distance relationship for about a year, and then she moved to be with him and they got married. Marta became a patient of mine as well, and I envied their relationship in a way.

But things are not always as they seem.

When I asked Brian at one of his yearly physicals "How's married life?" I expected a glowing response, but instead, his face became pained. Brian told me all was well when they were travelling to see each other, but once she moved in with him and they got married, things started to change. Brian was very active in the law society and would often have responsibilities that kept him away from home. He said Marta would become angry when he had to go out at night, and that would escalate into fits of rage if he had to travel without her. I found this a little hard to believe. Marta was smart, funny, and self-assured. I couldn't picture her flying off the handle with rage.

During an appointment with Marta, when I asked her about her parents and her childhood, she told me that both of her parents were alcoholics. She said she and her younger brother were always clothed and fed, their physical needs looked after, but after 6:00 p.m., "the booze came first."

Knowing this, I could clearly see why she would revert back to the attitude of an irate six-year-old when Brian left. It evoked the same feelings in her that she felt when her parents abandoned her in favour of alcohol.

So, it wasn't what Brian was doing now that was the cause of her alarm and rage; it was what her parents had done when she was young. She was regressing back to the little girl who had no idea why her parents left her every night. She had needed her parents to reassure her and diffuse her alarm, but they were the ones causing the alarm. She didn't have the help she needed to metabolize the trauma, and it was stored in her as background alarm.

Remember that a response driven by background alarm is activation of old energy and not so much about what is happening in this moment. Whether you're defusing a tense situation, like Brian's fights with Marta or my spat with Kat, or whether you are interested in your own healing, know that you will not fix the problem by only addressing the foreground alarm. Trying to reason with Kat about her driving would have been a useless strategy because it had nothing to do with the underlying problem. Similarly, taking deep breaths, doing qi gong or yoga, or inhaling essential oils will calm your foreground alarm—and that does reduce the intensity of background alarm and help to break the feedback loop—but for a lasting solution, you must address the root of the problem, your background alarm. You must stop bailing out the boat and instead focus on patching the hull.

47

The Autonomic Nervous System: The Engine of the Unconscious Power of Alarm

When I talk to patients about the autonomic nervous system, I often substitute the word *automatic* for autonomic. This is an easy way to remember what this system does using a word we all know. To review, the autonomic nervous system controls heart rate, blood pressure, gut motility and digestion, and many other functions of the body that aren't under our conscious control—and therefore seem to happen automatically. As you may recall from the diagram back in chapter 38, the autonomic nervous system has two components: the *sympathetic nervous system*, often referred to as the accelerator because it revs us up, and the *parasympathetic nervous system*, which we can call the brake because it calms us down. Remember, sympathetic = fight or flight and parasympathetic = rest and digest.

When one side is activated, the other side is never completely "off." One is dominant at any given time and the other passive. For example, if you've just finished a big meal and you're at home watching a movie, you're probably feeling safe and relaxed, with your parasympathetic nervous system dominant. But then your daughter runs into the house and tells you your son has fallen out of a tree in the yard and may have broken his arm. When this happens, you quickly flip into sympathetic activity. Your heart rate and blood pressure increase, your muscles tense up, and your breathing gets faster. You rush outside and assess the situation. As you talk with him and comfort him, you conclude that his bone probably isn't broken and he seems to be more stunned than injured. After about twenty minutes, as you become more certain he'll be okay, your body's sympathetic response fades. Parasympathetic activity takes over again, and you move back into "rest and digest" as you return to your movie.

This is how a normally calibrated autonomic nervous system operates. It rises to a challenge and then calms down when the challenge resolves. This on/off reaction is mediated by our experiences—and when we feel safe and connected during childhood, our autonomic nervous systems develop with proper calibration. Fight-or-flight foreground alarm activates in the presence of a threat, and this smoothly moves into parasympathetic activity once the threat resolves.

That's how it's supposed to work, anyway. But remember the parable of Restless Rusty and Stable Shirley. When traumatic experiences have taught us that it's best to stay on high alert, we have a hard time settling down. In those of us with background alarm, the sympathetic nervous system (foreground alarm) stays activated for much longer than is necessary or healthy.

On an airplane, we know the turbulence can only last as long as the plane is airborne. On the other hand, my father could teeter on the verge of psychosis for weeks at a time. As a result, my background and foreground alarm could have a very long game of ping pong, with no sign of resolution. My background alarm would often flare up as a warning when I saw mood swings or signs of mental instability in my dad. As adept as I believed I was at reading him, sometimes, when I thought he was fine, he'd wind up in hospital, and other times I thought for sure he was heading for the cuckoo's nest, and he'd land safely on the ground. All of this taught me to stay vigilant—in a constant state of sympathetic activation.

This reminds me of a story. Two monks walk into a bar … No, sorry, wrong story. Two monks were walking together, returning to the monastery after a long day of monking. It was the rainy season, and they saw a woman having trouble crossing a creek. One of the monks approached her, gently picked her up and transferred her safely to the other side. The monks continued their journey in silence. They had taken a vow not to touch women and after hours of walking in silence, one angrily said to the other "You know we are not to touch women. Why did you pick that woman up?"

The other monk said, "Oh, I put her down hours ago. Clearly, you are still carrying her."

I carried the stress from the turbulence. Shirley put it down before the plane landed.

I've never really been good at resting or digesting. I've rarely felt grounded enough to move deeply into parasympathetic mode. Even when I did make conscious attempts at relaxation, it was like trying to offer a large, frightened dog a piece of meat. You want it to go well but it could turn bad in an instant, so you need to stay vigilant. This kind of acute and prolonged sympathetic nervous system activation, with slow resolution, is a very common pattern for people with old, unresolved trauma stored in the body as background alarm. For those of us with unresolved trauma, our foreground alarm is like a coiled spring, constantly ready for threat.

Have you ever had the experience of anxiety making you lose your appetite? This is your sympathetic nervous system in action. As blood flow is diverted from your digestive system to your tensed-up muscles, the intestines grind to a halt—and your body rejects food when it senses it can't move through.

Another hallmark of sympathetic nervous system activation is adrenaline, also known as epinephrine. This is what primes your muscles with energy to fire and carry you away from whatever is threatening your survival. From an evolutionary perspective, for this system to be activated quickly and easily was lifesaving. When in doubt, it was better to assume danger than assume safety. If you assumed the crack in the reeds behind you was a predator and you ran, you had a better chance of survival than if you just assumed it was nothing and stayed obliviously munching on your berries and grubs. A hair-trigger adrenaline response may have saved many of our ancestors from perishing—but in the process, natural selection was favouring nervous and paranoid humans to pass a reactive (or even hyperreactive) temperament down the genetic line.

(As a little aside, in my informal polling of my hypervigilant patients, I've found that they universally hate scary movies. I know I do. I already have a nervous system that makes me jump—I don't need more of that!)

This is why exercise is so helpful in people with anxiety and alarm. It metabolizes the adrenaline that would otherwise stay circulating in our systems, maintaining a sense of agitation and hypervigilance, feeding both foreground and background alarm. Since we worriers can fire up this system with only the *thought* of danger (aka worry), we often have all this adrenaline running around for no viable reason. Thousands of years ago, when humans faced a physical threat, the sympathetic nervous system would fire up and help them fight or flee. This physical activity would metabolize the adrenaline, leaving them ready to stand down in parasympathetic mode once the threat was gone. Today, since we aren't fleeing and fighting and burning off our adrenaline like we did thousands of years ago, it stays in our system and maintains both foreground and background alarm.

48

Game Drive: How the Alarm System Works in Real Life

I remember being on a game drive in South Africa in 2003. On these game drives, you go out twice a day, dawn and dusk, in an open-air Land Rover. There is a guide who drives the vehicle and he has a rifle in a leather sling on the hood. I imagine this rifle is to protect the tourists from the animals, but this particular gun looked like it hadn't been fired for decades. I had never seen lions in the wild before, and I was nervous.

On the day of our excursion, a pride of lions had been spotted by some other guides, and we were driving to the lions' last seen location, about five kilometres away. Dawn was just breaking and the six of us tourists were in the Land Rover. Even though it was Africa, it's still very cold in the morning before the sun rises, so we all had wool blankets that kept us warm-ish. So we had the rifle and now the blankets to protect us from the lions. My alarm was certainly up, and I was looking for reassurance. Back to the gun. It was a bolt-action rifle that looked like it had seen better days firing blanks on the set of a 1953 Tarzan movie. It did not inspire much confidence. Did I mention this vehicle was an *open air* Land Rover?

But that didn't matter because we couldn't find the lions. Apparently they had moved on from their last seen location. If you don't know by now, I can be more than a bit of a chicken, and I was torn. On one hand, I wanted to see the lions, and on the other, I felt more than a little uneasy being in an open-air Land Rover with only a pop gun and a protective blanket.

As I mentioned, I had never seen a real lion in the wild before. The sun was coming up, and it was getting noticeably warmer, and I started to feel calmer. As my alarm came down, my irrational fear of being plucked from the Land Rover and disembowelled abating, I now wanted to see the damn lions. Before my disappointment set in too much, the guide got a message on the radio in a language I didn't understand. The guide swivelled around and said the lions were about one kilometre away.

Remember when I said the body goes into foreground alarm in response to a real or *perceived* threat? Just the anticipation of the lions revved up my alarm. Back in 2003, I had a full-blown anxiety (or, should I say, alarm) disorder, and while my conscious mind knew I was safe, my body wasn't taking any chances. My body had grown so used to always being in some form of fight or flight that it didn't take much to activate the familiar body state of alarm. My gut started to get queasy, my heart was racing, and I could feel my breath getting shallower and shallower. I was already halfway down the hill on my toboggan, with the runners cutting the familiar grooves of anxiety and alarm ever deeper.

At this point, the reaction I was experiencing wasn't about the lions. Yes, they are literally predators, but they were actually still one kilometre away. I couldn't see them yet, and therefore what I was experiencing was actually *excitement* that my sensitive nervous system was misperceiving as the presence of a threat.

The way alarm impairs the mind is actually not that different from what happens when we drink alcohol. With alcohol, it's in a different direction—sedative instead of stimulant—but it's impairment nevertheless. Imagine you go to the bar with your friends after work. As you're parking your car and heading inside to meet your friends, you wonder to yourself how long you're going to be there and how many drinks you can have and still be able to drive home safely. Skip forward to 11:00 p.m., and you've had a great time. You've had five drinks (give or take—at this point you're not quite sure) over the four hours you've been there. You have to work tomorrow, so you tell yourself you can drink a bunch of water and in half an hour you should be okay to drive.

If you'd asked yourself when you'd gotten there, "How many drinks can I have over four hours and still be okay to drive?" your rational mind would have said three, max. But now you've had five drinks and that same mind (or so it seems) is telling you to drink some water and you'll be good to go—and you believe it!

Both alcohol and alarm impair the mind, and both do so in a way that makes you think you're still using your rational capabilities. It's still *your* mind, after all!

Believing the mind to be a homogeneous, consistent, and reliable source of information is a fundamental misconception that makes us prone to believe everything we think. It is a profound problem if you have a tendency to worry, as a part of you will believe the worry simply because your mind came up with it. Your mind gives you the impression that it is a unique and reliable tool that operates independently and consistently, no matter what is happening in the body—but that is simply not true.

Here's an interesting analogy: As cell biologist Dr. Bruce Lipton asserts, a cell's environment is in many ways more influential than its genes. A cell's environment determines whether it goes into growth or protection mode—and a similar dynamic exists between the mind and the body. The environment of the body determines whether the mind goes into growth or protection mode. Do not make the mistake of believing that the mind operates independently and objectively from the influence of the body where it resides.

Once I started to see the same thought could lead me to two completely different reactions, things started to change for me. Here's an example from that same South Africa trip. During that trip, I had a total of fifteen flights in twenty-four days. There were points on the trip when all I could think about was what might go wrong—like turbulence, a midair collision, or running out of pretzels. Yet, there were other times I would think about an upcoming flight and feel elated by the sense of how much I loved flying. I was aware of this inconsistency at the time, but I didn't yet understand it.

But back to the lions. My brain had misread excitement over seeing the lions and pushed me down into my old groove in the snow—perceiving a threat and moving me deeper into survival brain, where everything looks more damn dangerous than it really is. If I'd taken a few breaths and made an effort to truly connect to myself, I could have reframed the experience as excitement. That would have allowed me to keep blood flowing to my rational mind, and I could have enjoyed the situation more, but I didn't know that then. I was in survival brain, and the idea of lions jumping into the Land Rover and ripping me clear of my safety blanket seemed plausible. There I was, in the same place I'd been so many times in my life, having an amazing experience ruined by the background and foreground alarm in my body.

Our guide slowed the Land Rover down as we got closer to the sighting area. We turned a corner in the bush and saw two full-grown lions beginning to mate about ten gun-lengths away. The guide kept inching closer until we were about fifteen feet away.

I didn't know this then, but when lions mate, they do it for forty-eight hours straight. Each coupling lasts for eight to fifteen seconds, and this is repeated day and night every thirty to forty-five minutes for two days. The female was getting pretty angry and growling very loudly and aggressively at the male during and after coupling. I can't say I blamed her. I believe if someone mount-ed me for ten seconds every half hour, I'd be irate as well.

Initially, being so close to those lions and having *them* in a state of high activation put *me* in a state of high activation—and not in a good way. But after about ten minutes, without me understanding yet what was happening and why, my foreground alarm started to resolve (which eased my background alarm), and I could better experience this awe-inspiring scene as I moved slowly out of survival brain.

This story illustrates a pattern that was so familiar to me. When my body was in alarm, my mind was tainted, and I perceived a threat when no real threat was present. I wish I'd known then what I know now. Back then, I was trapped in a cycle that I had no idea how to break. When my body was worn out by being in alarm all day, I would get some relief as evening crept in, only to restart the cycle the moment I awoke the next day. Now I am an expert at breaking the cycle—and soon you will be, too.

49

Potentiation: Deepening the Groove

Typically, in a well-calibrated autonomic nervous system, the degree of activation is proportional to the threat. Hearing a mosquito buzzing around you would elicit less of a response than realizing someone is trying to break into your home. But in those of us prone to the alarm-anxiety cycle, the sympathetic nervous system becomes both hyperactive and hypervigilant and often responds well in excess of the actual level of threat.

To understand how this works, imagine a fresh snowfall on a hill. You get your toboggan and climb to the top of the hill, put the toboggan in the snow, and have a fun ride to the bottom of the hill. Then you do this three more times. Now a groove is formed in the snow that toboggan will preferentially take. Each time you ride down the hill you go a little bit faster as the groove gets a little bit deeper and smoother.

In a nervous system that's used to the alarm-anxiety cycle, alarm becomes a knee-jerk response. After many runs down the hill, the grooves are deep and they carry you down quickly.

To ease the alarm, you must take a different path. You must pick up that toboggan and mindfully place it away from the well-worn groove (of thinking and worrying) it has made from previous trips down the hill. You must become aware of the seductive impulse of the mind to try to think your way out, knowing that thinking is like digging—the more you do it, the deeper and darker it becomes. Thinking, or adding worry, is not the answer. You must *feel* your way out of alarm.

In neuroscience, we call these metaphorical toboggan grooves *potentiation*, referring to the process that shows increasing strength and speed of nerve impulses along pathways that are well used. The classic example is the startle reflex. In people with an overactive sympathetic (fight-or-flight) nervous system, it is very easy to elicit a jump reflex if you startle someone. In most people, if you repeatedly startle them, say, every fifteen seconds, after a few startles the reflex diminishes. But in people with chronic anxiety and alarm, the reflex takes a long time to extinguish, so people with an uncalibrated autonomic nervous system will continue to jump each time they are startled.

I've got a friend who lives only a few blocks away. His family has one of those nervous, little dogs that barks at me the moment I come up the drive and continues to bark at me intermittently while I am there, with a reprise crescendo as I leave. Like Kat yelling at me from inside the Road Rage Mobile, the dog keeps on barking at me as I'm walking away, the barks fading but, I assume, continuing even after I'm out of earshot. I've met the dog many times and obviously am treated as a friendly figure by its owner, yet I always get the same reaction from the dog.

A hyperreactive sympathetic nervous system is like that dog—barking and barking even though there's no real threat. (Poor doggie, probably had a tough puppyhood.)

The dog's propensity to bark is another sample of potentiation. It keeps on doing it because that's what it's always done. Like riding a bike or driving a car, the more we do it, the more "at the ready" and automatic it becomes. This is great if you're practicing a skill like speaking Spanish, but not so great if you're reinforcing the habit of worrying. The more you practice Spanish, the more fluent you become. The more you worry, the "better" you get at worrying.

Since people in Madrid worry in Spanish, maybe this makes them better worriers. (Not funny? Hey, not all of my jokes can be *bueno*.)

A traumatic childhood—and the poorly calibrated sympathetic/parasympathetic balance that can result—layers complexity on a brain that is already born with a fear bias. Many psychological experiments have shown that human subjects are more disturbed by the prospect of losing an imaginary dollar than they are pleased by the prospect of gaining an imaginary dollar. (One of the measures used to detect discomfort was skin impedance, the metric used in lie detector tests. When we lie or are uncomfortable, we start to sweat, although it's barely noticeable to us. The sweat makes it easier for electricity to pass across our skin, so a decrease in skin impedance—meaning the skin impedes the electrical flow less or, rather, conducts it better—means we are uncomfortable. In these studies, people sweated more—and skin impedance decreased, indicating greater nervous system activity in response to the negative prospect of losing a dollar compared to the positive prospect of gaining the same amount.) Even though the two potential outcomes change our fortune by the exact same amount, the reaction is stronger to losing what we already have than to gaining what isn't ours yet.

Virtually every book on neuroscience includes some version of this concept: the neurons that fire together wire together (attributed to the Canadian neuropsychologist Donald Hebb). Although our nervous systems learn protective habits very easily, remember that potentiation applies to habits that serve us as well as those that hurt us. When you were first learning to drive a car, you had to pay close attention to every detail, but after years of practice, the program has been repeated so often that you don't have to consciously think about it. It gets recreated rapidly and unconsciously.

So potentiation isn't inherently harmful—in fact, we couldn't get by without it. Instead of being able to brush our teeth, mindlessly going through the motions while our mind is already on tomorrow's to-do list, we would be using up all of our brainpower on "First, I squeeze the toothpaste. No, first I unscrew the cap. No, first I pick up the tube of toothpaste." Potentiation helps us a lot—and we can consciously leverage its power to learn new habits that serve us.

Once we recognize that we have Stone Age brains in a digital world, we can work to bring back sympathetic/parasympathetic balance. We can know that we're here today because our ancestors were hyperreactive and passed down that tendency to us. (Because remember, that yappy little dog might be spending more time in agitation than it needs to, but it is *definitely* going to fend off an intruder better than a dog that's overly relaxed and greets both family friends and burglars by begging for a belly rub.) We can thank our nervous systems for being hard-wired to keep us safe, and we can choose to pick up our toboggan out of those well-worn grooves and start constructing a different path down the hill.

50

Sea Monster

I used to play this game with my daughter, Leandra, when she was about four. The game was called "Sea Monster." Leandra would run into the room and yell "Sea monster!" I, being the aforementioned sea monster, would jump up and chase the damsel around the house. She would squeal with a combination of fear and delight. After about three minutes, the sea monster would get tired. Sea monsters need to do more cardio. The damsel would invariably want to continue the game, but the sea monster would agree to throw the damsel on the sofa only one more time. Sea monster and the damsel would then have a cuddle until the sea monster had to go back to his medical studies.

I didn't know it back then, but I was calibrating my little daughter's autonomic nervous system. I would get her all riled up for a dangerous sea monster attack, with high-tone foreground alarm fight-or-flight activation of her sympathetic nervous system, and then calm her back down into parasympathetic tone with some safe, connected snuggles on the couch. I was teaching her body that she could get all fired up and then, in a safe and loving environment, the switch could be thrown to the opposite wing of the nervous system. In other words, her body learned to take the foot completely off the accelerator and put that foot firmly on the brake.

For many of us with anxiety and alarm issues, it's not that simple. Ideally, we should be able to press on *either* the gas or the brake. But if you grow up with uncertainty, abandonment, or abuse, your system never feels safe enough to take your foot completely off the accelerator.

I have a theory for those of us with trauma, especially if that trauma carried on over a long time, that we lose the ability to take our foot completely off the accelerator and place it completely on the brake. Our background alarm is never completely off, although there are times we aren't consciously aware of it. But like your startle reflex, it's ready to jump into action at the slightest provocation. (I also believe this is the case with PTSD. The body stays in a state of fight-or-flight foreground alarm, in relentless readiness to jump back into action in pursuit of safety). We always feel we have to maintain a little fight-or-flight energy to be ready to deal with a trauma that could arise at any moment. We might be braking hard to stop and relax but are still keeping one foot on the accelerator and revving the engine—which causes our shell-shocked nervous system to become even more confused, perceiving danger where there is none.

When we don't feel safe and connected as children, our autonomic nervous systems never adopt that beneficial "when one is on, the other is off" cooperation. We never feel safe letting our guard down because in the past when we relaxed and let the parasympathetic wing take over, we got blindsided. The longer my dad was well, the more painful the crash, so eventually I learned to keep one foot resting on the accelerator. I stopped allowing myself to rest.

The neuropsychologist Rick Hanson says we have minds that are like Teflon for the good stuff and velcro for the bad. This goes double for those of us who carry alarm in our systems. I took that fear bias, programmed into the nervous system of every human—telling me the sound in the reeds is a crouching tiger and not the wind—and I amplified it by telling myself it wasn't safe to feel safe. This "waiting for the other shoe to drop" mentality robs us of our quality of life.

It still happens sometimes that I'll be driving on a beautiful, sunny day, feeling good, and then my mind will suddenly conjure up a worry to bring me back down to earth. I recognize it now, but old toboggan tracks die hard. Now I just laugh at my mind trying to trick me into creating worry on a beautiful, sunny day, and I take a moment to reassure my younger self (who still lives in me) and acknowledge his fear that his dad is slipping away from him.

When we don't recognize our "it's not safe to feel safe" program, we are like an artist who paints a picture of a tiger and then finds the picture so realistic he scares himself to death. Our bodies create the alarm, and then we react as if the self-created illusion is real. We forget (or were not aware in the first place) that we created the alarm ourselves.

We are not doing this on purpose. This "not safe to feel safe" program hides in the darkness of our unconscious. Once we see it and bring it into the light, we can use it as a focus for change.

51

Heart First, Brain Second

Imagine you were just a brain, kept alive by artificially bathing in cerebrospinal fluid and receiving blood and nutrients via the cerebral arteries and veins. Would you feel anything? It is ironic that the brain has no pain sensors itself (you can cut right into a living brain and it will perceive no pain), but if that brain is attached to a body, it reads that body and creates an interpretation of pain that it doesn't experience in itself. If there is pain in the physical body (like stubbing your toe), the brain is very good at identifying the location and extent of the pain via its interpretation. But if we experience emotional pain, the brain's interpretations are ill-defined and often completely inaccurate.

The brain does not feel on its own. For perception of physical and emotional sensation, you need a body. So if feeling emotional pain requires a body, why isn't traditional therapy doing anything to treat the body? Why are we directing all of our treatments at the mind and brain? Why are we spending so much time treating the anxious thinking of the mind and paying so little attention to the alarm feeling in the body—especially when that is the most painful part?

I know I have alluded to this already, but it's such a critical point that I'm going to flog it again. The body has just as much (if not more) to do with healing from suffering as the mind. In our development as embryos, there was a body and a heart before there was a mind or nervous system. Heart first, brain second.

In this way, the source of alarm (the body) was present before the source of anxiety (the mind). It was key in my own recovery to give reverence to the body, to create a new paradigm where the locus of emotional pain was more in the body than the mind and to direct attention to healing with that in mind. Or should I say, in body.

After my decades-long search for relief, which included taking trips on psychedelics to get far, far away from my years of academic training and experience, I arrived at a new paradigm that I never would have seen had I stuck to conventional medicine and neuroscience. Under the influence, my scientifically trained mind was shown that emotional pain is rooted in the body and only interpreted by the mind. Seeing the source of emotional pain as alarm stored in the body, with the mind playing only a supporting role, has been invaluable as a healing construct for my own recovery, and I am confident it will benefit you as well.

52

The Purpose of the Alarm

If I had to sum up the purpose of alarm, I think I'd say protection. We activate alarm to protect ourselves from actual or perceived danger, which can be physical or emotional. When we are young and our minds are overwhelmed by trauma or separation that is too much for us, initially we create a foreground alarm energy of fight or flight (or pursuit). This puts our minds into survival brain and our bodies into high activation. If that boost of energy does not resolve the situation and because the sympathetic nervous system activation can only be maintained for so long, eventually part of us just gives up, like a cornered animal that stops fighting and freezes.

When my father first started losing his mind, my sympathetic nervous system would activate and I would go into an activated pursuit phase, using the classic fight-or-flight energy in an attempt to reduce that separation. When I saw that my pursuit was futile, as my dad was not able to connect with me no matter what I did, I would freeze. Remember Mitch, the guy I met at a retreat who had been physically abused by his father? It is likely he experienced the same "freeze" reaction, but he would have been in flight trying to escape from his abusive father. The difference was that Mitch's experience of futility was trying to get away from his father and my futility was in trying to get closer to mine. In both cases, our sympathetic nervous systems would be highly engaged but would meet with futility as our goals were blocked. The response to that sense of futility would be to freeze.

My sense is that the freeze state is a sign of complete overwhelm and is the immediate precursor to dissociation. Like when you hear people speak of being attacked or when escape from peril was impossible, they say they "just froze." At a conscious level, they may have felt immobilized, but at an unconscious level, the trauma was overwhelming the mind's ability to cope and was being shunted into background alarm to be stored in the body. As children, we would be overwhelmed and freeze, and then the energy would be added to background alarm.

Although Mitch and I both felt frozen, albeit, for different reasons, our energy sure wasn't. When I took physics as a prerequisite for medical school, I learned that energy can't be created or destroyed, only changed in form. This is a great analogy for how trauma overwhelms our system and is stored in the body as background alarm. In my communications with Mitch over the years since we met, we have been able to isolate where he feels his background alarm in his body (upper chest and throat). As you well know by now, my background alarm is in the right side of my solar plexus.

One of my relatives is a (now retired) pilot for a major airline. I am always fascinated by his stories. Every six months, he was required to get certified on a flight simulator that would simulate an emergency on his Airbus A320. In one of these tests, he was given a scenario of severe wind shear on takeoff. The correct response was to push the throttles up to one hundred percent to escape, and that was exactly what he did. This is where the story gets interesting. Apparently, modern jet engines are almost never used to even seventy-five percent of their capacity, and modern engines are so powerful they don't even come close to that in regular use. So if this scenario occurred in the real world and he used max power, both engines would have to be scrapped because maximum power can cause a weakness that will lead to future malfunction. He did what he needed to do to keep the passengers safe, but if the scenario had been real life, it would have meant throwing two, multimillion-dollar engines in the trash!

When I heard this story, my imagination took hold of it. Our nervous systems are like the jet engines—if they are too strongly activated, they are never the same. This is what happens when we experience chronic and repetitive trauma that forces our sympathetic nervous system to maximum output. If no resolution occurs, we freeze and dissociate, and the thwarted energy creates a pathway or shunt that stores the trauma in the body. The more the system is pushed to overwhelm and futility, the more that pathway becomes a deep groove that additional trauma can flow down with ease to add to the increasing reservoir of background alarm.

Like the jet engines, our nervous systems are not cut out to be used too much and too often. They have tremendous capacity, but it's meant to be used in the presence of actual threats to our lives—the kind we are supposed to encounter only rarely, not every day at home where we are supposed to be safe. In case of emergency, we can rev up our engines, but the system will experience some changes due to excessive demand. When that happens, we are like the car at a standstill, one foot on the gas and one on the brake—the engine spinning high RPMs but going nowhere.

Fortunately, when we overwhelm our nervous systems in this way, we don't have to throw the whole thing out. When we apply the tools of love and compassion to our protection instincts and background alarm, each of us can become skilled jet engine repairmen (and women).

53
Dark Night of the Soul

I didn't become the anxiety whisperer without earning it. My experiences with psychedelics were invaluable in getting me to consider a non-traditional approach. While it's true my "trips" on psychedelics were revelational and fruitful, those insights also came at a great cost.

While LSD was a very intense experience, full of alarm with both intensely beautiful and intensely frightening hallucinations, ayahuasca was the hands-down, unequivocal heavyweight champion of frightening experiences. In fall 2014, I was still recovering from a full Achilles rupture and the subsequent surgery eighteen months earlier. I was losing weight, not sleeping, and dealing with unrelenting background and foreground alarm for many hours every day.

I had friends who had significant recoveries from depression using this psychedelic "medicine" called ayahuasca, and I was desperate for relief. A year earlier in September 2013, I had limped my post-op leg 14,835 kilometres from Vancouver to Beijing to Bangkok to Chennai (Okay, okay, I didn't limp the *entire* way there, but I limped when I wasn't on an airplane or in a taxi.) to live at a temple in India, where I was assured by the monks that after their program I would be anxiety-free. Other than a ninety-minute episode of what I can only describe as an enlightenment, where I became one with everything, I can't express to you in words the disappointment when I returned home from Chennai to Taipei to Vancouver (still limping) to find that my anxiety had not significantly improved.

I still marvel at the fact that I actually made that trip because I was so mentally and physically impaired. To this day, I firmly believe the only reason I was able to make it was the support of my future wife, whom I'd met just weeks before the trip.

When I met Cynthia in June 2013 at a personal development retreat, I was at the lowest point in my life, both mentally and physically debilitated. But I also knew for a month before I got to the retreat that I was going to meet my future wife there. I don't want to weird you out, but I have clairsentient ability, and I've had it since I was a child. It makes me a good doctor in that I can read people and the energy around them, and it especially helps me see where someone's alarm is coming from. Much of the material from this book comes from my ability to see things most people do not. Curiously, it has grown in me since I left the practice of medicine—maybe something to do with not having to think in the linear terms of a physician?

When I met Cynthia, it was one of those meetings you just know are going to be life-changing. She was beautiful and vulnerable. I could see her energy was kind and giving, but I also saw her pain. There is a tremendous bond we have in healing ourselves and others. She has since become a somatic trauma therapist and we have learned so much from each other, both personally and professionally. She has shown me it is actually safe to love. The primary thing that's really kept me going, over the years, since leaving the official practice of medicine is my relationship with Cynthia.

Back to my experience with ayahuasca. Buoyed by my fellow comics' stories of miraculous relief from mental suffering and addiction, I was desperate and optimistic to try something that might actually work. I found a shaman who would, for a significant amount of money, guide me through a private two-night ayahuasca experience, in a small town in British Columbia, about a two-hour drive from Vancouver. I expected to find a shaman with a name like Arechron or Dorhuk or Norbundo. (These are real shamans' names.) But do you know what this eternal, divine mystic's name was?

Dave.

Yes, Dave. The name Dave didn't inspire a lot of confidence, but again, I was desperate.

So a couple of weeks later, in October 2014, I had two successive nights dancing with the snake called ayahuasca. The first night I sat in front of Dave while he mixed the medicine, and I was about twenty-two times as scared as I would be of flying—and I was pretty scared of flying. Dave did some more incantations. He had an assistant, Paul. Cynthia was there with me, but she did not want to do the medicine. Buddha was there, too, for canine support.

I took the cup from Dave and swallowed in one gulp. It tasted like bitter seaweed. I went back to my place across from Dave and waited. And waited. In a way, I was less scared than before because now I was committed. The long wait to do this was over.

I closed my eyes and started to see the most intense purple, blue, and pink geometric figures and shapes. Then everything seemed to disappear but the vivid colours. I was in a new world I couldn't even begin to explain. Even as I write this, I can feel my alarm come up.

I had the sense I was falling, which was very disturbing. More disturbing was that I was trying to understand what the word "falling" meant. I was trying to make sense of what was happening, but I had no brain function that I could understand. I felt I *did* understand and I *could* explain what was happening, but when I tried, there were no concepts I could use to explain it. Apparently, I kept repeating out loud—and I don't remember this—"There's nothing to hold on to."

I have no memory of saying this, but I have often felt, in times of deep alarm and anxiety, that there was nothing to hold on to. I think this is the same way I felt as a young teen when I was grasping for something, anything, to support me or give me a reference for what was happening. At the mercy of the serpentine mother ayahuasca, I was being shown the well-grooved pattern my mind and body had defaulted to—and it was terrifying. At least when I am going through anxiety and alarm in my daily life, I can do some yoga, focus on my breath, or even just distract myself. Now I was faced with my alarm and anxiety full force, and I had no defence—at all.

As I write this now, it makes perfect sense to me why this was so terrifying. I have decades of background alarm repressed and stored in my body. To get away from this pain in my body, I escaped into my head and became an elite-level worrier. I even went into a profession that required a massive intellectual investment and became even better at using my mind. I used thinking as a way of escaping feeling. Thinking and worrying in my head became my coping strategy to avoid feeling in my body. I ran up and hid in my head for decades.

And then I ingested a substance that removed any ability to think. All those decades of pain that I had avoided, I was suddenly defenceless against. In the open-air Land Rover that is life, I had removed my protective blanket of thought and was now face to face with the lions of my past—and they were ripping me apart. I have never experienced anything as ghastly, grim, hideous, and horrifying as that experience on ayahuasca.

If I got anything out of ayahuasca, it is that in life there is truly nothing to hold on to, *especially my thoughts.* There is no "thing" to hold on to. Ayahuasca showed me the only thing to hold on to is something that is not "hold on to-able," and that is faith.

Faith is not a tangible thing. You can't pick faith up and move it from one place to another. My mind-based world loved concrete concepts, but faith is ethereal. Faith is not of the mind as much as it is of the body.

With my ability to think removed, I could still have faith that this human experience is its own illusion and that we are truly connected to something that has no resemblance to a human body.

In that experience, I was shown there is a universal wisdom that has order, and death is sometimes a part of that order. Your human form may die, but the essence of *you* will always be a part of the fabric of consciousness.

I was shown the more I try to make sense of things, the more man-made and ultimately wrong it could be. I was shown that I am the grape-coloured Kool-Aid (there's the purple colour again) in the eternal water of existence and that my human form borrows the suspension of the water but is not it.

This sentence makes sense to me, and it likely won't make sense to you, but it will give you a sense of what my mind did on ayahuasca.

Here's another ayahuasca-ism: "I was shown that I don't know and trying to know is different from knowing." There. I know that sounds vague and non-sensical. That's a little taste of what psychedelics do to impair your reasoning.

I was also given a sense that I overthink (there's a big surprise!) but, more directly, that my mind-based perceptions were subjective and very often dead wrong. What I see as bad, may well be one of the best things that has happened and vice versa. For example, something I assumed was bad—my anxiety—has pointed me toward becoming more connected to myself than I've ever been. In contrast, something I viewed as good—getting into medical school and becoming a medical doctor—may actually have been one of the worst things for me. In many ways, becoming a doctor took me further away from my real self by forcing me deeper into my head and thus out of my body, with the massive amount of information I had to memorize. In addition, being a doctor put me in a chronic environment of illness (and more importantly, mental illness), which is where my background alarm originated as I watched my father become sicker and sicker. I had to realize that my perception of good and bad was a story I became locked into, and in my compulsion to reduce uncertainty and make sense of my life, I was unable to see the messages that would allow me to heal.

As Dr. Wayne Dyer put it, "If you change the way you look at things, the things you look at change." But if you never question (or renew) your perceptions, you'll never see the deeper meaning in your suffering. You'll live Groundhog Day over and over. You are a hostage to your own pattern of perceptions and the stories you create based on those rigid perceptions—most of which were created by the fearful child in you.

My perception was that being a doctor was saving me, when in reality it was sinking me. What I perceived as my anchor and a force keeping me grounded, was an anchor all right—but it was dragging me to the bottom! Ayahuasca allowed me to renew, or at least revisit, the perception that everything was up to me and I had to know everything.

With that experience, I saw I was like the tree surgeon who had to give it up because he realized he couldn't stand the sight of sap.

Although I certainly wouldn't describe it as pleasant, my psychedelic dance with the snake was enlightening. Ayahuasca showed me faith in a higher order that my simple mind-based interpretations, thoughts, and mental constructs of good and bad could not see. Because as a child I had not received the support I needed to resolve my alarm, I had concluded that I was solely responsible for protecting myself from the vicissitudes of life. Becoming a doctor furthered the illusion and kept me trapped in my belief that life could be "figured out" if I only tried hard enough.

Being a doctor hadn't helped with my chronic alarm. In fact, it reinforced my mind-based story that I had the power to go at life alone. Here's the kicker. I had adopted the unconscious assumption that I needed to look after myself (and my parents) around thirteen years old and had been carrying it around ever since. How accurate and complete do you think any thirteen-year-old boy's understanding of life is? I had built a house of cards based on my own intellect and pseudo-independence. Ayahuasca knocked it down.

There was tremendous, excruciating, confusing pain in my ayahuasca experience, but the gift was two realizations: that faith means I don't have to do it all myself, and my perceptions of what is good or bad for me may be entirely inaccurate. It allowed me to see there is wisdom that goes far beyond my own personal subjective experience. There *was* something to hold on to. I just couldn't see it because the mind can't see and touch faith. That is the job of the body, and I had left my body behind when I was thirteen.

In the days after ayahuasca, I was a complete mess. My only source of security, my thoughts, was not secure at all. In fact, my worried thoughts were one of the main reasons I was so miserable. But now I could not even hold on to them.

I could not go into my body because that is where my background alarm was, and now I'd been shown that my mind was also *verboten*. In the days following ayahuasca, I was as close to suicide as I have ever been. The background alarm in my body had reached nuclear proportions due to the destabilizing psychedelic experience, and my mind had been fractured severely by that same psychedelic. There was truly nowhere to go and nothing to hold on to for me.

Thank goodness for one last thing I did see on aya: slowly, I began to realize that I was somehow protected—by what, I do not know, but I could develop faith in that. I didn't have to do it all by myself anymore. I didn't have to be that thirteen-year-old who pretended he had it all under control when deep down he knew he was just a kid and woefully unprepared for guiding his own life, let alone being a physician to guide others.

With this realization, I understand why my whole career as a doctor, I felt like an imposter. I was just "playing doctor"—not in the way that Jack Hammer Johnson played doctor in some of his movies, but I did feel like a child in a doctor costume. Even though I did a good job as a physician and had an exemplary record, part of me felt I was a thirteen-year-old boy in an oversize white lab coat with a stethoscope around my neck. Ayahuasca showed me I did not have to only rely on that persona, in fact I could leave it behind and have faith in a new path—the path of belief that I am protected and guided and I don't have to do it all as my thirteen-year-old self.

As a child who took it upon himself to look after his parents and himself, I had given up on someone looking after me. Now I knew there *was* something that looks after me and that it came from faith inside my body and had nothing to do with the machinations of my mind. The security of that knowing is what brought me on the path to write this book.

I have talked to many people who struggle with chronic worry and doubt who became caregivers at an early age, and I've noticed that many of them lost faith in life. When you lose faith in life, you begin to think you are the ultimate arbiter of good and bad. I became an alpha child—very headstrong and *hated* to be told what to do—and that's because a part of me needed to know everything and do everything my way.

But in making yourself God, there is nobody or nothing to look up to or have faith in.

At the same time, I became overconfident in my own abilities, part of me knew I was overcompensating and had been overcompensating since I was thirteen years old. As a result, I developed a mindset where everything was up to me and, at the very same time, felt like a fraud, insecure about my abilities.

Of course, I was anxious! On one hand, I had convinced myself that I was the most competent person in the world and on the other, I knew I was in way over my head. It would be almost like having no experience whatsoever and being thrust into the job as the president of the United States and just faking my way through. Although that could never happen ...

That first night was not the end of my ayahuasca experience. Dave had told me in no uncertain terms that I must "drink" at least two nights. The first night is an acclimatization, and it is only on a subsequent "drink" that I would learn what I needed to begin healing.

I know I am a strong person because after what was hands-down the most terrifying, disorienting, soul-ripping episode of my life, to which nothing had come close before or since, the next night I went back for another round. The second night was less terrifying, but still highly disturbing. I again saw the purple, pink, and orange geometric hallucinations, but I hate to tell you I had no new profound shifts in my mind or body that relieved my anxiety and alarm. Dave was wrong.

The next morning as I was helping Dave load up his stuff in his car to leave, he told me he'd had anxiety for many years and had done ayahuasca close to a thousand times. He said it helped considerably with his depression, but in specifically addressing his anxiety, he said it hadn't really helped him that much. I said to him, "What the fuck am I doing here, then?!" Sorry for the language, but I needed the best word to express frustration and "hell" (although I had just visited there for two nights) didn't seem to describe the angst I felt when I heard that.

After my disappointment in India and then this, I was at an extremely low point. I'd had such high hopes for relief, and once again they'd been dashed. For the two days after returning home from aya, I did not have that sense of connection. I was "out of my mind." I had a real sense of what my father went through and to say it was groundless, terrifying, empty, confusing, disorienting, vacant and otherworldly would be an understatement.

At the time, I felt ayahuasca was a total bust, and I would never recommend anyone with anxiety or control issues put themself through it. It took away the anchors I had put in place to feel in control. And, in many ways, it retraumatized me, as I don't think I have ever been closer to suicide than in the week following those two nights with the snake of ayahuasca. When people with anxiety ask me if they should do it to heal, I ask them: "How much do you need to feel you need to be in control to be safe?" Typically, I find that when people feel a need to be in control, they depend on their mind to do that. Anxiety is an attempt to keep control of the uncontrollable and predict the unpredictable, so ingesting a substance that removes control (separates you from your mind) is bound to be difficult.

That being said, for some people, that may be exactly what they need to heal. Seeing your world without any control may be a "reset" that gives you the ability to accept uncertainty and unpredictability. At points, ayahuasca showed me I had to face my fears of uncertainty if I was to overcome them. It also showed me I was infinitely connected to the universe, whether I was alive in this human form or not. In a way, it showed me that there is no death—so what was I afraid of?

Often in Scandanavian cultures and folklore, a dragon is pictured on top of a treasure chest. I had seen that image in some of Dr. Neufeld's presentations, and I accept that you need to slay the dragon to get to the treasure. But for me, it took me a long time to really see that I had to face the fear before the treasure would be revealed. Until I learned to face my alarm and even embrace it, my battle with anxiety and alarm seemed futile and the dragon turned into a hydra. Whenever I tried to cut off its head, it seemed two more would grow back.

But the dragon was not my enemy. It seems I was trying to slay my protector. The dragon, I've come to see, is my protective ego. When I was a child, alone and fearful, and my attachment figures were not there for me, my younger self conjured a mythical protective figure, a powerful dragon to keep me from harm. But the dragon did its protective job too well, and it got all fired up over anything and everything that had caused me any trauma in the past. The amygdala and the dragon worked in concert to overreact to anything that had caused me pain in my past. The dragon used his mythical powers to stop me from getting close to anything that hurt me in the past. And what hurt me more than anything else? Love. The love I had for my dad was seen by my Ego

Dragon as something I needed to be kept away from. Once our Ego Dragons see love as dangerous, love is pushed away and fear fills the space left behind. Since fear is what drives the dragon, our lives become progressively ruled by fear and protection and less by love and growth—another cycle that perpetuates fear, all in the righteous name of the dragon we incarnated to protect us. Ayahuasca paralyzed the dragon of ego that my frightened child created to shield me from pain so I came face to face with my fears. It's no wonder I kept saying "There's nothing to hold on to."

Since the time six years ago I faced the dark night of the soul and danced with the snake for not one night but two, I've realized aya had many lessons for me. I learned that I am infinitely stronger than I give myself credit for. Going back for a repeat performance after that first experience showed me I would not allow myself to be a victim. If I could have the most terrifying experience of my life and go back the next night, I could go through anything. It also showed me how much I used my thinking and worry as a way of controlling and predicting and how excruciatingly painful it was when my ability to control and predict was removed. My experience with ayahuasca also showed me control was an illusion of the mind and faith in the feeling of the heart was critical. Faith allowed me to see that it wasn't all up to me. There are things beyond my control, and accepting and loving what is, with a sense of feeling, was a far superior way to live than being limited by the realm of thinking and its false promise of finding security in my head.

Feelings cannot be readily vanquished by thought, and there is a good reason for that. Feelings are where life is. Faith in something bigger than me (not a religious faith for me, but rather a sense of spirit) gives me a felt sense that I can focus on looking after myself, while knowing even that isn't completely up to me. It took months after the experience, but the snake did visit me and show me I was spirit in human form and I was divinely protected in both life and death. That knowing precipitated my next journey, the one I am still on—that of creating a feeling connection to my thinking self.

54
Feel It to Heal It

If I've shown you anything by now, it's that thoughts aren't the root of the problem. Thoughts make the problem feel worse, no question, but they are more of an effect than a cause. The feeling of alarm is the problem, the real source of our pain and the energy source for our worrisome thoughts. The root of the problem is the emotional energy that is trapped in the body. We are just less aware of it because it's harder to describe a feeling than it is to describe a thought.

Thoughts are already in our home language, the words we use to communicate with ourselves every single day. Feelings, however, are in a language of the body, and that is considerably less readily understood. When you see people having a peak experience, like a professional athlete winning their championship or a mother describing the birth of her first child, they often say that they can't describe it in words. The same is true for healing from anxiety. Words are not enough. We need to delve into the feeling.

In fact, words and thoughts often function as a distraction from the feeling. If we detour into words and thoughts, we never actually access the feeling, and for a long time that was just fine with me. I didn't want to access all that old feeling. That's why my system packed it away in the first place. But I've learned the hard way that you can't think your way out of a feeling problem. If that worked, saying "Just forget about her/him!" would absolve you of the pain of a breakup.

Now, if you know, on some level, a relationship isn't good for you or you need to get over it, you might purposely call to mind the bad memories and all the ways the person hurt you in an effort to try to get yourself to stop loving them. Although it may feel like it's working, by trying to think your way out of a feeling problem, you are bypassing true healing. I'm all for doing what you need to do to get through the emotional pain at the beginning when it's at its rawest, but just know, if you don't face the feeling, there won't be any true healing or learning for the next time. Take it from a guy who's been divorced twice.

We need direct access to the root of the problem—i.e., the alarm feeling—before we can change it. In other words, you need to feel it to heal it. You can temporarily make it easier by manipulating your thoughts, but this doesn't fix the root of the problem.

If I ask you "What are you thinking about right now?" you can probably tell me easily that you're thinking about what you're going to make for dinner or the errand you need to run this evening or your plans for the weekend. If I ask you "What are you feeling right now?" that takes an order of magnitude more attention, self-awareness, and introspection. If it takes you a minute to come up with an answer or if you maybe even draw a blank, you're not alone. It's actually pretty rare for us to talk about our feelings in everyday life. We are a left-brained, linear, logical, analytical culture that tends to look down on the right-brained feeling state as self-indulgent and nonproductive. On top of that, we tend to push away negative feelings and pretend they aren't a part of life.

In general, we are much more well-versed in describing thought processes than feeling emotional ones. And that focus on thinking is dangerous, as it makes us much more skilled at thinking than feeling—and in times of crisis, we are much more inclined to go for what we know (thinking) and bypass the source of the problem (feeling).

It is the feeling moments that give life its meaning. It is feelings that have the most important messages for us. And yet, at least in North America, we live in a society that denies feelings, especially uncomfortable ones. We are encouraged to live life from the neck up and not pay much attention to emotion and even urge people to discount or disown feelings that are unpleasant. Feeling sad after a breakup? Just forget about your former love! Buy a new car or binge watch Netflix!

In addition to it not working—because even if we manage to change our thoughts, the feeling underneath is still there—I believe positive psychology's focus on "thinking positive" actually harms us and holds us back. When we distract ourselves from or gloss over uncomfortable emotions, we lose the message the feeling is trying to give us. When we sit with the feelings instead of resisting them, we see that they, too, are transient. Feelings, both comfortable and uncomfortable, are woven into the tapestry of life. If we try to think our way out of every feeling, the feelings will not be processed and stay in a form of limbo as background alarm.

If your beloved pet has just died, forcing yourself to redirect your energy into happy thoughts of your wedding day, every time you feel sad, never allows you the opportunity to metabolize and integrate the experience. We are a highly intelligent culture in many ways. We greatly value technology and science. But when it comes to emotional intelligence, I'm not sure if we would even be given a passing grade. Our society is fixated on the idea that uncomfortable emotion is bad and must be avoided at all costs. Less explicit, but omnipresent, is the belief that we can buy our way out of negativity. (Retail therapy, anyone?)

I, myself, valued thinking over feeling for decades. In diverting my energies into my thinking mind, where I felt more comfortable, I increasingly lost touch with the feeling in my body. For many years, I didn't know I was doing this as a protective measure. Many of us with childhood trauma lost touch with our bodies because that was where our background alarm lived and we didn't want to go into that part of town. I did not sense I was hungry until I was ravenous or that I had to go to the bathroom until it was urgent.

I had to learn the hard way that staying in my head was a precarious place to live. To heal from anxiety and alarm, you must live in your body and make that place as safe as you possibly can. If you get trapped in your thoughts, the body is your escape route. Once the body is grounded, then and only then does thinking actually help. It took me years to figure out changing or controlling my thoughts was not the answer. I was already an expert-level thinker, and it was killing me. I had to direct my energy and attention away from the trap of the thinking mind and toward the feeling body. It was the feeling I had to become focused on and deal with directly. But my ego-mind did everything in its power to convince me my salvation lies in thinking. I had to escape that trap, and my goal with this book is to show you the way out too!

55
The Body Keeps the Score

If I hear about someone struggling with psychosis, schizophrenia, or bipolar disorder, a little alarm tripwire gets tripped in my mind and body. Although I have done a tremendous amount of emotional work in integrating the story of my father, I'll feel my background alarm perk up and I'll put my hand on my chest and take a few breaths and focus on the gratitude I have for my dad. I'll recall how he was there to teach me to ride a bike or throw a ball or get me my first job cleaning up the pool hall he ran. He was a great teacher when he wasn't incapacitated by the vagaries of his mind.

Hearing of someone struggling with mental illness is a trigger for me and, if I'm sleep-deprived or emotionally stressed, can easily send me into an alarm state, but, in general, I have integrated much of the trigger of seeing or hearing of someone in emotional distress. Oh, and by the way, my job is dealing with people in emotional distress.

Let me tell you about me and grocery stores. My wife knows I hate grocery shopping, but I still almost always go with her because I know she enjoys the company and appreciates the help. Sometimes I am funny and silly and I have a good time with her at the store, but most times we go, I dissociate a bit. I may become fixated on my phone and not very interactive with her. Those are my clues that I am heading into alarm, and I use that as a signal to reconnect with myself—and her too. (You'll learn in Part 3 how to recognize your own clues and what to do with them.)

My mind and body associate grocery stores with emotional pain. I never knew the exact reason, but shopping with my mother for groceries has been a painful memory for me. I have the distinct impression that it started when I was a younger child—perhaps about six—but I don't recall any episodes of food-based trauma, other than Cap'n Crunch cereal shredding the skin of the roof of my mouth. (And like a child with Stockholm syndrome, I always went back for another bowl. Cap'n Crunch is the most masochistic cereal I know.)

Anyway, I was never attacked by a head of lettuce or had a can of soup fall on me. I was curious about my resistance to grocery stores, so I recently asked my mother about it. "Did I have any traumatic events happen to me in a grocery store that I might not remember?" She thought for just a moment and said, "Well, I lost you in the grocery store in Ogdensburg once."

I was indeed six at the time. She remembers because at the time Canada was celebrating its centennial, so the year would have been 1967. She told me that in my usual style with stores, I was hyperactive, relentlessly exploring and running through the aisles. This was not unusual behaviour for me, and I would always find my way back to her. But on this occasion, we had gone for a quick trip across the international bridge at Prescott, Ontario, and entered Ogdensburg, New York. We were in the United States, and grocery stores are different there.

The layout of this particular Yankee store was different from my usual, normal Canadian grocery store. As my mother described it to me, my usual custom was to be wary of new things, as most sensitive children are. But I have another distinct side to me that runs counter my scaredy squirrel nature, and that more hyperactive side was often described by my dad as "Rusty's got more balls than brains (MBTB) today." (MBTB is the part of me that loves doing stand-up comedy.)

This particular day, the MBTB variety of Rusty had accompanied my mother to the store. As soon as we got there, I wanted to explore, and it didn't take me long to get lost. According to my mother, another mother of the American variety found me in tears after my foreground alarm pursuit energy failed to track down my parents. She took me to the store manager, who announced over the intercom that a child with more balls than brains had been lost and found and could be claimed by the frozen fish section.

I guess I blocked this out because I don't really remember it. When I focus, I have a foggy recollection of my dad claiming me and him being agitated. I'm actually not sure if this is a real memory or one I made up, because I remember losing Leandra in a store once and feeling that same combination of embarrassment, fear, and anger my dad likely felt.

To my point—and I do have one—this may be the reason I don't like grocery stores. It also may not be. I enjoy department stores that do not have food, and I love sporting goods stores. I only seem to react adversely to grocery stores. How I would know the difference as a six-year-old, I'm not sure—but sometimes things trigger our alarm and we have no idea why.

These are implicit memories, also called body memories. (You may recall we talked about them in Part One. Remember how much I love hearing someone practice the trumpet?) Implicit memories can trigger a fight-or-flight reaction in our bodies and we may have no idea what caused it. When triggered, it feels exactly the same way each time. I believe most panic attacks start when these implicit/body memories are triggered by stimuli we are not consciously aware of.

Over time, I've learned that the alarm in my body has its own "signature," meaning it feels the same way each time it is triggered. While the intensity can vary, the quality of it is the same, and it's the background alarm I was first able to visualize during my LSD trip.

The feeling of being triggered becomes its own implicit memory over time. The more the body has the experience of being alarmed, the stronger the memory becomes so that what's being triggered is not just the memory of the initial traumatic experience but also the memory of all the other times we've been triggered.

There is a theory that when you experience significant wounding as a child, like parental divorce or death, abuse, or abandonment, a part of you stays frozen in the trauma at the age you experienced it. This is consistent with my concept of background alarm, as well as Eckhart Tolle's concept of the pain body.

When our background alarm or pain body is triggered by implicit memory and we regress to the wounded child at the time our pain was frozen into us, this tends to separate us from ourselves. When we learn to soothe ourselves, we can reconnect with ourselves—and that is the path to recovery.

Yep, a medical doctor just said alarm is frozen into your body and fused with your wounded inner child. All that neuroscience and then this!

Still with me?

While in storage, our stored background alarm protects us from our direct experience of it, like mementos or photographs of a painful relationship that are stored in a box in the basement. In a way, it's like hiding a trauma from the mind *in* the body. When we experience trauma that is too much for our minds to bear (especially when we are children), we may repress it to a place that is "safer," where it is out of sight—but never actually forgotten. It may not be available to the mind, but that energy and information had to go somewhere, so it finds a place in the body. This is why people sometimes cannot actively or consciously remember the details of their overwhelming trauma. However there is always a remnant of it stored in the body.

I have seen many adults, when reminded of their childhood trauma, age regress back to the time that it happened. One of my patients, Jamie, had just had a baby with her husband, Ward, and things in their life and relationship seemed bright and connected. But in the first few weeks of her new baby's life, Jamie started to display some tendency to self injure. She locked herself in the bathroom and superficially cut her wrist with a knife and threatened to kill herself. Up until that time, she had shown no signs of significant mental illness other than some OCD, but even in her OCD, she had never been suicidal and certainly never anything as fragmented as she was experiencing now. I asked Ward about Jamie's own infancy and found out that Jamie's mother had been hospitalized for three weeks right after Jamie's birth and that Jamie had had limited contact with her mother for her first few months of life as her mother recovered. I suspect that in addition to feeling stressed by the demands of caring for a newborn, Jamie was also triggered by implicit memory of her own experience of infancy. Her alarm was activated and she regressed back to the time when she herself felt abandoned by her mother as a newborn.

On a lighter note, I have a friend who cannot even smell tequila without feeling desperately ill. I mean a full-body reaction, tight gut, watering mouth, instant headache. This is because he got so drunk on Cuervo at a New Year's Eve party in 1989 that he threw up for two days. Even now, thirty years later, if he smells tequila, he is taken right back to that New Year's Eve party and the subsequent vomiting and nuclear hangover he had for much of the first week of January 1990. The alarm is still stored in his body and can be awakened by the smell of tequila. We joke that he has PTSD—post-tequila stress disorder.

56
What A.L.A.R.M.S. Us

I know I have mentioned the word *alarm* a lot in this book. Like more than a thousand times. Believe me, I'm a little sick of it too. But it's important.

When I say alarm, I know what might come to mind is a fire alarm or an alarm clock—something that gets your attention and lets you know you need to do something. The alarm in my body was doing the same thing. It was showing the unresolved traumas that had been stored in my body so I could give them the loving attention they hadn't gotten in the past.

But here's the problem: I didn't know the alarm was my messenger. Because it hurt, I assumed it was my enemy. As I perceived it was hurting me, I either tried to push it away or distract myself away from it by chronic thinking and worrying.

Learning acronyms got me through medical school. I love making them. So, of course, I had to come up with one for alarm! Well, actually, ALARMS. It stands for:

Abuse – Any physical, emotional, or sexual abuse is overwhelming for a child and will be stored in the body as alarm.

Loss – We all experience loss as children. It is unavoidable. Even when children are supported around the smaller losses, such as a favourite toy or a beloved pet, major losses like the death of a parent or sibling can be overwhelming even in a family that is emotionally healthy and supportive. Loss that is overwhelming gets stored in the body as alarm.

Abandonment – When a child feels their caregiver has left them, it is completely overwhelming. Children know intuitively that they are not prepared to face the world on their own and are completely dependent on their caregivers to look after them and keep them safe. Remember that all anxiety is separation anxiety. Any sense of being abandoned or being separated from our protectors creates a tremendous energy of alarm in our systems. Abandonment can be physical, but it can also be emotional if our protectors are physically present but show little to no emotional connection.

Rejection – Being rejected by peers or family, as with bullying or ridiculing, can be completely overwhelming for a child. School can be a devastatingly alarming environment for a child.

Mature too early – Becoming a caregiver for parents, having sex too early, taking drugs or alcohol—anything that puts the burden of responsibility on the child before they are ready—will create and store alarm in the body.

Shame – Anything the child perceives as shameful will create alarm in the body.

57

Shooting the Messenger

So now we've established that if you had ALARMS in your childhood, they may well be the cause of (or at least *a* cause of) your alarm.

We know that alarm is the root problem we need to address if we're going to feel better. But I would suggest that it's also a treasure map. It points us back to the critical points in our life when we started to accumulate background alarm, so we can heal it at its source. Knowing this entry point, we can go back and give our younger self the support we so badly needed but didn't get.

I do not want to give the impression that I had all these revelations immediately after my LSD experience. I'm still working on processing my psychedelic experiences almost seven years later. What I did get initially was that the emotional pain I had erroneously attributed to the anxiety of my mind was in reality a state of alarm in the body.

In the years since LSD, I have made other observations, especially in meditation. I've seen that there was a part of me, around thirteen years old, that never had a chance to grow past that point as I began stockpiling trauma as background alarm in my solar plexus. A part of me was lost and abandoned at that age. My future still unfolded, but there was fundamental change in direction. Instead of the diffuse, amorphous organic unfolding of life that should be offered to a child so they can feel sheltered and protected to "find their own way," I was overwhelmed by my circumstances, and part of me decided I had to step up and be responsible. This was not a conscious choice that I had gradually matured into; part of me just saw it as a necessity. As a coping strategy, I became a different person and started taking on responsibilities far beyond my age-appropriate abilities. The certainty of my child self that I could relinquish control to adults and just be cared for and sheltered was shattered as I flipped the responsibilities on myself and became the carer and shelterer. I matured too early (the M in ALARMS) and became the man of the house as I saw my father failing.

As I moved from the role of eldest child to parent, switching roles with my dad, I was rewarded with praise from my mother, who appreciated the help. That inflated my ego and gave me a sense of control that I perceived I was missing, so I decided this caregiver role wasn't so bad and ran with it. Of course I knew deep down that this was way above my pay grade, and that increased my background alarm.

When children experience trauma in their family, they often blame themselves. Perhaps this is because to blame the parents would be a threat to that child's survival—that is, the child can't see a parent as fallible because the child needs to see the parent as competent and reliable. Because the problem cannot be seen as a parent's fault, the child assumes the blame, which gets poured directly into their background alarm.

There is a sad saying about this: If a parent mistreats or abandons a child, the child doesn't stop loving the parent, they stop loving themselves. When you stop loving yourself, that is too much for you to bear, so the negative energy is pushed out of your direct awareness of your mind and into the background alarm in your body. Much of healing is bringing this back to the surface; realizing it truly was not your fault; and reprocessing, metabolizing, and integrating that alarm. This removes the alarm from your body and gives your mind a chance to metabolize and integrate it so it no longer needs to be stored in the body.

What do you think would happen if you had a child come up to you crying in pain from ALARMS and you distracted away from them, withdrew into an addiction, or pushed them away? That child would get louder and pursue you more. Over time, that's what alarm does too: It gets louder and pursues you more. The alarm is your younger self asking for your attention and support.

With this awareness, we can see that "How do I get rid of my anxiety?" is asking the wrong question. Instead, I would encourage you to ask what inside of you—the emotional pain you could not metabolize or integrate back then— is asking for your love and attention now?

Just as we once engaged in pursuit to get back a secure attachment to our parents, your child self is now trying to close the gap with your adult self and get the nurturing it needs—and this pursuit energy is expressed as alarm.

If you deny and reject your younger self's attempts to connect, the energy goes into worry. You may temporarily be able to ignore, distract, or addict your way into suppressing that background alarm, but know that it *will* rise up again. I can't tell you how many times I had to increase a patient's antidepressant medication because it failed to contain their sensation of alarm. The alarm/ wounded child comes back because that wounded part of yourself has not been healed, only drugged so it's not as loud. It's like when the Honey Badger gets bitten by a cobra and passes out. He's only out for a short time, and he's right back to badgering again.

When you start to see that the alarm you feel is not an enemy to be defeated but a younger version of you that deserves compassion, the whole game changes.

If your mail delivery person rang your doorbell because they had an important letter for you, would you open the door and attack them and force them off your property? Instead of interpreting the alarm as the enemy that you need to get MAD at (that is, treat with medications, addictions, or distractions—see,

I told you I love acronyms), you can channel the sympathetic nervous system energy of pursuit created by the alarm into pursuit of yourself and use that energy to mobilize you to love and care for that alarmed, frightened child that is in you.

Getting rid of the alarm is throwing the baby out with the bathwater. Instead, we need to learn to embrace that child and the alarm that is in the child, even if at first it seems like learning to love what torments us. The good news is that you have the resources to address those old wounds now in a way you did not back then.

When you start the process of metabolizing and integrating old wounds, you welcome the background alarm. There is a process called integration that occurs when the alarm trapped in the body is brought to the surface and healed. According to Dr. Dan Siegel (the interpersonal neurobiologist and psychiatrist I mentioned earlier when discussing cognitively making sense of the story of what happened to you), integration is the process by which disparate parts are united to become a functional whole. When background alarm is suppressed, it is held in limbo and creates a tremendous amount of dysfunctional energy. When the alarm is brought to the surface and embraced (more on this in the last section of this book), it can be integrated and its energy used in a functional and beneficial way. When this happens, the energy of your alarm can be embraced as contributing to a constructive, functional whole instead of a destructive and disparate part.

When you view the alarm as some sort of weakness or punishment, you are likely to further separate from that wounded child by medicating it, overpowering it with addictions, or using distraction. But when you distract, reject, or worry, that alarmed child feels the same abandonment it did years earlier—creating more background alarm. As the alarm ramps up, it becomes less and less rational, like a lost child at the grocery store, freaking out more with each minute that goes by since seeing his parents.

But the alarm is actually not a threat but a messenger showing you the path to healing. For as long as you've been trying to "get rid of your anxiety," you've been shooting the messenger—but the messenger is you, so you've been shooting yourself.

Your background alarm is your younger, vulnerable self—not your enemy but your impetus for a closer connection with self. It's time to stop hurting yourself and start helping yourself.

58

On Integration

When you neutralize and integrate your old wounds, they leave the body and go back into the mind in an organized state where the energy can become integrated in a form of growth. It is the reverse of what happened when you were young when the energy was too much and you became disintegrated in a form of protection.

This integration is what happens during childhood in families with a strong sense of attachment that can fully support children through the trauma so that the negative emotional energy is metabolized, digested, and neutralized.

The story of my patient Alanna illustrates this concept of integration.

Alanna came to me when she was fifteen, just after her parents had divorced. Alanna developed a significant issue with OCD. (I've often joked it should be called compulsive obsessive disorder, because shouldn't we put it in alphabetical order?). Alanna would have elaborate physical movements like tapping her chest five times before getting in the car or turning around in a clockwise circle three times before entering a room. She also developed disordered eating (though stopping short of any clinical diagnosis).

Alanna's parents had an "amicable divorce," but Alanna felt very polarized— compelled to be close to her physically distant father and resenting her mother, even though her mom was the one that provided most of the support.

Over the six years we spent working together, Alanna did therapy that focused on her body, called somatic experiencing therapy, along with traditional psychotherapy. Somatic experiencing is a form of therapy created by Peter Levine, PhD, that tunes into the trauma stored in the body. My wife is a certified somatic experiencing practitioner, and she has taught me a great deal about the process of healing trauma using the body. Working with this modality has confirmed what I first saw during my LSD experience—that my pain had more to do with the alarm stored in my body than the machinations of my mind. Healing trauma, it has become clear to me, is less about talking about it and more about feeling through it. When I say you can't think your way out of a feeling problem, this is exactly what I mean. I believe that in the very near future we are going to see the field of psychotherapy as a whole move in the direction of using more of this type of body-based therapy, along with psychedelics.

When I met Alanna, she had a very rigid posture and her voice was tense and muted. In therapy, she was encouraged to trust her body and become aware of how tightly she held herself.

Alanna had been unable to feel (and therefore metabolize) the grief of the dissolution of her family. She would tell me that because the divorce of her parents never got "ugly" and because her mom and dad were amicable towards each other, she couldn't understand why they needed to separate in the first place. It was like she didn't believe it was happening, so she couldn't grieve a loss she didn't feel. Once her father found another partner, that caused reality to sink in for her emotionally so that she could process her feelings and access her grief. Over time, as she allowed herself to feel more, Alanna came to accept and even see the positives in her parents' divorce. In addition, Alanna's parents developed a friendship as they became committed to emotionally and physically supporting Alanna together.

Alanna's issues and obsessions with food resolved. Today she would probably say that although the divorce caused her great pain at the time, she could see why it had to happen and that it led to a connection with both of her parents that is actually closer in many ways than before the divorce. She also came to feel that talking about the divorce, although still not her favourite topic, did not trigger her anymore. (When you are no longer triggered by an event, this is evidence that integration has taken place.)

Initially, the divorce of Alanna's parents had created a vulnerability that was too much for her mind to tolerate and which, therefore, was stored in her body as that background alarm that drove her disordered eating and obsessive movement rituals. Once she understood how to feel and listen to the alarm in her body, and once her mind fully accepted the divorce and even grew to see the positives that came from it, the old trauma had been integrated. Alanna no longer felt so triggered when the old wound was touched, and her obsessions and compulsions no longer cropped up as a coping mechanism.

To reinforce the point of integration, the trauma energy is felt, metabolized, and neutralized in a supportive environment and no longer stays a trigger with the power to reignite alarm. Alanna had plenty of emotional support throughout her healing and learned how to connect with both of her parents—and, probably more importantly, with herself. Her background alarm was brought to the surface, metabolized, and integrated. Her OCD behaviours and disordered eating were signs she was dissociating because her mind was overwhelmed; once she was able to feel the loving association and connection with her parents and herself, she was able to come back into an associated and integrated state.

59

The Dissociation Association

Remember Jane, my patient who picked one alcoholic boyfriend after another like they were doughnuts at a bakery? I once had a session with her the same day one of her boyfriends had emotionally abused her. She was not physically harmed or even touched in anger, but her boyfriend had harshly berated her verbally for simply talking to another man.

When I saw her in my office later that day, she could not meet my eye. Her facial muscles drooped, and she talked with a weak, monotone voice. There would be episodes of five to ten seconds where her voice would just trail off. As I looked at her, with her shoulders hunched and her head hanging down, it seemed to me I was looking at an eight-year-old girl.

And I probably was, in a way.

When Jane was being verbally abused by her boyfriend, the similarity to her father's tongue lashings would have fired up her background alarm. Remember the amygdala, the structure in the brain that never forgets? If there is a situation that shares any similarity to your original wounding, the amygdala will flare up and fire both background and foreground alarm in an effort to protect you from what it perceives as the very same wounding happening again. The amygdala is very much like the hypersensitive smoke detector in my old condo, firing off not just at smoke but also at things that vaguely resemble smoke. Jane's amygdala would have fired up her background alarm, which would then have started the game of ping pong with her foreground alarm, and she would be in a full-body reaction. If the situation carried on and the abuse from her boyfriend kept going, her rational circuits would shut down and her survival circuits would engage, activating a maximal response in her alarm—like pushing the airplane engines up to one hundred percent in an emergency.

Because the mind cannot handle energy like that for long, a protective reaction called dissociation steps in. Dissociation is a type of escape when the present moment becomes too intense for the mind to stay engaged, so the mind leaves the present moment. When faced with an acute state that reminded her amygdala of severe trauma from her past, the "shutdown" of dissociation would occur to prevent the system from staying at the maximal response. (To make another analogy along the lines of the jet engines, over-revving a car motor can damage the valves and pistons; you could think of dissociation as a shutoff mechanism to prevent this.)

So why did Alanna's dissociation look different from Jane's? My theory is that Alanna's dissociation was slower because her trauma was not as acute. Alanna's trauma, although very intense and painful for a teenager, was never life-threatening, and she knew that. In contrast, Jane, being a young child when her trauma occurred, likely did fear for her survival on some level because of the abusive nature of her past experience. When Jane was faced with similar abuse from her boyfriend, her amygdala would fire her into full-throttle foreground and background alarm in a matter of seconds, so her dissociation looked more like the "freeze" response animals go into. If they've already expended too much energy fighting and/or know they have no chance of fleeing fast enough to get away, they feign death in hopes their attacker will lose interest. This is called "Dorsal Vagal Shutdown," and it frequently happens in humans that carry a lot of alarm, making connection (and healing) very difficult. (More on this coming up in the last section).

When we get knocked off balance and are acting from a disconnected, disorganized, and volatile place of alarm, our responses will be primitive and disorganized. Although we may appear withdrawn to an outside observer, there is plenty of volatility happening inside.

If eight-year-old Jane had had a secure attachment figure—another adult who could help her see through her father's tirades, love her, and make her feel safe—she may have been able to integrate the experience back then and keep the energy from flowing into her body. But instead, it is likely Jane dissociated when her father abused her. She would spend a certain amount of time in high activation and then her system would give up. She would then go into a dissociated state where she was "split from her self." While she was disconnected from herself, the normal processes by which she would connect and "associate" with her own self and others would be disengaged or at least compromised—

and when we disassociate this way as a survival mechanism, it overwhelms the mind and that energy flows into background alarm. This background alarm would likely stay active in Jane's system for hours to days, even after the abuse incident ended and her intense foreground alarm faded. Though less alarmed, she would have stayed in a vigilant state with limited ability to truly connect to herself or other people.

During our office visit, Jane began to come out of her dissociated state once she got some reassurance from me and started to feel safe. She started the visit as her eight-year-old self in full collapse but, by the end of the visit, was able to make eye contact, gain some strength in her voice, and even laugh with me about the fact that she had "picked another one!" in her recurring cast of questionable boyfriends.

Remember the social engagement system (SES), the innate part of our nervous system that allows us to connect with ourselves and others? This system is also sometimes referred to as human resonance circuitry because we literally use it to resonate in safety with another person. I used Jane's familiarity and trust of me to engage her SES and help her emerge from her dissociated state. Jane also had a counselor she felt safe with, and over the course of multiple sessions with her trusted therapist, Jane was able to become acutely aware of her compulsion to pick the "wrong" men. She came to see that she would dissociate and in her words "leave herself" when she accepted the advances of a man who fit the abusive or alcoholic profile of her father. In a moment I still vividly remember to this day, she even used the term "repetition compulsion" in describing her attraction to these guys! Jane is a great example of the power of bringing her alarm to awareness and the power of simple social interaction in helping us heal and calm our alarm.

60

The Effect of Dissociation

People dissociate in different ways, up to and including becoming fully unconscious (either falling asleep or fainting), but mostly it involves withdrawing from interaction. Eye contact is lost, the voice becomes monotone, and body movements are minimal.

My wife used to see me moving into this state on a very regular basis. An early telltale sign for her was when I would begin to lose my sense of humour. Normally, I'm always doing silly things around the house to make her laugh, but that would disappear as my mind and body headed into alarm and I began to shut down and dissociate. I would lose the warmth and play in my voice, and my voice would become flat and monotone. My body would turn inward, my head and shoulders slumping forward. Often I would withdraw into the bedroom.

We saw in the last chapter the healing power of the SES, but when we are in a dissociated state, we lose access to this powerful tool for self-soothing. I believe this describes the sequence of events that plays out with social anxiety. In a dissociated state with their background alarm triggered, social anxiety sufferers move into survival brain—and you can't be socially engaged and connected when you perceive (rightly or wrongly) that your safety is at risk. In this way, negative past experiences (in the absence of awareness and integration) hold them back from having the experience of connection that would help them heal. It's like being invited to play in the company softball match when you know you're a terrible softball player. Of course you're going to avoid the potential humiliation and get out of playing if you can.

I believe this also explains the phobia of public speaking some people experience. When a fear of being judged triggers someone's background alarm—for example, if they had a harshly critical parent who expected them to be perfect, like Kat—then their foreground alarm is also triggered. Suddenly the person is standing in front of an audience, wondering why their heart is racing and their startle response magnified like they're about to flee from a pack of hungry hyenas on the savanna. At some level they know the audience is probably just waiting with an open mind to hear what they have to say—but that's their rational mind speaking, and they don't have much access to their rational mind because they're in survival brain. At the time they most need to be connected and engaged with their audience, their human physiology has betrayed them. They start to speak in a monotone, moving stiffly or standing frozen in place, and their presentation does not include a single joke. The part of their brain that senses and produces humour (a form of social connection) has gone offline as the brain prioritizes survival over connection. So much of their energy is devoted to survival that they may not even remember the experience.

I experienced a similar type of shutdown myself when I started doing stand-up in 2000. When I would get onstage, my rhythm and timing would leave me. I can still send myself into a little bit of alarm by thinking back on those early stand-up gigs!

In my early days as a comic, the thought of going onstage alone and needing to make people laugh brought up such a fear reaction I needed more than a few shots of tequila to do it the first few times. (Fortunately, I don't have post-tequila stress disorder!) My nervous system wanted to shut down as it predicted a massive rejection and tried to protect me from the pain. Gradually, it got easier. I gained confidence and was able to connect with the audience without tequila's help as going onstage sober became my new habit, overwriting the implicit memory the early gigs triggered.

People with social anxiety who force themselves to go to parties—and a comic who forces himself to go onstage but needs tequila's help to do it—are taking a "sink or swim" attitude that can backfire just as easily as it can pan out for them. Sometimes new learning in the form of positive experiences does overwrite the old pattern, but on the other hand, survival physiology could take over and the person has a terrible experience with the result they will strongly resist ever going back. If I went onstage and froze in fear or "blanked" (forgot my material and stood in silence), that would have made me even more fearful of my next gig and more likely I would freeze the next time I got up to perform! When someone forces himself to go to a party and then gets there and speaks in a monotone all night, avoiding eye contact with his shoulders hunched, the party will likely be interpreted as a painful experience of rejection. Since he's unable to truly connect with fellow party guests, his SES never engages and can't do its job of creating warm, soothing connections. Then, he judges himself harshly, making it even more likely he will go into survival brain and again lock out his SES at the next social gathering. This fear creates a self-fulfilling prophecy that he is not able to connect with other people, feeding into an even greater sense of dread when the next party invitation arrives.

By forcing yourself into social situations as a way of "getting over" your social anxiety, you are creating more alarm for yourself and pushing yourself further away from access to your SES. I can show you a better way—an alternate route through the body that first opens up your natural calming physiology to quiet down the alarm, allowing your innate social engagement circuits to do what they're designed to do.

There were days when just getting out of bed to have a shower or take Buddha out for a walk seemed like a monumental task. While I know this narrow focus on life-sustaining functions was my nervous system's way of protecting me, it cut me off from nurturing, caring interactions with other people. In dissociation, there is a certain comfort in staying frozen and still. Dissociation and alarm are protective, but the price we pay for this protection is massive.

If we can understand this dissociative state as our primitive brain's way of trying to protect us and not some personal failing, we can see it, accept it, and neutralize it. I want to show you how to gradually introduce a new relationship with your SES that will help you ease into it. Practicing self-compassion and using sensation to bring you into the present moment are great ways of pulling yourself out of dissociation. This is what we will explore in Part 3.

61
Insights From MDMA

From the time I was a teenager, I had started to feel uneasy in my love for my dad. To see someone I loved in deep pain—to see someone I loved literally losing his mind—and not have a damn thing I could do about it was disturbing in a way that defies description. To an extent, part of me was beginning to feel that to love him was not safe, and if you push out love, that space is quickly filled with fear and alarm.

(You might ask whether another option might be indifference toward a parent who has abused, neglected, or otherwise failed you. Here's my more ethereal side coming out, but I do not believe we can truly be indifferent to a parent. We may tell ourselves we are, and we may even convince ourselves that we feel nothing, but there is an undeniable unconscious linkage we have to a parent, regardless of what they have or haven't done.)

Perhaps the biggest sin of an unworthy parent is that they engender a mistrust of love in their child. When your ability to trust love is compromised, fear takes over the empty space and pushes you into survival brain, further limiting your ability to mature your SES. As your SES is compromised, your ability to connect to love diminishes as well, and fear slowly gains the upper hand.

Early on in my teen years, when my dad would return from the mental hospital, I was quick to connect with him again, each time hoping that he was cured. But every single time, with sometimes as much as a year of relative normalcy in between, he would return to madness, and after a while, out of self-preservation, I started to withhold my connection with him.

My experiences with loving my father and seeing him in excruciating pain made me withdraw in self-defence. But when we withdraw love from a parent, we compromise our SES and limit the ability to love anyone else fully, including ourselves. When we withhold love from ourselves, we are unable to find solid ground and are left defenceless from the ravages of increasing anxiety and alarm. So allowing and accepting the feeling of love again is key to bringing the SES back online so we are open to loving connection. The more connected we feel to others, the more connected we will feel to ourselves, and this self-connection is the best route to integrating and dissolving our old background alarm. Just as when love is excluded and fear rushes in to fill the void, as love is allowed back in, fear is pushed out, and the SES comes back to do the job it's been designed to do for thousands of years of human social evolution.

I had shielded myself from love for many years, and while I still felt it, there was always a little "once bitten, twice shy" element to it. My trusted LSD guide suggested that I could try MDMA to really feel the unbridled sense of love I'd disconnected from after being disappointed so many times by my father. Once again, I was scared, but as I knew MDMA was not a psychedelic, I felt confident I was not going to have a terrifying journey—and it turned out to be quite the opposite.

So in the summer of 2015, at the ripe old age of 54, I took my first hit of ecstasy. All in all, MDMA was a wonderful experience that showed me when my brain had a healthy dose of love running through it, anxiety was impossible to conjure up. I could still academically bring up worrisome thoughts (even those of sickness and death), but they seemed trivial and did not disturb me in the least. My mind was full of love for everything and everyone, and my body felt a lightness and peace I never remembered experiencing before. MDMA didn't fracture my mind into a million pieces the way that the psychedelics (psilocybin, LSD, and ayahuasca) did. On MDMA, I had much more control of my mind, and I felt a sense of unity with my environment more so than I had with psychedelics. Even if it was drug-induced, I saw that love vanquished all anxiety in my mind and alarm in my body. MDMA showed me that I was repeatedly trying to mistrust something that I *was* at my essence—love.

As it began to wear off, MDMA helped me to see that I was very quick to sidestep positive emotions like love and joy. I found myself looking for reasons to jerk back into protection mode. I was still feeling this sense of love for everything and everyone, but my familiar pattern of recoiling from love and blocking joy started to creep back in. A benevolent part of me wanted to ride on in the loving experience, but another part (a part I was all too familiar with) started to mistrust feeling good. Perhaps fifteen minutes earlier I'd had nothing but love in my heart, but I could start to see the old pattern of discomfort in feeling "too good," and in real time observed how my pattern of familiar worry slowly but steadily began squeezing the unfamiliar good feeling from my experience.

What was curious is that I saw my worries in a new light. As I was still feeling warm and loving, I could watch those worries start to line up like excited children outside the gate at a swimming pool that was about to open. I realized I was seeing my worries in a way I'd never been able to before—objectively. Thanks to MDMA, I was not in alarm, so my mind stayed out of the typical survival brain that had always gone along with my worries before. For once, I could stay in my rational brain and really see the worries in a dispassionate, non-alarmed way that gave me a choice to believe them or not.

As I noticed my old protective habit starting to give the worries credibility, I wondered why I was "ruining" the experience and proposed to myself that I should just stay in love. In a moment of introspection, I asked myself why I felt the need to destroy this feeling. My answer was clear: "Don't enjoy it, because it's just going to be taken away from you." I was afraid those emotions would be ripped from me, just as I perceived my dad was ripped from me by mental illness. I saw that I didn't let myself stay in positive emotion for very long without sabotaging it by thinking of something scary or uncomfortable or discounting my own abilities. In short, I was learning how to remain separated from myself, and since all anxiety is separation anxiety, when you are separate from yourself, you have no chance of healing from chronic anxiety and alarm.

My unconscious self-talk had told me "good things don't last" and "don't get too comfortable, for this will all be taken from you." Those thoughts were repeated so often that they became an unconscious program, like an implicit memory, or body memory, I talked about in my unconscious aversion to grocery stores. The program, "Don't get too comfortable or all this will be taken away," had been just as deeply ingrained in me. My system had adopted the implicit program that I should not enjoy positive emotion because it was going to be taken away and the pleasure wasn't worth the risk and pain of losing it. This is exactly the "foreboding joy" Brené Brown talks about when she says, "When we lose our tolerance for vulnerability, joy becomes foreboding." To me, this means that when we block our access to love, we block our access to joy as well. It's like never allowing yourself to enjoy a piece of chocolate cake because you know you'll ruminate on getting fat the whole time it's in your mouth.

There's the old fear bias in action. Even the most emotionally healthy child is still programmed toward fear, so it doesn't take much in the way of experience to make that fear response a preferential groove in the snow. I needed something powerful to bump me out the deep groove of believing that love was too big of a risk to take. Luckily, my friend and trusted LSD guide came to my aid with another opportunity. He said that MDMA would help me feel love without the fear.

MDMA showed me I was disconnected from myself and that I should make an effort to allow the positive emotions to stay as long as they liked. MDMA also gave me the inkling that a compassionate connection to myself would go a long way in reducing my alarm and the anxiety that followed it.

I'd like to note that I didn't take any of these mind-altering substances until I was in my fifties. Although MDMA was an overall positive experience, the two to three days following it were difficult, as I experienced a rebound in my anxiety. So, like psilocybin, LSD, and ayahuasca, it had a significant downside for me, and I am in no way recommending someone with alarm experiment with these "medicines." I won't ever use them again, but in hindsight I'm glad I did. They gave me insights into my own mind and body that most doctors will never know. But we worriers cling to our thinking minds like a lifejacket in a tumultuous sea, and those substances take away that lifejacket, leaving us to face our feeling bodies without protection in the storm of our alarm.

Remember, it's not so much the trauma as the way that trauma was handled that determines the outcome—so I could have blamed my mother for her inability to fully look after my emotional needs, but I don't. She had her hands more than full. I love my mum dearly. She did remarkably well given all the demands on her. She was simply spread too thin. She is remarkably strong and resilient, and the family needed that strength to survive as well as we did.

When she was home, she did her best to be emotionally present, but the environment could often be dreadfully bleak if my dad was depressed or chaotic if he was manic. Mum was often at work to earn the money to meet our needs as a family, and I took it upon myself to look after dad when she was working. I also think that her work as a registered nurse was a place she felt some power and agency in the world. She retired over twenty years ago, and I still have people she worked with praise the fun and organized nature she provided on her ward. I'm very glad she had that praise and fulfilment at work because I think it kept her going during the really tough times when my father was close to suicide.

There was a point I actually did blame my parents until I came to see holding contempt for them locked *me* in contempt—and I could not afford the luxury of any more negative thoughts or emotions, since that just kept me out of my own SES, and in that state of contempt and blame, I had nothing to pull me out of the turbulent sea of alarm.

I saw on MDMA that I needed to be the connection to myself that my parents were unable and ill-equipped to give me. I had to see what both parents went through in their own childhoods made it virtually impossible for them to give me what they hadn't gotten themselves. The connection to them I refused would be the connection I refused to give myself. As a result, in maintaining my split from my parents, even if it was unconscious, maintained my split from myself. That, in turn, maintained the alarm in my system, which kept me in survival mode and out of touch with my own SES, which prevented me from healing my alarm. Simple, huh?

For many years, I was in an almost perpetual state of either alarm or dissociation/shutdown. In that withdrawn state, I was unable to connect with myself or others. I was trapped in a Catch- 22—in a constant state of alarm/pursuit yet unable to trust the connection I was so desperately pursuing. I repeated this in all my romantic relationships (and I had a lot of them). In the initial stages of my relationships, idealization and infatuation kept me in an MDMA-like state where love could flow readily. But my own "this is all going to be taken away from you" program always popped up, and slowly I became more dissociated from each partner—and then I would resent *them* for not keeping *me* in love! In some respects, I did the same thing with my parents, resenting them for my own feelings of dissociation.

It's been said many times that holding on to resentment is like drinking poison and expecting the other person to die. The bottom line was that maintaining resentment for my parents maintained my alarm, and maintaining my alarm maintained my anxious thoughts. You can see where this is going: As long as I maintained separation from my parents, I continued to recharge the alarm-anxiety cycle because separation is exactly what set off my alarm in the first place.

"All anxiety is separation anxiety." – Dr. Gordon Neufeld

"All alarm is separation alarm." – Dr. Russell Kennedy

I was about twelve when I first realized that my father was seriously mentally ill. I lost a bit of my innocence because there was a part of me that separated from him. Although it was a feeling much more than a thought process at that point, there was a sense I couldn't trust him. Not that I couldn't trust him not to hurt me, but because I questioned his ability to look after me. A son at that age always wants to completely trust his father, and I was beginning to have serious doubts. Over time and many episodes of mental illness, I saw that the more I loved him and empathized with him, the more I *was* going to get hurt. There was a sense that I needed to protect myself, as the pain of being close to my father was becoming too much to bear. It was too much for me to see him tortured by intense emotional pain and not be able to do anything about it.

As for my mother, I separated from her as well. I needed extra support from her because of the situation with my father, but she wasn't able to give it both because she had too many demands on her time and energy and because she didn't really know how to reassure me and connect with me, since she didn't receive much emotional support in her own family of origin. You can't give what you didn't get. A part of me simply gave up and shut down. Part of me separated from myself as I went into my mind and out of my body, separated from my own SES. That created a huge sense of alarm because the SES plays a significant role in giving you the sense of being calm, grounded, and stable.

As our society moves faster and faster with the ever-increasing pace and volume of information, we have lost the feeling sense in our bodies and learned to prize speed over substance. For the sake of neck-up efficiency, we have learned to accept the *description* of a feeling over the feeling itself. We live in a world that goes so quickly that our mind has adapted to the speed and even becomes addicted to it. Our brains love to learn, but there is a price. In stimulating our minds with speed and knowledge, we lose the meaning of life—because the meaning is in the feeling.

This is largely out of necessity. As life moves faster and faster, our brains are saying to us, "I feel the need for speed." (Sorry for the *Top Gun* reference, but I couldn't help myself.) We process things on a cognitive basis just so we can keep up. We are trading a *feeling* of life for a *thinking* of life, and it is killing us.

In my own case, separating from the feelings in my body started early. I began to split from the very thing I needed to connect to the most—my own self. As I became more numb and separate from myself, I became more alarmed, causing me to separate further from my body and to move away from my source of stability and grounding. As I numbed out my body in an attempt not to feel the alarm that lived there, I retreated into my head. At the time, I went along with traditional dogma that I could think my way out of a feeling problem, so I did all sorts of head-based talk therapy, but none ever really got me back into my body, where I could reconnect with myself and my SES. I was trapped in alarm with no way out until I started doing body-based therapies like somatic experiencing. I was chasing my tail up in my head. There's no tail up there, as far as I know—and neither was there a solution up there to my alarm and anxiety.

So let me ask you: When did you start to separate from yourself? Was there a point when you separated from your caregivers? When did you experience ALARMS: abuse, loss, abandonment, rejection (or bullying), maturing too early because of the demands placed on you, or shame?

As I go through the list, I can see not only the loss of my father to his illness, the abandonment I felt from both parents due to their own overwhelm, and being forced to mature too early—all of which I've already discussed at some length. But I also recall being bullied by kids in school and feeling rejected. I remember being ashamed of myself at times I felt weak or wasn't effectively carrying out my father's role in taking care of the family. I say all of this not to garner sympathy but to show you how many ALARMS one person might have. Don't minimize your own experiences and tell yourself they weren't that bad. This list of ALARMS shows us all the places we lost or abandoned ourselves along the way. Knowing where you split from yourself allows you to find yourself again. Just as the child lost in the store can feel safe again when parents are found, you can find yourself in your own ability to feel and create your own sense of safety.

62

When It's Not Safe to Feel Safe

I love getting massages, because it's one of the rare times my body completely lets go. It used to happen to me often that I would fall asleep during a massage and then awaken with a jolt.

Remember, for me it didn't feel safe to feel safe. I came to understand this was causing my reactions during my massages. I would get so relaxed, and then I would feel a jolt of alarm, like a milder version of a panic attack. This was my body falling into the old groove, "Don't get too comfortable because this will all be taken from you."

I realized this was a throwback to when things were going okay, even good, with my dad, and then it would all collapse, sometimes completely unexpectedly. In essence, if my dad collapsed, I felt everything would be taken away from me, so I could never let myself relax—either my father was falling apart or I was worried he was going to.

Normally, I had worries in my mind at all times. If a medical test came back normal, I'd immediately start to worry about something else. I invented all kinds of worries, and the more horrible they were, the more effective they were at keeping me in my head and out of my body. Of course I never felt safe; I made sure of it!

When the emotion held in the body is not expressed, this trapped energy wreaks havoc in our system. In medicine, the prefix *dys-* means abnormal, as in *dysfunctional*. The alarm-anxiety cycle is a dysfunctional relationship between the mind and the body. It's not so much they're cut off from each other as the relationship is skewed toward surviving rather than thriving.

For a long time, I had a relationship with myself that did not have the luxury of rest. In that hypervigilant state, it was very easy for my mind to focus on the negative. It was almost like there was a gate where the negative was let in preferentially but the positive had to be overwhelmingly positive before it was allowed admission. As a result, my mind and body remained dys-connected and dysfunctional and never learned to trust each other. Therefore, it was second nature for me *not* to trust positive feelings, to trust myself, or to trust in the general safety of life.

During a massage now, I actually allow myself to stop worrying and just settle into feeling. This had always been a recipe for disaster before, but now

I know that my body may still snap me back into vigilance and worry when I feel "too safe." But I am fully aware of what is happening, and I can consciously return to the sensation in my body and enjoy the feeling of safety. This ability to settle in and realize that it is safe to feel safe took a long time to cultivate, but I will show you exactly how to do it in Part 3.

63
Waiting for the Other Shoe to Drop

There are a few different origin stories for the phrase "waiting for the other shoe to drop," but the most common one seems to be that it originated in the nineteenth century, when people lived in wooden buildings with limited soundproofing. At night, someone above you would drop their shoe to the ground while getting into bed, which would make a loud sound. The person below would know there was no point in trying to fall back asleep until they heard that second shoe hit the floor. (Kind of makes you wonder what their upstairs neighbour was doing if too much time elapsed in between taking the first shoe and the second shoe off, doesn't it?)

That time spent in limbo, literally waiting for the other shoe to drop, was a state of vigilance not unlike the hypervigilance I've observed in myself and many of my patients who suffer from alarm and anxiety. We don't allow ourselves to feel calm and peaceful because of the fear of the inevitable loss that is coming. In addition, we worriers think that if we keep ourselves in constant readiness for trouble, we will be more prepared to handle it when it arises.

But we are wrong on both counts. One of my favourite stand-up comedians, Norm MacDonald, has a line I love: "What doesn't kill you only acts to make you very, very weak." Allowing ourselves to be calm and peaceful is actually what allows us to better handle pain when it arises. Your vigilance does nothing but tire you out so that you lose twice. First, you lose from the pain of keeping yourself in a constant state of worry and alarm. And, second, you lose when you lack the resources to handle the pain that does come up because you've exhausted your mind with hypervigilant worry and your body with chronic alarm.

I've mentioned her in passing when I talked about foreboding joy, but renowned shame and vulnerability researcher Brené Brown, PhD, talks about this. No matter how many times you rehearse that phone call from the school saying your child has been seriously injured, it does not help or empower you to deal with the situation. No matter how many times you worry about something terrible happening, the "practice" does not help you deal with it any better in the very unlikely event that it does happen.

Remember, worry is an illusion we use to trick ourselves into believing we are reducing uncertainty, when in truth what it actually does is the opposite. When we worry about something, we are not reducing the chances of it happening. If anything, we are creating more focus on uncertainty by chronically raising the worry (and the inevitable internal defence and reassurance), which by its very nature implies *more* uncertainty, since you can only worry about something that by definition is not happening.

I have seen that many of my patients dealt with painful uncertainty during childhood: "Am I going to run into my bully today?" "Will my mother be drunk when I get home from school? "Is there going to be anyone there when I get home?" "When are my parents going to have another huge fight and bring up divorce again?" "When's the next time I'm going to have to protect my mother from my father?" The list goes on.

In all of these questions, notice the uncertainty—the waiting for the other shoe to drop. This uncertainty was especially apparent in my patients who grew up with alcoholic parents. There would be a period of relative calm before the inevitable blow-up, binge, and chaos. When the binge ended, the chaos would resolve and there would be a period of relative calm again—until the next binge.

That cycle repeated itself countless times in many families I learned about in my work. As a child growing up with plenty of uncertainty around my father's mental state, I could relate.

When you grow up constantly waiting for the other shoe to drop, background alarm continues to accumulate, and with its accumulation, it brings a level of hypervigilance and hyperactivation of your foreground alarm in your sympathetic nervous system. Background alarm carries a perpetual activation of the nervous system—a preparatory, protective level of fight-or-flight readiness that keeps the system primed and ready for action. But the true need for action rarely comes, and we exhaust our resources in a constant preparedness, so if and when there is a real threat, we are too tired to be able to react to it. The more unresolved trauma gets added to background alarm, the higher the level of readiness for threat becomes ingrained over time—and the more we deplete ourselves by never allowing our bodies to fully rest.

I experienced a version of this (with less emotional charge than the hyper-vigilance related to my father) being on call overnight when I was a resident in the hospital. I would often fall asleep, but was still ready for the call. As an intern, if there was a cardiac arrest or other emergency, we were expected to get to the patient within two minutes. I would sleep in my scrubs so if the emergency pager sounded, I was ready. During these shifts, I never slept deeply, as my body was always waiting for the call.

When I was resting in the doctor's lounge, my parasympathetic rest-and-digest response was impaired by low-grade activation of the sympathetic fight-or-flight response because part of me knew that I may need to spring into action at a moment's notice. I'm sure every doctor has this to some extent, but because of the background alarm already in me, I suspect my inability to rest when on call was more pronounced than that of my colleagues who grew up in more securely attached and less traumatic homes.

When background alarm is active, even if you don't feel it consciously, at an unconscious level it is working to make your body feel unsafe. As an example, if I hear that someone committed suicide, my amygdala (because it recognizes the significance of suicide in my past) will fire up background alarm, which touches off a foreground alarm response. As this happens I'm not overtly feeling anxious, but when I check in with my breathing, it is shallow and superficial, evidence that my body is reacting to a perceived threat with an element of foreground alarm.

If you have chronic background alarm from unresolved pain in your past, it is likely your autonomic nervous system never properly calibrated the balancing act between the sympathetic nervous system and parasympathetic nervous system. The rest-and-digest part of the teeter-totter was never fully settled on the ground, as the chronic fight-or-flight activation held it suspended in the air. You never knew when someone would charge into the room and yell, "Sea Monster!" You just had to be ready.

In those of us with chronic alarm (more commonly known as chronic anxiety, of course—but we know the real truth), both foreground alarm and background alarm have been fired up so often that they've made their own grooves in the snow and can go from zero to sixty very quickly.

(Actually, you might notice an inconsistency with that last remark—and you're right. The foreground and background alarm in us worriers is never actually at zero. We always have a bit of that "waiting for the other shoe to drop" energy. Maybe I should have said "from ten to sixty.")

The good news is that you can recalibrate your autonomic nervous system. With time and practice, you can learn to feel safe feeling safe. But this recalibration must be done through the body—quieting the mind alone is not enough. Autonomic dysregulation is a feeling issue and needs a feeling modality to recalibrate it.

64
Am I Safe in This Moment?

Have you ever been ziplining? You clip yourself into a moving carriage that slides on a steel cable suspended above tall trees. Safely clipped in and secured, you can slide at high speed suspended at a terrifying height above a ravine or river.

This experience activates a bit of primal fear in our Stone Age brain. (One hundred thousand years ago, there were no circumstances in which it was safe to be dangling hundreds of feet in the air, or so I'm told.) But for worriers, ziplining can actually feel refreshingly safe, since tolerating a fear of heights feels easy breezy compared to the intense pain and uncertainty we experienced as a result of ALARMS.

Clipped to a wire hundreds of feet in the air, we were, at least in some sense, safer than we had been in our childhood homes.

My patients often say they felt like they "had to walk on eggshells" (or, sometimes, they were always waiting for the other shoe to drop) while growing up. When there is a dynamic like this in families, the members of that family often form what's called a *trauma bond* with each other. This is a bond based on fear. In my family, we each had a trauma bond to my father, loving him and fearing him at the same time. Although he was never violent or physically abusive, there was a sense he was not safe, and our ideas of love and fear became melded together.

This is also what I believe happened with Jane. She had a trauma bond with her dad where love and fear got fused together, which became her template for her future bonds with men—with disastrous consequences. Jane was a very attractive woman and could have had her pick of men, but when given a selection of perfectly good croissants and turnovers, she always picked the day-old doughnuts. She told me she was never attracted to the "nice guys."

Freud called this *repetition compulsion* and defined (paraphrased by me) as the need to recreate your adult relationships to fit the model of your childhood relationships. As I said earlier, not only did Jane recognize her repetition compulsion to recreate her trauma bond with a man like her father, but she even called it by name!

One thing I've noticed in dealing with thousands of people on a fairly intimate level over many years is that human children equate familiarity with security. What was familiar in childhood we unconsciously repeat in adulthood, for a deep unconscious part of us equates security with what was imprinted on us as children.

A part of Jane had falsely equated her alcoholic father, as perverse as this sounds, with security. Equating familiarity with security works fine if you grew up in a healthy, securely attached family but not so much if your family was dysfunctional or traumatized, as you'll unconsciously and compulsively recreate old pain.

In addition to placing ourselves in unhealthy relationships that replicate our trauma bonds, another way we enact the repetition compulsion is by staying disconnected from ourselves. This is another way of saying we choose to stay in our minds with our worries, not realizing the worries are keeping us out of our bodies where the path to healing lies. When we are used to spending all our time in our minds because the feelings in our body were too painful, what's familiar feels comfortable. We would rather stick with the devil we know than the devil we don't.

As a child, I never had a chance to connect with myself because all my attention went to reading my father and mother and trying to make sure they were okay. Typically, in families with trauma, the children don't get the luxury of being able to see how they themselves really feel inside because their focus is outside—on one or both parents. Many children who grow up to be alarmed adults had to look after one or both of their parents in some way. Their survival brain told them, "If my parent is not okay, then I am not okay." As a result, they made their parents' needs a priority over their own, and they lost touch with their own inner world. As adults, many of them are still great at reading and looking after others but struggle to read and look after themselves.

Since your relationship with others can be no better than your relationship with yourself, to break your repetition compulsion and stop finding yourself in relationships with trauma bonds, you must first foster a closer relationship with yourself than you've ever had before. Once you have a compassionate relationship with yourself, only then are you able to create truly compassionate relationships with other people in your life.

It's no wonder you weren't able to integrate your trauma during childhood. You can't break the alarm-anxiety cycle until you feel safe, at least for a little while. During my own childhood, conditions were never safe or conducive to give my background alarm a chance to die down. Many of my patients had a similar soul-crushing dynamic of looking for safety in a parent who was also the source of their alarm.

My dad could be quite caring and lucid for months at a time, and there were some truly wonderful times in my family. But there was also a profound sense that both my father and the foundation could crack at any moment. This kept my family perpetually off balance and never allowed us to truly connect to each other because the focus was always on my father and his state of mind. My mother, my brother, and I could also not engage each other's SES with more positive interactions because there was never a big enough foundation of safety to allow that to happen.

So how do you connect with yourself when the connection has been broken for so long?

Good question. And it's one that may elicit some frustration since it sounds so simple, and yet I'm telling you you've been in a chronic state of disconnection you haven't even been aware of.

But stick with me. It's easier than you think.

We can start right now with one simple question that has transformed many lives.

"Am I safe in this moment?"

In this moment, right now, reading or listening to this book, are you safe? Can you take a deep breath in and out and really sense that you are safe? Can you close your eyes and just sit in the experience of being safe, even if it is for just a few seconds?

"So often times it happens that we live our lives in chains and we never even know we have the key." – "Already Gone" sung by The Eagles

If you are safe in this moment, then you are safe because this moment is all we ever have.

Now you know you have the key the Eagles were singing about.

Maybe, in the time it took to keep reading, that sense of safety is gone. Maybe your mind has jumped ahead to your root canal appointment later this week or the sizable tax bill you have to pay. That's okay. Just observe what your mind has done—created a story to support a feeling of danger.

Then ask yourself again: "At this moment, sitting here reading this book, am I safe?"

Repeat as many times as necessary.

And know you can stop and ask this question anytime you are stressed or ruminating on your worries. You can relish your safety in the moment by focusing on your breath or by putting your hand on your chest to connect with yourself. This brings you into sensation in the present moment (you can only feel in the moment you are in) and pulls your attention away from the future-based thoughts your mind is trying to get you to believe. Remember, *don't believe everything you think.*

65
Find Your (Background) Alarm

Knowing that my alarm is an irregular oval-shaped purple crystalline density located just to the right of my solar plexus and lower sternum has been invaluable in providing me with a true focus for my pain. So, let's help you find your alarm.

Where do you feel your anxiety? When you get stressed and overcome by worry, where do you feel it in your body?

Go ahead, think of something that makes you afraid and zero in on the sensation in your body. Get really quiet and focused. Bring to mind a troublesome emotional event from your past (not too severe) and focus on the pain of it and then scan your body.

Most people will find it somewhere between their chin and their pubic bone, most often close to the midline (or centre of the body). For some, it feels like butterflies in the stomach. For others, it feels like nausea or a punch in the gut. It may feel like the heartache after a bad breakup or even a death.

Once you've found it, see how much you can observe about it and how specific you can get.

Does it have a shape? Is it circular or oval? Does it have a sharp border or is it fuzzy at its edges? Is it painful, and if so, is it sharp or dull (or both)?

Does it have a colour? A size? Does it radiate pressure, pain, or any other sensation?

As you feel it and connect with it more, it will probably reveal itself to you in more detail.

I know this sounds odd coming from a medical doctor, but localizing the sensation and characteristics of my alarm has been invaluable in my healing. It gives me something to "hold on to" unlike my terrifying experience on ayahuasca, where I felt there was "nothing to hold on to."

Don't worry (ha!) if you can't find it right away. I've had many patients who had to search for a while and just stay open and curious until eventually they became aware of it. Be patient with yourself. Finding your alarm is probably a brand-new concept, and it may seem more than a little strange. But I assure you, finding the source of your alarm in your body is an extremely helpful component to your healing.

Sometimes patients who initially can't find their alarm can do so as they repeatedly practice holding a fearful scenario or old grief in their minds while focusing intently on their body. I had one patent who was finally able to locate her alarm during a huge argument with her ex-husband over where their children were going to spend Christmas. (♪'Tis the season! ♫Alarm bells ring, are you list'ning"?♪)

Seriously, painful Christmas or holiday season memories are an absolute goldmine when you are looking to find your alarm.

Some people feel safer trying to find their alarm in the presence of a trusted person or therapist. Alarm can be buried deeply and surrounded by a lot of protective emotion—not to mention the hypervigilant, distracting mind whose job it has been to keep you out of this area in your body. If you are having a hard time locating your alarm, I highly recommend enlisting the support of a trusted friend or counsellor.

This is actually exactly what my wife does. Cynthia's job as a somatic experiencing practitioner is to take people close to their past wounding while at the same time helping them feel safe and keeping them oriented to the safety of the present moment. She does this by keeping people connected and present with their bodies and their SES.

This is where the previous chapter and this one come together. If you have trouble fully believing that you are safe, it may feel scary (even if the fear is beneath your conscious awareness) to get acquainted with your alarm and face something head on that you've been avoiding for so long.

Practitioners like Cynthia are experts at noticing when their clients start to dissociate because their old alarm has been triggered. She uses, among other things, her own SES to engage her clients' SES using tone of voice, body language, touch, and facial expressions to connect and create an environment of safety. Using the ancient human resonance circuitry that dwells in each of us, she creates the environment of safety that didn't exist for her clients when they were children and helps them stay present through the tremendous urge to dissociate when difficult emotions arise. With support in developing a tolerance for their old emotional wounding, her clients are able to integrate the trauma and stop following the familiar toboggan track of dissociation. If you are finding it triggering to isolate your old alarm or if there is a powerful urge to numb or withdraw and you keep finding yourself back in your mind with your worries, consider seeing a therapist who uses somatic (body-based) practices to help you.

Above all, be patient with yourself. We worriers needed our worries to keep us away from this alarm, so it may take a while to reveal itself.

In the meantime, you might use the heart space to represent your alarm temporarily until the real location becomes apparent.

Your alarm is where your younger, wounded self lives. Once you find it, you can use it as a focus for healing, along with the techniques you'll learn in Part 3.

66

Feeling Your "Anxiety" in Your Body

When I asked my patient Jane where specifically she felt her anxiety in her body, she seemed stunned by the question. She insisted that she felt confused and scared in her mind, waving her hands around her head.

I asked her another question: "What stops you from eating?" to which she replied, "I'm just not hungry anymore."

Next question. "Most people get hunger pangs in their gut area when they don't eat. Do you have any uncomfortable sensations in your stomach when you don't eat?" Jane answered, "No, but my tummy does get upset when I get anxious." Aha!

I asked her to describe this sensation. She said it felt like a rock (she squeezed her fist over her upper abdomen to illustrate) and that it would also feel like pins and needles. Then she said, "It feels cold and hollow and alone."

Wow.

Delving into it more, over time Jane found the feeling in her gut was the focus of her alarm—the residue of unresolved childhood trauma that still lived in her body—and the alarm represented her younger self that surely did feel hollow and alone.

Until I specifically got Jane to focus on her body, she assumed her issues were all in her head.

But in truth, the traumas she had experienced as a child that had made her feel too vulnerable for her conscious mind to bear had lodged in her unconscious mind and, from there, in her body as background alarm.

67

You Can't Change What You Can't See: Watching for the Hook

When I feel a sense of alarm in my body, I've developed a practice of watching for the "hook," my mind's attempt at solving the cause of the alarm. After all this time and work and study, I've become very aware of my mind's compulsive desire to reduce the dissonance I feel by developing an alarming story (aka worry) to explain it. Since I know it's coming, I can prepare for it and use the energy previously expended on worrying to instead focus on getting grounded in my body.

Have you ever had an itch and scratched it, but that just caused the itching sensation to intensify? This happens with allergic reactions to things like poison ivy. Scratching feels good for a moment but ultimately just makes us more miserable. And worrying is exactly the same.

Recognizing your worries aren't helping you is a great first step in shifting your focus. Remember, although worrying may seem to create a sense of certainty and control, it's actually increasing your alarm and forcing your mind to come up with ever scarier worries to match. Instead of obsessing about painting a more and more realistic-looking tiger that will ultimately just scare you more, you can decide to put down the brush.

It's not exactly possible to stop thoughts—they're just what the mind does. But what you *can* decide to do is to pull your energy and attention away from your thoughts. You can do that by changing your conscious focus to sensations in your body.

This can start with noticing your breath or putting a loving hand on your chest or rubbing your fingertips together—anything that pulls your attention away from the "hook" of compulsive worrisome thoughts and into the sensation of your body. This will create a positive focus on sensation, which brings you into the present moment and away from negative thoughts, which are always about the future.

Once you've gotten better at noticing the emotional signature of your alarm, you can look out for the hook. Or you might first notice the hook—the irrational horror story your mind is telling you—and then look for the alarm.

Just remember that you can't beat thoughts on their own turf. That hook may appear so seductive and lead you down the old familiar path, but you know it doesn't lead anywhere good. As soon as you notice you're in alarm, do not pass go—go directly into your body.

68

Sensation Without Explanation

In November 2014, I attended an eight-day residential personal development retreat close to Whistler, British Columbia. Four times during the retreat (so every second day) we did a three-and-a-half-hour process called Holotropic Breathwork®. This technique was popularized by Dr. Stan Grof, a psychiatrist who used to do LSD-assisted psychotherapy. When LSD became illegal, he remembered that many of his patients who'd had transformative experiences engaged in breathing patterns similar to hyperventilation. He wondered if the breathing alone could produce transformative experiences—and indeed, he found that was the case.

In Holotropic Breathwork®, you inhale intentionally and forcefully, then exhale more passively. The inhalation lasts around one second, and the exhalation two to three times that. This is often accompanied by loud trance music. Usually there is a "breather" (the person engaging in the breathwork) and a "sitter" (the person charged with helping them get to the bathroom and generally watching over them to make sure they continue the rhythm and don't stop the process). Sometimes people will fall asleep (even with the trance music blaring), which is usually allowed to continue, for many old emotions can be processed during this sleep. I have seen people jump up, dance, laugh, scream, cry, punch, and kick as part of this practice. It is said to induce a "non-ordinary" state that bypasses the protective ego, allowing the breather to get in touch with old, repressed stories, thoughts, and emotions.

Some people have profound revelations about their lives that change them forever; for others, they do not perceive much of a difference, but that is not to say there is no difference. Something may have shifted in their unconscious even if they don't see much in the way of conscious change. The first time I did breathwork, I had just come off my LSD experience a month earlier. In one of my breathwork sessions, I got this message: "Sensation without explanation." Much like the revelation I received during LSD, I didn't really know what to do with that insight right away either.

Around the fourth day of the retreat, I was having a particularly uncomfortable day. We were going into many of my childhood fears and traumas, and I had listened to many stories from my fellow participants about abuse, loss, abandonment, rejection, being forced to mature too soon, and lots and lots of shame. I could distinctly feel that familiar and intense sense of background alarm in my solar plexus. It wasn't even in the background at that time—it was in full "Purple Haze" mode with a hat tip to Jimi Hendrix.

The retreat facility was in this beautiful area in nature, right beside a rushing river and at the time the salmon were spawning. I tried to sit by the river in meditation but could not settle my mind. I felt distinctly lonely and agitated and wanted to leave, and then I brought to mind my ninety-minute episode of "enlightenment" on that temple rooftop in India fifteen months earlier. I conjured up as much of that scene as I could and found it to be easier than I thought it would be. My foreground and background alarm started to be washed away by the presence of the rushing river, and it crossed my mind that my mind and body were being cleansed. In this state, the phrase "sensation without explanation" came to mind. It was another example of being able to sit with pleasure, pain, whatever and just feel it without automatically adding thoughts to it.

I turned to the sensation of alarm in my lower chest. "Just feel it," I said to myself. This suggestion was met with considerable resistance. My mind started its compulsive, knee-jerk reaction to make sense of the uncomfortable feeling by explaining to me that *I was lonely, and why had I spent all this money on another self-help retreat. … And was the loneliness I felt there easier, the same, or harder than my time alone in India? … And what was I trying to accomplish anyway? Nothing was helping, and I was going to stay in this anxious state forever since I had been like this for decades and nothing had helped, and I was a lost cause and should just get up and go home.*

I felt that for the first time I was seeing my mind. I had seen my alarm in my solar plexus, but I never thought to isolate my mind in the same way. Sitting there by that river, I could watch my mind try to distract me back into my head. I repeated "Just feel it" in a way that reminded me of Nike's "Just do it." With more resolve, I made an intention to stay with the feeling without words or explanations—just the feeling. Just feel the alarm. Don't try to explain it. Explaining it was not going to make it feel better. In fact, trying to explain it only seemed to make it worse. I did a little experiment on myself. I would set the intention to feel the alarm and go into it as deep as I could and feel around.

I'd love to tell you the pain seemed to fade away completely when I isolated it. Although it didn't fade away, it did fade. Then I started to add thoughts in, and the pain increased noticeably. When I was on MDMA, I was overwhelmed by the sensations of love, and any worrisome thought seemed to have no foundation, to the point it bordered on ridiculous. But here in my "right" mind, my thoughts had tremendous power to amplify my alarm. When I consciously directed my attention away from thinking and into feeling, I had a sense I had stumbled onto something momentous. I had finally found something that gave me a sense of agency over the previously overwhelming feeling of alarm. Each time I tested it again by committing to the uncomfortable sensation without trying to explain it, the discomfort faded. With allowed and added thoughts, it got worse again. I was really onto something here.

The background alarm in my solar plexus still hurt. But for the first time, I had something that gave me a sense of control. Many people have told me the worst thing about alarm and anxiety is that they feel at its mercy and have no idea when it's going to end. Although I could not relieve it completely, I was curiously optimistic. Although feeling it was unavoidable, I had discovered that adding thoughts to it was optional. I found I could take the energy that I previously used to fuel my worries of my mind and redirect it into the focus of sensation of my body, and in so doing I felt a real sense of relief.

By allowing—dare I say, embracing—the uncomfortable sensation of alarm, I was dealing with it on *my* terms. I was no longer a hostage to my mind's compulsive need to overreact by compulsively explaining and worrying. When I took control and divorced myself from the previously overwhelming need to unconsciously and automatically follow the well-worn groove in the snow of relentless thinking, I could let the worry snowstorm calm and see a new path—one of feeling, of embracing sensation, of cleanly grasping the issue at its root without the muddying influence of my thoughts and worries.

In that moment, I saw a distinct change in my usual process of compulsive thought trying to explain the pain. I saw there was a space I had not been aware of before—a spot where I could be with the pain of the alarm but not automatically and compulsively fill in the perceived blank with an explanation. For perhaps the first time, I could see that I did not have to fill the space with thoughts and worries. I had the option of just leaving it empty. And in that emptiness arose a fullness I had never been aware of.

When I taught myself to just feel the alarm as sensation alone with no attempt to reason with it, or reason it out, it got much easier. If I just sat with the sensation itself and although it was still uncomfortable, it seemed to be contained. It didn't spiral out of control. I wasn't throwing matches on the fire. *Sometimes you can make something much better just by stopping what was making it worse.*

When we can't sit with our alarm, we never see the messages it may have for us. We don't learn that we can develop a relationship with it, even (dare I say) become friends with it. Picture a pool of clear water with a layer of silt at the bottom. When we muddy the water (our alarm) with the silt (our thoughts), the water becomes cloudy and obscures the message. We need to learn to let the thoughts settle to the bottom so we can see and feel our alarm for exactly what it is without being clouded by our worries.

I love the Michael Singer quote from *The Untethered Soul*, "The mind is a place where the soul goes to hide from the heart." This is exactly why we overthink. Rumination and worry are a way of not feeling that old alarm.

In an effort to do more feeling and less thinking, the phrase from that retreat has become my mantra, and I offer it to you: "Sensation without explanation." (Also, "Just feel it.")

This simple phrase allowed me a space between my feeling of alarm and my relentless need to add a corresponding story. I found that if I just stayed with the alarm sensation, although it was uncomfortable, I could breathe into it and just stay with it. Once I consciously stopped adding worrisome *thinking* to the alarm *feeling*, I gained a sense of control I had never felt before.

One thing that may help as you work with this is to give your mind something productive to do while you stay attuned to sensation. Try this: When you feel alarm, make a conscious intention to inhale the pain. That's right, as much as this sounds counterintuitive, I want you to focus deeply on savouring and relishing the pain as you breathe in.

Personally, I find this practice of embracing and taking the pain in quite empowering. The truth is, I am feeling the pain—so why deny it or run from it? When I deny or run away, I become a victim, and that changes my physiology so my brain actually perceives more pain. When I consciously embrace the pain and breathe into it, there is a congruence—it "makes sense." Instead of trying to escape from the pain by denying it, I am facing it and embracing it, and by breathing it in and embracing it, I take a measure of control and move out of victim mentality. I'm saying "This hurts, but I will deal with it on my terms," and as long as I stay in sensation and don't add thoughts to the pain, I find it much more manageable. Essentially, I am proving to myself that I am strong enough to handle it.

For me, there was a sense when I was a child that I was unable to handle the pain, so I pushed it away or ran from it. I avoided my pain for many years under that same childlike assumption. This may sound melodramatic, but when I acknowledge and embrace the pain by consciously breathing it in, I gain my power back because I am not running away anymore. I face and embrace it as a victorious adult rather than a victimized child who did not have the strength to deal with it back then.

You aren't a child anymore, and seeing you are no longer powerless, you are fully able to embrace the pain of your alarm and face it. Just stay with the pain and the pain alone; do not let your thoughts hijack you. Breathe the pain in and stay in sensation. Stay out of explanation at all costs.

We are constantly encouraged to push pain away in our society. This process of breathing in the pain is adapted from the practice of *tonglen* I learned from the Buddhist nun Pema Chodron. It facilitates facing the pain and even welcoming it by bringing it in with the breath. When we stop running and distracting ourselves from it in the form of compulsive thinking and worrying and, instead, willingly accept and encourage the pain to be present, we can begin to digest and metabolize it. Willingly breathing in the pain and savouring the sensation allows us to feel it and even puts us in control of it. When we feel more in control by willingly breathing in the pain, we don't feel we need to run from it—and because you've got to feel it to heal it, the more you can stay with your alarm, the less scary it becomes.

69
Changing Your Perception of Pain

I'll let you in on a big secret. Are you listening?

It is often our *interpretation* of a feeling as painful that actually causes the pain.

If we can sit with our sensation of alarm and learn to avoid adding worrisome thoughts to it (i.e., anxiety), we can stop the cycle in its tracks. We can stop feeding the feeling.

Psychiatrist Dr. Bessel van der Kolk (mentioned earlier as author of *The Body Keeps the Score*) has said that therapy is not so much about taking away the pain as it is about increasing the patient's ability to tolerate the feeling.

For me at least, the feeling is much easier to tolerate if I avoid attaching scary thinking to it. *Just feel it.* Sensation without explanation.

I recognize that this isn't always the easiest thing to do. But you're getting better at observing what your alarm feels like and where you feel it (or at least at asking the question and looking out for it), and in the same way, this is a practice that will get easier.

There is a Buddhist saying that pain is unavoidable, but suffering is optional. This is exactly how our alarm works—the pain is real but we don't need to let it make us suffer by packing on the fearful stories and thoughts.

To practice this, focus on your alarm (focusing on the heart area if you haven't located your alarm yet) and breathe into it. Feel it but do not add thoughts to it. Remember you have embodied practices to call on (rubbing your palms together, putting a hand on your heart, savouring your breath) to help ground you. When you connect with your body in a positive, loving way, the alarm will dissipate. You defuse negative worries by removing the attention they need to survive, and you diffuse alarm by creating a safe place in your body. You can learn that it is safe to feel again—and that's a good thing because feeling is where life is. In Part 3, I'll show you the practice I've used to connect my mind and body to diminish my alarm and the anxiety that goes with it.

70
What If You Are Pursuing Yourself?

Imagine a child in front of you, upset and holding up their arms to be held. Would you distract yourself from the child's bid for connection by using drugs, alcohol, sex, social media, or online shopping?

When you feel the pain of alarm, that may be exactly what you are doing. Your younger self needs attention and compassion and your help in the here and now to recalibrate a system that wasn't calibrated properly when you were younger.

This might feel like jumping into the deep end, but stay with me. There's a good chance the physical symptoms of your anxiety are really a part of your child self begging for the love, attunement, and attention it missed. The purpose of the background alarm in your system and the foreground alarm energy it creates is not to activate you to chase your tail by putting you into fight or flight against some perceived danger or imagined worry but, rather, to activate you to pursue a connection with your very own self.

Younger self? Inner child? If I had not experienced this firsthand, I would have discounted it as new-age hogwash. All of this talk of the child inside of us is so foreign to what I learned as a medical doctor—but doctors were never able to fix the problem with me. How are they doing with you? There were some MDs and psychiatrists that certainly helped me, but most relied on pharmaceuticals, and I would be shocked if any doctor asked me about my "inner child" or where I felt the alarm in my body. I love the saying, "When you're a hammer, everything looks like a nail." As medical doctors, we are trained to be pharmaceutical hammers, and we are very quick to look for a drug-based solution to any ailment or illness. I am not against using medications—in many cases they are life-saving—but I do feel that too often they are used to simply mask the symptoms.

One of my favourite stories is about one of my fellow comedians who was a heavy smoker. Smoking relaxes the muscle at the top of the stomach, so acid can wash up into the esophagus and cause heartburn. He wanted me to prescribe an acid-blocking medication for his discomfort. "Let me get this straight," I said to him. "You want me to prescribe you a medication so you can keep on damaging yourself by continuing to smoke?" He answered "yes" without missing a beat. Do you see how anxiety could be the same—you might be taking medication to paper over the problem instead of seeing that you have the option of making a behaviour change that would fix it for good?

My best estimate is that about forty million people worldwide take medications for anxiety. For this vast number of people—forty million patients who you can't really say are cured but, rather, are just managing their symptoms—why not try to heal the root of the problem if we have a way to do it? Medication can be extremely helpful and even necessary in some cases, but it shouldn't be the be-all and end-all of treatment. If you go to an M.D. as your primary care physician, there's a good chance you and your inner child will get a medication. Medical doctors want to help, but outside of psychiatrists, physicians get very little training in psychotherapy. Not only are primary care doctors not trained in psychotherapy, but we wouldn't have the time to do it even if we were, so medication is seen by many physicians as the best option. This isn't a value judgment or a condemnation of doctors; it's a statement of fact.

So back to that scenario of an upset child asking for your attention. Picture your own child self in front of you. Imagine Mom or Dad is drunk or raging or is about to hit you or that you don't know when they're coming home or that they're screaming and fighting with each other. Maybe they're incapacitated or addicted or ignoring you and expecting you to look after yourself and your siblings or being ravaged by some physical or mental disease. Or maybe your circumstances were less dramatic. No blowouts, no cataclysmic events, just an apathetic household with very little attachment. Dad was a workaholic and Mom was emotionally numb. That type of environment is alarming for a child, too.

Once you have called to mind a hurtful moment, look at your younger self as they are suffering. Imagine looking into the child's eyes as if they are your own (because they are), and in your imagination pick up the child and cuddle them, feeling their little body relax as they hold on to you. Feel their hand and arms around your neck. Place them so your adult heart is against their little heart. Feel their alarm. It should feel very familiar—but now you've started to break the spell.

It may take a little time to get over the idea that comforting yourself is someone else's job. You never got what you needed, and you're still waiting. Be gentle with yourself.

But know that once you do accept this truth—you are the secure attachment figure your inner child is waiting for—you can provide the love and care for yourself you've been wishing you had all along. You are your inner child's best bet.

71

Creating a Safe Place

All children need to feel safe, and usually that comes from attachment and connection. When children are in alarm, it is often because they are experiencing a lack of secure attachment and connection. The alarm can be acute, like when they lose their parent in the shopping mall, or chronic, when they perceive they are in a constant state of danger or uncertainty.

Even though there were many times when my dad was caring and nurturing toward me as a teenager, I made the unconscious decision to numb myself and become emotionally detached from him as it just hurt too damn much each time I lost him again. He would be quite functional for months at a time, but then I would inevitably lose him to mania or depression or psychosis. After a number of cycles of this, my nervous system decided it was safer to detach.

In short, I began to mistrust love. And since at our essence we *are* love, in mistrusting love, we mistrust ourselves. When that happens, we split into the part that is truly us, which is love and growth, and another part, which is fear and protection. Because the brain's automatic default setting is to ensure survival, I stayed in fear and protection for many years.

If you, too, have become stuck in the alarm-anxiety cycle, it is likely that you also disconnected from vulnerability.

The only antidote to fear is love—and you need to go back there because the place has changed! Meaning, you can create a safe and loving place for yourself that perhaps was not there when you were younger. It is now safe to feel safe.

Creating a safe place allows your mind and body to reconnect and recalibrate your nervous system, correcting the imbalance that was created by your unresolved traumas. The first step is always to connect with yourself. The alarm-anxiety cycle cannot survive inside a compassionate and functional mind-body connection.

Try this: Right now, rub your palms together vigorously for ten to twenty seconds until you create some heat. Then close your eyes and place the heels of your hands over your eye sockets. Mentally focus on the warmth and the feeling of paying kind attention to yourself. Now focus on your breathing and notice how your breath is always there for you. Repeat this as many times as you like. This is a taste of what a constructive mind-body connection looks and feels like. Know that this little practice is almost always available to you. (Except while you are driving. Or boxing.)

72

Alarm Blocks Connection

Here's the main problem with both foreground and background alarm. It keeps you in survival mode, and in survival mode you are not able to truly connect to yourself or others. You need a functional SES to connect to and soothe yourself, and the SES cannot function if the system is in alarm. Another way of saying this is you cannot thrive if your system is stuck in the perceived need to survive.

Imagine you got a call that your son had been injured at school, and then in the elevator on the way to your car to be with him, a coworker started talking to you about her relationship problems. You wouldn't be able to offer any meaningful advice, and you probably wouldn't even remember what she said afterward, right? That's because you'd be in alarm-based survival brain while worried for your son's well-being. The part of you that could be socially engaged and connected with your coworker is simply offline.

We all know this intuitively, but we may not be as aware the same applies to our connection to ourselves. When we perceive a threat, our evolutionary human wiring defaults to assume that threat is physical and external. Cue the alarm! But in the absence of a physical threat, all of this alarm just runs rampant in our system, escalating in a self-reinforcing feedback loop.

I'm sure you can think of examples of people who are totally and obviously disconnected from themselves. The man with a bad temper who keeps lashing out at his family members even though he really hates hurting them, but he can't seem to develop enough awareness of his emotions to stop. The woman who's so self-critical that she totally gets in the way of her own ability to relax and enjoy spending time with her friends, because the whole time she's comparing her body to everyone else in the room or silently berating herself for saying the wrong thing, completely unaware that her self-judgment is blocking her ability to be present in the moment.

We all know these people—and the problem is so clear to us from the outside. Yet they seem unable to see the issue clearly for themselves. Or maybe we *are* those people, and we haven't realized yet that the fundamental issue is disconnection from ourselves.

It may (at least sometimes) be obvious to outside observers when we are disconnected from ourselves, but we can't see it because we're in survival brain. We're not thinking logically. To see clearly we're the ones holding ourselves back, we first need to soothe our alarm with compassionate connection to ourselves.

My biggest issue with cognitive therapy is you have to remain cognitive to implement the strategies you are taught. They typically don't address why and how people spend so much time in survival brain, and what to do about it. This actually sets people up for failure in therapy—a very discouraging experience— since it will feel like they have the strategies but just can't seem to think of them at the very moment they need them the most!

A troubled marriage, an eating disorder, or an addiction is the effect of background alarm in the system. We have to go deeper to fix the cause. (As a side note, much of allopathic medicine in general is attacking symptoms in the hope that the underlying cause will go away or, at the very least, appear as if it is going away.) When I see programs for eating disorders that get into endless meal plans and weigh-ins and regimented eating, I just cringe. They are trying to treat the symptoms as the cause. While they may have some success in the short term adjusting the external situation, if the underlying emotional dysregulation in the body (the background alarm) is not dealt with directly, the eating disorder will sneak its way back in (especially in times of acute stress). Again, I am not attacking doctors; treating symptoms is simply the way we are trained.

Here's a practical example from my career. My patients Rob and Janice were in their mid-fifties, and had been married since their early twenties. You know those people who look great with gray hair? They were both like that.

Janice had had an affair more than twenty years earlier, at a time when Rob was putting in solid hundred-hour weeks in his construction business. At the time, Jan would tell him she felt alone, and Rob would spend more time with her for a little while but would soon go back to just sleeping and working.

Jan told Rob of the affair a year after it occured, and he was shocked but said he understood and then became quite attentive to her. But the resentment built over the two decades after. They had seen counsellors right after Rob was told, but the counsellors focused on resolving the *reasons* for the affair—Rob's compulsion to overwork and Jan's story that she felt alone.

I didn't know how to help them back then. I can be almost certain that both had unresolved trauma and subsequent background alarm that was stored in their bodies, and today I would have treated them completely differently. I would pay much less attention to the reasons in their minds and would, instead, guide them through learning to attend to the feeling of alarm in their bodies.

You see, what many counsellors do (especially back then but still to this day) is to try to fix the situation and develop a cognitive plan. Rob would commit to working less, and Jan would be shown how to develop her own hobbies so she wasn't so dependent on Rob. This is classic for the time, trying to fix the symptoms, hoping the disease would fade away. It appeared on the surface that Rob and Jan were disconnected from each other, when the real underlying issue was that each of them was disconnected from themselves. I've come to know unequivocally there is little point in "fixing" a couple's relationship to each other when they are cut off from connection within themselves.

Now, if I see a couple struggling to stay together after an affair or break in the relationship, there is little point at dissecting the reasons for the affair or event until I have been able to regulate each partner in their bodies. Both are in alarm and as such have little access to the parts of themselves that could integrate any potential academic solutions.

Until the body is regulated, little will be learned by the mind. When stressed, we follow our old grooves in the snow and regress into our patterns and our wounding. But once we treat the alarm, the anxious thoughts disappear or lose all of their power because the mind is no longer in survival mode and can rationally see the worries for the simple distractions they are.

We need to focus on and calm the alarm state of the body first, creating the necessary conditions for emotional healing by reengaging our connection with ourselves—and then and only then go after the external reasons that could be resolved cognitively.

* * *

If the book up to this point has done its job, it has shown you what you call anxiety has more to do with a sense of alarm in the body than with the thoughts of the mind. Of course, the mind still plays a significant supporting role, but "the body keeps the score"—it never forgets our old wounds and, courtesy of the amygdala, reacts instantly to even the slightest whiff of familiar threat with a well-rehearsed program of alarm that stays stored in the body, always at the ready to "protect" us. But in its childlike effort to protect us, it causes even more pain. With every activation, the alarm becomes more ingrained and powerful—and even worse, by flipping us into a survival-focused state, it locks us out of the connection to ourselves that we need to release the alarm and blocks us from connection with others that could be deeply healing.

When our minds are overwhelmed in childhood, our bodies take on the energy that overflows the mind, and that energy is stored in our bodies as background alarm. When one of my patients says "I'm feeling anxious," I encourage them to instead say, "I'm feeling alarmed," as that is a much truer statement. If you have a friend and they are trying to understand what you are going through, I urge you to use the term "alarm" instead of "anxiety." When you say, "I feel anxious," many people have no idea what you are talking about, but if you say "I feel alarmed," *everyone* can relate to that feeling.

So many of us became alarmed as children in response to a situation or event that was traumatizing and out of our control, especially if that situation or event would repeat itself. Our fight-or-flight nervous system naturally kicked in to protect us and to energize us in an effort to resolve the situation. If that alarming situation was then addressed and resolved by a loving parent or caregiver, our system could stand down and we could move into parasympathetic rest-and-digest phase. If the situation could not be resolved and a competent parent was not available, that fight-or-flight response would stay chronically active and our overwhelmed system would accumulate even more background alarm. Without a secure attachment figure to help us calm our fight-or-flight reaction and allow us to process our experiences in a healthy way, our system is like a one-way valve where more alarm can enter but none can leave.

Cells that fire together wire together in a phenomenon called potentiation. If I told you to forget how to ride a bike, could you do it? In the same way, you cannot "forget" how to ramp up your alarm. The background alarm stored from unresolved trauma and the foreground fight-or-flight activation become linked together in a unified program that activates easily like a well-oiled machine. Again, to borrow that saying by Joe Dispenza, DC, "The body has learned to do it better than the mind."

These familiar habits can be unlearned, but it takes practice. There's an engineer who designed a bike that when you turn the handlebars left, the front wheel goes right. It's pretty funny watching people trying to ride this bike. Not many of them get farther than two feet before falling off. The engineer himself took many months to retrain his implicit program so he could ride the bike he designed. But that's how it is when we're working to retrain our alarm.

I could describe to you in words how to ride the backwards bike. You could study the instructions in your mind for weeks, but that intellectual knowledge would only provide you with a fraction of the benefit of actually physically getting on the backwards bike.

Please know that just reading this book without trying any of what it recommends is about as effective as yelling "Stop!" when your alarm clock goes off in the morning. (Although you probably still get my point, technology has to some extent stolen this analogy from me because these days that actually does work. Thanks, Siri.)

Just as you can't talk your way out of a problem that requires action, reading about a body-based approach will only get you so far.

You won't be able to learn your new feeling-based program and reprogram your alarm until you actually get on the bike and ride it. You must say goodbye to your mother tongue, the mind's language of thinking, and become fluent in the body's language of feeling. Learning how you become fluent in how you feel is critical for the awareness of self you will need to heal from alarm and anxiety. In a way, it's like learning a language you have always known but have forgotten, kind of like learning the alphabet all over again.

So if you're ready, let's relearn our ABCs.

PART 3

AWARENESS OF SELF

73
Survival Versus Connection

We humans have two main drives: the drive to physically survive and the drive to emotionally connect. If you grow up in secure attachment, you learn life is about connection. If you do not grow up in a secure, attached environment, you learn life is about survival.

This is why childhood is such a critical age to feel cared for, loved, and supported. If you experience trauma that is too much for you to bear, a metaphorical crack forms in the hull of your metaphorical boat. Then, like the groove in the snow, that crack forms a preferential pathway for further pain.

If the crack isn't patched over with safety, secure attachment, and love during childhood, over time it becomes a full-blown hole as the hull's integrity weakens further. That is, as more trauma spills in through the crack, the crack gets bigger. This is what happened with me, and I imagine probably also with you. Once that area of weakness or damage forms, it becomes a preferential path and a reservoir for pain to accumulate—and as the pain accumulates, it blazes a deeper trail that makes it easier for more pain to follow.

The final section of this book will show you how to address and heal the background alarm stored in your body as a result of old unresolved emotional trauma.

Remember that you may be carrying unresolved trauma from your parents and grandparents. Scientists are beginning to understand (for example, through studying the descendants of Holocaust survivors) how trauma is passed down through the generations, not just through the behaviour children learn from their parents but also through our biology as the trauma is embedded in noncoding genetic material that influences how genes are expressed. (When you hear that health outcomes rely on both genes and environment, the *environment* doesn't refer only to lifestyle factors. If you have a genetic predisposition to cancer or heart disease, genomic factors along with lifestyle factors play a part in whether you actually develop that condition or not.)

This is one reason alarm can be seen in people who did not experience significant trauma themselves as children, and this might explain why some of my patients who have carried significant alarm can't point to any specific overwhelm from their childhood. (My friend and colleague Mark Wolynn has written a groundbreaking book about this called *It Didn't Start With You*, which I highly recommend reading, especially if your parents or grandparents had very stressful lives.)

As we embark on the last phase of our journey together, revisit the alarm you located in your body—where it lives and what it looks like. (And remember, if you're not sure yet, just focus on the space around your heart. When alarm has been with you for a long time, it blends into the furniture until one day you see it for what it is.)

Remember that there is no quick fix, no hack that is going to suddenly make you worry-free. Don't forget how long it took me to see my thoughts as brain droppings. Even after all I'd been through, I needed that experience by the river to see that I had the option of not thinking. Until then, I was convinced that I was my thoughts and my thoughts were me.

I love the quotes "The mind is a wonderful servant but a terrible master" and "There are no prison walls stronger than the ones you cannot see." For many years, I could not see I was in a prison of my own mind. I was chained to being both servant and master, never seeing that I had a choice to drop the chains by simply becoming the dispassionate observer of both.

Awareness was seeing I had a choice to *see* my thoughts and not *be* my thoughts, and that was the beginning of my liberation. By that river I learned that I didn't have to attach a thought to every feeling. I had spent so long in the dark, expecting someone else to show me the light when the light had been within me the entire time.

74
ABCDE

There's a process I developed and use every day to help me heal from the alarm-anxiety cycle. It follows the first five letters of the alphabet in a cycle (although the first three are the most important).

Awareness
Body
Connection
Discipline
Ego

(You'll see that a couple of them encompass more than one word with the same letter, but use what's up above as a simple and quick way to remember the process.)

First comes **awareness and acceptance**. By awareness I mean *conscious awareness* as discussed in the first part of the book. When you are aware of being aware, you embrace and become fully familiar with how the pain manifests in you. If you don't see how anxiety and alarm take you over, you can't change them, and you keep unconsciously biting your own tail in an effort to feel better. Seeing that you are in a state of alarm is the first step.

Body and breath is the next step. Thinking, however well-intended and "positive," is only keeping you in your head, and your attention needs to be grounded in your body. When you can find a safe place in your body, your anxious thoughts lose power because the thoughts' sole purpose was to distract you from your body. The key here is to recognize when you are in anxiety and alarm and make a firm intention to move into sensation and away from thought.

Next comes **connection and compassion**. Once you've opened the door for your SES to come in and soothe you, you can connect with yourself from a place of compassion. This is where you neutralize your old wounds by being the parent for yourself that you wish you'd had. In this section, you'll learn a lot more about how to get past the blocks that can hold you back from relating to yourself with connection and compassion. Imagine you have a box and inside it are both love and fear. For a long time, fear has squeezed the love out of your box. It's time to let the love squeeze the fear out instead.

Discipline is next on the list. It's like the old joke goes: A man is lost looking for the theatre, so asks a woman on the street, "How do you get to Carnegie Hall?" She replies, "Practice, practice, practice." You've lived in the groove and false belief that your thoughts have been keeping you safe for a very long time. By overthinking, you've been digging yourself deeper into a hole while thinking you are digging yourself out. Doing it another way—staying out of future worries and staying in the moment, in your body—is going to take practice.

Lastly (for now), **ego**. This is the one-trick pony (or perhaps a better metaphor is one-trick dragon) that makes you avoid vulnerability. It never forgets and will shy away from anything that has ever caused you pain. While that is functional and adaptive in making you never touch a hot stove again, if you avoid love out of the perception that love hurts you, love is squeezed out of your box and fear jumps in to steadily fill the space left behind.

Even for those of us who don't have old pain to heal and trauma to process, there's something to be said for reconnecting with the child self. On that note, let's take our ABCDEs one by one.

75
Awareness Gives Choice

You can't change something you can't (or your ego refuses to) see. Before you can change it, you need to see it—and feel it.

Have you found your alarm—the part of you that lights up when you feel anxious? This is the feeling I want you to become acutely aware of. This is the source of your pain.

One of my patients, Kelly, had abandonment issues in her childhood. In the present, she was having intrusive thoughts about Paul, her devoted husband of twelve years. Kelly had convinced herself that Paul was preparing to leave her. It's important to know that Paul had never given Kelly any rational reason to think he would leave. When he would go off to work, she would have intrusive thoughts about him not coming back. She would even look through the house, searching for a suitcase Paul might have packed to prepare for a quick exit.

My work with Kelly focused on making her aware that her anxiety had nothing to do with Paul. The real issue was old unresolved alarm in her system from when she was ten years old. One day her father left for work and never came back. He'd been killed in an industrial accident.

Kelly had done hours and hours of cognitive therapy trying to minimize her intrusive thoughts, which helped for a time. But the abandonment worries always came back, often more intense than before.

Kelly and I went through a similar exercise to the one I laid out for you in the last section. Under my guidance, she imagined Paul leaving for work and then zeroed in on where and how she was experiencing alarm in her body. She found it in her upper abdomen, where it showed up as a sense of pressure that seemed to radiate up into her chest and throat. Over time, she was able to describe it in great detail. It was a hollow, black, empty, foggy, diffuse hourglass shape that squeezed in the middle over her heart, expanding above and below.

Once upon a time, my friends and I had a regular poker night. In poker, there is something called a *tell*, a mannerism or habit that gives away signals about whether a player had a strong hand or was bluffing. For example, my friend Tom would always look at his cards over and over when he had a strong hand. If he was bluffing, he would barely look at them at all. These were his tells. Once I figured this out, I rarely lost big hands to him.

Like poker players learning to read each other's tells, we can look out for our own tells once we know what they are. In Kelly's case, when she would catch herself looking around the house for a suitcase or when she'd find herself off in her head somewhere spinning a story about why Paul was leaving her, these were the tells. Once she noticed them, she could remind herself that the worry was not the problem (and, in fact, it was making the problem worse). Instead of letting the worries spiral, she could get in touch with her alarm and get grounded in her body.

Once Kelly became familiar with her alarm and knew what to look—or, rather, feel for—she noticed it more and more. She became extremely skilled at localizing her alarm and learning to recognize it when it came up. She described it as a messenger telling her to get out of her head and into her body. It became like a kind of early warning system for her.

My hope for you is that you'll learn to see your own tells and be able to use that information to address the real problem: the alarm in your body.

What are your most common intrusive thoughts? (For the sake of getting our definitions straight, let's set out exactly what intrusive thoughts are. In a popular context, this phrase may have the connotation that the thoughts are extremely disturbing or violent, but for our purposes, an intrusive thought is simply any unwelcome thought that takes over your attention and that you'd rather not be having but it seems you can't help it.) What are the paths of worry you most commonly find yourself going down?

Once you identify a worrisome thought, such as "I'm scared my husband will leave me," and name it as an intrusive thought, you welcome it into your curiosity, and in the light of that objective awareness, the thought loses much of its emotional power. You've moved from survival brain into rational brain, and instead of going off down the path with the thought, you can direct your energy into the present moment sensation of your body.

We worriers often make an automatic right turn into worry when we feel alarmed, but awareness allows us to see there is another option: to turn left and go into the body. This may feel unnatural at first, like steering the bike to the left when you actually want it to turn right—but with practice, your new way of doing things will start to feel more natural. Remember that you've automatically and unconsciously trained yourself to overthink, and so, when you try to do the opposite, you may "lose your balance" a few times and find yourself right back in your thoughts. Keep practicing, and soon turning left will be your new habit. Your automatic, unconscious reaction to worry will be replaced by a willful, conscious choice to redirect your energy from the future-based worries of the thinking mind into the present moment of the feeling body.

It's natural to wonder why you would want to move deeper into the painful sensation of your alarm. Remember that your alarm is your younger self crying for your attention. The more you connect with your alarm, the more you connect with the part of you that needs to heal.

Also remember that you are in charge of creating a safe place for your alarmed younger self, and you have the (cognitive, emotional, developmental) resources to do that now. You are no longer defenceless. As you get better at pulling your intrusive thoughts out of the dark and into the light of awareness, you take the critical first step in healing from chronic worry.

76
Body and Breath Break the Cycle

There's an old joke about a man who constantly hits himself with a hammer. When he's asked why, he says he keeps doing it because it feels so good whenever he stops.

This is exactly how worries work. Remember the sense of relief I'd feel as a child when I got myself all worked up envisioning horror stories each time my mum was late coming home from work? It felt so good each time those stories in my head turned out not to be true!

But just because there's sometimes a payoff (in the form of feel-good chemicals flooding our brains) when worries turn out not to be true, does not mean it's a good idea to pour our energy into worrying. Remember, worrying actually contributes to the feedback loop of chronic alarm. By worrying, we are making the problem worse.

So what's the solution? I'm so glad you asked!

Once you become aware of your tells that you're heading into alarm, you can change your focus from the thoughts in your mind to the sensation in your body. This move away from hypervigilant thinking may go against every coping strategy you learned in childhood, and your ego may get all fired up trying to suck you back into your worries, but I promise you can do this—and it may even save your life. I know it saved mine.

One way to begin to step away from the worries of your mind and into the stillness of your body is to intentionally focus your attention on the sensation of your breathing. We might think of the breath as neutral or "just there" without any particular quality, but you really can go into quite a bit of detail if you tune in. At any given moment, your breath has a sound, a scent, a temperature, and a speed. How deep is your breath? What parts of your lungs is it touching? What other parts of your body do you feel moving? There's so much to notice when it comes to our breath.

What's interesting is that hypervigilance often gives us a fine attention to detail. Remember how I read the tone of my father's voice and all the other nuances I hoped could give me clues about his mental state? We worriers are actually quite good at noticing the minute details of things like our breath—all we have to do is direct our attention there. Finally, a productive use of this tendency to overanalyze!

Note that (especially at first) the sneaky ego tries to swoop back in. Make sure you are staying with the sensation and not inventing stories about it. Noticing a slight smoky smell in the air is being with sensation. If you find yourself thinking, "Is there a forest fire somewhere?" you've drifted back into your thoughts, and it's time to reorient yourself in sensation. *Just feel it.*

Here's how this might look for me. I'll become aware that I've been taken over by some worry, like "I wonder if I might have prostate cancer?" Once I become aware of that, I almost always find the feeling of alarm is there in my solar plexus as well. I will use that point of awareness and say to myself, "This worry about cancer is an intrusive thought." Then I'll take a second to just *stop* and acknowledge that I'm aware of the anxious thoughts and/or the alarm in my body and look at both the thinking in my mind and the feeling in my body with curiosity.

When I adopt an attitude of curiosity, it allows me a non-emotional aware-ness. The questions might look like: "Hmmm, I wonder why I need to think a painful thought right now?" or "Hmmm, there's my old familiar feeling of alarm. I wonder why that's there?" The attitude of curiosity gives me a degree of separation from the emotion because it is grounded in the rational mind, not the survival brain. In this grounded space, I can set an intention to move into my body and breath.

When you make a firm intention to direct your attention specifically into the sensation of your body, you remove the energy and attention that were previously fueling your worries. This is the moment when you separate the thoughts of the mind from the alarm in the body. With your intention, you rechannel the destructive energy of anxious thinking into the constructive en-ergy of present-moment sensation. When you are in conscious control of your attention, you can create, perhaps for the first time, a safe (or at least neutral) place in the sensation of your body.

You can't stop thinking. It's just what the mind does. But you can starve it of its energy source—and this is the main goal of the letter B. Redirect the energy and the thoughts have less ability to aggravate your alarm.

When our worries trap us in the future, we have no grounding or secure place to do anything else but more worrying. When we stop and create a space between feeling and thought that connects us to the present, we have solid ground to stand on—and with that solid ground, we can go from a fear-based belief system (governed by worry and focused on the future) to a love-based belief system (based in compassionate connection to ourselves).

Your adult self is exhausted by the chronic need to think and distract. Your coping strategy of worry has turned from an asset into a liability. But by becoming grounded in your body and breath, you can begin to overwrite the childhood programs that are now creating much more pain than they are relieving. You can stop hitting yourself with the hammer of your worries.

Remember that just because something sounds simple does not mean it is easy. This takes practice.

But don't worry, Carnegie Hall is just around the corner.

77
Your Thoughts Are Your Sirens

Before we move on from the letter B, I want to tell you a related story from Greek mythology: that of Odysseus and the Sirens. On their long journey by sea (the Odyssey), Odysseus's crew hears beautiful voices singing to them. They've been warned about these singers in advance—so powerfully beautiful is the Sirens' song that it's enticed many a ship to steer onto the rocks. So as they prepare to approach this area, Odysseus orders his crew to plug their ears with beeswax so they cannot hear the song. He is so curious to hear the song that he leaves his own ears open, but straps himself to the mast of the ship with strict orders to his men not to release him under any circumstances. As the ship passes close to the Sirens, Odysseus hears the song and sees maidens of indescribable beauty beckoning to him. He struggles so hard to get out of his restraints that the ropes cut and tear his skin. Meanwhile, for the crew members who cannot hear the song, the Sirens appear as grotesque monsters.

In this scenario, your thoughts are the Sirens. They seductively promise to be the answer to your fears, but they hold nothing but pain. Awareness and seeing your thoughts for what they are—and that you have a choice not to believe everything you think—is like plugging your ears to the Sirens' song. Only once you do that, can you keep rowing past their island and get into the sensation of your body, where you have the chance to heal.

You must be steadfast in your intention and commitment not to fall prey to the siren song of your worries (more on this when we get to the letter D). When you get away from the rocks and reach the sanctuary of your body, you break the spell. You may need to strap yourself to the mast—and this is why setting an intention is a pivotal step—but once you learn to resist the seduction of your worries, you can undertake the next hero's journey: the letter C, developing a compassionate connection to yourself.

78
Connection and Compassion Push Out the Fear

Developing a compassionate connection with myself has been the cornerstone of my recovery from chronic alarm and its accompanying compulsive worry. This is my secret weapon, and the part of healing from anxiety and alarm that virtually nobody addresses.

The reason I needed to dump all that trauma into my solar plexus when I was younger is precisely because I did not have a secure attachment that could support me in neutralizing it. I had to teach myself how to be the security now that I needed back then.

When I am truly connected with myself, I do not need to conjure up a convoluted rollercoaster of worrisome twists and turns to distract me from the pain of alarm. I can bring awareness and compassion to the alarm at its source. I can go right to the heart—or, in my case, to the solar plexus—of it.

Go ahead and try it for yourself. Place your hand on your chest or over the site of your alarm if you have found it. Form an intention to connect with yourself. As you breathe in and out, focus on the stillness and sensation of your body. Savour the air as it comes in and out of your nostrils and chest. Stay focused on your sensation of your hand against your chest, and focus deeply on the sensation of your chest rising and falling with your breath. As you stay with the sensation of your breath and body, close your eyes and stay with these sensations for five slow deep breaths.

As you breathe in, imagine the breath traveling right into the place of your alarm. Summon as much compassion and love for yourself as you possibly can, knowing that the alarm you feel in your chest is your younger self that would have given anything to feel this safe, connected attention from one of your parents. Stay keenly aware of the sensation of alarm in your body, sending it breath and love and holding your alarmed younger self in loving presence.

What I wouldn't give to be able to collapse time and show my med student self a glimpse of future me. He'd probably think he was hallucinating because there's *no way* Dr. Russell Kennedy is ever going to be talking about meditation and breathwork—*especially* not as being more effective than pharmaceuticals and talk therapy. He might even say, "Don't listen to that guy, no matter what you do! He's a quack!"

But if I know one thing, it's that developing a compassionate connection to myself has allowed me to heal my alarm at its source and has been infinitely more effective than the traditional treatments I received in mainstream Western medicine.

Physician, heal thyself.

Now, this is not to say that you may not need some additional help at points in your healing journey. The approaches described in this book can work hand in hand with Western medicine, and doctors these days (at least in some cases) are more open-minded than they were thirty years ago about their solution not being the only solution. But if you can master the ABCs as given here, it will vastly improve your quality of life, either on their own or in conjunction with other treatments.

Reintroducing a loving relationship with yourself must be done in manageable increments so you can gradually overcome your ego's resistance. If you spook the ego by trying to say "I love myself" too early and go straight from fear into love, you run the risk of activating the very same alarm that blocked you from trusting love in the first place. Be patient and compassionate with yourself as you learn to allow love in again.

It's like if you've always been in abusive relationships, and finally you learn to understand your patterns and end your repetition compulsion. Even once you choose a partner who is going to treat you well, it's still going to take you a little longer to trust them, whereas someone whose relationships have always been healthy and peaceful can trust from the beginning, since their experiences haven't shown them any reason not to.

Time and patience will help as you stay committed to your intention of treating yourself with compassion. But later in this section, you'll also learn some tools for overcoming the ego's resistance. The ego doesn't keep us down on purpose; it's often just very guarded against positive emotion. It's kept you safe by keeping you in a narrow range of emotion for many years. Just like my father once told me I should probably set my sights lower than medical school because he didn't want me to experience disappointment and have my confidence crushed, my ego doesn't want me to experience love only to lose it again.

79

Discipline Versus Distraction

You've been seduced by the siren song of your worries for a long time, and this distraction provides a sense of relief—but it's very short-term. As you continue to practice your ABCs, distraction will continue to call to you and there will be a compulsion to reach for the addiction of worry, especially at first. As much as the protective dragon of your ego is going to try to convince you that thinking is the answer, it's a trap. You must stay in sensation.

As you learn to be your own self-healer, it may feel as uncomfortable as Odysseus resisting the Sirens. You may want to rip off the ties holding you and rush to be with your worries. But as you sail past the Island of the Sirens and resist the call of your worries—once, then again, then many more times—you will feel a liberation unlike any you ever have felt before.

Remember that in some ways worry operates like an addiction, rewarding you with dopamine each time you do it. Just as smokers know they shouldn't smoke but the urge is too great, worrying is something you know you shouldn't do but you just can't help yourself—but people *do* stop smoking, just as you will stop being seduced by your worries. You will teach yourself to stay present with yourself in compassionate connection in your body versus abandoning yourself to the self-abuse of worry up in your mind.

Even though the pain of alarm will still be present, once you learn this, you've stopped throwing matches on the fire. So even though you still feel pain, for the first time, it is pain you have some control over.

I can't tell you how many times (especially when learning the ABCs) I've gone into awareness of my tells and triggers and moved into my body and breath, only to be yanked back into anxiety and alarm. I cannot tell you how many times I thought I grounded myself in my body with sensation, touch, the smell of an essential oil and a focus on my breath, only to find myself right back into anxious thoughts of my mind and alarm in my body. The same goes after I have moved into compassionate connection with myself, only to "wake up" and find myself right back in anxiety and alarm. The healing process is not linear.

Especially early on, the Ego Dragon is relentlessly going to try to pull you back into the place it feels most in control—frozen in immobility, trapped in your worries and alarm.

There is a process that neuroscientists refer to as neuroplasticity. This is the brain's ability to make new pathways. Even though there are "critical periods" for certain types of brain development, the brain also has a phenomenal ability to learn and develop throughout our lifespan, given the right conditions. Neuroplasticity has its work cut out for itself when there is a previous pattern (or groove) to overwrite, but I am living proof of someone with severe anxiety that has started with a deep groove of protection that has used the ABCs process and created a deeper groove for growth.

This took trial and error, and early on I didn't feel a great deal of progress, but I intuitively knew I was definitely on the right track. As I cultivated a deep commitment to awareness and perhaps an even deeper commitment to being kind and connected to myself, the process progressed and I "broke through" to a new way of thinking and being.

In the time I've been using the ABC process (a few years now), there are two parts that seem to be the hardest: (1) developing awareness of the anxiety and alarm cues that allow me to initiate the process in the first place and (2) staying with the process.

When I worked with patients who were trying to quit smoking or drinking, many times they would describe finding themselves with a cigarette or a drink in their hand, not really knowing how it got there—the habit was so strong that it didn't take a conscious decision and overrode what their rational mind wanted to do. The human program to fall into addictions as a way to distract from our pain is an automatic and unconscious one. Worrying is like this too—we suddenly find ourselves back in it without any idea how we got there.

This only gets worse when your mind is impaired by the alarm in your body. I still sometimes spend some time in anxiety and alarm before I notice what's happened. But with practice, the time it takes me to notice has decreased.

As you train yourself to recognize your signature worries and state of alarm, you'll get better at bringing awareness and dodging your ego's efforts to sabotage you. And for this, you need discipline.

One way you can start practicing awareness to make it a habit is to just pause a few times a day and ask yourself with loving compassion, "Where are you right now?" Are you in your body, feeling life, being connected and open? Or are you in your head? Are you here in the present moment, or are you off somewhere in the future worry? Then, with intention, put a hand over where your alarm usually is and check in with yourself.

I go through a version of the ABCs multiple times a day, and it takes me only two to three minutes each time. I close my eyes, check into my physical connection to myself with a hand on my chest, savour a few breaths as my hand rises and falls, and focus on something I like about myself—like my sense of humour, or my generous spirit, or my intuitive gifts. Sometimes I will bring up a mental image of my wife or my daughter or one of my grandkids, or if I'm at home I'll go over to one of my dogs and give them a cuddle and a few kisses on the snout. I'll end by thanking myself for taking the time to take care of my own needs, and I'll move back into my day.

The discipline of doing the process, especially when I am not worrying or in alarm, is invaluable. The better you get at the ABCs during good times and bad, the more it will become a part of you and the better it will serve you.

With discipline I found a place where I felt the alarm in one part of my body and my presence in another *at the same time,* and it didn't take long to create that experience. If this seems like too much trouble, consider that spending time practicing your ABCs is infinitely better than spending time practicing your worries, which is what you're probably doing now if you've turned to this book for help.

You may have noted that nowhere in the ABCs do I go after the worries directly. That's because it's a losing battle. Remember, you can't overcome thinking with more thinking. I repeat for emphasis: you cannot beat thoughts on their own turf! Trying to disprove or mentally argue with your worries is like trying to reason with the Sirens. If the temptation is strong to examine your worries (and most likely go off down a path to other worrisome scenarios), remember that you have a simple question to use as a tool: "Am I safe in this moment?"

80
Let's Practice Our ABCs

Awareness is the start of taking your life back. Training yourself to be aware of your mind and body from moment to moment gives you tremendous power. And all it takes is developing a ritual of sorts, in which you ask yourself "Where am I right now?" multiple times a day.

1. If you find yourself feeling grounded and your breath is slow and deep, continue on with an intention to move deeper into your body, putting your hand on your chest, closing your eyes, and focusing deeply on sensation.

2. If you find yourself in a worry or rumination, simply stop and make a conscious intention to move into your body and breath and, therefore, away from your thoughts. Close your eyes (unless you are driving), put your hand on your chest, and move fully into breath and sensation. (We don't want the ABCs to be Awareness, Breath, Collision.)

3. If you find yourself in alarm, put your hand over the alarm and breathe into it. Close your eyes and, as you focus on the sensations of your breath and your hand rising and falling, create a place where you can focus on a pleasant (or at least neutral) sensation. Allow the sensation of alarm to be present, but focus your attention on savouring your breath and the pleasant and supportive feeling of your hand over your alarm.

4. Once you've grounded yourself in your body, move into a state of compassionate connection by bringing to mind something you like about yourself (or a person or place or pet that brings you joy) and staying with the emotion of that. Generally, the more anxious thoughts you have and/or the more alarm you feel, the longer you can stay in B and C. You can often tell you need to go back and start the ABCs over again if you are still focused on the original thoughts. The goal is to break the destructive alarm-anxiety cycle and start reprogramming a new, constructive path that connects you to your true, innocent self. The more

connection you can create to your innocence, the more you interrupt the need for the Ego Dragon's "protection" of worry and alarm.

Doing this several times a day retrains your nervous system to move into a parasympathetic, relaxed state. It also gives you something constructive to do with your mind and keeps you away from the ego's destructive habit of compulsively worrying in a futile effort to keep you safe.

CHEAT SHEET: THE ABC PROCESS IN A NUTSHELL

I know there is a lot in this book. What you really need to know is to follow this process:

(A) Develop intentional **A**wareness of your "tells." Train yourself to call out the repetitive scary thoughts of your mind and the familiar feelings of alarm in your body.

(B) When you sense worries or alarm, immediately move your attention into your **B**ody and **B**reath (no more thinking!). Put your hand over your alarm and focus on making a connection with that *alarm sensation.*

(C) In grounded present moment sensation in your body, make the specific *intention* to practice acceptance, **C**ompassionate **C**onnection, and love towards yourself.

The more you practice this ABC process—becoming aware of awareness, breathing into your body, changing your focus from thinking to sensation, and compassionately connecting to yourself—the more you will start creating a more positive environment where your true self can emerge. Over time, you'll spend more time embodying your authentic self, and it will happen less often that your nervous system unwittingly slides back into anxiety and alarm like the smoker who's trying to quit yet finds himself with a cigarette in his hand.

The ego is tenacious and it will do everything in its power to undermine the ABCs. The best way to deal with this masterful saboteur is to develop a ritual that you do the same way every time, so when you do spot the ego's tricks you can go right into the ABCs.

Just a word of caution: If you find that your alarm is especially strong and that you are still getting sucked into the endless loop of triggers and worries, please call on a therapist who knows how to deal with trauma and alarm stored in the body. You should not be afraid to try the ABCs—in and of themselves, they'll be healing—but there is no harm in enlisting additional help while you're learning to untangle your well-worn patterns.

81
Ego Awareness

E is for ego.

Remember the image of the dragon sitting atop a treasure chest? I interpret this image from Scandinavian folklore to represent the ego, evoking a fiery sensation of protective alarm in our bodies. The treasure inside is our innocence, our authentic love for ourselves. And you have to win over the dragon to access the treasure.

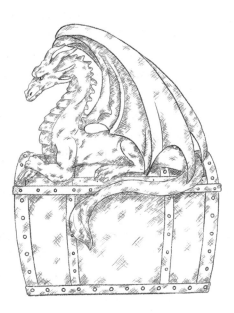

By winning the dragon's favour, we can turn it into an agent of growth and love—just as fierce in love as it once was in protection.

Not to put too fine a point on it, but the ego *is* our love for ourselves, and it is fierce. This is why it has fought so hard to protect us.

The ego's job is to keep you alive no matter what. And the sad truth is that on some level, the ego is "comfortable" with the alarm and anxiety in your system because you haven't died yet—and it's taking the credit for that. If the ego creates worry that hurts you but keeps you from moving into new territory that might harm you, it's done its job.

Pain is a prerequisite for growth, so by shielding you from getting hurt, the ego is also shielding you from growth—and at the same time, the ego is causing you an enormous amount of pain under the guise of protecting you.

So if pain, in general, leads to growth, why doesn't this pain inflicted by the ego lead to growth? Well, if you're reading this book, it has. I know without a doubt you've been strong enough, many times in your life, to "feel the fear and do it anyway" (to borrow a phrase from Susan Jeffers, PhD, who wrote a book by that title). By the fact that you're here, I know you've experienced enough growth to know you want to find a solution for your anxiety.

But since the pain caused by the ego is mostly an incarnation of our inner child's wounding, this pain causes us to regress back to the time the pain occurred—and then since we are not feeling the pain from the awareness of an adult with ample emotional resources, we react in an unaware, childlike way. The purpose of this book is to guide you to meet your pain as a resourced adult, so you can climb out of the hole instead of falling back on the childlike response of digging yourself deeper.

This may sound melodramatic, but I would like to propose that the most heroic journey you can take is gaining your innocence back by seeing that innocence never left; it just got trapped inside that protective chest, which is being guarded by your Ego Dragon. The chest acts as a protective structure, shielding you from painful experience but, at the same time, preventing you from expanding beyond it.

Goldfish secrete a substance that limits their growth to prevent them from growing too large for their pond or bowl. In the same way, your protective strategies minimized the pain you felt in childhood but at the cost of keeping you small and separate from the fullness of your authentic self. Your innocence and your authentic self are locked inside that chest made up of all the mechanisms that sheltered you from both the bad and the good, and they're blocking your access to the love in you.

For example, friendships thrive on trust and vulnerability—qualities you had as a child that may have been stamped out of you by traumatic experience. Perhaps now you have a strong desire for deeper friendships, but you can't seem to let anyone get close to you and really get to know you.

You're not defective. You have the same human capacity for trust and vulnerability as everyone else. It's just locked away in the chest.

And it's not your fate to stay cut off from social connection this way. You have the ability to slay your Ego Dragon (or rather, make friends with your dragon, which is honestly an even more badass thing to do). You can open that chest and get at the glittering riches inside.

Patients often say to me, "I don't know who I am anymore." Disowning their wants and needs and the dreams of their authentic and innocent heart—because someone hurt them or didn't have the capacity to care for them or just wasn't paying attention—has left them, so many years later, not knowing how to get past their defense mechanisms and tune in to those authentic wants and needs and dreams again.

Remember, all anxiety is separation anxiety and all alarm is separation alarm. By allowing the dragon to keep sitting on top of the chest, you've unknowingly been reinforcing its reason to guard the chest so tightly. First, your alarm came from separation from a caregiver—but what's feeding your alarm now is separation from yourself.

So, come on. Let's make friends with that dragon, shall we?

82
Ego and the Abuse of Power

Your ego is supposed to protect you, but in many ways it is like leaving a frightened child in charge of your safety. Indeed, part of you still believes you are back in your childhood pain, and that dragon will fight to the death to protect you. Ego will act automatically and unconsciously to protect you at any sign of threat. Oftentimes, that threat is not even real. Much like a fire-breathing dragon, it is something we created in our own imaginations.

Remember my story of having my alarm triggered at a concert when I heard a trumpet? When my protective ego took over, I lost the rational ability to see I was perfectly safe. Part of me was transported back to a time where hearing a trumpet was a sign that I was trapped in a situation where I felt fearful and powerless. I turned into an angry teenager in an instant. The anger took me over, and I *was* it.

The reason I gave myself for wanting to leave was that the music was too loud and there were too many people. And that over-reaction was evidence of the immense power of the protective ego—I convinced myself of something that just wasn't true.

Luckily, I was able to get curious about my reaction and come to understand it after the fact. The trumpet still triggers me to this day (especially if the trumpet player is not so skilled). But now I'm fully aware of what's happening. I can *see* it so I don't have to *be* it—and not only that, but my Ego Dragon and I can even laugh about it … sometimes.

Again, it's not about defeating the Ego Dragon because the dragon cannot be defeated. You must learn, young Jedi, that the more you fight with the dragon, the more it feeds your alarm, which drives you deeper into an age regression. In many ways, the ego is your younger self, for the amygdala has frozen you there. But now, when I notice the pull to be dragged into the past, I use my ABCs to keep me firmly rooted in the present moment.

When I see the pull to be dragged into the past, I use the ABCs to ground me in present moment awareness and then I am able to resist my ego's urge to regress me back into an old childhood place of survival.

Our ego, like our amygdala, will reject anything it perceives has ever hurt us. But what if the thing we perceive as hurting us is actually part of us? I can avoid trumpets, but I can't avoid parts of myself.

As you already know, I was a sensitive child. Up until about eight years old, I would cry openly if I was hurt. But according to cultural norms of masculinity, if a boy is still crying at age eight, it's gone on about four years too long. So I rejected that part of myself that cried. I stopped crying when I was hurt because I correctly perceived that crying was going to create even more pain as I got teased for it.

You know the prototypical dad figure that says, "Stop crying or I'll give you something to cry about"? That's what I became for myself. (Now that I think about it, if there is no situation in which crying is acceptable, I don't even know what dads meant by that. Must be some nuclear-level pain they had in mind that would make it okay to cry).

Once I stopped crying, I found that I wasn't being hurt as much, but the price I paid was I had to stuff down my sensitivity. I perceived myself as weak for crying, so I rejected that part of me. I have since come to understand my sensitivity is a gift and an integral part of my being, but back then, my ego saw my sensitivity as something it could blame for my trauma—so it split from that sensitivity in an effort to reject anything it perceived as causing me pain. That's what the ego does.

This rejection of my sensitivity caused a separation from my true self. When we reject a part of ourselves, it starts a whole cascade of negative emotions that knock us off balance. In being both the judger and the judged, we lose our centre.

When we say "I don't like myself" or something similar, that essentially creates two entities inside of us—the part that doesn't like and the part that isn't liked. A child might say out loud, "I don't like myself," but more often it's an internal split that is more felt than said. The same is true for "I blame myself," creating a split between the blamer and the part that's blamed. This internal separation is a significant source of alarm that needs to be repaired if we are to heal our anxiety.

Acceptance and compassion for ourselves is the best way to heal that split. Do you see how when we judge ourselves harshly for being anxious, we are furthering the split that is already there? The split needs love and connection to heal. We need secure attachment to feel whole and regain our balance.

To heal, we need to embrace ourselves and see the part we judged and rejected may actually be among our best qualities. For example, my sensitivity connects me with compassion for self and others. It's an integral part of my SES—and in rejecting my sensitivity, I block access to the very compassion I need to heal. My guess is that your dragon has exiled some of the very best parts of you as well, keeping you split from yourself and inflaming your alarm.

When my Ego Dragon blocked my ability to let love in, I had nothing to counter the ever-increasing fear. The ABCs do not create love—they merely reveal, and allow access to, the love that was always (and is always) there.

When we compassionately "come alongside" (to borrow a term from Dr. Neufeld) our Ego Dragon, we let the dragon know that it's safe to open the chest. In compassionate connection to yourself, you not only accept your "flaws" but you embrace them and are even grateful for them. And you let the dragon take a smoke break. (Yes, that's a fire breathing dragon pun right there.) We can thank the Ego Dragon for doing what it thought was best (no blame) and come to a new understanding.

In accepting all parts of ourselves (especially the part that is anxious and alarmed), we create a secure connection to all parts of ourselves and correct the separation. If all anxiety is separation anxiety and all alarm is separation alarm, when we win over the dragon by showing it that it can stand down, the alarm is able to be released since it is no longer needed.

83

Innocence

We are born innocent, and that is our true self. We are all innocent souls at our core, and if we are lucky enough to be securely attached to a parent or caregiver without significant trauma, we can hold on to that innocence for as long as possible. Even as adults, we have faith and trust that most people will not let us down, and we know that even if some do, we will be okay.

But if our attachment is not secure and we experienced pain and trauma that was beyond our ability to cope, that's when we develop adaptations and coping strategies that favour protection over growth.

When a child is abused, experiences great loss, or is abandoned or rejected, we often say the child has "lost their innocence." What people usually mean by this is the child lost their opportunity to be "just a kid" and not worry about their safety and security. But using the terms of this book, we can say the child's innocence is not *lost* but, instead, stowed away under lock and key. It can be reclaimed later, but until it is, the person may lose access to many of their gifts and much of their loving nature as those gifts are held back from self and others.

Nobody has gone into a nursery and said, "That baby is a narcissist" or "That baby is a people pleaser" or "You see that baby over there? It is clearly a compulsive liar." A newborn baby cannot be a narcissist or a people-pleaser or a compulsive liar. These attributes aren't born—they're made. We develop traits and behaviours that society deems unacceptable when we see the world as a place we need to guard against.

We are not born addicted to shopping or sex or lying. We adopt those addictions because on some level we perceive them as buffering our pain. Then, because all addictions have negative consequences, we judge ourselves for those addictions. In strongly judging ourselves for our "flaws," we become locked in them. Something I learned from Brené Brown: you cannot heal an addiction if you are still holding yourself in shame and contempt for that addiction. You can't shame someone into changing. In fact, shaming someone (including yourself) for an addiction will only increase the destructive influence of that addiction.

Addictive traits or behaviours are hard to change because (1) they helped us feel better at one time (usually in childhood), so they served some adaptive purpose; (2) we fail to see them—or if we do, we minimize their impact; and (3) you can't change something you haven't accepted and embraced in yourself.

Addiction is one of those topics that deserves a book of its own. I don't have space to explore it in detail, but I did want to note that alarm and anxiety play a massive role in developing addictions. Although more intensive help may be required, the ABCs will help you get out of your shame and break the cycle that keeps pushing you back into the addictive behaviour—and it starts with truly seeing your own innocence.

Once you fully accept your innocence, there's a flow that allows you to stay more in your parasympathetic rest-and-digest nervous system. From there, you can enter a place of engagement with yourself and others, using the SES that is wired into all of us as a factory setting at birth.

Nurturing and engaging this SES would help or resolve so many emotional disorders since the vast majority of them have their roots in the loss of connection in childhood, compounded by the reproach—separation—we inflict on ourselves for the disorders that follow. Even for such severe conditions as narcissistic, antisocial, and borderline personality disorders, connection with self and others can contribute significantly to healing.

When you rediscover your innocence and allow it to come out and play, you no longer need the overprotective ego. You realize you've been creating your own alarm all along, and you can move into loving growth and away from fearful, alarm-based protection. But like anything, if you don't clearly see how you separate from yourself, you can't change it, so let's spend some time looking at the tricks the ego uses to keep you split.

84
Connecting With Your Inner Child

With all of this talk of reconnecting with the inner child, does the idea bring up some resistance for you?

I ask because the term *inner child* does bring up resistance with a lot of people. Many view it as overly "woo woo" and spiritual. For me personally, it has been one of the most important concepts in my healing.

This is not a concept that was introduced to me in my training as a medical doctor, and, in fact, I suspect that if you ever used the term *inner child* with your doctor, most doctors would roll their eyes so far back in their head they'd risk losing their balance and falling off their stool. But although they may not be on board with using that term just yet, there is an increasing awareness of the importance of childhood experiences, and physicians are starting to ask routinely about traumatic events in childhood.

The Adverse Childhood Experiences (ACEs) Study, published in the late 1990s, made a crucial contribution to our understanding of how trauma in childhood leads to physical and mental illness in adulthood, and doctors receiving their education today do learn about it. Examining a sample of more than seventeen thousand people in the U.S., the study found that ACEs like neglect, physical, sexual or emotional abuse, parental addiction or alcoholism or any significant loss greatly increased the risk of mental and physical illness and disease in adulthood.

Another sobering finding was just how common ACEs were. The study did not look at the most at-risk populations (e.g., low-income, unemployed, or homeless). Participants in the study had solid income and steady employment with access to high-quality health care since the prerequisite to enroll as a subject was to be a member of the health system that conducted the study. Yet, in this relatively well-off population, more than one-quarter reported being physically abused as children, and more than one-fifth reported being sexually abused. About two-thirds of the sample reported having at least one ACE (a list that also includes parental divorce, death, incarceration, or mental illness).

In my terminology, ACEs lead to background alarm. Remember, when we cut ourselves off from our bodies for fear of running into that old pain, we also deny ourselves access to the child in us. We keep the child protected, but it's more like solitary confinement as we learn to cope alone, cut off from the connections that are an essential part of life. This is where the dragon gets its wings.

Your inner child is waiting for you to stop judging, alienating, blaming, and shaming them. That child wants to be seen, heard, accepted, and loved.

And you can do that with the ABCs.

Become *aware* that your hurt little self is inside you, and make an effort to see them. Move into your *body*, which is their body too, and both of you can learn to feel together. Show them that it is safe by providing them with the *compassionate connection* they needed when they experienced those ACEs. Be the comforting, competent parent to them now they so desperately needed back then.

People often tell me they've been trying to reconnect with their inner child but they just can't seem to reach them—and I just tell them to keep trying. Imagine that you have numbed, medicated, judged, abandoned, blamed, and shamed that child for so long they've lost the ability to trust you or have faith in you. Isn't that an understandable response? Show that child you're not going anywhere and you will be here whenever they're ready.

There's a story about a stonecutter who is faced with the task of breaking a large stone in half. His tools are so heavy that he can only manage a few strikes before resting. He examines the stone and sees the line he must strike in order to split the stone evenly. When he begins his work, each blow is precise and delivered with intention.

After one hundred well-placed strikes over many days, the stone is still intact. As the sun sets on another day, the stonecutter sets down his hammer and chisel and walks home with a heavy heart, wondering if he's taken on an impossible task.

But he wakes up the next day with renewed determination. When he examines the stone that morning, he sees a crack he's never noticed before. When he places his chisel in this crack, the blow breaks the stone clean in half. A passerby witnesses this strike and exclaims in wonder, "You broke that stone apart with a single blow!"

That's how it is with connecting to your child. It may seem like nothing is happening, and then, suddenly, you break through.

Each time you practice the ABCs is another strike to the heart of the matter.

Some people may feel an immediate connection to self, like they've found the missing piece of the puzzle. For others, it may take a while for the ABCs to break down the massive stone of your anxiety and alarm.

85

Ego Tricks That Keep You Separate (JABS)

When I first met my patient Anne, she described herself as high-strung. In her early forties, with short blonde hair and intense blue eyes, she was one of those people who always seemed like she had just drunk three cups of coffee. She spoke quickly, and when she talked her hands flew everywhere. This dynamo was a tiny, wiry person—just a little over five feet tall—but she carried a lot of alarm from the neglect she experienced in childhood. Her anxious thoughts mostly involved her three daughters, who at the time ranged in age from thirteen to nineteen.

Anne was a classic people-pleaser. Her husband and kids always had fresh lunches and fresh laundry. She was very good at keeping her family fed and taken care of, but she rarely looked after herself, especially when it came to food.

She had grown up the oldest of three sisters. Her mother was narcissistic and demanding, and Anne performed the vast majority of the work around the house, along with looking after her two younger sisters and having dinner on the table when her mother got home. Her mother was tall and striking and garnered a lot of attention for her looks. She would often comment to Anne "Don't ever let yourself get fat," even though Anne was naturally slim (even tending toward skinny). Every few months, her mother would go into a fit of rage, which was almost always directed at Anne.

Anne learned that she was not important for who she was but for her looks and what she could provide for others. Her only measure of control was the rare praise she got from her mother for being responsible enough to look after her sisters. Her father was affectionate when he would come home after a few drinks, but without alcohol, he was unemotional and seemed to "go through the motions" of being a father, attending school plays and community events without much apparent interest.

Remember, when a parent abuses, abandons, or rejects a child, the child doesn't stop loving the parent—the child stops loving themselves.

Anne became the poster child for the acronym for the JABS you learned about in Part 1. She **judged** herself as being unworthy or only worthy when she was helping others. She **abandoned** herself and her own needs to look after others. She **blamed** herself for her mother's rage (or any of her family member's anger) and **shamed** herself for eating because she feared the dreaded weight gain her mother had warned her to avoid at all costs.

Your ego (the dragon that is supposed to be protecting you) takes JABS at you because it doesn't want you to be vulnerable to being hurt by others. It's like Rebel Wilson's character in the movie *Pitch Perfect* in which she introduces herself to the *a cappella* group she hopes to join by saying, "I'm Fat Amy. I call myself that so you twig bitches don't do it behind my back."

JABS show up in many forms—resistance, victim mentality, inability to receive love (or even compliments), defensive detachment—and they all block access to your ability to heal. You just keep on hurting your inner child, not realizing that the enemy you're trying to protect the child from may not even be around anymore.

Anne started taking ego-based JABS at herself as a reaction to her trauma. When we are routinely mistreated by others (especially an important figure like a caregiver), on some level these JABS decrease the dissonance we feel. The hurt we experience at the hands (literally or figuratively) of those we love just blends into the pain we are causing ourselves with the JABS. This reduces our uncertainty. There is no longer a question of whether we'll be in pain or not. We know with certainty that we'll be in pain because we are inflicting it on ourselves.

As Anne rejected herself, she created a deeper split between her authentic self (her innocence) and her ego-created self—and as this split grew wider, she fell into the need for more and more protection, and redoubled her JABS at herself. In a feedback loop, Anne's Ego Dragon was becoming bigger and stronger each time she took JABS that made her feel less safe. Her ego protection manifested as JABS and disordered eating.

When I explained all this to Anne, just hearing it gave her some immediate relief. She told me for the first time she could see that what happened was not her fault. And over time, as we worked on accepting and loving the lost parts of herself, she was able to regain control of her life.

Anne, too, was a sensitive person by nature, and she had cut that sensitive side of her off to protect it. Once she became aware of where she was judging, abandoning, blaming, and shaming herself, she started to see she was worthy of her own compassion, attention, and self-care.

There is no healing from anxiety and alarm until you gain access to your innocence. You can do that by becoming aware of the JABS you take at yourself and using each incident you notice as a reminder to begin the ABC process.

These, too, are some of your tells.

For example, when Anne would feel shame as she was about to eat something, once she became aware of it, she could label it and then set the *intention* to shift her *attention* to *sensation*. Once she placed a hand on her chest and connected with her breath, she could move into a compassionate connection with herself, using phrases such as "I like that I've made a safe and comfortable home for my family" and "I accept and embrace all parts of me" to release shame and move herself into a state of acceptance.

Anne felt better quickly when she practiced the ABC process multiple times a day. It worked well for her, in part, because she was disciplined about it. She started to have an easier time looking after herself, telling me, "The more connected I felt with my body, the more I wanted to take care of it." She told me the process helped her feel more empowered and less like a helpless victim just waiting for her anxiety and alarm to pass.

86
Ego Trick: Self-Judgment

In the coming chapters, we'll look at some of the Ego Dragon's common tricks because (all together now!) when you can *see* them, you no longer have to *be* them. Along with JABS, the ego uses victim mentality, resistance, compulsive thinking, inability to receive, and defensive detachment among others (I told you the ego was crafty!) to trap you in alarm. With all of these, the ego unwittingly creates pain in its efforts to shield you from pain.

Along with each trick, you'll learn a strategy to move past it. Know that these are not a replacement for the ABCs; they are meant to help you gain awareness of the ego in real time and move into the ABCs when you notice one of your tells reveals your Ego Dragon in action.

Let's look first at self-judgment.

We may have been born sensitive, but we weren't born specifically judging and disliking parts of ourselves. Two-year-olds don't tell themselves they are too fat or they should stop crying because that makes them look weak.

Tibetan monks live in an environment of compassion and acceptance and find it hard to believe it's possible for a human being *not to love* themselves. But in an atmosphere of trauma and compromised attachment, being compassionate to ourselves is difficult. With no direct experience of compassionate attachment, it's difficult to conjure it up on our own.

As noted before, when there's trouble at home, children often blame themselves as the cause. On that foundation, it's not hard to see how you probably wouldn't have a positive self-image if you judged yourself to be the cause of problems in your family. Because we depend on our parents for our survival, it's too painful to believe they are the cause of the problems in the family—so the cause must be us.

It makes perfect sense where self-judgment came from. But over time, it's learned and ingrained with repetition until it has nothing to do with our parents anymore—we just do it because it's what we've always done. Self-judgment, like all of the ego tricks I'll show you, is self-reinforcing, just like the groove in the snow we make deeper and deeper and faster and faster the more we follow its track.

The solution is to be aware of judgments you make toward yourself. What does your judgmental ego tell you and when?

This most often shows up with statements that sound like "I'm too _____" (anxious, fat, selfish) or "I'm not _____ enough" (nice, smart, productive). But see what it looks like for you. View it as detective work—you are a private investigator gathering intelligence on the habits of your Ego Dragon.

If you have a supportive friend or partner you can share this journey with, I'd recommend asking them to tell you when they notice you judging yourself. Sometimes it takes a while for it to sink in how harsh our self-judgment really is—and how it's everywhere!

When you notice that you're being critical of yourself, you've taken the first step of bringing your unconscious habit of self-judgment into the light of conscious awareness. By labeling it as an intrusive thought and not something you need to believe, you are taking away its power and starving it of its energy source.

Now, recall that we're not trying to slay the Ego Dragon; we're trying to make friends with it. So the solution is not to "think positive" and tell yourself the opposite of the negative thought ("I'm so unselfish! I'm very svelte! I'm sooooo productive!") This is where the self-help movement gets a bad name. We are not Stuart Smalley (the Al Franken character on *Saturday Night Live*) looking in the mirror saying to ourselves, "I'm good enough. I'm smart enough. And doggone it, people like me!"

Instead, we need to bring compassion to the qualities in ourselves we've thought were not acceptable—but first we need to get grounded in the body.

My Ego Dragon often judges me for being too sensitive. Once I notice it (use my awareness to label the thought as intrusive and self-judgmental), I'll pause and move into my body and stay there in sensation until I feel grounded. I'll place my hand over my alarm and savour my breath in sensation—by now you're getting to know the steps to create a sense of secure attachment to yourself.

Once you've mastered the basics of getting grounded in your body, there's a way to work with the body that's a little more complex—and I think this can be especially useful in dealing with self-judgment. It involves focusing awareness on your own sense of being and feeling before you even address the self-judgmental thoughts you are having.

Remember that awareness is not so much thinking; it is an openness to what may be present outside of your habitual and judgmental way of thinking. Thinking is expressive; awareness is receptive. We are not trying to replace or contradict our expressive thoughts as positive psychology would tell us to do. Awareness is not a convergence to a specific goal but a divergence into a curiosity. In awareness, we first pay close attention to cultivating a receptive feeling state before we move toward expressive thinking. Grounding ourselves in feeling and compassion for the innocent child in us is the platform from which we can change our habitual, judgemental perceptions of ourselves. Simply stating an affirmation by rote will do little unless there is a connected, compassionate feeling underneath it.

This is a practice from somatic experiencing therapy called *pendulation* in which we move our attention back and forth between two sensations—typically one comfortable or neutral and the other uncomfortable.

So when I notice my self-judgmental thought that I'm too sensitive, once I've settled into my body, I focus on the cool, soothing sensation of my breath. I put my hand over my solar plexus and connect with my alarm, consciously accepting it and embracing it—even though it hurts.

Alternately shifting between the pleasurable sensation of breath and the painful alarm breaks the illusion that the alarm is infinite.

It's like adding a bit of ice-cold water to a cup of too-hot tea so it's no longer hot enough to burn my mouth. I can now take a sip of the alarm and see it no longer has to burn me. I always have a safe place in my body to return to—the place I've created with my own caring and compassionate touch and the reassuring sensation of my breath.

Now moving on from B to C, I will take the original thought and, with compassionate connection to myself, say "My sensitivity is a gift" or "My sensitivity is what's allowed me to help so many people in my career." Or it could be a broader statement like "What I used to see as a weakness I now fully accept, love, and embrace as a gift and a strength."

Do you see how this is all different from Stuart Smalley's approach? Poor Stuart is trying to counteract his self-judgments, but he's probably just digging himself deeper into a hole because he doesn't believe what he's saying to himself in the mirror. There's no feeling to what he says to himself, only words. Feeling is what changes our thinking—not so much the other way around. Statements grounded in the feeling of compassion let us know that we no longer have to hold ourselves up against the yardstick of perfection our parents or our childhood bullies expected us to measure up to.

Let's explore how the statements might look for some other intrusive thoughts of self-judgment. For "I'm too fat," the statement of true compassion could be something like putting your hand on your chest, connecting to your breath, and then *feeling* the words "I accept my body exactly as it is" or (with feeling) "My value as a person does not depend on the size of my waist." For "I'm not smart enough," once you create a connected feeling of yourself through your touch or breath, your statements might be "I don't have to be perfect. It's okay to be wrong sometimes. I accept myself—yes, even my airhead moments because I can laugh at myself and the people who love me laugh with me."

When we are able to reframe our "flaws" and view them with compassion, we integrate traumatic thought with grounded feeling. And the best part is we're not trying to fool ourselves by quoting some rote phrase like Stuart Smalley— our statements of compassion are true! I now fully embrace my sensitivity, as I know that without it, this book would never have been written. My sensitivity has become one of the things I am most grateful for in this life.

The emotional component of the ABCs is why the process has been so healing for people. If we could simply think our way out of emotional issues, talk therapy would work wonders and only take about twenty minutes—but you need more than a cognitive solution to fix an emotional issue.

When I started with the ABCs, every time I got to the compassionate connection part, I would find a way of discounting myself. You may find this as well, but as you persevere, you build more faith in your connection to yourself and the reservations fade. I found this fascinating.

When you do the ABCs and focus deeply on the positive parts of yourself, you begin to break down the Ego Dragon's strategy of self-judgment. You'll notice that I say "the positive parts of yourself" and not "the parts you love about yourself." If you do have parts you love about yourself, then by all means use those in your ABCs—but many of us had a hard time with love. Our Ego Dragons specifically tried to resist it because that was easier than letting it in only to lose it.

Finding and focusing on something you love about yourself can be a tough proposition, especially early on in the process. Don't feel that you have to "love yourself" before you are ready. When you've had many years of unwittingly focusing on the negative parts of yourself, it may take a while to create a new groove. But once you commit to developing a compassionate connection, you might be surprised how much you start to see what you truly *do* like about yourself. What you focus on, you'll get more of—so if you focus on what you like about yourself, you'll see more of it.

Your statements are so powerful because you're taking the time to get grounded in your body and connect with emotion before saying them—unlike poor old Stuart, who's just repeating words into a mirror without any feeling behind them. The more intention and feeling you invest into your words, the more power they have to create change in your system.

87
Ego Trick: Self-Abandonment

There is perhaps no greater propagator of chronic alarm than self-abandonment.

Self-abandonment typically begins (1) automatically, (2) early in childhood, and (3) under the guise it is keeping us safe. Over time it becomes a pattern, and this is why we find ourselves still doing it as adults. The antidote to self-abandonment is to (1) see it consciously; (2) act as your own connected "parent" now as an adult; and (3) keep yourself feeling safe by consciously and compassionately connecting with your authentic, innocent self.

One of the most devastating ways self-abandonment shows up is putting others' needs ahead of your own. In medical school, we were trained to do exactly this. It didn't matter if you had been awake for the previous thirty-six hours; you still had to be there for your patient. The doctor's code is that the patient always comes first. Every med student accepts it, and nobody is allowed to complain about it. Nobody spoke up to say this was unrealistic and unsafe.

Self-abandonment arises when we get into the habit of putting our own needs last, or we stop speaking up for ourselves because we have learned it doesn't do any good and may even hurt us. Sometimes we come to believe our only value lies in what we can do for others, and sometimes we give up our own dreams and passions because we've been told they are unrealistic or impractical—or simply because they take time or attention away from another person.

I have a friend, Emily, who grew up with a single mother who had her own history of unaddressed trauma. Because Emily's mother had trouble coping with difficulties in life, in general, the demands of motherhood were often overwhelming for her. As a result, Emily grew up feeling at times like her needs were irritating, annoying, and simply "too much" for her mother, and at other times like she simply didn't exist and was talking to a wall when she would try to express herself to her mother. This was the primary relationship in Emily's life as the only child of a single mom, and since she didn't have much else to go on in terms of examples of healthier patterns, she adapted to her environment as all children do. When children are told, or made to feel, they are "too much," they come to the only conclusion available and assume they themselves are the problem. Because the child depends on the parent for survival (especially if it is a single parent), the child cannot see the parent as fallible in any way since that would threaten the child's already tenuous sense of security. Emily adapted by catering to her mother's needs and swallowing her own since the child in her saw there was no point in voicing them anyway.

In her teenage years, she started to notice that she would repeat this pattern of not speaking up for her own needs and desires. When talking with friends about simple topics like choosing a restaurant, she would stay silent, assuming that no one would listen or care about her opinion anyway. When she would do this, she would experience what she described as "a hot, dense, collapsing sensation" at the base of her throat and her upper chest. She didn't understand her own behaviour since she was among friends who actually *did* care about her opinion and preferences, but the feeling felt familiar. Eventually, she recognized it was the same way she felt when dealing with her mother.

When Emily left her childhood home for university, she knew her relationship with her mother wasn't healthy, and she wanted nothing more than to get far away and forget all about it—but the patterns followed her as they tend to do. In her first serious relationship, she ended up with a boyfriend, Scott, who was extremely jealous and controlling—to the point that she didn't feel comfortable following her own dreams and passions because Scott felt so obviously threatened by them. This came to a head when she came back from studying abroad in Russia for the summer. While showing Scott the photo album of her travels and expecting him to share her excitement at what she'd experienced, the only response she could get out of him was jealous rage as he pointed out all the male students one by one and asked which ones she had cheated with. Desperate to calm him down, Emily threw the entire photo album into the dormitory's dumpster, seeing that the only way to salvage the relationship was to forsake her own excitement at the happy memories of something so important to her—and there again was that familiar hot, dense, collapsing feeling in her chest. The person she loved couldn't share her joy, so she might as well abandon it (and herself).

Although Emily hadn't noticed the similarities between Scott and her mother (and particularly the similarities in dynamics of how she related to them), the hot, dense, collapsing sensation clued her in. It was the common thread showing her that in both situations (as well as the interactions with friends where she swallowed her own opinion), she was abandoning herself. With practice, you can start to notice the "tell" of self-abandonment in the same way you notice your self-judgmental thoughts. It may have a physical and emotional signature that is different from the "garden-variety" alarm you've been getting acquainted with.

I haven't addressed this much for fear of making this book too complex, but alarm can show up in different ways, with different emotional and physical characteristics, for the same person. Typically, people have a predominant alarm, but they may well have different sources of alarm in different places in the body. As you become more attuned to your own predominant source of alarm, you may also discover the nuances of the others. Patients often report to me that once they attuned to the alarm in their body, they couldn't believe they had missed it for so long, and they often find alarm in other parts of themselves like their throat or pelvis. I remind them that their ego had a vested interest in keeping them locked in the worries of their mind and out of their body, so it was no wonder they couldn't see it.

Just as Emily used her "collapsing" feeling of alarm to connect the dots of a similar disempowerment with her mother with her controlling boyfriend, as you get more in tune with your own alarms, you too can use them as a beacon for your own understanding. As you become more familiar with your alarm and know what you are looking for, the alarm sensations in your body can act as a brilliant "tell," acting as a signpost to show you where you abandon yourself or ignore your own needs. Once you tune in to your particular sensation of alarm, you can see it as a friendly signal (although, at first, it likely won't feel that friendly) to compassionately connect to yourself. Prior to this awareness of her collapsing sensation of alarm, Emily would continue down the old path of abandoning her own needs while carefully attending to others, just as she did with her mother. Now in her awareness of that sensation, she knows she must put herself first. In putting herself first, with a comforting hand over her alarm sensation and connection to her breath in the present moment, the alarm settles and so does Emily.

Once we become aware, we can stop the automatic, unconscious alienation from ourselves and make a choice to consciously connect. Before becoming aware of our tells, we'd miss the sign and just proceed straight down the superhighway into Survival City. Now, we can use those tells as signals to move into our ABCs. And when we connect with ourselves, we get on the road to growth and off the highway of protection. Maybe an even better metaphor is a roundabout you can never exit but just keep going around in circles—until your awareness shows you the exit ramps and you set an intention to follow one of them.

Before I leave this chapter, I want you to see a deeper meaning. Of course it is important to see where you leave yourself for others, but it's more important to see when you leave yourself, in general. Since all anxiety is separation anxiety and all alarm is separation alarm, it stands to reason you need to separate from yourself for you to experience anxiety and alarm—and when you engage in any of the ego tricks, you leave your innocent self. Much of the power of the

ABC process is in the ability to keep you connected to yourself—to put your connection to yourself first. When you connect to yourself, the alarm dissipates because getting you to compassionately attend to yourself is the reason the alarm is there in the first place.

88
Ego Trick: Self-Blame and Self-Shame

We blame to discharge energy. It feels good to us to see someone held accountable for their negative actions. When someone is sent to prison for a crime, we feel justice has been served and any negative energy experienced has an outlet for discharge. Humans have an innate sense of justice, and the urge to blame serves that desire for justice—the desire to see wrongdoing named and atoned for. We use blame as a way of making sense and discharging pain. So self-blame is related to self-judgment but not quite the same.

In a situation where we can't blame our parents because we depend on them for survival, we turn the blame back on ourselves as we've discussed earlier. This has the illusion of "settling the score" because at least somebody is being held responsible for the suffering that's happening.

But when we use blame to push the pain out, it keeps boomeranging back in an endless loop. I view blame as a child's way of holding ourselves in prison forever for something that was truly not our fault.

Blame and shame are similar but manifest very differently. Self-blame is summed up with the statement, "I have made a mistake." The blame keeps what I have done in my awareness, and although it hurts, I can use that self-blame as a way of preventing me from making the same mistake. Although it is self-punitive, blaming ourselves can lead to change. Because it is present in conscious awareness, we can use that blame in a productive manner as an impetus for change.

Shame, while also self-punitive, is summed up with the statement, "I *am* a mistake." What shames us is who we are, not some past action we can now act differently to correct. For example, when I was being teased as a child about my facial tic (more on that below), I felt it wasn't something I *did* that was wrong; it was *me* that was wrong. It was so painful I had to bury it, and that is the hallmark of shame. We can't use it to improve ourselves because we don't allow it to come into the light of awareness. You can't change what you can't (or refuse to) see. I shamed myself for many years until I saw my daughter had the very same neurological tic. (I'll tell you the whole story soon.) When I saw the issue wasn't some personal fault but a medical condition, I was able to move it out of the shame category, address it, and allow it to heal.

Entire books have been written on shame, but the works that have had a tremendous impact on my own healing are from Brené Brown (see the resource guide at the end of the book for more on her work). She says shame is toxic because, from an evolutionary perspective, we feel it threatens our very survival. To be shamed in our history as humans could mean ostracization for our tribe, and that would literally be a death sentence.

Shame is an extremely potent potentiator of self-separation and alarm because it lives in the shadows and feeds our dragon big chunks of our self-esteem (or whatever dragons eat). I cannot tell you the number of people I've known or treated who see mental struggles as shameful and held off on getting the help they needed because of it. The dragon has a field day with self-judgment, alienation, blame, and shame over having a "mental illness" or even having it in a family member. I remember being deeply ashamed of my dad, even though I knew his illness wasn't his fault. One of the biggest sources of shame I see in people is the shame over having to take psychiatric medication. I've written many thousands of prescriptions for different kinds of medications, and I've noticed that people never shame themselves for needing to take antibiotics to treat an infection, but they sure do when the prescription is for a psychiatric medication.

There is much more I could write about blame and shame, and you'll find additional resources at the end of this book if you want to learn more about these topics. For now, let's help you find how they might be showing up for you.

When I was in elementary school, I had a nervous tic: a twitch around my cheeks and nose. That area would itch, and I would rub, pick, and scratch at my face and nose. I got teased for it quite a bit.

First, I blamed myself for the bullying I experienced—the kids wouldn't have been so mean to me if I just didn't have the habit of picking at my face. Then, when I tried to stop but couldn't, the shame set in.

Shame will probably be familiar to anyone who has experienced bullying as a child. In blame, you can discuss *what you did* that was bad, but in shame you bury it because you feel *you* are bad.

Shame festers over time. For me, it festered for twenty-five years, until one day I went to pick up Leandra from school. As I got closer to the playground, I heard one of the kids teasing her about a twitching around her nose. Of course, this brought back painful memories for me, but the doctor in me thought, could this be genetic? Leandra had a much milder form than I did, but I shamed myself for that for two and a half decades. When I eventually learned that I have a mild form of Tourette's syndrome, of which facial twitching can be a part, I felt liberated. This was a neurological condition: I couldn't control it if I wanted to. Quite the opposite—the more I tried to stop it, the more stressed I got, and the more stressed I got, the more my face would twitch, and then kids would tease me more, which would stress me more, so my face would twitch more ...

You get the picture.

To this day, when I'm stressed it can come back in a lesser form. In fact, when I notice it now, I use it as a tool because it's definitely one of my tells that I'm falling back into old patterns that are feeding my alarm and subsequent anxiety. Even my wife knows when I'm stressed because she sees me rubbing and picking at my face and nose. She will often say, "I see you going at your face. Are you okay?" Often she'll notice it before I do. What was once a troublesome symptom has become a valuable messenger.

Even though the twitching happens much less often now, I feel it and use it as an entry point to the ABCs. Now, when I feel the urge to start going at my face, I ask myself, "What is going on that is making me nervous?" or "Am I alarmed and not aware of it?" I am very aware now, when I start rubbing or picking at my face and nose, that I am on the express bus into Survival City and I should pull the cord to get off at the next stop.

When we see our self-blaming and shaming in the light of awareness, often we can use what we blamed and shamed ourselves for as an avenue to connect with ourselves. There is tremendous power in embracing a part of you that you previously kept in the shadows. When you see it (and accept and embrace it), you don't have to be it. You have broken the spell that prevented you from changing it. The tell gives us a direct link to healing the issue.

So what are you blaming and shaming yourself for? Chances are your dragon is using it to keep you separated from your authentic self and, therefore, exacerbate your alarm and anxiety. You may hold shame from decades ago, and it's still keeping you in alarm. If you feel a lot of self-blame and shame, that will supercharge your foreground and background alarm.

Telling another person about what shames you is a powerful practice in itself. Just by doing so, you are giving yourself the message you don't need to be ashamed and there's nothing to be embarrassed of. The shame is pointless because now somebody knows! Whatever you were or are ashamed of, even if it's still not something you're immensely proud of, getting it out into the light removes that "I must keep this hidden at all costs" energy. Not only that, but telling a trusted friend or therapist engages your SES, forming a connection with someone who can help you hold compassion for yourself—and you might even be surprised how many people have a story similar to the one you were hiding, thinking you were the only one.

There is nothing you have said, thought, or done that is unique to you. (Said with love: Get over yourself! You're not that special or unique.) There is nothing you could shame yourself for that has not been done by countless people before you and will be done by countless people after you. There are no new shames, only recycled ones.

Shame cannot live in the light of conscious awareness. Bring it into the light. You don't have a secret; a secret has you. Your dragon is blackmailing you and holding you hostage. Are you going to keep paying the ransom in alarm, or are you ready to escape?

Gila Golub is one of the teachers who has impacted me the most in my life. During her workshops, if someone would go on a rant about some perceived injustice done to them or by them, Gila would sharply interrupt them and ask (using words that were always the same, and I can still hear in my head like a refrain), "Who are you and what are you here for?"

She had taught us the answer: "I am an innocent soul and I am here to remember that." Still, people would often continue on with their reasons to condemn themselves or others—so Gila would interrupt them and repeat the question again, louder this time: "Who are you and what are you here for?" This continued until the person answered, "I am an innocent soul and I am here to remember that."

In Gila's meetings and workshops, I must have heard her ask that question to people hundreds of times and get the same answer hundreds of times. She wanted to show that at the heart of everything we blamed and shamed ourselves for was an innocent child asking to be seen, heard, and loved. It all comes down to seeing your innocence.

Gila also liked to say, "Anything that comes out of your mouth is love or a cry for love." This is the truth of our innocence. I don't know a person who has not hurt another person in one way or another. I do not know a person who has not hurt *themselves* in one way or another, either. Personally and professionally, I've known people who are manipulative, aggressive, people-pleasing, greedy, codependent, compulsively self-absorbed, arrogant, and narcissistic. Remember, those traits (and many others) were not born in them; they are manifestations of their Ego Dragon as a result of experiences they had.

Many maladaptive coping strategies came from perfectionism, and perfectionism is often the child's attempt to be seen, heard, and loved. You believe that if you could only do something more, better, or different, then everything in your family would be okay. That if you could just be "good enough," you would stop being such a nuisance to your parents (when really you just had the needs of a normal child, and their failure to respond had nothing to do with your not being perfect). When we are rewarded with attention and "love" for being a perfectionist, the straight-A student, or the child who can look after the whole house by themselves, it creates an impossible standard for the rest of our lives.

If you have been rewarded for being a perfectionist, you learn to have very high standards for yourself, and often you will project those high standards on others. I remember when I was about fifteen saying to my dad, "Nobody is happy with a perfectionist, especially themselves." I was onto something—it just took me a while to take my own advice to heart!

If you have unattainable standards and have been rewarded for them (by becoming a physician perhaps), you may well feel that self-acceptance and self-compassion are going to derail your plans to "rule ze world!" But nobody is happy with a perfectionist, especially themselves. To quote a line from the song "Desperado" by the Eagles, "These things that are pleasing you will hurt you somehow." Perfectionism may seem to please you in the short term, but over time it will hurt you because being perfect is actually not humanly possible.

Your authentic, innocent self knows that your ego's perfectionism is hurting you, but your ego wants to carry it on because your ego feels like if you are more, better, or different, you will be happy. Take it from a recovering perfectionist: More achievements are not going to ease your anxiety and alarm.

In fact, it is likely that your perfectionism is making you more anxious and alarmed because it is feeding your ego and starving your sense of innocent connection with yourself. It is only in truly seeing your innocence that you can heal from anxiety and alarm, for attaching to your true self is the only way to emotional peace.

Perfectionism is like gambling. It can be won in the short term but, in the long term, is always a losing proposition. It is the game adopted when you were a child, trying to get your needs met by being more, better, or different. My ex Katerina was a perfectionist, and she suffered greatly, but at least at the time I knew her, she could not escape the seduction of her ego.

Note that I am not giving people a hall pass to be manipulative, aggressive, people-pleasing, greedy, codependent, compulsively self-absorbed, arrogant, narcissistic, and perfectionistic! I am saying you need to see those traits as ways your protective ego used to get your needs met and you are no longer that child who had to do whatever they needed in a compulsive attempt to be seen, heard, and loved. I am saying to accept and embrace those traits, and even commit to loving those traits, for they served you at one time. (I am also not saying you have to accept this kind of behaviour from other people. You can draw boundaries and point out the behaviour for what it is while still feeling compassion for the wounded person behind the behaviour. I call this "seeing someone's innocence through their ego protective behaviour.")

You cannot change something you continue to reject in yourself.

I'll give you an example. I have something in me I call the "pusher/driver," and it has nothing to do with dealing drugs out of a vehicle. My pusher/driver is a remnant from my childhood that forces me to achieve things. My pusher/driver has told me the key to being happy and relieving my anxiety and alarm is in accomplishing more things. The trouble is, much of why I have anxiety and alarm is exactly because I am pushed and driven, but my pusher/driver conveniently forgot to factor that in. It would tell me how great it would be to accomplish this or that but would neglect to mention that these accomplishments would come at a significant cost to my peace of mind.

My pusher/driver is a part of my ego. Its action to push me into relentless accomplishment separates me from my true self and, in typical ego fashion, causes more harm than good. But my ego doesn't want to let me know that uncomfortable truth and, instead, really focuses on the great things that I'll get if I listen to it. It is seductive, no question about that.

To be bluntly honest, because I didn't get enough secure attachment in childhood, I never felt like I was "enough." I didn't feel confident in myself enough to get my needs met. So my ego created the pusher/driver to push me to achieve things, believing that the more I attained, the more I would be seen, heard, and loved.

For those who see self-judgment and perfectionism as what was needed to survive as children, this self-acceptance and self-compassion is going to sound like the exact opposite of what you need to achieve the goal of being seen, heard, and loved. You may well engage in ego-driven behaviours that are manipulative, aggressive, people-pleasing, greedy, codependent, compulsively self-absorbed, arrogant, narcissistic, and/or perfectionistic in an attempt to get your needs met.

It is very easy to judge and shame yourself for those behaviours. But as you judge yourself for those traits and states, you lock yourself in them. Until you accept and embrace yourself and all those traits, you are blocked from seeing your innocence—and without that innocent, true self on your side, you'll never be released from anxiety and alarm. You can't change something in yourself until you fully embrace it and accept it.

Once I learned to accept and embrace my pusher/driver, I could converse with it as a friend and not a taskmaster. I no longer feel forced to accomplish; I'm so much easier on myself than even five years ago. My pusher/driver is still there, but now we laugh together at his relentless goal-setting. Ten years ago when I was still practicing medicine in an office, I spread myself way too thin and overcommitted myself. I now can *see* my pusher/driver, and I don't have to *be* my pusher/driver. In seeing my innocence, I now peacefully give myself the choice to take on a project—or not. What was an unconscious compulsion has now become a conscious choice.

Ironically, when you accept your "negativity," you move away from ego and toward your innocence. As you accept and embrace your "faults," you are choosing to see and embrace your innocence. When you see the option to embrace all parts of you in compassionate connection with your innocent self, it becomes a choice, whereas, before, the only option you saw was self-judgment and its resulting self-separation. When you commit to your innocence, you begin to see your faults are not truly a part of you but an ego strategy you adopted as a child to be seen, heard, and loved.

Choose to see your innocence. It's who you are and why you are here.

Here's a little exercise you can do. Make sure you're alone and that nobody can hear you (ideally somewhere with a mirror, like the bathroom). The bathroom is good—and private. In the mirror, smile at yourself (I promise I'm not going all Stuart Smalley on you) and, in a calm and soothing voice, admit your shames to yourself out loud. Then add at the end, "And I love that about myself!" (This is a slight twist on a trick I learned from Kyle Cease, a fellow comedian who is now a gifted author and transformational speaker.)

So standing in front of the mirror, smiling at yourself, you might say in a loving, compassionate voice, "I am an anxious mess today ... and I love that about myself!" You might also say things like, "I am addicted to conflict and drama, and I create it all the time ... and I love that about myself!" or "I compulsively judge myself as unworthy or useless ... and I love that about myself" or "I am a manipulator. I manipulate people to get what I want ... and I love that about myself!" I invite you to really go for it! It adds a different perspective and also some humour. Consciously adding "and I love that about myself" has been very effective in breaking my habit of self-judgment for a particular trait or behaviour. (And remember, it works because, unlike Stuart Smalley, you're not lying to yourself about your perceived shortcomings—you're deciding to accept them as a way to bring you closer to your true self.)

Don't go for a highly emotionally charged "shame" right off the bat. When I did this exercise myself, I always thought of Johnny Cash's lyric: "I shot a man in Reno, just to watch him die ... and I love that about myself!" It always makes me smile and reminds me that there is no shame too big to use this with. But that might not be the one you want to start with. Start small.

As you do the exercise, note the resistance to even saying what shames you out loud or acknowledging it in any way. I can pretty much guarantee you the more trauma you had as a child, the more shame you have.

Or, rather, you don't have shame; shame has you.

Shame is one of the most powerful producers of alarm, and neutralizing shame is one of the most powerful ways you can neutralize alarm.

89
Ego Trick: Victim Mentality

The ego trick of creating a victim mentality deserves a chapter of its own because it is as debilitating as it is invisible. A victim mentality forms when we blame everything on the outside for our problems and shame ourselves on the inside. It is also the attitude we adopt when we shame ourselves for not being able to handle life. A victim mentality grows like a cancer because the weaker it makes us, the less able we are to stand up to it. If you're already starting to feel bad about yourself reading this first paragraph, know that you're not alone. I've never seen anyone with significant anxiety and alarm who *did not* adopt a victim mentality—myself included.

The more alarmed I became, the more powerless I felt and the more I adopted a victim mentality. Faith in myself leached away, and thus I abandoned my true self. As a result, I increasingly blamed the world and shamed myself for not being able to heal my own alarm. I poured my energy into achievement in an effort to regain faith in myself, but no matter what I accomplished—as a physician, as a speaker, as a comedian—it was never enough.

Believing your alarm will be soothed by something outside of yourself is a fool's errand. The famous Canadian comedian Jim Carrey talks about this. He wishes everyone could be famous so they could see for themselves if you're searching for your self-worth in validation from others, no amount of attention is enough to fill that gaping void. I could have become a rocket scientist neurosurgeon race car driver movie star, and it still would not have been enough. I had lost faith in myself at a deeper level than any accomplishment could assuage.

When we lose faith in ourselves, we lose connection with ourselves. We lose the ability to see our innocence and the innocence of the world outside of us. (And, yes, I do maintain the world has a basic innocence. Beneath any tragedy or injustice is the perception we've applied to understand it as such. There is no pain without our experience of it; the meaning of every event is derived from our interpretation of it.) You are whatever you perceive yourself to be, and that perception of yourself will reinforce itself. Whatever you focus on, you will get more of. The outer blaming and inner shaming recapitulates itself, trapping us in a faithless world where we are both the persecuted and persecutor. Then, we are in a roundabout without an exit until we consciously make one. That "exit" is a commitment to awareness of the ultimate innocence of the world along with truly appreciating your own innocence, for you are, indeed, an inextricable part of that world.

I know, seeing the innocence of the world is a tough one to grasp when there seems to be so much pain. The short answer is like the woman who forgives her rapist, not for the rapist's sake specifically, but for herself—as holding contempt for the world trapped her in a world of contempt of her own propagation. When you are angry at someone else or at God for something painful that happens, you are trapped in your own contempt (just as you are when you deem yourself to be the perpetrator). This feeds your shadow side, which creates more pain. In blaming and judging the world, you are trapped in your own blame and judgment, the same way you are trapped when you blame and judge yourself. When you blame and judge yourself you separate from your innocent self and that creates alarm, which creates anxiety.

Obviously, releasing blame and judgment is easier said than done. The same innate human sense of justice I spoke of earlier will rise up to reinforce your judgments. To rise above a little higher and see innocence is one of the most difficult things we can do. I am reminded of the saying, "Do you want to be right, or do you want to be happy?" Although this sounds trite, it belies a real truth. Judgment is a prison of our own making, and I am telling you, you have the key in seeing the innocence of everything in the world both inside and outside of your very own self.

I realize this goes dead against our sense of fairness, but here goes. When you refuse to see your innocence or the innocence of the world, you are imprisoned in a victim mentality. The person who was assaulted is only free when they refuse to be a victim and, instead, embrace the innocence of the world. Their ego wants to blame, for it perceives blaming and judgment to be forms of protection, but in truth they are the opposite.

The same is true for your ego telling you lies that purport to lead you in the direction of being seen, heard, and loved. Like the Sirens on the rocks, these lies may look appealing, but they are a trap that will keep you locked in victimhood.

The most common form of victim mentality I see is blaming one's parents. It took me a while to see this in myself as I blamed my parents for my alarm. Eventually, I saw they got their alarm from their parents, and their parents got their alarm from *their* parents. The vast majority of compromised parents were compromised children themselves.

If your parent was abusive, narcissistic, rejecting, abandoning, or addicted, it is because their Ego Dragon had to adopt that strategy to protect them. They became that way to get their needs met. It's not personal to you.

Again, I have heard some horrendous stories of parental dysfunction, but please believe me when I tell you the only people I've known who've been able to move out of alarm have been the ones who've been able to break the victim mentality of blaming their parents. This is not to say they did not have "good reason" to blame their parents—only that those who were trapped in a victim story about their parents never were able to resolve their alarm.

Just reading this may feel alarming. Blaming your parents can be a way of making sense of your life, and know that you have my complete sympathy if you had a horrendous parent. So many people with anxiety disorders had caregivers that were absolute nightmares. I get why they deserve to be blamed—I really, really, really do. I just don't know of anyone who still blames a parent who's been able to resolve their alarm.

I am not saying to immediately gloss over pain by simply seeing and realizing the innocence of your parent(s) and the world at large. There are losses that absolutely need to be grieved. The inability to do so contributes greatly to unresolved trauma that leads straight into background alarm. There are millions of people who had a dysfunctional or abusive parent who still carry that pain.

But I know this: horrendous parents almost always had horrendous childhoods themselves. I have seen many a wounded child inside of one of my adult patients soften when they accept and embrace that their parent was steeped in alarm when that parent was themselves a child. I know for a fact my father was highly traumatized and alarmed. I saw a picture of him in school when he was about ten, and I could feel the intensity of his alarm just looking at his eyes in the photo. Seeing the innocence of my dad has allowed me to take a detour from those dark streets of blame and judgment and find a new avenue where I can see him in the light for the innocent soul he was. I needed to hold that view of his innocence while, at the same time, holding the view of his "crimes" to complete the grieving process so I could heal. It was only when I pendulated back and forth between my dad's innocence and his ego that the side of his innocence overwhelmed the side of his guilt.

Remember that even when we have devastating things happen to us, we have a choice in how we respond. Several Holocaust survivors have written or spoken about how their mindset—specifically, forgiveness and taking absolute responsibility for their thoughts—enabled them to survive the concentration camps and the emotional aftermath. Now, obviously, there were also physical factors that contributed to survival—millions of people died for reasons that had nothing to do with their mindset. But even for those who did survive, the emotional burden of coming to peace with something as momentous as their experience was immense, and a common theme for at least some who went on to live happy lives was they were able to let go of blame. It's not to say what the Nazis did was right or any less terrible—the survivors just decided to stop fixating on what happened so they could be present in their lives instead of stuck in the old trauma of the past.

We move out of victim mentality by realizing it is our ego trying to trick us out of taking responsibility for our own healing. Your ego does not want you to take any risks; it wants to keep you frozen right where you are. Once I became aware of the tendency to fall into victimhood, that awareness allowed me to take responsibility for my own life. By simply seeing it and saying to myself, "I am blaming others" or "I am shaming myself" was a massive awakening for me. Then adding "... and I love that about myself" allowed me to really see it, accept it, and ultimately take responsibility to heal it. As I did this, I started to see how it impacted all aspects of my life—and it astounded me how pervasive it had become in my system.

There have been times in my life when I was afraid to leave my condo and the only reason I did was because Buddha needed to go out. I would often inspire my own anger by telling myself in a tongue-in-cheek way that I was clearly too weak to get out of the house, go to work, or go do that stand-up gig. I would do it in a playful but biting way that would mobilize me. Note that the exact same method might not work for everyone; some people may feel worse or demeaned by pointing their sarcasm toward themselves, but for me it was a semi-humorous way to stop taking my fears so seriously.

I am willing to bet that, even while in the grip of your Ego Dragon, there have been many times you were afraid to do something but you felt the fear and did it anyway. It might be a relatively big thing, like speaking in front of others, or a relatively small thing, like taking your dog to the park. Perhaps it was going to a social gathering where you didn't know anyone. In those moments, you made a choice not to be a victim. Now, when I see myself adopting a victim stance, I use my compassionate connection to myself to mobilize me in a much more caring and loving way ... and I love that about myself!

Whatever method works for you, the important takeaway is to use your awareness as a point of choice to flow into the ABCs. Just the awareness that you are making yourself a victim ("Just my luck," "I can't do that," "Why me?" etc.) can be life-changing.

Once you find yourself there, get mad if you have to. Dance, move around, do anything that mobilizes you to overcome the paralysis of victim mentality. Then, you have the building blocks to adopt the opposite mentality, which substitutes victimhood with faith in the world and faith in yourself.

The more faith you create inside yourself, the less danger you will feel. Because faith is a belief from the inside, it's not something that can be manufactured or outsourced. Faith is an inside job.

Your faith in yourself will grow from the inside, and your victim mentality will have no choice but to be pushed out by your increasing faith.

In yourself.

And instead of unconsciously feeding into the problem, you are now consciously part of the solution.

90
Ego Trick: Inability to Receive

When we don't receive the care and support we needed as children, we will often adopt a coping strategy of telling ourselves we don't need it. If we deny care and support from others, we see that as less painful than experiencing the repeated disappointment of anticipating care and having it not be available to us.

In adulthood, this shows up as a dynamic where the ego resists positive attention from others and, more importantly, resists positive feedback from ourselves. You can see how this might be an especially sneaky trick, since the ABCs rely on us being kind to ourselves, and the Ego Dragon is trying to block us from precisely that!

Many worriers develop a coping strategy of putting our needs below the needs of others on the priority list. This is the beginning of codependency and people-pleasing. We literally stop being able to see what we need in favour of looking after someone else, usually a parent. But the irony is that, even if that parent or caregiver were to give to us (which in most cases they did, at least sometimes), we would block ourselves from receiving that which we so deeply crave.

My patient Anne blocked her ability to receive, and it showed up most in her relationship with food. She was extremely good at looking after the needs of her family but very poor at looking after herself. She would feed her family elaborate meals while she would restrict her own food. I believe this is because she lost touch with her body and wasn't able to detect when she was hungry. I'm sure her mother's comments to instill fear of gaining weight played a role as well.

Once Anne became aware of her pattern, when she would notice that she was denying herself food, she would say to herself, "This is my inability to receive." Then she would get grounded in her body and usually observe a sensation of desire for the food she had just made. She would put her hand over the area where she felt hunger and really connect with the sensation, while at the same time feeling the pleasant sensation of her own touch and the flow of her breath. She told me how she always got a feeling of reassurance from sensing the rhythmic rise and fall of her hand with her breath. Then she would give herself a taste of the food and savour that sensation as well. Finally, she would cap it off with a compassionate connection, saying how proud she was of her own creative cooking and appreciating herself for how good she was to her family. And, she didn't just say it, she felt it.

When Anne was able to connect with her body and become aware of her hunger, she was able to observe and respond to her own needs. She went from being blocked from receiving the pleasure and nourishment of a healthy, delicious meal to the opposite—gratefully receiving. I like to think she was both allowing herself to receive the food and receiving herself.

When we can't feel ourselves and our bodies, we may start to fill our needs in maladaptive ways. This is often how addictions start. When our powerful Ego Dragon blocks us from connecting with our bodies, addictions (food, porn, sex, gambling, drugs, alcohol, etc.) can become the only way we allow ourselves to feel pleasure. (I came up with this idea while reading Russell Brand's book *Recovery: Freedom From Our Addictions*, which, by the way, is excellent.)

How we respond to a compliment can be another tell that we are blocked from receiving. If you tell your friend you love her new haircut and she says,

"Really? I thought it might make my nose look too big," this may be a sign she's not comfortable receiving or entertaining kind thoughts about herself.

Sometimes I use this idea of giving one of my patients a compliment as a way to assess their ability or inability to receive. (I always give a true, genuine compliment that I mean, not just one made up to test them.) If someone responds by simply saying "Thank you" or "I appreciate that," they probably don't have a lot of negative self-talk and are able to easily receive. But if they temper it, deflect it, or make a joke, that means receiving is something we may need to work on.

The inability to receive is devastating. But like all the other tricks of the ego, it can be unlearned with the help of the ABCs.

Literally and figuratively, after you feed yourself, you can feed others if you choose to.

A critical part of the ABCs is to give to yourself—to create a compassionate connection where you are both giver and receiver. As you learn to give to yourself, you reactivate the part of you that shut down when you learned to deny yourself. This puts you in a sustainable position to help others because you are continuously filling yourself up. When you consistently give to yourself, you take responsibility for your own life. Further, receiving love freely from yourself and others is also a powerful antidote to victim mentality.

91
Ego Trick: Defensive Detachment

"Defensive detachment" is a term Dr. Neufeld uses to address the dissociation and withdrawal that occurs to protect us when we feel too emotionally vulnerable or threatened. It is exactly what I did when dealing with my father as I got older. Loving him and seeing him suffer became too much for me, so my dragon stepped in to block my vulnerability and I went into withdrawal and dissociation. Because my ego perceived that connecting emotionally was too risky, I closed off to real connection.

Over time, I started going into defensive detachment more and more to protect me from any kind of emotional pain. I'm sure you can imagine how this affected my intimate relationships as an adult. If you've suffered from chronic alarm, there's a good chance that you, too, adopted this ego protection strategy of defensive detachment.

Defensive detachment is withdrawing from connection because of the fear it will be taken away.

Using defensive detachment as a form of protection does block out some of the acute feelings of pain, but it comes at a cost. Going into defensive detachment creates more alarm in the long term, because when you detach from connection, you are separating from your true self and denying your own human need to be seen, heard, and loved.

This is why it's so hard to connect with people when we are anxious. I often tell the partners of my patients with anxiety about defensive detachment and why their partner seems to "leave them" in an emotional sense. I explain to the partner that their mate is not detaching from them but, rather, from their own self. This helps clear up confusion and helps the partner not to blame themselves for having done something to push their "anxious" partner away. You can't connect when your body and mind perceive you are in danger, even if that danger is purely imaginary worry.

The ego trick of defensive detachment is very hard on relationships because, whenever we get close to the other person, our dragon gets scared and pulls us away. It is so important to see when you are heading into a defensive, closed state and use the ABCs to bring you back into a compassionate connection with yourself so you can then provide that to your partner, parent, friends, or kids.

The tricky thing is, it is often hard to spot because there is a real sense that you need to withdraw. But just like when someone has a panic attack in a grocery store and then will avoid grocery stores, they are misunderstanding and mislabelling the problem. The goal in reducing alarm is to minimize the separation from yourself and others. Once you see you are withdrawing, you can use that as an entry point to the ABCs to reconnect to yourself, correcting the need to detach at its source.

I still hit the odd "anxiety patch" (like black ice, you don't see it until you're on it and start sliding) and still feel like I want to withdraw into defensive detachment. But it no longer surprises me—I recognize my dragon at work in this old pattern. I can notice my solar plexus alarm going into high gear, and this is my tell that it's time to follow my ABCs back to connection to myself.

Once I have reconnected to myself, I'm back in a place where I can reconnect to the other person.

When I see my urge to defensively detach, I call it out: "This is my old habit of defensive detachment, and I love that about myself!" I can breathe into my alarm and find something I really like about myself and about the person or people I am detaching from. This helps me get back into social engagement with myself and others, which gets me out of defensive detachment. This one realization has changed my life. It allows me to connect to myself and others before I am so deep into detachment that I become frozen in it.

92
Ego Trick: Resistance and Regression

Just like I have never met a person with anxiety and alarm who did not have a victim mentality, I've never met a worrier who wasn't full of resistance—often resistance to change and uncertainty, but the most devastating kind is resistance to love and connection.

The Ego Dragon wants to keep you exactly where you are, frozen in anxiety and alarm—again, not because it wants to hurt you but because it wants to keep you "safe," and it perceives that if you move you will put yourself in even greater danger. For me, because connection to my father was so painful, I learned to resist it. To allow love was to put myself in danger of losing it (again). In blocking my connection to my dad, I blocked connection to everyone else, including the connection to myself!

The ego acts like you are behind a tree, hiding from a predator or some ill-defined danger. There is real safety a relatively short distance away, but you resist allowing yourself to break cover long enough to get there. You are paralyzed with fear, but the ego resists any chance to escape, as it tells you things may get worse if you try to move. Of course, in this state of alarm, you believe your anxious thoughts—that your alarm is protecting you and that you'll be worse off if you dash to safety.

The amygdala never forgets, so if there's a situation remotely similar to the original trauma, you're emotionally transported back to that time—with the same emotional resources you had at that time. So if you experienced being verbally abused by a parent when you were six, today, if someone starts yelling (even if it's not at you personally), your amygdala will light up, and in some sense you're experiencing life as that frightened six-year-old.

Now, if you know hearing someone yell is one of your triggers, you can use your awareness of that as a switch to move you into your body, using sensation to keep you in the present moment so you don't get whooshed back into the past. But sometimes the trigger is just too powerful and the groove of the old trauma too deep, and you will slide into dissociation. This is exactly what happened to me when I heard that old musical phrase my father used to play on the trumpet. I got triggered and regressed before I realized what was happening. Even now, as I write this, I can feel that teenage-boy anger and resentment in my solar plexus as I imagine that damn trumpet.

But for me, that was the last time. Since then I've heard people playing the trumpet and, although I felt I did not like the sound, I didn't dissociate. I recognize that the sound of the trumpet is a trigger for me (even the thought is a trigger!), and I use it as an entry point into the ABCs. With awareness, I move into my body and breathe and connect with that boy who endured the opening phrase from "Dream a Little Dream of Me" thirty times in a row. I now move into compassionate connection with that boy and support him.

Anytime you feel pain, if you set an intention to stop resisting, the pain may not go away completely but it will be less. The psychiatrist and spiritual teacher Dr. David Hawkins tells the story of cutting his thumb in a mechanical saw and not being able to tolerate anesthetics, so he just had to accept the pain. He said that when he resisted the pain, the discomfort became intense, but if he stayed in full acceptance and flow, the pain eased considerably.

By definition, resistance blocks flow. When you consciously move from A to B to C, you are creating a flow state that allows you to move through your worries.

The energy around worries is very easy to fight and resist because you don't want those worries to be true. When you resist something, you close around it. Your goal is to let it pass through, not grasp it tighter. What we resist persists, but what we can yield to, we can heal through.

Here is a massively important point: Your ego will resist you doing the ABCs. Your dragon will try to dissuade you from doing anything that moves you out from behind that tree.

Fortunately, we know how to deal with this.

Feel your body right now. What is your jaw doing? Is your breath easy and slow, or is it shallow and tense? What are your shoulders doing? Are they relaxed, or are they up around your ears? Consciously make a point of slowing your breath and relaxing your jaw and shoulders, with an energy of allowing, not forcing. You can even close your eyes for a moment and put your hand on your chest. You are consciously easing your resistance. This awareness of your body and the grounding it creates is available to you in every moment. And it's what enables you to flow out from behind that tree and live your life, not resisting fear but using it as a reminder to connect.

93

Ego Trick: Compulsive Thinking

Compulsive thinking is nothing more than resistance to a quiet mind. As you learn to use the ABCs to create and move into a safe place in your body, your resistance to calm is reduced. You redirect the chaotic energy that was previously devoted to distracted and disorganized thinking and funnel it into the presence of being. The chaotic energy that was keeping you frozen behind the tree is consciously directed into flow and ordered movement.

Strange that movement is more orderly than being frozen, right? But that's how it works. Think of a computer with so many programs open that it just freezes and you get the spinning wheel of death. Your cursor will move a lot faster and you'll be able to work more effectively once you close down some programs—your anxious thoughts, alarm, and ego tricks—and free up some space to get things moving again and focus on the task at hand.

When our minds are worrying at gold-medal levels, it makes us feel like we are doing something. But although it may seem like we are moving, we are essentially digging ourselves a hole in place. The more we think, the more we dig. It was something we did as kids to help us feel like we were doing something when in reality we were powerless, but now it's just keeping us stuck. And it's another distraction the dragon uses to cut us off from connection.

If you get nothing else from this book, know that when you are in alarm, thinking will only make it worse. You have a choice to turn left into your body and feel, instead of turning right into your mind and hoping that magically "this time" you'll find the answer. It's like going to the hardware store looking for peanut butter—you're not going to find it there.

To be in alarm and choose to feel, instead of think, is the most powerful advice I can give you. I cannot tell you how liberating it is to be in alarm and make the conscious choice to redirect energy away from the thinking of your mind and into the feeling and sensation of your body.

You aren't the powerless child anymore. You have the power to establish a place in your body that is safe and give yourself what you never had.

When you can stay in the presence of the sensation of your body safely, you no longer need to regress back to the time of your original wounding. And the more you practice the ABCs, the more this safe place in your body expands.

You are no longer a slave to the need to ruminate, to solve, to be locked in your head with your only option to be stuck in the illusion you can think your way out of a feeling problem.

You now have a way to *feel* your way out.

94
Moving a Body That Is Frozen in the Past

For many of us with alarm, our bodies are frozen in the past. As children, it was progressively less safe to be in a body that was filled with alarm. The ego has actively and passively resisted allowing us to inhabit our bodies, and we have lost sensitivity to the ego's wisdom and grounding. Perhaps the most detrimental byproduct of having alarm in our body is that we live life in a "neck-up" cognitive space and not a truly feeling one—and feeling is where life is truly lived.

I gave a tremendous amount of credibility to my thoughts and, as a result, paid much more attention and credibility to my worries than those worries deserved. The more I ruminated on my pink elephants, the more real they appeared—becoming not only plausible but probable. In the process of absorbing myself in the world of my thoughts, I lost feeling. I lost much of life, and I regret that more than almost anything else. Hopefully this book will help you find feeling again, because living in your head is a waste of your life.

I was divorced twice because I was unable to feel connected. I told myself that it was that I was disconnected from my partners because of something in *them*, but in truth my body and my mind were separate, and I was disconnected from my own ability to feel. Since my relationship with others could be no better than the relationship with myself, the disconnect I felt from myself was the real cause of my failed relationships—but just as we might expect from an overprotective dragon, it's much easier to blame failure on someone else. I was pinning my hopes on outside relationships with others to save me, but saving me was something I had to do from inside myself.

There is no question that other people can help you along the way, but you can't simply offload all the responsibility onto them. In addition to my work with practitioners of somatic experiencing therapy and other body-based practices, I have found my own yoga practice to be one of my most powerful tools in getting myself out of a frozen state into flow. When your mind is in resistance, your body can be used as a powerful tool to release that resistance. Besides overcoming the resistance and stiffness in the body, qigong, tai chi, and yoga also create a flexible mind.

I became a yoga instructor because I had a felt sense when I did yoga that I was connecting to a place of comfort. I also had the distinct sense this place had been untouched for a long time.

The word yoga literally means to "yoke" or to join. (Fun fact: Sanskrit and English descended from the same ancient proto-Indo-European language.) Yoga helps me join my mind to my body and feel more grounded and present. I especially like yin yoga, which is very slow and focuses on holding relatively easy poses for a long period of time. I have found yin yoga to be very beneficial in calming alarm and connecting me to my body. But again, it's not just yoga—I have also found that tai chi slows mind and body down to a speed where it's easier to connect and that qigong nicely matches movement and breath together. In fact, anything you do, even random movements that match breath and movement, will connect and calm your system.

There's a typical body language and somatic signature that goes along with dissociation—slouching and shallow breathing. These movement practices will break that pattern in a way that is gentle and safe. When you are in movement and flow with your breath, you are showing yourself a direct way out of harm. The deeper your breath, the deeper your ability to feel.

The practices described above (yoga, tai chi, qigong) also increase flexibility. While any type of exercise gets us into our bodies, certain types of movement are more effective at bringing us into the present. Personally, I find it very hard to motivate myself to move when I am in alarm. There is a frozenness to it. In a meditation years ago, I was shown an image of myself with my body frozen in ice and was given the message that my anxiety (I had no concept of alarm at the time) was the ice, freezing my joints. As I imagined moving those joints, I felt and heard the cracking of the ice as I saw and viscerally felt it fall away.

That was an image I received years ago and to this day, whenever I do yoga the image of moving and freeing my joints, breaking the stagnation of alarm in my body, comes to me. There is a point, usually about ten minutes into my yoga session, where I enter a flow state. My breathing changes markedly from shallow to deep, and I feel like a weight has been lifted from me.

I do believe anxiety and alarm keeps me frozen in both body and mind. One of the reasons I believe yoga is so helpful is that it not only joins, or yokes, body to mind, but it creates a flexibility in both body and mind. When both body and mind are flexible and flowing, they more easily join together. For me, yoga creates a flow state that dissolves the emotional and physical rigidity that fuel alarm.

I have heard from countless patients how hard it is to exercise when they feel alarmed. It makes sense that if you are frozen, it's hard to move! Sometimes I have to prompt myself by counting down 5-4-3-2-1 and just get up and do a few stretches. More often than not, this flows into doing a few more, and then my breath settles and my body opens into a flow state. You don't have to run a marathon; simply stretching and moving your joints will begin to unlock the rigidity you hold in your body, and that quickly moves into your mind as well. The trick is to start.

When our bodies are rigid and inflexible, that state is transferred to the mind. The mind may be going a million miles a minute, but it's not flexible—it can't escape from the compulsion of ruminating on the same worries. And when we improve flexibility in the body, the mind follows. When you connect your body and breath in reciprocal flow, you've broken the anxiety/alarm feedback loop and started a new virtuous cycle. Congratulations!

When I was really suffering in alarm and anxiety in the early 2000s, moving into the body was easier said than done. For many years, I resisted breath and touch, yoga and meditation, tai chi and qigong. I *hated* my early yoga classes. At the time I told myself it was because everyone was better than I was, and my ego hated that—I felt like an elephant in a ballet class. But in retrospect, I think it was because it brought me into my body, and my ego hated that too. Still, I kept going back. Some part of me knew it was good for me.

I would repeat the same pattern: resist going to yoga like the plague, but then get there and go through class and finish it out feeling a sense of peace—a very rare occurrence during a very troubled time in my life. I am sure that I forced myself to sign up for yoga teacher training as a way of forcing myself not to quit yoga. If I became a yoga teacher, I thought I would be forced to practice, and if I felt competent by actually learning how to teach yoga, I would be much more likely to continue the practice. I knew my ego would resist, so I needed to cut off my escape route. As Tony Robbins says, I got to the island and burned the boats by signing up for teacher training.

And I absolutely loved it. For twenty-eight days in a row in the summer of 2007, I took the intensive yoga teacher training under Shakti Mhi at Prana Yoga in Vancouver. It gave me a brand-new relationship with my body.

Now you can start developing a new relationship with your body. You can regain access to its truth and wisdom.

One of the saddest things to me is when people who are out of touch with their bodies assume it's too late in life for it to be any other way. It is such an ingrained and unconscious habit to remain up in their thinking minds that they've completely abandoned the idea of going back to feeling inside their bodies. It reminds me of a sad story about how they keep elephants from running away. They keep a shackle around their leg tied to a thirty-foot chain that is tied to a stake in the ground. For the first few months of the elephant's life, it is bound by the chain, so it can only move within the thirty-foot radius. When the elephant is older, the chain isn't needed anymore—with the shackle on its leg, the elephant stays within the thirty-foot radius, even if the shackle isn't attached to anything. Metaphorically, I think we worriers assume we are unable to move to freedom in a similar way.

No matter how old you are, no matter how silly you might feel trying a yoga class when you've never heard the names of any of the poses and don't even have any idea what to expect, I promise you, it gets easier. And it is such an incredible gift.

If your experience in class is triggering, just remember your ABCs. Bring awareness to the reaction you're having. You're already in touch with your body and breath by being in class as long as you stay grounded in the present moment. And you can show yourself compassion by telling yourself things like, "I can't even touch my toes … and I love that about myself!"

In the disconnection where the mind moves too quickly and the body hardly moves at all, there is no reciprocal flow. We need a flow of energy to be in optimal physical and mental health. Your body holds the treasure—your innocent self. Embracing movement and flow can greatly enhance your ability to feel safe in your body. And remember, living in your mind is what got you where you are now. Isn't it worth at least trying a different way?

95
A New Default Setting

I remember that, while under the influence of LSD, I saw an image of my father in which he appeared to be dancing with an orca. I also had an experience of not being able to understand why I could not form water into a shape like a sphere with my hands, as you might make a snowball out of snow. I was genuinely perplexed by this.

After my trip, I was also curious as to why psychedelics allowed me to see the alarm in my body that had been invisible to me when my mind was not impaired. A frequent observation of people on psychedelics is they seem to lose the boundaries between self and not self and between conscious and unconscious—essentially, there is no separation. They feel "one with everything."

This is opposite of what the ego does. The ego reinforces the separate idea of self. The ego also keeps our conscious, "accessible on demand" mind separate from the deeper unconscious, "hidden" mind.

Now let me introduce to you a network in the brain called the default mode network (DMN). The DMN has been a relatively recent discovery in neuroscience. In short, it is a pattern of brain activity that occurs in identifiable brain structures that link together in a firing pattern when we are not focused on a particular task. Think of it like the daydreaming mode of the brain. The DMN may be a type of protective state when we are not actively involved in conscious processes like reading a book or solving a math problem.

The ego seems to be housed in the DMN. This would make sense, since for us worriers, rumination and worry seem to be a default state. That is, we fall into unconscious, compulsive worry automatically, seemingly by default. There is evidence that the DMN is linked to rumination, worry, self-judgment, and shame. So in effect, we can be worrying automatically, unconsciously, and passively when we fall into the brain's default mode.

Research has shown that under the influence of a psychedelic, the DMN shuts off. Since, as described above, when on psychedelics people seem to lose their ego as well, this has led to the hypothesis that the protective ego may be functioning from the DMN. This may be a biological explanation for why, when I took LSD, my ego was temporarily disabled and its protective function of keeping me out of my body dissolved, allowing me to connect with myself. But you know, I don't think you need to use psychedelics to get the same insights. Present moment awareness also brings us out of the daydreaming DMN, which limits the power of the ego to create separation in us.

This is why awareness is so critical. Advanced brain imaging studies show that when we focus on something specific, we "switch out" of the DMN. Those imaging studies also show that psychedelics shut down the DMN. In other words, activity in the DMN is diminished by both conscious attention to a task and psychedelic substances. The DMN lives in the past and the future but has no life in the present. Ironically, when you focus specifically on the DMN or the ego, they both disappear, as neither has life in the light of present moment awareness! The DMN acting in concert with the ego creates a type of anxiety and alarm daydream so, as you fall out of awareness, you fall into the nightmare of anxiety and alarm. When you are present, aware, and connected to yourself, the DMN and ego do not have the power to keep you in their daydream of anxiety and alarm. That is, awareness snaps you out of the grasp of the DMN and ego. This is one of the reasons I spent so much time showing you exactly what anxiety of the mind and alarm in the body looked like in the first two sections. On a physical level, it is the DMN that is probably responsible for projecting the pain of our past into our future as a way of warning us, but in doing so it uses the ego to create warnings, what ifs and worst case scenarios that only wind up creating more alarm. The Ego Dragon is back to its old tricks of separation, but if we can *see* the dragon's tricks, we no longer have to *be* them.

96
Change Your Focus

The dragon wants to keep you in your head, but that is a trap you'll never escape from.

On some level, you must use your head in awareness to see how to get out of your head—but the dragon doesn't want you to see you have a choice. When your overprotective ego scares and distracts you with worry, all your energy goes into survival concerns and there is no energy left for rational awareness in the present.

It is critical you bring yourself into the present moment and be able to see you have a choice. Again, the Ego Dragon and the DMN are like vampires— they cannot live in the light of present moment awareness. So let's make an intention to move them into that sunlight, shall we?

The ABCs at their core are all about creating the intention to stay in present moment awareness so you create a new pattern that becomes the new default setting—so instead of unconsciously making the problem worse, you can consciously start to make it better.

Much of this book has been about learning to see exactly where you have unwittingly turned right into thinking and been trapped in that overthinking cycle. By learning the ego's tricks—judgment, alienation, blame, shame, resistance, defensive detachment, inability to receive, compulsive thinking—you can recognize them and call them out.

But even if you don't know which trick the dragon is pulling right now, it doesn't matter. When you feel alarmed or catch yourself in worry, the path is always the same. Just get into your body and breathe. Do not try to fight with your anxious worries or alarm; change your focus.

As you become more aware of your own personal dragon's tricks, you will spot them earlier. And you will see the trap and move away, into your body, faster and faster. You will see how your body never lies to you, even though your mind constantly does.

Your ego's traps and tricks are like Lucy pulling the football away from Charlie Brown when he goes to kick it. You know what has happened every single time you've tried to kick the football before. This time, make a different choice. Resist the Siren-like appeal of that football and, instead, move into your body.

97
Moving Into the Present Moment Body

Here is a quick way to tell if you are in your body or in your anxious mind.

YOUR BREATH

When you are predominantly in your anxious mind, your breath will be high in your chest, with frequent, shallow, and relatively fast inhalations and exhalations. This is not to say you are breathing quickly; it's more like you are *not* breathing slowly.

When you are in your body and with your non-alarmed, authentic, innocent self, your breath will be slow and deep.

When you are in your head, your dragon is breathing you. It's keeping you frozen behind that tree. Your dragon believes you need to stay with short, shallow breathing so you won't get spotted by a predator. In other, deeper words, the peaceful innocence that is your underlying and perpetual presence is not breathing you into expansive growth and movement. Rather, your protective Ego Dragon is breathing you with the mandate to keep you protected and frozen in place. Anyone who has been too afraid to get out of the house or even move from the bed to the shower knows exactly what I mean.

Our minds and bodies take their cues from our breath to assess safety or danger. If our breath is shallow and rapid, the unconscious message is that we are in need of protection, and the shallow, quick breath of protection continues in a feedback loop. This is why it is so important to move into body and breath with the ABCs. When we consciously move into our bodies, our breath naturally slows, switching the control away from the unconscious, mind-based, dragon-controlled ego protection. Remember the analogy of the two tuning forks that vibrate to the same frequency. When one is struck, they both start to vibrate—unless one is tamped down with a weight to keep it from vibrating. Your ABCs are the weight that keeps your foreground alarm from feeding into your background alarm. They are your tool to break the cycle.

Your breath is the best, conscious link to your parasympathetic nervous system—but when your dragon is in control, it won't let you go there. I would sometimes go for hours before I checked in with my breath and realized I'd been in shallow, rapid breath for who knows how long. This is why it's so important to make a habit of checking in with yourself and why awareness is such a powerful tool. You have to see it to change it.

Right now, pause for a second and check the depth and quality of your breath. Put your hand on your chest and connect with your touch as you feel your chest rise and fall. See how your breath naturally becomes slower and deeper as your focus drops out of your head and into your body. If you have an essential oil that calms you, breathe that in. Close your eyes (if you're not driving) and really savour your breath.

Go ahead, I'll wait. It's worth it.

Welcome back. Now think of something you appreciate or are grateful for about yourself, like appreciating yourself for reading this book. Don't resist! You can receive this. Compliment yourself and say thank you in appreciation and gratitude for your own self-care.

Go ahead, I'll wait again. It's worth it.

That's a mini version of the ABCs. and you can do this multiple times a day. Now, there are other ways to tell if you're in your body. Here are a few:

YOUR JAW

When I talk about breath as a barometer of being in body or anxious mind, my wife always reminds me to remember to talk about relaxing the jaw. She likes to tell me that you can't breathe fully when your jaw isn't relaxed, and while I remind her she is not a doctor, she reminds me to try breathing with a tight jaw and then with a relaxed jaw, and there is a marked difference. (I guess doctors aren't the only people who know anything.)

So, what is your jaw doing right now? Is it relaxed and loose or are you holding it tight? Make a conscious effort to allow your jaw to loosen and relax.

SMELL

I discovered essential oils a few years ago in my search to help people relieve anxiety and alarm and found they are often very helpful in getting people into sensation. I look at essential oils as a kind of switch to make it clear to the system that the focus is to be on sensation and not on thought. I also think a strong scent (pleasant or even unpleasant) breaks the daydreaming DMN and helps bring us into deeper conscious awareness.

Out of all of our senses, the sense of smell is the only one that goes directly to the limbic, or emotional, brain. Touch, hearing, sight, and taste are all "pre-processed" in the brain centre called the thalamus before their information reaches the other parts of the brain. Smell is not filtered by the thalamus; rather, smell sends the raw data to the limbic brain, and it has an immediate and powerful effect.

This is a throwback to thousands of years ago when we relied on smell to warn us of danger and give us pleasure (which had the biological function of drawing us closer to food or an attractive mate). This was information we needed quick access to for survival purposes. Although we don't have the same keen sense of smell we had thousands of years ago, this sense is still strongly linked to emotion and memory, and it is still something we can use to calm our limbic brain and bring us out of thinking and into sensation.

I have found that telling my patients to have a little vial of an essential oil they find grounding and stimulating is a great "shortcut" for moving into sensation. If you imagine a boxer being brought back to his senses with smelling salts, an analogous thing happens to us when we smell something pungent like an essential oil. In the ABCs, after the awareness phase, I often suggest people use an oil they like as a way of making a distinct signal to move into sensation, and the essential oils do that quite well. Aromatherapists have made entire careers on finding essential oils that help people soothe pain, anxiety, and myriad other conditions.

TOUCH

Touch is a key part of getting into your body. Your awareness will automatically go to the place of sensation. In my wife's work as a somatic experiencing practitioner, she uses touch to bring her clients into sensation of safety of the present moment. But even touch on your own self is grounding. Touching the area around your heart or putting your hand on your belly to feel the rise and fall of your breath is soothing and grounding. If you feel your alarm in your belly, you can touch there. If your alarm is in your throat, touch there. Keep it slow and focused—the opposite of the superficial quick pace of the regular world. The slower the better.

I find touching my chest over my alarm and really savouring the sensation of my breath helpful. Once I see that I am being seduced by thoughts, I call out those thoughts as intrusive and set an intention to move into sensation. I use my hand on my chest and savouring my breath (often with smelling an essential oil) as ways of reinforcing that intention, telling my entire system we are moving into present-moment sensation.

You don't have to rely on putting your hand on your chest and focusing on your breath. That is what I find works best for me, but there are other options you can use. The point is to get out of your head into your body—so whatever *you* find works best, use that.

Patting your shoulders and upper arms with opposite hands, rubbing your hands or fingertips together, or rubbing your face like you are pretending to wash it are great touch exercises to redirect attention from thinking to feeling. Because so much of your brain is devoted to the sensation of your hands and face using these areas at the same time, it gets your brain's attention.

Doing a rhythmic beat with your hands on your chest (or over the place you feel alarm) is a wonderful way into savouring sensation in the present moment and out of ruminative thoughts of the future. When you withdraw energy from rumination and worry and bring yourself into the present moment, you lessen the power of those ruminations because the mind energy that was solely devoted to the rumination is now split with the body energy of relaxation.

Here's another exercise you can do. This one is like giving yourself a hug. Take your right hand just under your left armpit and your left hand over your right shoulder. Squeeze to the level you feel most connected. (And remember, with a hug you don't want to be the one who lets go first—take a minute to receive it!)

Some of my patients really love support on their head and neck. Although most people experience their alarm in the torso and abdomen, I've seen more than a few who feel their alarm in the back of their neck and even their forehead or face.

Go ahead and try it now. Put one hand behind your neck and the other across your forehead. Many of my patients have told me the hand on the neck reminds them of supporting the head of a young infant. Who knows—it may even bring back a distant sensation of physical support when you were an infant. For me, my mother would use her fingertips to make circles on my forehead or rub my back when I was child, and I still ask my wife to do the same thing. I find it very relaxing. Replicating a touch or smell that calmed you and brought you into sensation when you were young is a very potent way to induce that relaxation response in the body.

Berns Galloway, one of my wife's instructors for her somatic experiencing training, teaches another technique for getting into the body that I've found quite helpful. Berns suggests getting a towel or a scarf and wrapping it around you at various levels like hips, waist, chest, and shoulders, kind of like you are drying yourself off when you come out of the shower. But instead of sliding it back and forth, you just hold the towel with your hands in front of you so the towel makes a horseshoe shape and, as you push forward with your hands, the towel puts pressure across your back. Many people will have a preference for a level where the towel feels best. Try it at different levels and find the best place for you. I know this sounds odd coming from a medical doctor, but I was surprised by how helpful it has been for both me and my patients.

Know that your tools for getting into your body don't have to be anything fancy or even a specific "practice." They can truly be whatever works for you—even if it's something silly. My friend Angela bought me one of those soft rubber stress balls. It feels really squishy and changes colour when you squeeze it. She bought it for me as a kind of a joke, teasing me about being a stress doctor (she's a lawyer)—but I love that thing and I use it all the time. It sits on my bedside table and I squeeze it every night. I really devote my attention to all the sensations with it. It feels soft and pliable. It's yellow but it turns to orange when I stretch it. I'll hold it up to my ear and listen to it as I squash it against my face. I'll even smell the rubber. I know I am more than a bit obsessed with it—but that's okay because it really is good at bringing me into sensation, which is such a welcome change to being up in my head.

One thing to keep in mind in moving into your body: Go slow—and then slow that down by half. Your mind goes very quickly, and that becomes a habit. The mind is whirring away and you probably don't notice how fast it's going until you decide to move into sensation. One of the reasons our mind and body get out of sync is because, in many ways, the body moves much slower than the mind. When we slow down, in general, the mind and body have a chance to sync up.

Now, when we speak of our "no thinking" rule, there is one exception. Of course, I would prefer you see when you are in an ego-based coping strategy and proceed directly to letter B, immediately moving from thinking to feeling. However, I know firsthand that there are times when the urge to think is so great that you just can't avoid it. (I have been there more times than I can count.) In that case, I allow myself one thought. It is actually a question. That question is: "Am I safe in this moment?"

If you must think something, think this.

You learned the power of this question from Part 2. In almost every moment of your life—unless you are in acute alarm because your physical safety is at risk in which case you need to run or fight and not be asking yourself questions—the answer to this question will be yes.

If I am so activated I'm on the verge of panic, I have a hard time moving into my body and breath. I find that it helps if I say to myself something like, "I know you're freaking out right now, but are you safe in this moment? Can you look around and see that in this moment, right here, right now, despite the alarm feeling and the anxious thinking, in reality you are perfectly safe?"

This question has helped me more times than I can count, especially in the middle of the night. It helps me see that I am truly safe. It helps me find some grounding, and from that grounded place, I can move into the sensation of my body and breath. Perhaps I will smell an essential oil to further bring me into sensation. Then I can focus on the hand on my chest, and my breath, and find a safe place in the present moment of my sensation.

98
Social (Dis)Engagement System

Did you know the face is the only place in the human body where the muscles are attached directly to the skin? That is because so much connection and warmth can be transmitted through our facial expressions. We are social animals, and social connections start as early as birth. I delivered many babies

282 | ANXIETY RX

in my medical career, and over the course of my years as a doctor, getting the baby to the mother as soon as possible after birth became more and more of a priority.

Early in my career, when a baby was born, the nurses would dry the baby off and we'd do an examination. And that took time. The medical community has since realized how important it is to start the mother-child connection as early as possible. Provided the baby is not in distress, it gets skin-to-skin time with mom before anything else happens, such as cutting the cord and washing and weighing the baby. This first moment of connection is often referred to as "bonding" and is a way of engaging the child's SES from the start.

The SES is a two-way system that has both expressive and receptive qualities that guide interactions between people. Put very simply, the SES modulates the expression and reception of love and compassion *from* ourselves to others and the flow of love *to* ourselves. Starting from infancy, the more secure connections you have with your mother and other important people in childhood, the more the SES matures. And the more the SES matures, the more capacity is created to give and receive love with others and ourselves.

The opposite is also true. If you do not get enough engagement, love, and compassion from your caregivers from birth onward (or worse, your caregivers are the source of alarm), the SES fails to fully mature, and your ability to self-soothe and give and receive compassion and love (both to others and yourself) is also impaired.

We learned a lot about how this system develops from heartbreaking research on Romanian orphans in the 1980s. While living in orphanages, these infants received no emotional nurturing—no touch, no play, no books read to them or "baby talk" to help them get used to their caregiver's patterns of speech and expression—even when their physical needs (food, clothing, toilet, bathing) were met. This wasn't your typical randomized, controlled trial (to treat children this way would actually be completely cruel and unethical), but given the conditions in the orphanages because of Romania's economic and political situation, researchers followed the children through life to see the lasting impact of their early years. When the country opened up after dictator Nicolae Ceaușescu was overthrown, child development researchers who visited the orphanages reported the eerie silence inside; the children had simply stopped crying because they had learned that nobody would respond. Compared to children who had not been raised in institutions, the orphans had different patterns of electrical activity in their brains, and their brains were observably physically smaller, with lower volume of both gray matter and white matter.

Foster and adoptive families that took in these formerly institutionalized children noticed a pattern: The children would hold their arms up to be picked up and held, and when they were, they pushed to get away and be put back down. This process would repeat itself over and over. It was like they craved love and attention, but once it was available, they were unable to tolerate the connection. I find this both fascinating and curious, as it is reminiscent of many people with anxiety: They want to trust the nurturing and connection, but they can't seem to sustain it.

When the SES fails to mature, we develop strategies such as resistance, inability to receive, and defensive detachment in a pattern similar to the exaggerated version seen in the Romanian orphans. The good news is the brain is incredibly plastic. I, for one, believe that you *can* "pick up where you left off"—you can mature and enhance the brain's ability to connect with self and others at any age. (There is hopeful news about the orphans too: their language, IQ, and social-emotional functioning improved as they spent time in loving families, especially if they were adopted out of the orphanage before the age of two.)

If we are going to embark on this project, it might help to know a little more about how the system works. Polyvagal theory, first named and studied extensively by Dr. Stephen Porges and adapted specifically to therapy by Deb Dana, LCSW, has provided valuable and practical insights to understand how anxiety and alarm affect the human nervous system.

One of the main nerves involved in the SES is the vagus nerve, the longest nerve of the parasympathetic rest-and-digest nervous system.

The vagus plays a major role in the SES, relaying the presence of safety and connection and inducing relaxation. The vagus is also thought by many to be intimately involved in the more emotional "heart-to-heart" connection that is so important in the feeling of comfort and safety. And if you've ever wondered why you have trouble eating when you are alarmed, look no further than the influence of the vagus nerve, as it stops gut motility. When your gut stops moving, the urge to eat stops with it.

In the polyvagal theory, the vagus nerve has two main branches—the dorsal vagus and the ventral vagus. The dorsal and ventral refer to the differing positions of the nerve, the dorsal toward the back of the body (think of the dorsal fin on a whale) and the ventral toward the front. The ventral (front) side of the vagus nerve attunes to cues of safety and emotional connection. It supports a sense of physical safety and calming emotional connection to others. The dorsal (back) part of the vagus nerve responds to cues of potential trouble.

If you grow up with trauma, the dorsal vagus learns to be on a hair trigger, ready to spring into protection at the slightest provocation. In those of us with stored alarm, we see threat in things that are not threatening and produce threat by our own worry, so our dorsal vagus gets lots of practice. When we experience a cue of danger (and this can even be just worry), the dorsal vagus will shut off social engagement and we can even feel frozen. This makes sense from an evolutionary standpoint since you do not need to be socially engaged and connected when you are in physical danger—your energy is needed elsewhere, and there's no need to be "open" to social connection when you are face to face with a poisonous snake, especially if it's your ex.

The dorsal vagus, in concert with the amygdala and the Ego Dragon, pulls us away from connection, out of awareness, and into a state of social disengagement. I have called this protective mobilization with loss of emotional connection the *social disengagement system* (SDS), in contrast to the SES you know about already.

For our purposes, it's useful to know about two chemicals in the body that play a role in the SDS and the SES: *cortisol* to move us into protection and away from perceived danger (the SDS) and *oxytocin* to move us toward growth and love (the SES). Cortisol is often referred to as "the stress hormone" because it acts in concert with adrenaline (aka epinephrine) to mobilize the body for protection, and oxytocin as "the love hormone" because it creates a sense of bonding between people. When you start a new relationship and you are smitten with each other, oxytocin is secreted in great quantities, and you just want to be around your new mate all the time. Oxytocin is also responsible for bonding between mother and child during that skin-to-skin time after birth. Cortisol plays a role in protection through the dorsal vagus, and oxytocin acts in connection through the ventral vagus.

The ventral vagus is the main pathway used in the SES. The ventral vagal system relies heavily on input from the head and neck, especially tone and prosody of voice, facial expressions, and eye contact. When we feel safe, calm, and connected, we are in a ventral vagal state. We feel relaxed and receptive to connecting with others. When the ventral vagus is active, we make eye contact, our voice has a pleasant and even lilting quality, our facial muscles are relaxed, and we readily smile and laugh.

If you struggle with significant anxiety and alarm, your "set point" is likely leaning in the dorsal vagal direction. Your system resists connection because your mind and body simply aren't open to warm human contact if you sense a danger that is real or simply imagined. (As an example, I had a tendency to believe connection was not safe because of what connection to my father meant in my childhood, so when faced with connection, I tended to separate and disengage in defensive detachment as a form of protection.) This resistance keeps you separate from others, which activates your sympathetic nervous system, aka foreground alarm. In resisting connection, your body secretes cortisol and epinephrine, giving you that "flushed" feeling so many of my patients complain of. The foreground alarm activates your background alarm, and your system moves into dorsal vagal shutdown, even further blocking the very connection you need to move out of foreground and background alarm.

One of the most frustrating aspects of alarm and anxiety is that we become alarmed at the prospect of human connection because of what that connection meant in our childhood. The Catch-22 here is that human connection is exactly what we need to mature our SES and make a connection to ourselves that would break the cycle of alarm and anxiety. In essence, anxiety and alarm are so hard to treat because we have trained ourselves to resist the connection that we so desperately need to heal.

As an aside, this is what happens in social anxiety disorder. Imagine you want to go into a party but you struggle with anxiety and alarm and fear connection. As you get closer to going into the party, you move into dorsal vagal immobilization and maybe become frozen in outright dissociation. As you move into alarm, you lose access to ventral vagal SES skills. You can't make or hold eye contact, your voice is flat and monotone, and you cannot read other peoples social cues or body language. On top of that, when your SES is offline, you are much more likely to read neutral signs as negative. Someone politely excusing themselves to go and talk to someone else is seen as a personal affront when it was merely that they hadn't seen that friend in a long time. Your alarm deepens and your dorsal vagus is activated more, encouraging your system to disengage.

If you are in alarm, of course you are going to shy away from social interactions. Without access to your ventral vagus and SES, you can't "speak" the social language, so you go into a protective freeze state, which locks you out of any possibility of being social. I believe social anxiety disorder should be called social alarm disorder or maybe even social freeze disorder because that is exactly what it is. You simply cannot be social and connected when the physiology of your mind and body is telling you that you are in danger.

99
A System to Engage Your Social Engagement System

You may have noticed above I mentioned something called a vagal "set point." You've probably heard this phrase used when it comes to our weight and the fact that for some people it settles within a small range and it's very difficult for them to gain or lose weight outside of that range, regardless of diet or activity levels. What if there is also a "set point" for intrapersonal and interpersonal engagement that is mediated by the vagus nerve based on the quality of social engagement, love, and connection we had in our childhood? We still go into and out of dorsal and ventral activation at different times, but the "set point" we return to varies from person to person and is influenced by our experiences. In addition to governing how much time we spend in alarm, your vagal set point would determine how lovingly and compassionately you see yourself.

Albert Einstein is reported to have said, "The most important decision we make is whether we believe we live in a friendly or hostile universe." While I don't disagree, I don't believe it *is* a decision until we are aware of the question. I believe we see the world the way our nervous system learned to perceive the world, and this happens mostly outside of our awareness. In other words, we see the world now in a way that is determined by the way our nervous system experienced the world back then in our childhood.

Have you ever thought of yourself as someone who directs your empathy and attention towards others and not enough into yourself? I have seen many people like my patient Anne who looked after her family but abandoned herself. I would propose to you that you can shift that self-abandonment by bringing your level of love and compassion for yourself into your awareness. Just making yourself aware of your ability to love and be empathic towards yourself can break a very old program. In addition to being more fulfilled and connected to ourselves, this shift inwards makes us less vulnerable to alarm and dorsal vagal shutdown and more able to access and stay with ventral vagal activation and peaceful connection. The more you commit to ventral vagal connection, the more you deepen that groove of caring for yourself. The groove in the snow can work *for* us too! The more we commit to ventral vagal connection, the more we feel connected to ourselves and others. We heal in relationship to others because it uses the same SES we use to relate to ourselves.

Remember, it is *in* us to be connected to each other. That is the way it's supposed to work. You have a system innate in you that is designed to connect mother to baby and person to person. The system is optimized when it has a healthy dose of connection and compromised when it doesn't. This social engagement system circuitry is in all of us. Let's make a firm intention to let it do its job of creating an empathic connection to our own selves and others that it's been designed to do with thousands and thousands of years of practice!

Perhaps there are some people out there who are incapable of empathy for themselves or others, but it's only because they are not interested in cultivating it in themselves. They are not reading this book. You are—and the fact that you are here, wanting to work on this, makes me very confident that you can improve your SES and boost your vagal "set point." The system is in all of us; it's just that sometimes it gets very out of practice and just needs some loving attention of its own.

So, what can you do to consciously work on this? We always come back to the ABCs as our foundation, and here are some additional tips:

EYE CONTACT

One of the things that helped me greatly was very simple. Before I even knew much about the ventral vagus and polyvagal theory, I had read an article in a psychology magazine about increasing eye contact with someone you feel connected to as a way of increasing oxytocin and soothing anxiety. I tried it with my wife and the results were immediate. It wasn't to the point of a staring contest; it was just to make a commitment to do it more often and hold it for longer than usual. If you are lucky enough to have a person in your life you trust, this is a great way to deepen your connection. (P.S. This even works with your pet—especially dogs.) Remember that eye contact is part of your SES and that your ventral vagal nerve helps process the sensory input from eye contact. So it makes sense why this would work, even though I didn't understand the reasons then.

At first, I noticed I had some resistance to eye contact, and that didn't surprise me since my Ego Dragon's job was to protect me from connection and vulnerability. The resistance was there, but I also felt a distinct benefit, so I stuck with it. And, initially, I didn't tell Cynthia what I was doing, so there was no pressure from anyone but myself to maintain my little eye contact experiment.

SINGING, CHANTING, VOCALIZING, LAUGHING, CRYING, FACE YOGA!

The vagus nerve has a branch that connects to the larynx, or voice box. Vibration and stimulation of the voice has a calming effect on the system. When you sing, chant a mantra, or use any form of rhythmic vocalization, you stimulate (i.e., create more tone in) your ventral vagus, releasing oxytocin and building capacity in your SES.

Laughter, by the way, has oxytocin-releasing power all by itself. In addition, laughing creates a form of breathing that is soothing and stimulates your vagus nerve. Thousands of years ago, laughing was a sign of safety and connection as we would laugh in a safe group of our tribe, and laughter in a group setting especially releases oxytocin. I saw this for myself—there were few feelings as good as when I did stand-up and had a great set!

Crying also has oxytocin-releasing power all on its own and also sometimes involves vocalization. Tears are a powerful mechanism for self-soothing and connecting with ourselves after a painful event such as a death or a breakup. After a good cry, the reality of the loss is the same, but the emotion (or at least part of it—we might have several good cries after some events) has moved through us. I think this is why men have a much higher suicide rate and rates of addiction than women; crying has been taken away from us by cultural norms that shame men and boys who cry. This isn't popular for a man to express, but I can feel when alarm energy is building in me and I know I need to cry to release it. With my old conditioning, I still find it very difficult to access tears, but I know I need to. Accepting and allowing my tears, although it strongly goes against my conditioning, is a small price to pay to get myself to discharge that energy, because I know that if I don't, I'll experience a significant rise in my alarm. Admitting this is hard, but it's part of accepting myself and the gifts of my sensitivity.

Lastly, there is something called face yoga. Yes. It's a thing. I won't get into it too much here, but there is evidence that the tone of your facial muscles play a role in your mood by sending signals back to the brain. It's been shown that if your facial muscles are formed to create a smile, you feel happier, and if your facial muscles are formed in a frown, you'll feel down. I include it as a bit of fun, but it may well show some promise in mood disorders. Certainly laughter yoga in which people gather in a group to laugh has a positive effect on mood.

COMPASSION

You probably knew this would be on the list. We've talked about it a lot.

Giving of yourself releases oxytocin. Giving *to* yourself releases more. Oxytocin opens the treasure chest that holds your innocence and your true, authentic self.

You can't feel loving compassion and alarm in the same moment. (Go ahead, try it). So all you need to do is expand the time you feel compassionate and loving and you automatically decrease the time you spend in anxiety and alarm. It is a form of the concept where love crowds fear out of the box. Easier said than done, granted, but this book is designed to show you exactly what you need to do to increase compassionate connection to yourself and others.

Building compassion into your life as a recurring theme, a daily practice, and an intention you set is a signal to the universe that you view it as friendly rather than hostile—and remember, what we focus on, we get more of.

RHYTHMIC BREATHING

Your vagus nerve innervates the throat and lungs, and breath is a highly effective way of moving into a ventral vagal state that is more socially engaged and connected. When you are alarmed, your shallow, rapid breathing is an indication the dorsal vagus is more active, but note that this is both cause and effect. Just as vagal nerve activity influences the quality of your breath, consciously taking control of your breath can influence the vagal nerve activity. You can use deep, connected conscious breathing to move into a state where the ventral vagus is dominant.

In yoga, we have breathing practices called *pranayama* that are tremendously effective in creating a more grounded state in our minds and bodies by consciously breathing slowly and deeply and bringing a keen sense of awareness to the breath.

You don't necessarily need to do much. When you stop and focus on your breath, it naturally slows and deepens. Any process (even holding your breath) that puts you in control of your breathing will break the pattern of the alarm breathing for you. There are lots of breathing techniques that break the cycle of the alarm. One involves breathing in, holding it for a few seconds, and making your exhalation slightly longer than your inhalation. A favourite of mine is to draw a deep breath in, hold for a count of four, and then breathe out through slightly pursed lips so it lengthens the exhalation and I can feel some resistance to my exhalation.

I encourage you to look up Ujjayi breath as it is a very potent way of stimulating the vagus nerve. To give you a brief sense of it, put your hand up to your mouth and pretend you are fogging up a mirror or the lens in your glasses so you can clean them. Now see if you can hold your throat in that position as you breathe in and out. Darth Vader was very good at Ujjayi breath. (He did seem to hold a lot of alarm, though.)

You might also look into Holotropic Breathwork®, which you learned about in Part 2. (Remember, the technique invented by the doctor who was trying to help people reproduce the effects of LSD without actually taking LSD?) Personally, it's been very beneficial for me, and another benefit is that you don't have to take LSD to do it.

MOVEMENT

There's a whole chapter on the power of movement above, but I wanted to include it here because when we're talking about ways of connecting with ourselves, you really can't leave this off the list. Yoga, qigong, and tai chi are my favourites for connecting the body and mind. When we are relaxed and comfortable—which is the effect movement has on us—that's a sign of ventral vagal activation. Lastly, who knows what kind of connections you'll make at yoga class?

MEDITATION

If you suffer from anxiety and you find trying to meditate difficult, you're not alone. I can offer you an explanation of this difficulty that is true for me. Meditation brings me into direct contact with the alarm in my body because I am unable to distract into my thinking. You likely know all too well how your Ego Dragon will swoop in with distracting thoughts to keep your mind from stillness.

But I promise that after you practice meditation for a while, you'll get more skilled at separating from your thoughts.

For a reason I can't explain—and I usually try to have an explanation for *everything*, so maybe I am finally getting out of my head?—once I started following the ABC process regularly, I found it so much easier to stick to a regular meditation practice. Before that, I was very inconsistent with meditation. I believe that the more I practiced the ABCs, the more of a place of comfort I created in my body, so I didn't resist wandering in there during meditation.

When you're starting out, don't set a goal of sitting and meditating for half an hour. This will be the longest half hour of your life and, probably, the only half hour you ever spend meditating!

I often tell people to use the 2-3 Rule: two to three minutes of focusing on your breath two to three times a day for two to three weeks. "Start low and go slow" is a line we use in medicine to describe starting someone on a medication; the same can be said for meditation!

CREATE RITUALS

Rituals are conscious activities in a repeatable sequence. I believe one of the reasons our culture is in chaos and alarm is that there is so much inconsistency in the world. As the world gets busier, we've lost touch with our rites of passage and our rituals—and without rituals, our days have no bookends, no boundaries, and no grounding.

Rituals create certainty and structure because they are performed the same way, which is why they are so reassuring to children. If your childhood lacked rituals and structure, it's time to create some for yourself and bring that sense of grounding and predictability to your relationship with yourself.

If there's one thing I know for sure, it is that people who struggle with alarm and anxiety tend to unconsciously create chaos in their lives as a form of distraction. They also create chaos because of its familiarity (this being a theme from their childhood). Remember way back in Part 1, where I talked about Freud's concept of repetition compulsion, such as the urge to equate familiarity with security by reproducing the chaotic events of your childhood? You may know at a conscious level that chaos in your life creates alarm, but at the level where your unconscious behaviours and motivations lie, there is a pull to repeat the turmoil. This is driven by the false impression that uncertainty must be avoided at all costs because it's the unknown that creates pain while what's familiar will keep us safe.

But now that you know better, you can do better. You can create your own rituals for yourself.

There are morning rituals, prayer rituals, meditation rituals, and lots of internet posts and articles on creating rituals in your life. It is really about finding what resonates with you. A ritual is often about creating a repeatable, safe place for yourself in your body and mind.

The ABCs are one of my rituals, although there is a great deal of flexibility in the way I practice them. That flexibility is available to you too. Trust yourself to find what works best.

AVOIDING SOCIAL MEDIA AND MEDIA IN GENERAL

Three quotes that highlight the effect of social media:

"Comparison is the thief of joy." – Theodore Roosevelt

"Don't compare someone else's outside life to your inside life." – Anne Lamott
(my paraphrase)

"Only an ego compares." – Gila Golub

I do think we get a hit of dopamine from social media that makes us temporarily feel good—temporarily being the operative word. Even though that hit is instantaneous and doesn't last, we worriers crave any positive hits we can get (this is also why we are sitting ducks for addiction). If you struggle with alarm, the risks of social media outweigh the benefits because the dorsal vagal cortisol response keeps us clicking for the next hit of dopamine—and we worriers need less manipulation of our neurotransmitters, not more.

In addition to being addictive, social media is a fantastic way to distract yourself from your actual life. There's nothing wrong with spending a little time on social media, but if you're using it as an escape and if energy you could be putting into mindful connection with yourself is being sidetracked into mindless pursuit of other people (like "haunting" your ex), it's not serving you. It's actually keeping you out of your ventral vagal-dominant state. Pretend connections (or at least connections that are way less satisfying than time spent together in person) are stealing your attention from improving your connection with yourself.

Remember, sometimes you can make something much better just by stopping what was making it worse. Having your system awash in cortisol from the twenty-four-hour news cycle and comparing yourself on social media is not helping you. Of all the items on this list, this is definitely the easiest one to find time for. You don't have to do anything extra—just stop doing something that will open up space and time for you to connect with yourself.

PLAY AND CREATIVITY

In ayurvedic medicine, they say that creativity is the cure for anxiety. In the coming years, I believe we will see play (defined simply as finding what you like and doing it) incorporated more and more into therapy for anxiety and depression. Engagement in play is one of the most healing and most underrated modalities. I cannot emphasize enough the role of finding what you enjoy—and doing that.

Many of my patients say they don't know what play is for them anymore. A good place to start is what you liked to do for fun when you were a child. Was it riding your bike or singing or dancing or drawing? Playing a sport or playing an instrument? Pick one of your favourite childhood activities back up and see if you still like it. It might take a little while to relax and enjoy it since we are so used to telling ourselves that play is a waste of time, but that's just your Ego Dragon talking.

Play and creativity have been shown to mobilize the ventral vagus and sympathetic nervous system, so they can be powerful tools as you work to develop social engagement with self and others. And think of the fun you'll have while doing it!

LOVING THE LOVE

There is something I've observed in myself and most of my "anxious" patients. We actually love and crave connection from others, especially our family and friends. One of the "crimes" of the protective Ego Dragon is that it directs us away from love and connection under the guise of protecting us. That being said, I've observed that people with anxiety and alarm are almost always very sensitive and really crave connection but are afraid to have it and to trust it. One of the reasons we are so alarmed is that we are pulled in two opposite directions: to relish the love and resist it at the same time. Our SES and SDS are active simultaneously. No wonder we are alarmed!

When you block attachment as a form of protection, you are starving for it when you finally allow it. Wanting the love and being resistant to it becomes this deep inner conflict that freezes us in dorsal vagal immobilization. It reminds me of the saying, "You can't have your cake and eat it too."

What the hell good is cake if you can't eat it?

So, how *do* you "love the love" if your system has been programmed to fear it?

Let me answer you with a story of one of my patients, Anna, who was recovering from anorexia nervosa. I met Anna when she was thirty years old. She was upbeat and quirky with youthful, childlike energy. She was tall, about five foot nine, and looked to be very fit and muscular. Anna had for the most part recovered from her eating disorder, although she told me I was not allowed to ask her to get on a scale, and she also told me she would not allow herself to go to a restaurant to eat (which made dating difficult). From her medical records, I could see that at sixteen years old, she had weighed eighty-six pounds (and presumably was already a tall young woman at that time).

Anna was one of those patients with whom I had an intimate and easy rapport right from the start. When I asked her how she changed her relationship to food, she told me that one day she woke up in the hospital, attached to tubes and wires. When she looked at the IV in her arm, she saw it as a symbol that someone cared. Somebody had placed that needle in her arm to help her, so why couldn't she help herself? Her doctors had been telling her in no uncertain terms for months that she was on the verge of death. In that moment of awareness that someone really did care if she lived, Anna realized she wanted to live, and if she was going to survive, she would have to accept nourishment in the form of both food and love.

Anna became acutely aware that if she was to heal, she had to accept the love and nourishment from herself that her Ego Dragon had starved her from for so long. It is the same for those of us with anxiety: We need to accept and embrace the love and nourishment we have allowed our Ego Dragon to "protect" us from.

After Anna had restricted her food so severely for so long, she could not start eating normally right away. Her system couldn't handle it. She had to begin with small meals—a bite at a time—and fill in additional calories intravenously while she gradually built up the amount of food she could eat. It took her almost two years to get back to eating the amount that was appropriate to nourish her body without causing any upset to her system. So as not to over-whelm her system emotionally, she also allowed herself progressively bigger bites of "love" along the way, building that up too.

I'm happy to say that Anna recovered from her disordered eating, but to this day she still has to work at it. That program of self-starvation is still in her, but in slowly learning how to accept physical and emotional nourishment, she was able to live a full life. Despite being told she'd never be able to have children, she was able to fully nourish herself through two pregnancies and is now a wonderful mother to a boy and a girl. Anna is a testament to rewriting old programs and learning to give herself the love and attention she needed to not only survive but thrive. It is incredible what connection to yourself and others can heal.

Like someone with anorexia who starts to eat normally again, we need to open up to love bit by bit. If we flood our system with love all at once, it will overwhelm us. Our old ego tricks will cause resistance and cause us to shut down—the very opposite of what we need to do to heal.

If you have unconsciously resisted love and connection for a long time, becoming connected again—and being someone who loves to feel love!—is not going to happen overnight. Nor should it—and nor should you feel bad if it doesn't. Actually, that means you are moving at just the right speed. Start with small things like holding a hug a little bit longer, maintaining eye contact for a little bit longer, consciously smiling a little bit more. Anything that creates a feeling of connection will bolster your SES, but especially things that promote more face-to-face and physical contact will renengage your innate ability to connect. And before you know it, you're loving the love.

I believe that as we develop our SES, we are able to metabolize, resolve, and integrate our own traumas so much more. "Increasing tone in your ventral vagus" may be a more scientific explanation to the saying "be your own wise inner parent." The more you focus on creating a compassionate connection to yourself, the more you can bring the SES back into a greater level of functionality.

If you would have asked me about my father five years ago, I probably would have told you he was severely mentally ill and I wasn't able to trust the love I got from him. If you would ask me that today, I would tell you my father showed me he loved me in many ways and that it was not his innocent self but his illness that created such turmoil for him and our family. I would add that I am grateful to him in many ways; if it wasn't for him, I wouldn't be able to put this book into the world in the hope that his pain would lead to healing for so many others. I would add that I was very proud of him for coping with a devastating disease and for being able to take the pleasure in life that he did.

So what used to be a tale of victimhood became a tale of victory through the process of integration. I have become more connected to myself than I had ever dreamed possible.

Practicing compassionate connection for yourself releases chemicals in your body and brain that foster more attachment. The more your innocent, loving, compassionate self comes out to feel safe, seen, heard, and loved, the more your engagement system matures. The safer you feel, the safer you *will* feel. It's a virtuous cycle, or feedback loop, as opposed to the vicious cycle of alarm and anxiety. Self-connection becomes the new groove, and the more you focus on it, the more of it you will get!

There are so many ways to be compassionate to yourself. One of the most powerful compassionate connections you can use when you get to the letter C is acknowledging what a wonderful parent you are being for yourself. That child in you is so used to being shunned that it has given up hope and faith a rescuer will ever come. Be that rescuer.

It is critical, when you get to compassionate connection with yourself, that you really feel your compassion. Just saying the words that you will take care of your inner child can trigger your child's resistance, inability to receive, and defensive detachment. But if you set the intention to feel that compassion for your entire being, both adult and child, you will create a feeling of safety that is believable and nourishing to your child self.

Ideally, the awareness you came into the ABCs with should be reflected in the compassion part of the ABCs. For example, if you became aware you were in defensive detachment from your partner and had withdrawn, when moving into compassionate connection (after taking time to ground in your body), you could bring to mind a time you were very close and connected with your partner (maybe your wedding day or a holiday you took together) and sit in the feeling of that connection. The point is to draw on an emotional, compassionate connection that runs counter to the awareness that started you into the ABCs in the first place.

It is in your nature to be compassionate to yourself. But it takes discipline and practice to commit to that compassion because, chances are, that inner child has felt judged, abandoned, blamed, and shamed for a long time and is wary of showing their authentic, innocent self. You need to show them—and believe yourself—that there are no reasons *not* to be loving and compassionate to yourself. You need to know that every person has an innocent being at their core. My dad did some crazy and damaging things to our family, but when I choose to see him as an innocent soul, I am being loving to both myself and to his memory.

100
Hello? Is It Me You're Looking For?

The thirteenth-century Sufi poet Rumi wrote, "What you seek is seeking you."

You have worked so diligently to learn about your alarm, to understand that you are not your worries and that they are not serving you. You've practiced your ABCs to help you choose to stay present instead of spiraling into worry. You have learned all about your Ego Dragon and how you can make friends with it so it will let you open up the treasure chest. You've learned how to activate your ventral vagus and reconnect with your child self.

You've shown your inner child that they are safe. Now it's time to ask them what they want.

And then listen for the answer.

Because your child self has been there all this time, just waiting for you to ask.

It's so important to open up a line of communication with your younger self to let them know you are there for them. And I mean this literally—I have actual conversations with my inner child, Rusty (my childhood nickname). Not out loud in public, but rather when I feel calm and resourced. (When I see people on the street having a heated conversation with themselves, I sometimes wonder if they are arguing with their tantruming inner child. These days, though, they usually have earbuds in.)

One of the ways I have a conversation with Rusty is by expressing empathy and telling him I understand how he felt. I place my hand over my heart and focus on my breath, just like I do in my ABCs. When I feel I have a connection with myself, in the most compassionate tone possible, I say something like "It must have been really hard for you to watch your dad taken away in an ambulance" or "It must have been really hard when the kids at school teased you."

Then I wait. Or sometimes I ask him, "What do you need to feel safe?"

Sometimes I reach him and he responds, and other times I don't feel his presence. His answers to me are often nothing like my adult self thought they would be, and those answers give me incredible insight into his pain—and his strength. The more I create an intention to connect, the more he hears me and responds. Over time, we've developed a relationship, and it's begun to feel more like we are one, as opposed to an adult talking to a child.

As he began to trust that I wasn't going to leave him by distracting into my thoughts and worries and as he felt my compassion for him, he became more a visceral part of me. We could have conversations, and I learned much more about his life from how he perceived it, rather than my memory of it. We could converse about where he felt judged, abandoned, blamed, or shamed, and I could reassure him that I loved him and cared for him no matter what he ever said, thought, or did.

When you try connecting with yourself, remember that it's not a "one and done." Just as it takes time to develop trust and increasing levels of intimacy in a romantic relationship, it will take time to develop trust and intimacy in this one too. I have had hundreds of conversations with Rusty. If you had a childhood nickname, I suggest you try using that too, as a way of connecting to your younger self.

Your inner child must not only be encouraged by your words but must also *feel* that it is safe with you. Remember the importance of staying present and grounded in a state of connected compassion.

Give it time. You need to keep throwing your child a life preserver with your adult self holding the rope at the other end. That child needs to know beyond a shadow of a doubt that if they grab the life preserver, you are going to consistently pull them to safety and not just drop the rope and leave them stranded to tread water on their own yet again.

It is your job to give yourself now what you didn't have then—to take your child self by the hand and see them, hear them, love them. That is all any of us want.

101

Use It or Lose It: Self-Compassion

For many of us worriers, compassion and empathy are inherent in our (over) sensitive nature. But ironically, it is exactly our heightened sensitivity that has made our inner critic and Ego Dragon so powerful and cut us off from feeling that same compassion for ourselves.

The muscle is still there. It just hasn't been exercised in a while.

Our sensitivity is fertile ground for our self-compassion. When we re-engage our sensitivity, we can create more compassion and care for ourselves. Bit by bit, it will come more naturally as our sensitive inner child realizes it is safe and they won't be chastised for being too sensitive.

Make yourself this promise: I will love, guide, and care for you, no matter what you have ever thought, said, or done in the past or do in the future.

Then, be persistent and patient. As you reconnect to your authentic, innocent self, more of that self can emerge.

When you soothe your alarm with connection, compassion, and love, the alarm can stop flaring to get your attention. Your alarm has no need to activate if it gets the love and compassion it needs.

Inability to receive and resistance have blocked our kindness to ourselves for a long time. Now, with consistent self-compassion, the innocent child innate in you will begin to integrate with your adult self.

If Humpty Dumpty had some self-compassion, he wouldn't need all the king's horses and all the king's men for he could probably put himself back together again. And while we are on that subject, I can see the king's men being of some help with the dexterity in their opposable thumbs, but what good were the king's horses? Surely they were useless with those big hooves?

But I digress. Compassion and care for yourself matures the system for connection in your mind and body, enabling you to increase the connection both inwardly to yourself and outwardly to others.

102

The Biggest Obstacle to the ABCs

Perhaps the most poignant thing a patient has ever said to me is, "Dr. Kennedy, to be blunt, I get worried when I'm not worrying."

Nothing captures the Ego Dragon's essence better than that statement. I knew exactly what she was saying. The moment she said it, I *felt* it.

Before I learned the ABCs, I could stay in this worried state for hours. I had no idea what to do. It was like worry was an old familiar friend whom I didn't like very much but still found a perverse comfort in their presence—a strange security in the familiarity of rumination and worry. I had been there thousands and thousands of times.

This feeling that there is no escape from anxiety is devastating, and it came close to killing me. I've had people tell me my anxiety couldn't have been that bad because I worked as a doctor and could do stand-up comedy. I would say that many of us worriers are infinitely stronger that we give ourselves credit for. We grossly overestimate threat and grossly underestimate our ability to cope. That being said, chronic anxiety and alarm take a toll, and things can sometimes overwhelm us.

To win over your Ego Dragon, you will need discipline. It will be a fight, but it's one worth winning—because you are fighting for your life, or at least the quality of it.

Discipline yourself to show compassion to yourself and others.

Discipline yourself to limit social media or news.

Discipline yourself to stop taking JABS at yourself.

Discipline yourself to receive so you can drop your resistance to giving and receiving love.

Discipline yourself to recognize compulsive thinking and move, instead, into sensation and feeling.

Discipline yourself to recognize when you are making yourself a victim, and discipline yourself to see that you can absolutely do things your dragon tells you that you can't.

Discipline yourself to see when you are going into defensive detachment and separating from the people close to you, and discipline yourself to lean into connection.

Acknowledge your sensitivity, and discipline yourself to limit stressors that are avoidable.

Discipline yourself as a wise and guiding parent, knowing that discipline is always carried out in a compassionate way.

If this sounds overwhelming, know that it can be done—and it gets much easier with practice. You can do this. I did it. I didn't stop worrying overnight; in fact, I'm still working on it. I work on it every day.

Stop being afraid of living. For the vast majority of us, life is safe. You're still here, right? How many times have you assumed the worst—and yet, here you are. I can't tell you how many times I have diagnosed myself with some terminal illness and then convinced myself that I was not going to survive, yet I'm soon heading into my sixties and I'm still here. Not only that, but I'm thriving.

Just like me, you've probably needed your habit of worrying to avoid going into your body, but there is a way out.

It's your choice. It really is. You don't have to be a frightened child anymore.

103
And I Love That! or Embrace Your Dragon

It's hard not to think of the Ego Dragon as an enemy or villain. It's not that your dragon is bad—it's just misguided! Your dragon needs love too.

I'll often talk with my Ego Dragon just as I talk with my younger self—in quieter moments, asking it what it needs to feel safe. Much of my healing has come from disciplining myself to give the dragon love and compassion too, as it was created by a child and is a child itself. The answers I get back from it have been invaluable in coming alongside it and seeing it as a messenger and guide.

Although the ego is often regarded as some kind of omnipotent deity, it is a child's manifestation. It may appear large and foreboding, but it *had* to appear that way in order to protect you. We must always remember that as a child's incarnation, it acts in a single-minded way that does not see the big picture.

To overcome anxiety and alarm, we must see through our ego. By that I mean we must see its attempts to "help" us and compassionately tell our dragon, "Thank you for trying to protect me. Can you help me do this another way?"

Coming alongside our dragon with compassion and gratitude for its service keeps the dragon in perspective because we do not want to repeat the situation in our childhoods where our Ego Dragon became responsible for our entire world view.

Fighting the dragon is counterproductive, just as arguing with thoughts makes them appear more dangerous. As the dragon and the thoughts get bigger, they obstruct our field of view so they look like the only option (just as they were in our childhoods).

When we vilify and separate from our dragon, we are failing to see its innocence. We are also vilifying and separating from the child who created it and failing to see that child's innocence as well. It's like creating an imaginary friend to help you and then treating that friend as an enemy.

I know loving something that hurts you sounds counterintuitive, but, in general, my healing from alarm and anxiety has been a highly counterintuitive process. Perhaps that is why anxiety is so hard to treat long-term, as practitioners are treating it intuitively—like ascribing the source of anxiety to the mind and missing the more important role of the body. Healing from chronic worry has often been an exercise in accepting the exact opposite of what I used to think, so adding "and I love that" to a statement about a perceived shortfall makes perfect sense to me. It also automatically adopts an accepting framework around something that you perceive is hurting you. The change in perspective when you claim to love something that is "negative" is immediate and curious. It opens the door to seeing something painful in a brand-new way.

Some people live their entire lives in the "protection" of their Ego Dragon. I'm glad you're lucky enough to read this book and see another way.

The idea is to *see* the dragon and fully accept it as a *part* of ourselves, rather than *be* the dragon and feel it is *all* of ourselves. In this process, the dragon becomes smaller—perhaps so small it can perch on our shoulder. We don't want to lose it; we just want to put it into perspective and see that it's not so big and all-powerful after all.

Let's see how this applies to each of the ego tricks.

SELF-JUDGMENT

Our society and our economy run on self-judgment. If none of us judged ourselves, we wouldn't have to buy stuff to make us feel better. Now, if I need to, I put on a video of a dog that's been rescued and I release my alarm with my tears.

And I love that about myself.

I embrace the part of me that embraces my tears. I cry when I feel deeply hurt. I can express my vulnerability in this book. And I love that about myself too. I embrace my sensitivity, and my so-called "feminine side," but my friends would tell you that I don't shy away from a fight, either. I can be very competitive, especially with other men. I used to be very driven to win, and that came from my pusher/driver part of my personality. As much as I embrace my tears and don't judge myself for them, I also need to embrace my pusher/driver, and love that about myself just as much.

So where do you judge yourself? It is keeping you separate from yourself and increasing your alarm, so call it into the light and label it. Are you too weak, fat, skinny, dumb, sensitive, or fearful, according to your dragon? Say to yourself, "My dragon thinks I'm too sensitive, *and I love that about myself!!*" While this sounds trite, I guarantee you that when you say you love something about yourself, it opens up a whole new way of thinking about that judgment, and it shows you how much you really do it!

SELF-ABANDONMENT

I can knock off two Ego Dragon tricks in one paragraph. Compulsive thinking and worrying is a form of self-abandonment. When you find yourself in ruminative, worrisome thoughts, call it out: "I am in compulsive worry, and I love that about myself!"

When you distract into social media, food, shopping, sex, drugs, or alcohol, you are also abandoning yourself. Not always, of course, but be aware of your motives. Are you using these things primarily to give yourself some pleasure, or are you doing it because you are attempting to avoid pain? Call it out: "I am distracting right now to avoid pain, and I love that about myself!" It doesn't even mean you have to *stop* distracting, but if you are conscious about it, you can see it and then have the choice to be it or not.

Let's say someone cuts you off in traffic, and at that moment you have a choice to yell at them and ratchet up your own stress and blood pressure or just take a breath and let it go. I always say that as long as you give yourself the conscious choice—as in, "I could yell at this guy, or I could just breathe into this experience"—I have no problem if you yell. I really don't. The point is, rather than unconsciously and automatically beginning to scream at the other vehicle, you gave yourself a choice. And then decided to yell.

And I love that about you.

SELF-BLAME

There is a surefire sign to see if you are blaming yourself for something: Guilt.

You don't have to look too deep into guilt to see what you are blaming yourself for. The blame may be justified, but remember that the things we do that we are not proud of we likely did because of our past wounding.

Of course, this is not always the case, nor is this a "get out of jail free" card absolving you from responsibility. Guilt is often a useful emotion, in that it shows us where we can do better. But you can't change anything until you accept and embrace it in yourself.

Acknowledging, "I feel guilty about _____, and I love that about myself!" changes your relationship to guilt. After connecting with your body and breath, seek compassionate ways to see your guilt as a messenger for change.

SELF-SHAME

We can look guilt in the eye. It's uncomfortable but it's doable. Shame is different. Shame hides in the shadows. We are much more open to looking at what we feel guilty about than what we are ashamed of. But we can add "and I love that about myself" to guilt *and* shame. This is where you can start to see and even embrace your shadow side.

It seems almost wrong to address a topic as big as shame in just a few paragraphs, but it's important to include here. Seeing your shame, labelling it compassionately, and saying "and I love that about myself" is a great way to start bringing it into the light so you can change your (likely fixed and alarming) perception of it. When it comes to shame, the Ego Dragon becomes a monstrous size in an attempt to protect you. Your dragon will bury your shame very deeply. And like guilt, shame becomes more powerful over time if you do not address it.

Aside from intergenerational trauma and wounding, typically, you aren't born with shame. It is our experience of wounding, and the subsequent alarm that is created and stored, that often makes us do things we are ashamed of.

Shame is the place where self-compassion from your ABCs may have the most benefit. Say to yourself, "I have love and compassion for us, no matter what we've ever thought, said, or done." Repeat it out loud two more times (if you aren't on the bus or at the grocery store). Bringing our shame into the light of full acceptance and embracing it is the only way to get free from it.

You are not your shame, but unless you acknowledge it and love it, it will always have you and hold you hostage. Again, you don't have shame, shame has *you*.

INABILITY TO RECEIVE

How did you respond to Gila Golub's statement that I quoted earlier, "You are an innocent soul and you are here to remember that"? Did you receive and acknowledge that was true? Or did you resist or reject the premise?

The next time you get a compliment and watch yourself deflect it, say to yourself, "I don't allow myself to accept compliments, and I love that about myself!" For a long time, I had a hard time receiving gifts, even small things like when a friend wanted to pick up the cheque for dinner. If you find yourself rejecting a gift or show of affection, call yourself out. I am much better at receiving now than I ever have been, and I've found that when I give to myself without reservation, other people give me more! My theory (and you know by now I have theories on everything) is that I was blocking love from others as a way of protecting myself, and they felt that, so they just stopped trying.

DEFENSIVE DETACHMENT

This is an ego trick that kills relationships. Sometimes you feel like you need to end a relationship because that's the healthy choice, but often we break up because we feel vulnerable with attachment. In psychological parlance, this is often referred to as an "anxious avoidant" pattern of attachment. The person wants intimacy but becomes uncomfortable when things get too close. This pattern has destroyed countless relationships.

When I engage my awareness and find myself pulling back, I call it out, saying (sometimes out loud), "I am going into defensive detachment, and I love that about myself!" I put my hand on my chest, take a breath, and step back in awareness of my protective reflex to resist loving connection.

Every time I go through a successful cycle of calling out my defensive detachment in awareness, I find a little more love for myself—a little better ability to engage my SES and connect. My dragon gets a little bit smaller and allows me a little more access to the treasure chest containing my innocent, sensitive, and truly loving self.

VICTIM MENTALITY

Victim mentality thrives on a principle called secondary gain, which means that as victims we get some sort of payoff or reward. We all appreciate being helped out and taken care of at times, but for someone with unresolved trauma and wounding, this feeling can be downright addictive. They have such a strong sense of lack, left over from childhood when they weren't taken care of, that they keep on trying to force others to fill the void instead of recognizing that they are mature adults who can take care of themselves.

For an example, let's look back to my friend Emily (the one who learned to abandon herself after observing that her needs were too much for her mother to handle). While Emily was growing up, her mother fell into a pattern of getting fired from jobs repeatedly. Each time she would get a new job, Emily could see the pattern unfolding: Things would go great at first, and then slowly her mother would start to come home with stories of how her coworkers and her boss didn't appreciate the hard work she was doing. They were asking her to change things, but Emily's mother refused because she insisted her way of doing things was the right way—and once again she would get fired.

Each time she would get fired, Emily's mother would call on her siblings for emergency help. She seemed unable to see that her own victim mentality was causing this to happen over and over. The first time she got fired and a relative bailed her out, it soothed her wounded inner child. Finally, someone was taking care of her! But the feeling was so seductive that she pursued it over and over, instead of pursuing professional success. On a conscious level, she was asking, "Why do I always get fired?" and "Why is this happening to me?" instead of "Why is this happening for me?" Although at a conscious level she felt embarrassed about her work history, the secondary gain of being taken care of by her family was keeping her stuck in a maladaptive pattern of victim mentality.

When we victimize ourselves, our subconscious does know what is happening, and as a result we carry shame. This leads us to separate from ourselves more, leading to more alarm and, in turn, more of a feeling that we need to be taken care of—and the cycle strengthens as our self-esteem weakens.

It's so critical to call out your victim because it grows in you like a cancer. Victim mentality is self-perpetuating. Although there is a "payoff," in that we appear to get pleasure or relieve pain in the short term, the more you act and feel like a victim in the long term, the more you disempower yourself—and the more you disempower yourself, the more attached you'll become to the secondary gain because you won't have to do what scares you. This is what's known in psychology as negative reinforcement—reinforcing a behaviour by removing a painful stimulus. While being a victim appears to ease your pain in the short term, it magnifies it greatly in the long term by ultimately adding to your alarm.

It's hard not to feel like a victim when you are in alarm. I know. Been there, done that—more times that I can count. But the first step is always awareness. "Oh, I see that by avoiding this event, I am making myself a victim, and I love that about myself!" When you label it and call it out in awareness, you can make what was invisible visible.

By now you may be thinking how trite this "and I love that about myself" can sound, but do not underestimate its power as a tool of self-awareness.

During the worst of my anxiety, almost always after going out and doing what I was afraid of, I felt much better. I didn't know this specifically at the time, but I was creating an ally in myself, whereas, before, I would separate into the part of me that knew I should go and the victim that didn't want to. When I became aware of my victim, connected with him in my body, and fully embraced his victimhood, I began to integrate into a cohesive whole. When I embraced my innocence and felt whole and connected to the parts of me I judged as unworthy, I created an unwavering confidence and faith in myself—and the world.

RESISTANCE

Alarm cannot be released if we resist it. There is an exercise by Kathy L. Kain, one of my wife's somatic experiencing teachers, called "Objecting without Contracting." The exercise involves bringing to mind something that bothers you and then consciously staying open and letting go of any resistance. If you're feeling pain, chances are you're resisting, so say to yourself, "I am in resistance right now, and I love that about myself!" When I did this, I was amazed at how much I resisted, how intense that resistance was, and how unconscious and automatic it was. Then, I would move into the ABCs and have deep compassion for that place in me that was so resistant!

When you call out the ego's tricks, you can love your dragon for trying to protect you. When you do this, the dragon sees it doesn't have to be so dominant and intrusive.

Try this exercise. Bring to mind one of your ego's popular tricks. See if you can feel it in your body. For example, when I think of resistance, I feel a diffuse pressure just above my solar plexus that radiates strongly into my back.

Now say, "I see I am in (*insert ego trick here*), and I love that about myself!" Touch your chest, take a breath, and physically smile down at the child in you. That child has been waiting to feel this love from you for a very long time.

One more thing. If you can stand in front of a mirror and follow this same practice with the same statement, you will supercharge the effect.

Embrace the dragon. Embrace its tricks to keep you safe. And most of all, embrace your innocent, true self—because as you give yourself the love and compassion you need, the dragon can stand down and you'll gain access to the treasure chest and feel more of your authentic, innocent self.

104
Carrot and Stick

I am not against thinking. I *am* against thinking when you are in alarm. If you struggle with alarm, you've probably been living in your thoughts for a long time—so long that you've forgotten what it is like to live in the only safe place there is, your body.

We need to be able to think, but there is a big difference between thinking and rumination. There is also a massive difference between conscious, aware thinking and the rumination of the DMN. In the former, *you* are in charge, and in the latter, your Ego Dragon is running the show, fuelled by both background and foreground alarm.

Conscious thinking has an endpoint or goal that is constructive. Rumination is endless and is destructive, creating a vicious cycle that feeds on itself, driving you deeper into rumination and alarm. And you can only distract for so long. Eventually being in your head all the time catches up with you. As the alarm gets more powerful, the distraction no longer works.

For a long time, your body wasn't safe. To avoid the discomfort, you retreated up into your head, and drowned in rumination. But you are growing a safe place of presence and wisdom in your body. Now, you have the blueprint to connect with your body in a sustainable and self-reinforcing way. The more safety you create in your body, the less you will need to distract and dissociate into compulsive, worrisome thinking.

With the help of the ABCs, you can smash the one-way valve where alarm gets in but doesn't get out. In compassionate connection with yourself, your SES becomes engaged and your ventral vagus activated. You are able to see your ego's manipulations in a new light and choose to do the opposite. As you move out of victim mentality, you feel more and more empowered as your successes increase your ability to feel good about yourself. You no longer feel you *need* to heal yourself; instead, you *want* to heal yourself—and this is a crucial distinction.

I've known I *needed* to heal for decades, but it hasn't been until recently that I *wanted* to heal. And this has changed my whole approach.

In doing the ABCs, I have seen, especially in part C where I focus on my positive qualities and compassion for myself, what a truly caring and giving person I am. For much of my life, my pusher/driver personality made me strive for accomplishments and to help others as a physician. But that came at a price because I wasn't giving enough to myself. It's no wonder I felt like I was giving and not getting anything back for I saw myself as a victim, deep in resistance and unable to receive. So when I felt that angst, my pusher/driver thought that if I worked a little harder and gave more, I would be alarm-free and feel fulfilled. My attempts to give were compulsive, exhausting, and often not appreciated. That is why I am actually grateful for my Achilles rupture because, when that happened, it clearly showed me I had nothing left to give—to others or myself.

At that moment, my tank was empty. I had burned out. I loved helping people, but pushing myself harder was creating more pain than pleasure. When being a doctor wasn't enough, I had tried harder, becoming a yoga teacher and stand-up comic. It was just another attempt to get the love and attention from others that I was, as it turned out, unwilling to receive (or give to myself). If I had carried on that way, I'm not sure I would still be alive.

There is a metaphor about a carrot and a stick. If you have a mule and you want him to move, you can hit him with a stick or entice him with a carrot. I spent much of my life hitting myself with a stick, and now I am enticing myself with carrots. It's a much kinder and more productive way for me to be.

105

Your Thinking Hurts More Than It Helps

On your journey to healing, your ego will try to convince you that there is a thinking solution.

There isn't.

Of course, you need your thinking mind to be aware of the ego's tricks and to label them and embrace them. But after that awareness stage, most of the *healing* comes from *feeling*.

You can't heal what you refuse to feel. But when you are on your own side, using carrots instead of sticks, feeling becomes the better option and your emotional range increases.

On the other hand, when we are stuck in compulsive thought, afraid to go into the body and feel, our emotional range narrows in a form of protection. It's almost like we sign an agreement as children to live in a narrowed range of emotion if that prevents us from feeling deep pain. Any time we venture out to feel and go into our bodies, we use the sticks of thoughts and worries to beat ourselves back into our heads.

If emotional range was measured on a scale of one to ten, with ten being nirvana and one being deep depression, most worriers seem to live their lives between four and six to avoid pain. And we use our thoughts to keep us there. Ever had a really good day and then forced yourself to think a negative thought to bring yourself down? I know I have.

You are more than your thoughts. Your thoughts and worries (brain droppings!) are only a small part of you. You have a complete and beautiful range of emotions you can live in, now that you've convinced your Ego Dragon to let you see that range.

And love is always trustable.

You may perceive the *person* may not be trustable, but love is love. I know my father loved me very much, but as he got older, his illness got in the way. You can be sensitive and thin-skinned in a safe environment or you can be thick-skinned in a challenging environment, but both my dad and I suffered the worst combination—being highly sensitive in a challenging environment. And the odds are strong that you had that latter combination as well or, at least, the sensitive part.

I've learned a new feeling story with my father. He loved me very much, and I remember all the things he would do for me as a young child, taking me fishing, showing me how to ride a bike, catching and hitting a ball, and playing chess with me. The more I focus on the good memories with my father, the more good memories I recall. What you focus on, you get more of. I am lucky in many ways because I knew my father loved me, and I can focus on the feeling of that.

So I focus on that part of him. It's much more compassionate than the alternative—to myself and to him. He did the best he could, and his real self would shine through sometimes, even in the late stages of his illness.

It is so easy to blame our parents, but I always ask my patients, "How was your parent's childhood?" Then I remind and assure people that for the most part, you can't give what you didn't get. Even just before he died, my dad would share music with me, or a book. I even believe his suicide was a way of releasing the family from more pain, as in lucid moments he could see how hard it was on all of us—but especially on him, of course.

The more you focus on practicing the ABCs and embrace feeling over thinking, the more you'll heal. And the more you heal, the easier it becomes to feel (and *be*) truly connected to yourself.

106
Belief

I said earlier that I would return to beliefs. Did you believe me?

(If you don't understand why I'm asking … read that again.)

Just because you believe something, does not make it objectively true. Beliefs can be an accurate representation of reality, or not. Of note, for we worriers, if we are in survival mode created by alarm, the chances that our belief is valid and true decrease significantly when compared to the exact same belief when we are in a calm, peaceful state in the mind and body.

As an example, if I have a thought that "this book is ahead of its time and may do poorly," that thought is far more likely to gain traction in my body if I am already in survival mode and alarm. In survival mode, my system preferentially looks for threat, and, as a result, I create a vivid picture of what it would be like to have a book that fails to make a difference, which makes me feel disappointed and apprehensive, which leads to more worrisome thoughts of failure. This is all before the book has been fully written! But these worries keep me in a state of alarm and separation, which is not where I need to be to do my best work on the book. Thank goodness for the ABCs!

The experiences we have gone through have shaped our perceptions of ourselves and the world. The ego gathers information throughout our existence and, along with our amygdala (and other brain structures), guides our subsequent perceptions and behaviours based on those earlier perceptions. If those perceptions are repeated, we create a belief system that we rely on to inform us if the world is safe or not. The more unresolved trauma we carry (as background alarm), the more our perceptions will reflect that world view—and the more we will perceive our environment as a place we need to be protected from.

Beliefs begin as thoughts, which, with repetition, are then elevated to perceptions. Those perceptions turn into hypotheses. If those hypotheses are confirmed by repetition, they become beliefs. Much of this goes on outside of awareness, usually in childhood. Here is a critical point: Those perceptions and subsequent hypotheses are subjective. The child-generated hypothesis can be (and often is) completely false. (Remember how children wrongly blame themselves for the pain in their households?)

I'll always remember the poignant way one of my patients, Carl, gave voice to some of the false beliefs he'd developed as a child to make sense of his pain. When Carl was young, his mother would fly into a rage every couple of weeks, then would lock herself in her room and typically not come out for two or three days. Carl told me each time she would do this, he would think, "I wonder if I've done something to upset her" or "She's hiding because of me." The more his mother withdrew, the more the thought "It's my fault" was repeated, which became his go-to perception, which repeatedly confirmed his hypothesis, which became the firm belief that he was completely to blame for his mother's withdrawals. When he came to me, we used awareness to dismantle this entire process. Carl discovered how to use the ABCs to create a safe place in his body and, from that grounded place, question the groove he created as a child to constantly blame himself for things that had nothing to do with him.

Now, here's the complicated part.

Some beliefs are conscious and explicit. Drawing from my earlier example,

I could believe that Toronto is the capital city of Canada or that I was born in the province of British Columbia. If someone then told me I was mistaken and Ottawa is the capital of Canada or I was actually born in Ontario, I could change that belief almost instantly. Easy peasy.

But other beliefs are unconscious. We call these implicit beliefs, and I'll propose a new term as well: "body beliefs." (Remember how implicit memory is held in your body? It's like that.) Body beliefs are those ingrained perceptions of self that form after a child has listened to the Ego Dragon for years. These implicit or body beliefs are much harder to change, because they have emotions wrapped up in them. I am not emotionally attached to believing the capital city of Canada is Toronto, so I can change that belief in an instant. But if I have unconsciously adopted a protective emotional "body belief" that I need to detach from the people close to me because love can't be trusted, that belief can be both devastating and difficult to change.

Body beliefs are not going to be changed by simply correcting them factually. If simply telling yourself not to believe something would actually heal it, a full course of psychotherapy would last about twenty minutes. We need to see those implicit, body beliefs in awareness first and then use a process to rewire them. That process is the ABCs. As you get more adept at the ABCs, you'll be able to use compassion to counter your initial awareness and actually overwrite the damaging implicit belief with a loving one.

We give our beliefs so much power, and in that power they are hard to change. *Without awareness, we see our beliefs as who we are.* These beliefs form deep grooves because they have been ingrained by the Ego Dragon since we were young children. Many of my protective beliefs were in me for more than fifty years!

When I left the practice of medicine, my Ego Dragon went nuts because it had built up a belief that as long as I was a doctor I was protected (although in actuality the reverse was true)! It wasn't until I was able to see I held the belief, "I am safe if I stay in medical practice," that I truly saw practicing medicine was killing me—and that's when I was able to make the compassionate choice for myself to leave.

THE POWER OF BELIEF

As you learned way back at the beginning of this book, your thoughts need belief to have any power over you. But if you struggle with anxiety and alarm, your beliefs have been pre-stored in your body and kept alive by your dragon. They are beneath your awareness, yet it takes very little to fire them up.

A belief being held outside of your awareness is a monstrous force. But once you make the unconscious conscious, you can make a different choice than to be led by your anxious thoughts. And simply bringing awareness defuses much of the pain behind the beliefs and anxious thoughts. You have a friend in yourself to help you share the burden of that pain.

You know how you watch a movie like *Star Wars* with a fantastical premise like laser swords or talking aliens in a bar and you're just supposed to suspend disbelief? Well, I am asking you to suspend *belief*. You can think the thought but allow it to sit in awareness before you compulsively believe everything you think.

This suspension of thinking is in contradiction to much of what I've read about healing or diffusing anxiety. I do not agree with authors that suggest critically appraising your thoughts for truth with the assumption that if you see your thoughts are false, those thoughts will disappear. Like seeing that your odds of dying in a plane crash are twenty-six million to one will magically extinguish your anxiety about flying, or seeing that your worries are irrational will somehow cure you. Spoiler alert: It won't. You can't think your way out of a feeling problem.

If you ask me, there's no point in trying to change your mind—but I do see a lot of point in changing your body, because that is where your alarm and your implicit beliefs are stored. Your body must be calmed before your mind will change. There is no point in trying to think when you are in survival/alarm mode. It's like trying to solve an algebra problem while you are being held at gunpoint.

So instead of trying to think while you are alarmed, wait to look at the objective facts of the situation after you've gone through your ABCs. Once you've moved out of your survival brain fostering compulsive future-based thinking and worry and into the present-moment sensation in your body, the things that overwhelmed you will look much more manageable. You'll be in a better position to help yourself once you've gotten into your body so you can meet your implicit beliefs on their home turf, as that is the only place they can be changed. Your body keeps the score (and the scoreboard!) and that is the only place that score can be changed.

107

Faith

Simply and truthfully put, faith is often difficult for those of us who did not have secure attachment as children. It is hard for us to have faith in other people and the world when our trust was broken so many times by people who were supposed to have our best interests at heart. Children are inherently fragile and eminently impressionable. Without inherent faith that we are seen, heard, welcomed, supported, cared for, and loved, the fear bias of our brains has nothing to balance out its relentless focus on signs of danger. Like fear and love being mutually exclusive in the box of your psyche, faith and danger have a similar adversarial relationship.

I had a profound awakening after I formed and committed to my intention to bring awareness to my anxious thoughts and my alarm. *It was a deep realization that when trauma took my innocence, it took my faith with it.* When that happened, I lost the innocent, childlike view that I was whole and complete. I know now that in order to regain access to our innocent self, we must have faith. Without it, we will be trapped in the ego-based protection of victimhood forever.

To put it in very simple terms, faith is growth. Victimhood is protection. As long as you are a victim, you have no access to faith because your dragon will not allow it.

As a child, I developed a perceptual framework that the world was a dangerous place, and this framework was reinforced by the lack of trust in my caregivers to look after my emotional needs. As a result of this loss of faith in my caregivers or the world to provide a safe place for me, I created a protector and transferred my safety to this omnipotent Ego Dragon. When we regain our faith in the innocence of ourselves, other people, and the world at large, we can thank the dragon for its service and tell it it's time to stand down.

This is not to say we trust people who have shown themselves to be untrustworthy. We can see through someone's negative ego tricks and behaviours to see their innocence, but we don't have to allow those people into our trust.

As we feel and connect to our own innocence, we will find we do not need to look so much to others for reassurance since we can learn to have faith in ourselves. As we become more connected to ourselves, we gain confidence in seeing our true nature and are able to create our own boundaries. From that grounded place, we can clearly see we do not have to look to other people to get our own needs met. We can move away from victim mentality and move into our own power of looking after ourselves. Of course, when we have children, there is an imperative to put their needs ahead of our own—but even then, not all the time.

There is a reason why you put your own oxygen mask on before your child's in case of trouble in an aircraft. The point is, you're no good to your kids if you're not conscious. If you sacrifice your own needs to those of your kids, you are setting a dangerous precedent for your children by teaching them to place someone else's needs above their own. If you model that "selfless" behaviour, your kids can grow up to be anxious people-pleasers just like you.

Note that I am not saying we don't need other people. Yes, we can meet our own needs, but sometimes this happens through communicating with other people: asking for help when we need it, speaking up when someone is hurting us, or just letting someone know we need a hug. These can be huge accomplishments for the child who grew up learning they shouldn't need anything and should never ask for anything because they are afraid it may not be there. It's having faith in others that we can ask them for what we need and having faith in ourselves that if they say no, we will be okay. We are not those children who were dependent on support that never came; we have confidence and faith in our adult abilities to look after our own needs now and can lean into the support of others. This is how faith creates healing.

As my wife, Cynthia, says, "We heal in relationship." The SES that is innate in all of us needs connection and interaction. No (hu)man is an island. Even the most well-cared-for children still need peers for their optimal development. Remember how I helped Leandra settle down after our games of Sea Monster. Hugs and cuddles helped her sympathetic nervous system downregulate. Yes, we can give that to ourselves—but it doesn't mean we have to get it from ourselves, and only ourselves, all the time.

What I am saying might seem contradictory—that we can meet our own needs, but we still need other people. The difference lies in our ability to have faith that we can find other people who can be trusted with our hearts and that on the occasions they do let us down, we don't fall apart because we also grow faith in our ability to compassionately connect to ourselves.

Children growing up in traumatic environments lose faith that the world has their backs and often resolve not to need anything—just to have no needs—because this seems like a better option than dealing with the hurt of being disappointed over and over. As they get older, this self-denial is often accompanied by a coping strategy to be there for others, and they learn to become much more adept at meeting other people's needs over their own. This may give the illusion of being in control, but this lack of self-reference and self-care deepens background alarm because the child in them is still starved for attention. As they give to others while blocking their own ability to receive, they lose even more faith in the world, failing to see that they are the ones blocking the very care that would build their faith in their world. As faith decreases, alarm increases.

Since people are wired to lovingly connect to other people, continually giving yourself the message that you can't depend on anyone for anything, coupled with believing you are responsible for other people's needs over your own, makes the world feel like a very destabilizing place. When you are unable to connect, not only do you make it impossible to release the alarm you already have, but you create even more. As alarm increases, faith decreases.

Do you see how someone acting from alarm would have issues with maintaining relationships? As I've said throughout this book, your relationship with other people can be no better than your relationship with yourself. If your alarm disengages your SES, you can't connect with yourself or others, and as a result, (1) you can't meet your own needs, (2) your relationships with others often become focused on meeting *their* needs, (3) the child in you feels abandoned by yourself, and (4) the child in you feels abandoned by others because you won't let them meet your needs for fear that they will take their support away in a throwback to your original childhood wounding. All four of these decrease your faith and increase alarm.

When you recognize that you can meet your own needs, then it becomes okay to depend on other people. You can ask people for things and know you'll be able to handle it if they say no. Acting from a place of awareness and compassionate connection with self, you can take it one step at a time without spiraling into "all or nothing." And the more you practice this, the more it will feed into your faith in yourself—and others and the world.

Faith is the antidote to uncertainty.

Uncertainty is not the enemy we once thought it was. It's actually a beautiful thing, and as you work with your ABCs, I think you'll come to see that too. Imagine if we knew everything that would happen to us in life at the beginning.

Some of the unexpected twists and turns it takes, and the people we meet along the way, are some of the best parts. Even when I was deep in my anxiety, I could see that although I fought tooth and nail to maintain a resistance to uncertainty, that *protective* resistance also closed me off to the *growth* of new experiences.

You don't have to have perfect faith right away. You can start with just a little. When you meet someone new and start to assume they'll eventually hurt you or disappoint you so it's not worth getting to know them, you can bring awareness to that thought, notice how it feels in your body, and have compassion for the person inside who was hurt so many times. And from that place, you can choose to take a chance and believe that this person just might be worth letting in—not necessarily every person in the whole wide world. You can start with one person.

And that person is you. Having faith in your own compassionate connection to yourself by doing the ABCs on a regular basis will help re-establish the faith you lost as a child. What you seek is seeking you; you just have to open up and allow it. As you see that you are not going to withdraw from yourself and that you are a consistent loving and compassionate presence, you learn to be the parent you wish you had. As your faith in yourself increases, you develop a stronger relationship with yourself, and that leads to a stronger relationship with others.

Whatever you focus on, you'll get more of. Faith creates more faith, and victimhood creates more victimhood. Faith, along with being the antidote for uncertainty, is also the path to escape from victimhood. Faith in yourself and the world doesn't mean you aren't going to face challenges. It does mean that you don't have to know the outcome before the start of the game.

Worry and faith cannot coexist.

Faith embraces uncertainty for it knows uncertainty is the mother of opportunity and growth. Victims pull back in the face of uncertainty and withdraw into protection and feel alone and helpless, just like when they faced painful uncertainty in their childhoods. In victim mentality, we rely on hope that someone or something external to us will come to the rescue.

"... take a chance on faith—not religion, but faith. Not hope, but faith. I don't believe in hope. Hope is a beggar. Hope walks through the fire. Faith leaps over it."
– Jim Carrey, Maharishi University of Management Commencement Address,
May 24, 2014

Victims cower in the face of uncertainty, as opposed to people with faith in themselves who can embrace it, even if it is painful.

Those with faith expand into growth and learn to rely on themselves and, as they gain confidence in their ability to connect and soothe from the inside, realize they are never alone.

I don't want to sound like I am blaming victims here. In many ways, adopting victimhood was a way the childhood ego could survive, and I know that I was a victim for a very long time. Even now, when I feel alarmed, I can still drive myself straight into Victimtown. But in growing faith in my compassionate connection to myself, I recognize the landscape and turn around much earlier.

When you have faith in your world "Things don't happen *to* you; they happen *for* you." This is a saying that people with faith tend to, well, have faith in. I know I perceived my Achilles rupture as one of the worst things that ever happened to me and getting into medical school as one of the best. The truth may have been the opposite. The Achilles rupture led me to growth and to faith in myself to leave medicine and create a career I love and produce this book. Getting into medical school drove me deep into protection and really took what was just a sensitivity and predisposition to anxiety and alarm into a full-blown disorder.

If events in your life seem to form a repeating pattern, can you get curious about what message they might be trying to show you? The next time you find yourself thinking "Why does this always happen to me?" can you flip it to "How can I see this as happening *for* me?" or "what opportunity to rely on myself am I missing here?" (After doing your ABCs, of course, because the first question is a telltale sign you're in alarm.) I know this sounds a little Pollyanna, and "turn that frown upside down, mister!" but I assure you, faith is a mindset, just as victim is a mindset. Like anything else, the more you focus on it, the more you'll see its influence in your life.

In short, having faith is the ability to not only let the uncertain remain uncertain but to embrace uncertainty as fertile ground for growth. And as you build up your track record of tolerating uncertainty, you also build your confidence that you'll be able to do so in the future. And you begin to see yourself as victor instead of victim.

When I speak of faith, it is not so much faith in a higher power (although that can help) as it is a faith in your own innocent self. Much of why we develop a victim mentality is because we have given over our power to something or someone else. I am in no way against a belief in God, but as the psychologist, speaker, and author of *12 Rules For Life*, Jordan B. Peterson, points out (and I am paraphrasing), you can believe in God but take responsibility for your own damn life.

The more I adopted victimhood as a coping strategy, the less I was able to take responsibility for my own damn life, and the more alarm I put into my system.

At its core, victimhood is making someone or something else—really, anything but your own self—responsible for your life circumstances and changing them. When I placed that responsibility outside of myself, I lost my true connection to myself and my own well-being. This is the difference between accomplishments based on belief in self and feeling grounded in ourselves, on the one hand, and the empty accomplishments driven by the taskmaster of the ego, on the other hand. I became a "superachiever" because I felt I had to prove my worthiness, but even after the pusher/driver of my Ego Dragon shoved me into becoming a doctor, a yoga teacher, and a stand-up comedian, I still didn't feel worthy. Nothing was enough, and nothing ever would have been enough.

VICTIMS HAVE NO FAITH, AND FAITH HAS NO VICTIMS

Victims give up their power in the hope that someone or something else can save them. When our caregivers were unable to meet our needs, we never stop hoping they will come back and do their job. This is how a traumatic childhood so often leads to a state of victimhood later in life—we are still waiting for our parents to see us, hear us, and love us.

But no one is coming to save you—and by practicing what's in this book, eventually you will see that's a good thing. You could say when you stop hoping someone will come along and save you, this is happening for you and not to you. Instead of getting into another relationship where you give someone else responsibility for your happiness (which so many of us do when we have unresolved trauma), you can step up and develop the emotional capacity to save yourself.

As a teenager, I waited in vain for the old dad that I knew to return, to be happy and healthy and pick up where we left off when he was relatively well, taking me fishing, playing chess, throwing and hitting a baseball—you know, dad stuff. I can't tell you how many times he would return from a stint in the mental hospital and tell me he had found a new psychiatrist, was on a new set of medications, and he felt much better. In my adolescent mind, I believed he would stay well for the first three or four times I heard this optimistic story, but then he would invariably collapse again months later, and the cycle would repeat itself. I lost hope that he would ever get better. I lost faith.

I lost even more faith in the world waiting for my dad to "come back" and put me first again, to become the leader he once was. But even if my father magically returned back to life today, mentally healthy, strong, and fit, and showered me with the love and attention that I missed after he got so sick, it *still* wouldn't be enough. There will never be enough love, attention, and admiration from the outside to heal the alarm I felt inside.

I can tell you that some part of me is still waiting for my dad to return and give me the guidance and love to help me feel cared for, whole, and worthy—to be the teacher and protector he was in the first ten years of my life. There is a part of me that wants my father back the way he was when he was healthy and strong. I am aware of that part, and through the practice of making a conscious, compassionate connection to myself, I have taught myself to have faith in my own ability to give that lonely child in me the love, compassion, care, and teaching he needs. To have faith in myself to become my own wise father.

Waiting for a figure to come back and save us or putting that responsibility on a partner, friend, child, or anyone else keeps us in a victim mentality. In addition, I can tell you from personal experience that believing we will be healed by some doctor, treatment, supplement, patch, drug, psychedelic, guided meditation, yoga nidra, hypnosis, meditation, or therapy is a fool's errand. As The Holistic Psychologist, Nicole LePera says, and I unequivocally agree, "There is no quick fix." There is no doubt those things can help, but to truly heal on a deeper level, we need to relentlessly regain faith in our authentic, innocent selves and stop being victims by hoping that something outside of us will magically save us. We must place the faith we need in ourselves.

"What progress, you ask, have I made? I have begun to be a friend to myself."
– Hecato

Hope is a victim (victims hope to be rescued by someone or something outside of themselves). Victors keep the faith (faith in the moment being perfect for our growth and faith in ourselves for us to heal). We need to create faith that we can handle life and that the universe is a safe place regardless of our ego's relentless predictions to the contrary.

Look back at all the traumas you've had. Did you handle them? Are you still here? Sure, you may be suffering emotionally, but you made it through. And now you are reading a book that will show you how to empower yourself to begin to release your alarm and the subsequent anxiety that alarm creates. We need to realize we are not the alarmed children we once were.

And we need to regain faith in our innocent selves again. We need to develop the faith in ourselves and the world that we lost as children. Taking responsibility for things you have no control over (the future) is a victim's hope-filled stance.

This is one of my favourite quotes (and I am paraphrasing Larry Eisenberg): "Today I officially resign as the general manager of the Universe."

Taking responsibility for embracing uncertainty is an act of faith. I know that making a committed, conscious intention to have faith in the future—and to let the uncertain be gloriously uncertain—has been one of the best things I have done for my mental health. Instead of worry and rumination, I choose to use the ABCs and go into my body to find sensation and present-moment awareness. I have faith in that process because it works.

The more we use our awareness to stop being tricked by our dragon, the more we release it from the impossible and endless victim-based task of protecting us from everything. The more we consciously release the dragon, the more we are led to gain faith in our innocent selves. With faith in ourselves, we break the habit of victimhood and find our true power. With faith, you can embrace and find peace and opportunity in uncertainty in the safety and grounding of your body instead of endlessly searching for certainty in a place you'll never find it: your mind.

This takes courage. But you aren't a child anymore. You have this courage inside you, and you will connect with it the more you practice the ABCs.

Courage is facing and embracing the unknown. Faith and courage are brothers in arms. It will take courage and faith in yourself to embrace the ABC process and do it consistently, especially early on when your Ego Dragon resists and puts up a fight. But when you tell the dragon "I've got this" and remove its responsibility to protect you, it has no choice but to recede. The dragon won't acquiesce without resistance, but although you may not know it, you are the Dragonmaster. It must obey you if you command it with faith and courage, but if you fall back into victim, the Dragon can rise up and burn you.

The tangible evidence I've observed by using the ABCs to regain faith in myself is that I look after my own needs much more—genuinely, proactively caring for myself with the achievable goal of *growth*, as opposed to worrying with the unattainable goal of *protection*. The more adept you get at the ABC process, the more you'll see yourself looking after your own needs—not just because you know that you should but because you truly *want* to.

Being compassionate and connected with your innocent self when you are alarmed is probably the opposite of what you have been doing all your life. It is an unfortunate feature of the human species that we deal with emotional "threats" in the same way we deal with physical ones: by moving into dorsal vagal survival physiology that locks out the ventral vagal SES we need to connect and resolve the emotional pain that sparked this reaction in the first place. The ABCs are designed to circumvent this evolutionary bug in the system.

When we commit to connecting to our true and innocent selves instead of abandoning and separating from ourselves during emotional stresses, we break that old habit and can move toward thriving instead of constantly focusing on surviving. But this takes time and practice. We must know our innocence and be patient and fully committed to our own connection. To heal from anxiety and alarm, we must have faith in our ability to connect and nurture our younger selves.

"Be here now." – Ram Dass

Faith is being present. Faith is consciousness. Faith is in us; we are faith; faith *is* us. As children, when we lost our innocence, we lost our faith as well, and that is one reason childhood trauma is so devastating. When we lose faith in the world, we lose touch with our true selves and part of us stops growing, so the only remaining option is to go into protection. We invent a protector that blocks some of the pain, but at the cost of blocking love and connection to ourselves and others (which is the worst deal ever). Without that connection and ability to be open and vulnerable, our nervous system is forged in protection, and alarm gets in but it can't get out. Unless we can return to seeing ourselves as innocent souls and truly let love back in to push out the fear, we will be trapped in protection, anxiety, and alarm forever.

Love is a path to faith, and faith can be a path to love. Faith in ourselves, to quote the title of a wonderful book by spiritual teacher Marianne WIlliamson, is a "Return to Love"—to consciously choose love and compassion over fear and protection. Faith, love, and connection are all linked and self-perpetuating, as are fear, worry, and alarm. When you see you are in anxiety or alarm, you can use the ABCs as a path to the true, authentic self you left behind. That innocent child is still waiting for you.

Moving from victimhood to faith at the level of *thinking* is short-lived. The Ego Dragon (like the Sirens) will always be able to seduce you back into victim mode, as there is not enough grounding resonance in thought alone. The ABCs change your perception at the level of *feeling*, and feeling does have the resonance to keep you grounded—and as you do this more, your faith grows.

Throughout this book, I have maintained that protection and growth are mutually exclusive, but faith may be the exception where they intersect. Having faith both protects you and allows you to grow at the same time. Ego-based protection is an illusion because it precariously and relentlessly exhausts you by trying to predict the future from a place of fear. Ego-based protection has no substance to it because it is a prediction of the future that is, by definition, unknown. Faith, on the other hand, acknowledges that your need for protection is neither helpful nor necessary, for faith comes from inside of you and can never be taken away. Faith does not require an elaborate series of unpredictable events to be analyzed and protected against. The ego has a multitude of complex options to consider for the future; whereas, faith is a single, simple pathway that is clearly present in every moment we choose to trust in it. It is awareness that allows us to see and choose the path of the ego or the path of faith.

In our awareness, we always have a choice to choose faith in every moment. Faith is always one conscious decision away in every circumstance. Faith is a singular path on the solid ground of courage and trust, grounding us in the reality of the present moment. Worry, on the other hand, is an infinite ocean surrounding us in all directions, in which we are treading water that chronically threatens to drown us in our imaginings of the future.

When we are in alarm and separate from ourselves, our need for ego protection dominates and we inadvertently create pain by trying to avoid pain. When we are connected to ourselves, we can rest in faith that we will deal with whatever arises, just as we have dealt with painful losses in our past.

Despite being a complete anxious mess upon entering medical school, I had faith in myself. Deep down I knew I could do it. My ego challenged me greatly, but through the pain of chronic, intense daily alarm, I had faith in myself—and I graduated four years later with two academic awards and as president of my graduating class. (I am just going to pretend I didn't mention these graduation distinctions before)

I truly believe that faith in myself (facilitated by my ABCs practice) has changed my physiology and my psychology. This did not happen right away since having faith in the unknown was a change that I initially found very stressful. I was moving from a fear-based belief system that I created as a child, in which I needed my dragon to protect me, to a love-based belief system where I could be fed by my connection with my true, innocent self. Faith allowed me to take responsibility for my own life and to live much more in growth and much less in protection. As I gained confidence in myself, my physiology changed from victim-based survival mode to that of a growth-based victor. The more my physiology reflected confidence and safety, the easier it was to stay in the sensation of my body and not be seduced into the victim mentality of compulsive worry and rumination. My physiology then reflected my psychology. Faith allowed a grounded presence in my body so I no longer had to retreat into the trap of my mind.

Finally, for the first time in my life, I have a safe place to go in my body.

Faith is embracing uncertainty and not going past the moment you are in. Faith is avoiding the need to predict or control. Your whole journey with anxiety and alarm stems from your child self's desire to control and avoid uncertainty because that uncertainty was excruciating. What if you just stopped trying to control it? A mantra for this is: "This is uncertain ... and I love that!"

You can only allow and embrace the unknown from a place of faith in yourself, a grounded physiology that ultimately comes from knowing your own innocence. And regardless of what you have ever thought, said, or done in the past or think, say, or do in the future, I guarantee you that you're an innocent soul and you are here to remember that. The call to judge, explain, predict, control, and worry has led you to immeasurable pain. But it is a habit based on protection. It is a habit based on the experiences of the child you were then. You have a choice to make that need for (over)protection no longer true for the adult you are now. In compassion for yourself, you see there is no anxious thought worth having and the most loving action is to let go, ignore the sirens (or Sirens!), and use that energy to create faith in the moment and yourself.

I cannot tell you the number of times in my life I have been sure I was dying of some disease or condition, beyond panic, collapsed in my bed in terror, certain I was doomed. That went on for forty years.

Forty years.

I cannot tell you what a relief it is to trade that for faith in myself, faith in love, and faith that when my time comes, it is what it is. I do not have some magical power to change the future by worry and rumination, so instead, I leave it to faith in myself and in the safety that is inherent in the world. The safety that your child self could not see—because it was not there back then—is available to you now.

There is no treatment, vitamin regimen, workshop, book, medication, drug, or addiction that is going to heal you. *You* have to heal you, and you do that by minimizing separation from yourself. Because the real truth is, you can't leave yourself anyway. And you'll see and feel that reconnection when you do pass from this life. But you don't have to wait. You are innocent love and consciousness at your essence and the only thing that can separate you from that is your own perception. Your child formed your dragon to keep you connected to love and safety, but it did the opposite. It's okay—now you know better; you can do better.

As hard as it may be for you to believe, you do love yourself. You have always had love for yourself, but your psyche has blocked it. It is time to remove those blocks to loving yourself and to find connection and faith in your true, innocent self.

Choosing the ABCs over your Ego Dragon requires a leap of faith. And you can find the courage to make that leap when you get grounded in your body—when you get out of your thoughts and into your feelings.

The start is the most important, so awareness is your biggest ally in breaking the alarm-anxiety cycle for good.

It is not your dragon that will save you. It is the child in you. What you seek is seeking you.

Once you have learned to embrace uncertainty as the spice of life, your confidence increases in your own ability to overcome—to be victor instead of victim. By releasing the need to predict the future, you'll stop feeding your powerless victim and, instead, pour your energy into growing your faith and self-confidence. As you create a caring connection with your innocent self, faith is a natural byproduct of that loving commitment to yourself. You can give yourself now what you needed back then.

A victim must make sense of the uncertainty.

Faith is the cure to victimhood. Faith takes its power in peacefully filling the space previously held by the compulsion to know the unknowable. Faith does not need to know, and I love that about faith!

Before I leave this critical chapter, I want to show how faith takes the fire out of the Ego Dragon. In us worriers, discipline is absolutely critical when it comes to faith. The seduction to fall into worry is considerable, to say the very least, and you can use faith as an entry point to the ABCs, as well as developing faith as a practice of its own. Again, this is not faith in a higher power so much as it is faith in yourself, but you must discipline yourself to avoid the siren song of your worries and move to a place of peace.

Awareness gives choice, and seeing that you are in alarm and anxiety gives you the choice to draw on faith to continue with the ABC process.

Faith grounds you in a sense that you can suspend the urge to fall into worry.

Because discipline is so important in deploying faith, I want to use the same type of repetition here that we did when discussing discipline. The groove in the snow runs deep when it comes to defaulting to anxious thoughts, so we have to wear a new groove in the snow.

Faith in yourself disarms self-judgment by focusing on the best in you.

Faith in yourself disarms self-abandonment by joining your child self to your adult self.

Faith in yourself disarms self-blame because it fosters responsibility over guilt.

Faith in yourself disarms self-shame because it creates forgiveness and understanding.

Faith in yourself disarms inability to receive by constantly giving to you.

Faith in yourself disarms defensive detachment because it attaches you to yourself.

Faith in yourself disarms compulsive thinking by showing thoughts are simply not needed.

Faith in yourself disarms resistance by providing a place to flow into the peace of the moment.

Faith in yourself disarms victim mentality by building your courage and self-reliance.

As a final critical point, faith allows you to sit with the uncertainty now that was unbearable back then. Like the smoker who wants to quit smoking but finds a cigarette in their mouth with no idea how it got there, we worriers will often fall into worry so quickly and so insidiously we don't see a moment when we could have stopped it. In a commitment to a practice of awareness and faith in ourselves, we can create that space between stimulus and response that Viktor Frankl talks about. In that space of awareness, there is choice where before there was only the path to worry. If you can consistently fill that space with a commitment to faith in your connection to yourself, you can create a new, self-deepening groove that tracks you consistently *toward* the faith in yourself and the ABCs and *away from* automatic and compulsive worry.

There is a reason this is the longest chapter. Faith really is the crux of everything. You need a leap of faith to jump over the fire of the Ego Dragon and reconnect with the innocent self that the dragon hid inside the treasure chest in order to keep your child "safe." This faith arises from your awareness and intention to access the chest and connect with the child in you that was hurt. Revisiting that traumatized child is hard, but relentless faith in the bond you make to yourself and the belief in your innocence is exactly the key to your healing.

Your younger, traumatized self is still in you, and that part needs to know you are there to comfort them in love and growth, as opposed to leaving them in the chest alone under the dragon's protection. While you are split from yourself and your innocent self is sequestered away, you are powerless to overcome your alarm and anxiety. We heal in relationship, and there is no relationship more important to have faith in than the one we have with ourselves.

The leap of faith comes when your adult self opens the chest, pulls out your innocent child self, and fully accepts, embraces, and loves them. This allows us to learn that we are indeed safe in our own love and do not need the dragon's protection to face the world anymore. We have something infinitely more powerful: our faith in our connection to ourselves.

The ABC process connects your thinking adult self to your feeling child self and dissolves the separation that caused the alarm and anxiety in the first place. Whenever you are worried or alarmed, it is because you have become split and fallen back into the proverbial hole of believing you can think your way out of a feeling when really you're digging yourself in deeper. When you get caught in the trap of overthinking, you lose focus on the feeling child in you. The ABCs are there to show you how your child can feel their way out (with your love and connection to support their growth).

A part of us stopped growing at the time of our trauma. When we are alarmed, our amygdala sends us straight back to the helpless child we once were. We need to go back and retrieve that child, and creating faith in our connection does just that. The more faith and effort we put in that connection, our child sees they can trust our adult self, and our adult sees they can trust our child self.

Anytime you become aware of anxiety and alarm, relief always starts with a connection to yourself. Having faith in your innocence of your whole being—no matter what you have ever thought, said, or done—will dissolve the separation that is at the root of your alarm and anxiety. A leap of faith that to love and embrace your inner, younger self will accomplish what no medication, doctor, supplement, or spell is going to be able to do.

We heal by creating wholeness from the inside. Our commitment to faith in ourselves is what will heal the separation that is at the root of our alarm and anxiety. The ABCs at their core are a vehicle to develop an unwavering faith in our connection to ourselves.

If we worriers fear uncertainty most of all, faith—specifically, faith in ourselves—is our most powerful ally. A simple touch of your hand to your chest and a deep breath in reassuring yourself of your own presence can make the difference between a life spent in self-abandonment, alarm, and anxiety on the one hand, and a life spent in flow and connection with your authentic, innocent self on the other.

Using the ABCs trains you to consciously go to faith in your connection to yourself, creating a new groove that consistently and relentlessly tracks you away from worry. Ultimately, the worry was a distraction from the pain of alarm, and as you connect with yourself, that alarm dissolves, since the alarm was simply your younger self asking for your connection and love. If you give yourself that connection, the alarm fades away as it is no longer needed.

I have no doubt this book will have helped you understand and heal from chronic anxiety and alarm. But the information is of limited benefit unless you make it a part of your daily life. Be warned, your Ego Dragon will try to convince you to abandon faith in your authentic self and slide back to the familiar groove of anxiety and alarm. That may simply look as insidious as abandoning the ABCs and just settling back into your old habit of worry. Worry will be your alarm signal that you have fallen back into the groove of fearing uncertainty.

Uncertainty will be your greatest teacher and your greatest opportunity to call on its antidote, faith in your present moment connection with yourself. Know you will be faced with uncertainty and your ego's automatic reaction will be to transport you into alarm from your past or to start to worry about your future. In both cases, you abandon yourself because you leave the present moment. Staying with yourself, putting a hand on your chest, and taking a breath in teaches you that uncertainty is bearable and you do not have to retreat into past alarm or leapfrog into future worries. Further, faith in the moment flows with and completely embraces uncertainty and shows you that uncertainty can be pleasurable because, perhaps for the first time in your life, there is truly nothing to do and nowhere to go! Over time, you teach yourself that uncertainty does not have to be a one-way superhighway to anxiety and alarm that it has been in your past.

At their core, anxiety and alarm thrive on intolerance of the uncertainty of our future.

Turning to faith in your present-moment connection to yourself when you are faced with uncertainty will always soothe you, no matter how much the worrying sirens of your ego tell you otherwise. Faith shows you that the answer to "Am I safe in this moment?" is always "Yes, I am here with you and I am here for you."

And you can love that about yourself!

108

Gratitude Is the End and the Beginning

Wow. You ok? That chapter on faith is pretty intense. I'll let you get your breath (haha) and we can bring our journey to a close. Thanks for taking this "trip" with me. My father and I deeply appreciate it.

So we have our ABCDEs, and with F we added faith. To close this book, I will add G for gratitude.

Many people keep gratitude journals, and I do think that is a good idea, as it does change your physiology and psychology. Often this gratitude journal is for external things in your life that you're grateful for, like people or events. But I want you to develop a gratitude journal or practice specifically to capture and reflect on traits and characteristics you appreciate in *yourself*.

Make an intention to focus on, and really *feel*, compassion and love for yourself—and not just for you now, but gratitude for yourself at every stage of your life. Gratitude for the scared child who needed protection, and gratitude for who you were during the times you were lost in your anxiety and just doing the best you could. This process will supercharge your faith and connection with yourself. (Bonus points for doing it in front of a mirror to fully engage your SES and ventral vagal response in service of yourself. However, this experience may be too intense at first; it took me almost a year with the ABCs to be able to do them consistently with a mirror.)

Just as discipline and faith work together, the C and G in this alphabet can work together. If during your compassion practice you call to mind reasons you are proud of yourself, then when it's time for gratitude, you can bring those traits or accomplishments to mind and really feel into gratitude for the gifts you have. The key is to connect with the feeling and not just think (or say or write) the words. I can say to myself, "I am proud of you for writing this book," but If I take a breath, say it out loud, and commit to feeling that sense of pride, it will change my physiology—and I can feel it right away as my heart expands and my face starts to move into a smile.

If you are having a hard time finding things you love about yourself, please know that's not at all uncommon among worriers! On the resources page, I have included a link to a list of positive traits so, instead of trying to generate ideas from a blank slate, you can start with a list and choose the ones that resonate for you.

In addition to reflecting on what you're grateful for in yourself right now, I would encourage you to set an intention to find qualities to be grateful for in your child self as well. You can tell yourself things like "I loved how sensitive and caring you were" or "I loved what a great swimmer you were" or "I loved how you took care of your dog"—and really *feel* each one.

Building a positive self-image and connection to yourself helps you build faith. As you build faith in yourself, whatever you focus on you get more of and your confidence increases and you see more of your positives of your innocent self. If all anxiety is separation anxiety and all alarm is separation alarm, then as you cultivate compassion, love, and gratitude for yourself, you heal the separation—and when the separation heals, the alarm disappears. As the alarm disappears, the anxious thoughts go with it.

When we were younger, uncertainty made us feel powerless, but it turns out that this is actually where our power lies: in our ability to embrace and love uncertainty and the unknown, full of faith and gratitude; in our choice to see the innocence of our inner child and the innocence of life in general.

Seen from a grounded commitment to present-moment awareness, the unknown can now be a place of possibility and faith instead of apprehension. We can have gratitude for our ability to embrace uncertainty as part of the fun and feeling of life. When we view uncertainty this way, it has a peaceful, open quality, and loses the sense of urgency that creates such alarm in us. As the pain of uncertainty was often our biggest challenge in childhood, it requires a special awareness in adulthood; when we *see* it, we do not have to *be* it.

You may get some help along the way from therapists and counsellors—and for many, the old wounds heal faster with the connection of another person, especially one who knows how to work with trauma stored in the body—but true healing is an inside job. After trying just about every kind of therapy, medication, plant medicine, yoga, and meditation, I found that healing is based in my reconnection within myself and, specifically, within my own body.

I couldn't think my way out of a feeling. To heal, I had to feel my way out.

Even today, I feel that frightened thirteen-year-old boy looking out his bedroom window some forty-six years ago, watching his father being taken away. But he is with me now as I bring my younger self out of his past loneliness and into today. Rusty lives with me now, safe in the knowledge that we are present together, here and now. He never has to be back there alone ever again. I see my younger self and my father, and I love them both. I am deeply grateful for both. I love my dad for the kind, sensitive, innocent soul he was, and I love my younger self for the kind, sensitive soul he was. I can feel that my dad lives in me, and I welcome and cherish his presence and know that we are connected in a loving and compassionate way. I can feel that my younger self lives in me and that we are connected in a loving and compassionate way. I love the innocent soul I found dead on that January day, who chose to exit the world with his last written words, "It's not your fault. It's no one's fault. Love, Dad."

It truly was no one's fault. The world is innocent. We are all innocent souls, and we are here to remember that. It is only our self-created blocks and perceptions that make it appear any other way. If you commit, and I mean really commit to the ABCs, you can find a place of peace, faith and gratitude where you increasingly renew more of your *perceptions*, and less of your *prescriptions*.

THE 109TH BEAD
Acknowledgment of My Teachers and Guides

When I returned home from India, my now wife, Cynthia, made me a Mala, a string of beads I use in meditation to keep track of a phrase or intention that I repeat 108 times. She made it from 108 beads of rose quartz, the stone of unconditional love, and a slightly larger 109th bead of malachite, the stone of transformation. When one uses a Mala, every time a mantra or intention is repeated, a bead is moved. When you finish the 108 repetitions and reach the larger 109th bead, it is a time to be grateful for your teachers and guides who have helped you on your journey.

As this is the109th chapter, or final "bead," on my journey of writing this book, I want to acknowledge those who have helped me along the way and made this book possible.

My acknowledgement of my father is bittersweet. As he is the most important influence in this book being produced, I feel it only right to give him the longest acknowledgement. From the time I watched out my bedroom window as the ambulance took him away, I told myself I would make sense of this mess. I know my dad wanted much more from his life than his illness would allow. From his early days in radio, he had something special, and his sense of humour and intelligence shone through. But he was also handicapped by severe emotional and physical childhood trauma.

On October 5, 1934, my father was born Beverly Lorne Germa in Sudbury, Ontario, Canada. Beverly was a common boy's name until 1955, but as he grew older, it was more known as a girl's name. Another strike against him. He was born premature, weighing just over twenty-five ounces. Yes, twenty-five ounces. That is just over a pound and a half. I remember my grandmother telling the story of how she could get her wedding ring up to his shoulder and that they brought him home in a shoe box with the expectation he would not survive.

But he did survive. Babies born today at that weight have a very poor prognosis even with all the advancements in Pediatric ICUs. He is a miracle.

I acknowledge his pain in just surviving. I do regret withdrawing emotionally from him in my late teens, as his psychotic breaks were often as heartbreaking as they were embarrassing. In many ways, I am much closer to him now than I was when he was alive. I see him in a different way now. I can see that it was his illness I was seeing and not the man himself. Looking back, I have some shame in telling you I was embarrassed by my dad. When I got into medical school (a success of mine he never saw as he died five months before I learned I had been accepted), I changed my surname from Germa (my birth name) to Kennedy, my mother's maiden name.

I like to joke that Dr. Kennedy sounds infinitely better than Dr. Germa.

Jokes aside though, I remember him the way he was in his more functional days, taking me fishing, teaching me to play sports and billiards. In a way, I feel that I am fulfilling part of his destiny to make a difference in the world, a way he could have never made personally. So if this book has made a difference for you, if you would take a second and send him some gratitude for his sacrifice, I would deeply appreciate it and so would he. My dad just wanted what we all want: to be seen, heard, and loved. Thank you, Dad. I see you, I hear you, I love you.

My mother kept our household together, and I am very grateful for her. She emigrated to Canada from Scotland in 1958 and worked as a registered nurse. In fact, my father was one of her patients and that is how they met. My mother had been listening to my father on his radio show and was a fan and, soon after his recovery, became his wife.

My mother is tough. Through so many of my father's suicide attempts, depression, manic phases, and just general craziness, I only saw her cry a handful of times. We always had a place to live and food to eat because of her Scottish work ethic. She would often take extra shifts to help us make ends meet, and I have an immense amount of gratitude for my mother and her many sacrifices. Her life has not been an easy one, and she has always supported my brother and me in a selfless and relentless code of honour. The Kennedy clan motto is *Avise la fin* (Consider the end), and she always made sure we were safe in the end.

My mum has always supported me, and she supported me in this book. She knows exactly what anxiety and alarm feels like for she has felt it for over eight decades. Throughout it all, she has maintained a brilliant sense of humour that I inherited to become a stand-up comedian, and the funny parts of this book come from her love of laughter.

My wife, Cynthia, essentially saved my life and, therefore, played a big role in getting this book to you. It would have been very difficult to compile this book if I were dead. In 2013, with a ruptured Achilles and a ruptured mind, I could not have envisioned this day when I would be able to put my knowledge into the world. At the start of this journey of healing, Cynthia was there for me, nursing me back to health. It is a gift to be able to learn with her as we have taken many trainings and workshops together. Being able to draw on her expertise as a somatic trauma therapist has been invaluable in the creation of this book. "Cyn-Cyn" is a truly beautiful soul and a gift beyond measure.

There are some family members I need to acknowledge. My brother Scott, who experienced our dad's craziness first-hand and has raised a thriving family of his own. My daughter, Leandra, who has had her own struggles with the anxiety monster (and the Sea Monster!), has always lovingly supported me in my personal and professional endeavours. Leandra also showed me love was safe, and her ability to make me laugh is second to none. I am very grateful to my first wife Ginny for giving me Leandra and getting me through the darkest days of medical school.

To my teacher Gila Golub I am eternally grateful. I still remember the day in October 2014 that she and her right-hand man Dave Romer and right-hand woman Britta Frombach picked me up from an emotionally devastating journey on ayahuasca (remember my Shaman, Dave?). The teachings and support I received from Gila, Britta, and Dave would set the stage for this book, and I will be forever grateful to them for giving me some hope in some very dark nights of the soul. Britta lives close to me, and we still talk every week. She is one of the wisest souls I've known.

Gila introduced me to the work of developmental psychologist Dr. Gordon Neufeld and the Neufeld Institute in Vancouver. As I grew in emotional strength, I resonated deeply with Dr. Neufeld's teachings. Much of the basis of my theory of alarm comes from Dr. Neufeld. This book would not have the same resonance and depth without what I received from him.

There are some doctors who have made a real impact on me in my life and career. Dr. John Noseworthy (who is now the CEO of the Mayo Clinic) was one of the kindest and most compassionate doctors I have come across in supporting me over the years of Medical School. Also, Dr. Bruce Yoneda of Victoria, British Columbia, a fellow physician (and a former ice hockey teammate), is a man of great character and help to others and really went above and beyond the call of duty to surgically repair my ruptured left Achilles tendon. Bruce really looked after me and helped me get back on my feet emotionally and physically. Dr. Saul Isserow and Dr. Michael Mulvey have also been outstanding physicians who have propped me up at some very dark times. Mike is a psychiatrist and has always been very supportive of my non-traditional theories! Also, thanks to Nima Rahmany, DC, for our endless conversations about human emotion and healing from trauma and to my Aussie pal and colleague Dr. Jen Draper for her wisdom and support. Special thanks to Todd Caldecott, a brilliant teacher and great friend.

I do have my more ethereal and spiritual side, and I am grateful to medium Debra Doerksen for helping me access my intuitive nature, which played a big role in understanding the messages needed for the creation of this book. Also, thanks to Edward Dangerfield for helping me to use my breath to access a deeper place of peace and wisdom that also shows up in these pages.

A special thanks to my Florida connection, fellow physician Dr. Keith Holden, who inspired me by following his own atypical path to healing himself and others; to my pal and intuitive coach extraordinaire Heather Alice Shea, MS; and Sifu Anthony Korahais, the best qigong and tai chi teacher I've ever known.

Many people have helped me with the manuscript by giving me invaluable feedback and supporting me over the years, especially my good friend Angela Rinaldis. Thank you, Ang, you have always been there for me!

I am thankful to my Facebook friend Galina Singer, who encouraged my writing a couple of years ago when I asked her for advice. She planted the seed that I could actually become a good enough writer to write a book. Galina didn't know me from anyone but helped me for no other reason than she is a good person. You never know what simply helping someone can lead to!

Therapists Ginger Henderson and Kim Fraser-Harrison contributed to making the book more practical, and their feedback from the front lines was invaluable.

I am also grateful for the teachings of Nicole LePera, PhD, also known as "The Holistic Psychologist." Nicole's work has had a distinct impact on my own, and the world is fortunate to have her.

I am eternally grateful for the comedians that I learned from and got me through: notably, Sacha Baron Cohen, Bill Burr, Jim Carrey, John Cleese, Norm Macdonald, Bill Hader, Kate McKinnon, Eddie Murphy, Jerry Seinfeld, Mike Myers, Seth Meyers, and Kristen Wiig. They say laughter is the best medicine, which I mostly agree with unless you've contracted an STD; then laughing just makes it burn more, and then penicillin beats laughter in the "best medicine" department by a considerable margin—so there's that caveat.

A special note of thanks to Robin Williams. When he was in Vancouver to shoot a movie, he would often drop in to do a spot at one of the venues there called the Urban Well. I won a comedy competition at that club, and Robin signed a card I still have. It says, "You Won! – Robin Williams." I talked with him a number of times. He knew I was a physician, and we talked about anxiety and life in general. It was a thrill to perform on the same stage—I deeply miss him.

And now I come to Amanda Johnson, the founder of Awaken Village Press. Amanda really helped me bring this book to fruition. I told Amanda I had been working on this book for many years, but I really didn't know how long until I talked to my friend Robyn Ellingson (who played an invaluable role in exposing me to yoga and suggesting I become a yoga teacher), and Robyn told me I had been working on this book before I went into the teacher training program in 2007. Thirteen years later Robyn is still helping with edits and advice!

Back to Amanda and Awaken Village Press ("AVP"). We have been through a lot together. I have stretched her patience (understatement!!) but she always remained focused. At points, this book was well over 300,000 words. Amanda knows my tendency to over-explain. She has been my cheerleader, my taskmaster, my inspiration, and the person who brings me into reality. Many times I hit emotional walls, not wanting to go into my past. Amanda patiently listened to me and offered a way forward. Sometimes there were carrots, sometimes there were sticks, but always we kept going.

In June of 2020, Amanda and I had a serious conversation about the size of the book. It was big and messy. We needed to cut it down from the Titanic (I even called it that) to a yacht, and she found Elizabeth Gudrais. Elizabeth has written and edited science pieces (among other topics) for the Harvard alumni magazine and personally knows the subject of anxiety. She was the perfect person to clean it up. She reminded me of Harvey Keitel's character in *Pulp Fiction* who had to come in on short notice and do a big purge.

And she did. Amanda got the ship built, and Elizabeth finished it beautifully. I have so much gratitude and appreciation for both of them. A special thank you as well to Marianne Johnson for her final passes to make sure all the fittings and joints were polished properly with no leaks!

To round it out, my book designers, Tim Murray and Daniel Holloway; project manager, Carrie Cojocari; and the entire team at AVP have been absolutely outstanding at getting this project across the finish line.

Finally, I have seen people acknowledge their anxiety as a gift. While I'd love to say that my anxiety was a gift and that I am grateful for it, I'm not quite there yet. What I can say is there are parts of anxiety that have certainly led to things I am deeply grateful for.

Being grateful for all of anxiety and its lessons would be a way many people would end their books. Thing is, we have a relationship now and I haven't lied to you yet and I am not going to start now. If I could find the guy that invented worry, I would still punch him in the balls.

What I am grateful for, and anxiety and alarm have certainly helped me with this, is the opportunity to see and embrace my innocent self and to take Rusty Germa with me wherever I go. He is my treasure.

340 | ANXIETY RX

RESOURCES

Dr. Kennedy is finding great new resources all the time, so please go to https://dr-russ.com/anxiety-rx/resources/ for the book's webpage and links to the very latest information.

You can also join the book's specific and private Facebook group at www.facebook.com/groups/anxietyrxbook for discussion and further reference material to help you on your healing journey.

An A-to-Z List of Good Personality Traits: https://penlighten.com/good-personality-traits-list

Here are social media sources for Dr. Kennedy personally, along with accounts specifically for the book:

YouTube Channel for Dr. Kennedy, The Anxiety MD: https://www.youtube.com/c/DrRussellKennedyTHEANXIETYMD

Video on panic attacks referenced in the book is here: https://www.youtube.com/watch?v=5GYDLVN4Oyw

Instagram for Dr. Kennedy, The Anxiety MD: https://instagram.com/theanxietymd

Instagram for Anxiety Rx book: https://instagram.com/anxietyrxbook

Facebook Page for Dr. Kennedy, The Anxiety MD: https://www.facebook.com/theanxietymd

Twitter for Dr. Kennedy, The Anxiety MD: https://twitter.com/THEanxietyMD

Twitter for Anxiety Rx book: https://twitter.com/anxietyRxbook

REFERENCES

Amen, Daniel G. 2020. *The End of Mental Illness: How Neuroscience Is Transforming Psychiatry and Helping Prevent or Reverse Mood and Anxiety Disorders, ADHD, Addictions, PTSD, Psychosis, Personality Disorders, and More.* Carol Stream: Tyndale House Publishers.

Bird, Nicola. 2019. *A Little Peace of Mind: The Revolutionary Solution for Freedom from Anxiety, Panic Attacks and Stress.* London: Hay House UK.

Block, Peter. 2003. *The Answer to How Is Yes: Acting on What Matters.* San Francisco: Berrett-Koehler Publishers.

Block, Peter. 2008. *Community: The Structure of Belonging.* San Francisco: Berrett-Koehler Publishers.

Bradshaw, John. 2005. *Healing the Shame That Binds You: Recovery Classics Edition.* Deerfield Beach: Health Communications, Inc.

Bradshaw, John. 1999. *Homecoming: Reclaiming and Championing Your Inner Child.* New York: Bantam Doubleday Dell Audio.

Brand, Russell. 2018. *Recovery: Freedom from Our Addictions.* London: Pan Macmillan.

Bridges, William. 2003. *Managing Transitions: Making the Most of Change.* Boston: Da Capo Lifelong Books.

Brown, Brené. 2019. *Braving the Wilderness: The Quest for True Belonging and the Courage to Stand Alone.* New York: Random House Trade Paperbacks.

Brown, Brené. 2010. *The Gifts of Imperfection: Let Go of Who You Think You're Supposed to Be and Embrace Who You Are.* Center City: Hazelden Publishing.

Brown, Brené. 2013. *The Power of Vulnerability: Teachings of Authenticity, Connection, and Courage.* Louisville: Sounds True, Inc.

Carbonell, David A. 2016. *The Worry Trick: How Your Brain Tricks You Into Expecting the Worst and What You Can Do About It*. Oakland: New Harbinger Publications, Inc.

Cease, Kyle. 2017. *I Hope I Screw This Up: How Falling in Love with Your Fears Can Change the World*. Webster: Audible Studios.

Chodron, Pema. 2018. *The Places That Scare You: A Guide to Fearlessness in Difficult Times*. Boulder: Shambhala Publications.

Dana, Deb. 2018. *Polyvagal Theory in Therapy: Engaging the Rhythm of Regulation*. New York: W. W. Norton & Company.

Dr Russell Kennedy - THE ANXIETY MD. (n.d.). Home [YouTube Channel]. Retrieved from https://www.youtube.com/c/DrRussellKennedyTHEANXIETYMD

Frankl, Viktor E., H. S. K., William J. Winslade. 2006. *Man's Search for Meaning*. Boston: Beacon Press.

Gilbert, Elizabeth. 2006. *Eat, Pray, Love: One Woman's Search for Everything Across Italy, India and Indonesia*. New York: Penguin Group.

Grof, Stanislav and Christina Grof. 2010. *Holotropic Breathwork: A New Approach to Self-Exploration and Therapy (SUNY series in Transpersonal and Humanistic Psychology)*. Albany: Excelsior Editions; Illustrated Edition.

Hanson, Rick and Richard Mendius. 2009. *Buddha's Brain: The Practical Neuroscience of Happiness, Love, and Wisdom*. Oakland: New Harbinger Publications.

Hawkins, David R. 2014. *Power vs. Force: The Hidden Determinants of Human Behavior*. Carlsbad: Hay House Publishing.

Huber, Cheri. 2014. *Unconditional Self-Acceptance: The Do-It-Yourself Course*. Louisville: Sounds True, Inc.

Jeffers, Susan. 2012. *Feel the Fear and Do It Anyway*. London: Vermilion.

LeDoux, Joseph. 2016. *Anxious: Using the Brain to Understand and Treat Fear and Anxiety*. New York: Penguin Books.

Levine, Amir and Rachel Heller. 2012. *Attached: The New Science of Adult Attachment and How It Can Help You Find—and Keep—Love*. New York: TarcherPerigee.

Levine, Peter A. 2008. *Healing Trauma: A Pioneering Program for Restoring the Wisdom of Your Body*. Louisville: Sounds True, Inc.

Levine, Peter A. and Ann Frederick. 1997. *Waking the Tiger: Healing Trauma*. Berkeley: North Atlantic Books.

Lewis, Thomas, Fari Amini, and Richard Lannon. 2001. *A General Theory of Love*. New York: Vintage Books.

Lipton, Bruce H. 2016. *The Biology Of Belief: Unleashing the Power of Consciousness, Matter & Miracles*. Carlsbad: Hay House, Inc.

Miller, Alice. 2005. *The Body Never Lies: The Lingering Effects of Hurtful Parenting*. New York: W. W. Norton & Company.

Miller, Alice. 2008. *The Drama of the Gifted Child: The Search for the True Self*. New York: Basic Books.

Myss, Caroline. 1998. *Why People Don't Heal and How They Can*. New York: Harmony Books.

Paul, Sheryl. 2019. *The Wisdom of Anxiety: How Worry and Intrusive Thoughts Are Gifts to Help You Heal*. Louisville: Sounds True, Inc.

Peterson, Jordan B. 2018. *12 Rules for Life: An Antidote to Chaos*. Toronto: Random House Canada.

Porges, Stephen W. 2011. *The Polyvagal Theory: Neurophysiological Foundations of Emotions, Attachment, Communication, and Self-Regulation*. New York: W.W. Norton & Company.

Rankin, Lissa. 2016. *The Fear Cure: Cultivating Courage as Medicine for the Body, Mind, and Soul*. Carlsbad: Hay House, Inc.

Robbins, Mel. 2017. *The 5 Second Rule: Transform Your Life, Work, and Confidence with Everyday Courage*. Brentwood: Savio Republic.

Schaub, Friedemann. 2012. *The Fear and Anxiety Solution: A Breakthrough Process for Healing and Empowerment with Your Subconscious Mind.* Louisville: Sounds True, Inc.

Sharma, Robin. 2007. *The Monk Who Sold His Ferrari.* New York: HarperCollins Publishers.

Siegel, Daniel J. 2010. *Mindsight: The New Science of Personal Transformation.* New York: Bantam Books.

Siegel, Daniel J. 2011. *The Neurobiology of "We": How Relationships, the Mind, and the Brain Interact to Shape Who We Are.* Louisville: Sounds True, Inc.

Singer, Michael A. 2007. *The Untethered Soul: The Journey Beyond Yourself.* Oakland: New Harbinger Publications.

Tatkin, Stan. 2018. *Relationship Rx: Insights and Practices to Overcome Chronic Fighting and Return to Love.* Louisville: Sounds True, Inc.

Tolle, Eckhart. 2005. *A New Earth: Awakening to Your Life's Purpose.* New York: Penguin Books.

Tolle, Eckhart. 2004. *The Power of Now: A Guide to Spiritual Enlightenment.* Vancouver: Namaste Publishing

Van der Kolk, Bessel A. 2015. *The Body Keeps the Score: Brain, Mind, and Body in the Healing of Trauma.* New York: Penguin Books.

Wolynn, Mark. 2017. *It Didn't Start With You: How Inherited Family Trauma Shapes Who We Are and How to End the Cycle.* London: Penguin Life.

About the Author

Dr. Russell Kennedy (born Snaffy McWeaselnuts), and also known as "The Anxiety MD," is a medical doctor, anxiety expert, corporate speaker, yoga and meditation teacher, father, grandfather, and hypochondriac.

To become "The Anxiety MD," Dr. Russ has earned university degrees in medicine and neuroscience, and he has had over 100,000 patient encounters in his medical career. In addition, he believes the vast majority of mental dis-ease starts in childhood, and to that end, he has taken master's level training in developmental psychology at the Neufeld Institute in Vancouver

Russ's own anxiety started as he was growing up in a chaotic and confusing household with a father who suffered from schizophrenia and bipolar illness. Once he became an adult, healing from his own anxiety took him on a long and frustrating road with plenty of dead ends. As a doctor, Russ had full access to the best methods and medications "modern" traditional psychology and psychiatry had to offer for many years, but traditional methods only provided limited relief. Desperate to find a solution, he forged an unconventional path, and many of his breakthroughs came from pursuing distinctly non-traditional, atypical, and counterintuitive sources.

He has often said he is driven by a need to help others in a way he could not help his father. He has also often said he does not want people to have to suffer as he did, and strives to make his father's painful life and death to mean something by helping other families heal from emotional illness. It's not all serious though, as for many years he was doctor by day, comedian by night, performing in comedy clubs across the country.

A physician who is a stand-up comedian is unusual, but Russ freely admits to being atypical for a doctor. He studied meditation and intention while living at a temple in India, became a certified yoga and meditation teacher, practiced Holotropic Breathwork®, and has taken psychedelic (plant) medicines to see and experience as much of his mind as he possibly could. While under a therapeutic dose of LSD he discovered what his "anxiety" truly was and used that knowledge to develop a theory that would allow him to ultimately heal himself. That theory is found in his book, *Anxiety Rx*. There are no better guides than the ones who have been in the maze themselves and can show the way out.

Continue the journey with Russ at www.dr-russ.com.

Made in the USA
Middletown, DE
07 October 2022

12254344R00205